WE MARCH AGAINST ENGLAND

OSPREY
PUBLISHING

WE MARCH AGAINST ENGLAND

OPERATION SEA LION, 1940–41

ROBERT FORCZYK

First published in Great Britain in 2016 by Osprey Publishing,
PO Box 883, Oxford, OX1 9PL, UK
1385 Broadway, 5th Floor, New York, NY 10018, USA

E-mail: info@ospreypublishing.com

Osprey Publishing, part of Bloomsbury Publishing Plc

A CIP catalogue record for this book is available from the British Library.

Robert Forczyk has asserted his right under the Copyright, Designs and Patents Act, 1988, to be identified as the Author
of this Work.

ISBN: 978 1 4728 1485 2
PDF ISBN: 978 1 4728 1486 9
ePub ISBN: 978 1 4728 1487 6

Index by Zoe Ross
Cartography by Bounford.com
Typeset in Adobe Garamond Pro
Originated by PDQ Media, Bungay, UK.
Printed in China through Everbest Printing Ltd.

16 17 18 19 20 10 9 8 7 6 5 4 3 2 1

Osprey Publishing supports the Woodland Trust, the UK's leading woodland conservation charity. Between 2014 and
2018 our donations will be spent on their Centenary Woods project in the UK.

www.ospreypublishing.com

Imperial War Museum Collections
Many of the photos in this book come from the Imperial War Museum's huge collections which cover all aspects of
conflict involving Britain and the Commonwealth since the start of the twentieth century. These rich resources are
available online to search, browse and buy at www.iwm.org.uk/collections. In addition to Collections Online, you can
visit the Visitor Rooms where you can explore over 8 million photographs, thousands of hours of moving images, the
largest sound archive of its kind in the world, thousands of diaries and letters written by people in wartime, and a huge
reference library. Imperial War Museum www.iwm.org.uk.

Contents

Introduction

After winning a stunning victory in France in June 1940, on 16 July Adolf Hitler issued Führer Directive No. 16, which initiated preparations for a potential invasion of England, designated as *Unternehmen Seelöwe* (Operation *Sea Lion*). Consequently, the German Kriegsmarine (navy) and Heer (army) began improvising an invasion fleet, initially by gathering large numbers of river barges and small motor vessels and assembling them in the occupied Channel ports. Regarding air superiority as a sine qua non to ensure the success of any amphibious operation, Hitler ordered the Luftwaffe to crush the Royal Air Force (RAF) and obtain air superiority over the English Channel. Yet despite two months of intensive air operations in August to September 1940, the Luftwaffe could not defeat the RAF and Hitler became uneasy about the Kriegsmarine's ability to conduct *Seelöwe* without adequate air cover. Furthermore, the RAF began bombing the invasion barges in the Channel ports, inflicting considerable damage. Unnerved by the prospect of failure, on 17 September Hitler decided to postpone *Seelöwe*.

By standing firm against the Luftwaffe, 'the Few' of RAF Fighter Command frustrated Hitler's plans to invade England and thereby inflicted the first major defeat upon the Third Reich. In short, this is the standard orthodoxy about Operation *Sea Lion* and the Battle of Britain: England saved as a result of the RAF winning a two-month air battle, and the Third Reich chastised by its first strategic defeat. This heroic orthodoxy was promoted first by Winston Churchill and British wartime propaganda, then in the official post-war histories. The 15th of September was officially made a day to commemorate the Battle of Britain and, implicitly, the day the battle was decided. The British film *The Battle of Britain* (1969) reaffirmed this thesis for the general public, by promoting the notion that the German threat to England essentially ended after the climactic air battles on 15 September 1940. In a memorable scene at the film's conclusion, ostensibly depicting the day after, RAF fighter pilots are shown sitting in lawn chairs for raids that no longer come while, over in France, German soldiers are shown throwing their life preservers into a huge pile – representing the cancellation of *Sea Lion*. Some modern historians, such as John Keegan, have continued to endorse the heroic orthodoxy. Keegan stated that, by defeating the Luftwaffe over England, Great Britain remained in the war and this outcome 'determined the downfall of Hitler's Germany'.[1] Leo McKinstry, another adherent of the orthodox theory, absurdly concluded that 'the deterrence of Operation Sea Lion was the beginning of the end for the Reich'.[2] As if to add insult to injury, the standard orthodoxy usually includes some mention that Hitler was never really serious about invading England and that *Sea Lion* was something of a Potemkin village-type fraud. Former members of the Luftwaffe, such as fighter ace Adolf Galland and Generalfeldmarschall Albert Kesselring, are particularly dismissive of *Sea Lion* and have been used to lend credence to the idea that the invasion preparations were nothing more than a bluff intended to intimidate Great Britain into considering a negotiated peace. Although *Sea Lion* remains an item of historical curiosity in Britain, British historians have generally treated *Sea Lion* with contempt and in absolutist terms. Peter Fleming stated that 'Operation *Sea Lion*, as planned and mounted, was doomed to failure and, had it been launched, could only have ended in disaster'.[3] Ergo, the threat of invasion was never really a threat.

Yet the standard orthodoxy has been under attack since the 1950s, particularly on the active role played by Fighter Command versus the deterrent role played by the Royal Navy. Hubert R. Allen, one of 'the Few' and author of *Who Won the Battle of Britain?* (1976), was one of the first to openly criticize the RAF's performance in the campaign. Newer accounts of the Battle of Britain, such as Derek Robinson's *Invasion 1940* (2005) and Anthony J. Cumming's *The Royal Navy and the Battle of Britain* (2010) have tried to acknowledge that Hitler's fear of the Royal Navy played an equally important role in frustrating Operation *Sea Lion*, but still tend to fall into the trap of evaluating events in an overly narrow and deterministic context. Max Hastings noted that Britain might have defied the Luftwaffe in September 1940, but this did not advance the goal of defeating the Third Reich – which was accurate, but really only an admission of the obvious.[4]

While the question 'Who won the Battle of Britain?' has merit, it has always seemed to me an attempt to divert attention away from the unpleasant fact that Great Britain's military position remained extremely perilous long after the so-called Battle of Britain. Despite what happened in the skies over England in mid-September 1940, Great Britain's military situation was far more precarious than Germany's for another two years. The defeat of the Luftwaffe's large-scale daylight raids over Great Britain only curtailed one aspect of the Third Reich's capabilities, but had negligible impact upon Germany's overall ability to inflict pain upon Britain and its people. The mythology of the Battle of Britain and 'the Few' conveniently avoided mentioning that Fighter Command was virtually impotent to stop the Luftwaffe's night raids during the Blitz, which killed another 14,715 civilians in the next three months, or to prevent German long-range Fw-200 Condors from mauling convoys west of Ireland. Nor could 'the Few' do anything to prevent U-Boats or surface raiders from savaging British convoys during 1940–41. Curiously, the Blitz receives far less attention in English-language historiography than the Battle of Britain even though it lasted three times as long. While it is true that the presence of the Home Fleet did help to deter Hitler from attempting an invasion in 1940, it was also relatively impotent to prevent the growing menace of U-Boat Wolfpack attacks on convoys or disguised commerce raiders (*Hilfskreuzer*) from threatening British trade in the Atlantic, Indian and Pacific oceans. Even the more clever analyses, such as Stephen Bungay's *The Most Dangerous Enemy* (2001), remain entrenched in parochial interpretations that deny a priori (i.e. before examining alternative analysis) that Germany had any chance of achieving its objectives against Great Britain. Claims of victory in the skies over England notwithstanding, Fighter Command's efforts did not deprive Hitler of the overall strategic initiative any more than the Royal Navy did. When all was said and done, at the end of September 1940 Hitler decided what was going to come next, not Churchill. Hitler had allies, Churchill had refugees. Without powerful allies or significant offensive capabilities, Great Britain had no potential for achieving its war aims on its own, whereas Hitler had multiple options to try to pressure Great Britain into a negotiated peace; despite the RAF's impressive defence of Britain's airspace, Hitler still held the strategic initiative going into 1941, not Churchill.

Another troubling aspect of the standard orthodoxy about this period is the manner in which many post-war historians have segregated 'the Battle of Britain', 'the Blitz' and 'the Battle of the Atlantic' into discrete and non-contiguous boxes, which is rather bizarre, given that these were concurrent campaigns and were all part of Hitler's effort to force Great Britain to submit to a negotiated peace. From the point of view of Führer Directives Nos. 9, 16 and 17, these actions were all part of the same campaign. As an example of this kind of historical de-linking, most standard histories count Luftwaffe bomber losses over Britain in 1940 but ignore British bomber losses over Germany and occupied France occurring during the same period. The fact that both the British and German strategic bombing offensives and other air-sea actions were involved in the kind of action-reaction cycle characteristic of schismogenesis, where the action of one actor drives the actions of the other, has been ignored because of this artificial compartmentalization scheme. Rather than the iconic Bf-109 versus Spitfire model, Great Britain was in fact being assailed by everything from U-Boats and disguised merchant raiders to precision night-bombing and delayed-action bombs. Britain's ability to withstand this ferocious onslaught – which stressed the nation's defences to their limits – was due to the active efforts of 'the many', i.e. the scientists, the photo interpreters, the WAAFs, the merchant seamen and many others. The problem for historiography has been that the truth of Britain's salvation in the World War II has been too eclectic to fit well into narratives written primarily for general audiences – tales of Spitfire aces sold books, but the other details were too obscure.

There have been many books about *Sea Lion* – why another? My approach is intended to be different from previous histories that deal with Operation *Sea Lion* and the Battle of Britain because it will holistically link a number of intrinsically related and concurrent activities into a coherent narrative and analysis, not as separate subjects. I also intend to demonstrate that Germany's efforts to coerce Britain to accept a cease-fire involved not just a simplistic daylight duel between fighters for air superiority, but a much larger air and sea campaign as well as diplomatic efforts – which did not end in September 1940. During the period July 1940 to May 1941 Germany conducted three major inter-related campaigns intended to apply increasing pressure upon Britain:

1. An air-sea campaign against British commerce, involving U-Boats, surface raiders, *Hilfskreuzer*, mines, long-range bombers and S-Boats.
2. A terror campaign against the British civilian population, involving precision night-bombing and a new type of delayed-action bombs.
3. Invasion preparations, for an amphibious landing to be conducted in either September 1940 or May 1941.

In addition to artificial compartmentalization, most previous works addressing *Sea Lion* have lacked balance and critical military analysis. Most books on this subject have been written either primarily from the British viewpoint or the German viewpoint, with little effort to integrate actions and intentions. Information about the inadequacies of British defences has been glossed over. Topics such as the possible British use of chemical weapons to stop the invasion have been uncritically accepted at face value. Furthermore, I intend to demolish the long-cherished notion that the preparations for *Sea Lion* were a waste of time and resources for the Third Reich. In fact, the amphibious capabilities developed for the invasion of England proved to be of vital importance to sustaining the German war effort in 1942–45 and contributed to several later Allied defeats. *Sea Lion* was not a chimera.

As part of lending balance to the historical scales, I intend to demonstrate that the British made their share of mistakes and laboured under misconceptions, just as the Germans did. While the German wartime leadership involved in planning *Seelöwe* has often been accused of substituting 'fantasy' for reality, post-war British discussions of Operation *Sea Lion* have also been permeated by several recurring fantasies. Three in particular are intrinsic to the British dismissal of *Sea Lion*:

1. The idea that the Royal Navy would easily intercept German invasion convoys in mid-Channel and destroy the bulk of them in a massive 'turkey shoot' type scenario.
2. The idea that the Royal Navy could easily sever the sea lines of communications of any residual German landing force, causing that force to surrender within a matter of days.
3. The idea that the British Army could have contained, then quickly eliminated, any German beachheads.

The famous war game on *Sea Lion* conducted at Sandhurst in 1974 concluded that the Germans would have been able to establish a beachhead in southern England, but that the Royal Navy would have soon severed their sea lines of communication. The war game assessed that, once isolated, the trapped German troops in England would have surrendered within just four days. Little regard was given to the ability of the Luftwaffe to mount aerial resupply missions or the fact that trapped German formations in places such as Stalingrad, Demyansk and Korsun demonstrated a marked ability to fight on for weeks or months on minimal supplies. Unlike the Russian Front, German troops in England would not be freezing to death or surrounded by an enemy with vastly superior numbers. In North Africa, even when Rommel's *Deutsche Afrikakorps* (DAK) troops were short on fuel and ammunition, they were repeatedly able to repulse British infantry and armour attacks; the idea that German forces in England would simply surrender because a number of supply ships had been sunk is preposterous and without any basis in wartime fact. The German soldier of the World War II repeatedly demonstrated an ability to fight through adversity, not wilting because of supply disruptions.

Equally invalid is the commonly held fantasy about the British Army's ability to contain and quickly eliminate any German lodgement. British assessments of *Sea Lion*'s prospects stressed that the British Army had recovered considerably by September 1940 and was capable of fighting on equal terms with German ground forces; it was reckoned that 30 British divisions ought to be able to defeat the ten German divisions in *Sea Lion*'s first wave. Yet sober analysis of ground combat between German and British units in the period 1940–43 indicates a significant disparity in tactical competence between the two opponents. In North Africa, German ground forces were often at a logistical disadvantage but still managed to best their British opponents, through superior leadership and tactics. While British troops demonstrated considerable prowess on defence, their ability to conduct successful attacks against German units remained poor until after the 1944 Normandy Campaign. The record of failure in numerous attacks – which have great bearing upon the British Army's ability to defeat a German invasion – is often conveniently swept under the rug. While it is true that British troops would likely have fought very hard to defend their own soil, this patriotic fervour would do little to ameliorate consistently weak tactical leadership and lack of tactical agility.

It is not my intent to present a counter-factual or conjectural history of an operation that did not occur. That exercise has already been conducted by others. I also intend to be very restrained in the use of 'if' as a qualifier. Rather, my intent is to demonstrate that history at critical moments often has options – it is not pre-determined to proceed down the path that it actually did move along. Anyone familiar with military planning process is aware of branches and sequels that are developed to provide senior leaders with a variety of options to meet various circumstances. In the case of *Sea Lion*, Hitler was not pre-ordained to cancel the operation because the Luftwaffe failed to break the RAF's Fighter Command. In fact, he continued to have the same strategic options after the Battle of Britain that he had before. Nor was Hitler pre-ordained to eschew *Seelöwe* in favour of *Barbarossa*, and a well-planned invasion attempt in spring 1941 might well have been the decisive moment of the World War II. This is intended to be a complex historical narrative, premised on the idea that the outcome of significant historical events – like Germany's efforts to force Britain to the peace table in 1940–41 – were driven by multiple factors and that there was no single explanation.

CHAPTER 1

Strategic Setting, June–July 1940

The Legacy of Dunkirk

Britain had not begun to prepare seriously for war until after the 1938 Munich Crisis and then most of the resources were devoted to the Royal Air Force and the Royal Navy, not the army. At the start of the World War II, Britain had 224,000 trained personnel in its regular army, which formed the bedrock of its ground combat capability. Although much of the army's equipment was of World War I vintage, new weapons like the Bren light machine gun and the 2-pounder anti-tank gun were modernizing the regular infantry divisions. However, the regulars could never provide more than a fraction of the manpower needed for a European war and Britain relied upon 173,000 regular army reservists and 200,000 personnel aligned with the Territorial Army (TA) to provide the necessary bulk – yet both groups were virtually untrained. Conscription was enacted under the provisions of the National Services Act, which would enable the British Army to add another 600,000 personnel by spring 1940.

In April 1939, Prime Minister Neville Chamberlain's cabinet approved a plan to outfit 32 divisions (6 regular and 26 TA) by September 1941. The decision was made to double the size of the Territorial Army to over 400,000 men. In addition, several armoured divisions would be formed and all infantry divisions motorized. This ambitious plan envisioned increasing the size of the army ten-fold, as well as equipping them with over 200,000 motor vehicles and 7,000 tanks. Four days after the British declaration of war, First Sea Lord Winston Churchill vehemently argued to increase the army to 55 divisions, including 23 from the Commonwealth, but this suggestion was shelved.[1] As it was, transforming over one million untrained recruits into an effective army of more than 30 divisions was a gargantuan task and the War Ministry anticipated that 20 divisions would be ready by September 1940 and 12 more by September 1941.[2] Chamberlain's army programme made no provisions for enemy action or losses and training of the second-tier TA units was deferred. Thus, when the German Blitzkrieg opened in the west on 10 May 1940, the timetable for the British Army's expansion plan was completely wrecked. Instead, Britain went to war with an army that was intended more to demonstrate diplomatic resolve rather than to engage in large-scale combat against a skilled opponent.

Prior to the war, Chamberlain's cabinet planned to equip ten divisions for continental deployment in the event of war. On 4 September 1939, the British Expeditionary Force (BEF) under Lord Gort began arriving in France and initially consisted of two corps (I, II), each comprising two regular infantry divisions (1, 2, 3, 4). In December 1939, a fifth regular infantry division was sent to France, followed by five TA divisions (42, 44, 48, 50, 51) in January–April 1940. In late April, three second-line TA divisions (12, 23, 46) were also sent to France, as well as the incomplete 1st Armoured Division. By May 1940, the BEF on paper consisted of 394,165 troops in 13 infantry and one armoured division.[3] However, only the five regular infantry divisions were adequately trained and equipped, even though civilian vehicles were still being used until sufficient military lorries became available. The newly raised TA divisions were much further behind and the equipment they were provided was obsolescent. Particularly egregious was the dearth of tactical radios at brigade level and below, which made command or control of mobile operations problematic. British training was also highly deficient in a number of regards, being still primarily geared towards 1918-style tactics and unconcerned with the possibility of air attack. British armoured units were far from combat ready, with a mix of poorly designed tank types and saddled with an incoherent doctrine. Optimistically, the British leadership hoped that the much larger French Army, which had 74 divisions facing Germany, would conduct the bulk of any ground operations until the BEF was fully trained and equipped.

On 18 December 1939, the lead elements of the 1st Canadian Infantry Division arrived at Aldershot in England – the first major Commonwealth contribution to the British war effort. Prior to the war, Canada had a tiny regular army of only 4,500 personnel, backed by a 10,000-man militia, but the decision was made to send troops to Great Britain as soon as possible. The Canadian soldiers arrived without steel helmets, equipped with worn-out Lewis Guns and 18-pounder artillery pieces; Britain would have to outfit them with virtually all their equipment, adding to the delay of outfitting the TA divisions. Furthermore, three-quarters of the Canadians were untrained recruits. By March 1940, the Canadian 1st Infantry Division grew to a 23,000-man force and a second division was being readied in Canada.[4] Australia also promised to send a corps with two infantry divisions to join the BEF in France, and New Zealand promised one division, but most of these troops were still training in Palestine or en route when France capitulated.

When the German Western offensive began on 10 May, most of the BEF moved into Belgium along with the best French divisions, intending to block any German turning movement into northern France – as had occurred in 1914. On the same day, Winston Churchill succeeded Neville Chamberlain as prime minister. Yet the German invasion of Belgium was not the main effort – that came further south at Sedan, where Generaloberst Heinz Guderian's Panzers from the XIX Armeekorps (motorized) smashed through second-rate French divisions and quickly achieved a major breakthrough. Guderian's Panzers advanced westward to the coast and as fate would have it, the only Allied formation in their path was the 12th Infantry Division, a second-line TA formation assigned to protect the BEF's lines of communications into Belgium. On 20 May, all three of Guderian's Panzer-Divisionen overran the dispersed British Territorials, completely demolishing the division; its battalions suffered 80 per cent losses and the division was permanently disbanded. With that minor obstacle removed, the 2. Panzer-Division reached the English Channel near Abbeville and pivoted northward. Lord Gort's BEF and three French armies were now isolated. For a few days, the Allies attempted to mount a counteroffensive to re-open land communications to the south, but these efforts failed.

As France wilted under the German onslaught, Churchill made a number of hasty decisions. He quickly realized that the BEF was in serious danger and that possession of the Channel ports was crucial to sustaining, or evacuating, Lord Gort's forces. The Royal Navy was already beginning to plan for an evacuation of the BEF, designated Operation *Dynamo*, but the Channel ports needed to be secured from Guderian's Panzers, sweeping in from the south. In order to demonstrate British resolve, Churchill ordered British units sent to reinforce the French garrisons in the vital ports of Calais and Boulogne. On the morning of 21 May, Colonel William Fox-Pitt's 20th Guards Brigade was dispatched from England by sea to Boulogne, where two battalions arrived the next morning. Fox-Pitt's brigade was sent so quickly that his soldiers arrived in France with only 50 rounds of rifle ammunition each, no grenades, no anti-tank mines and no vehicles. Only eight hours after the Guardsmen began disembarking, the vanguard of the 2. Panzer-Division reached the outskirts of the city. Local French troops, equipped with anti-tank guns, knocked out a few German armoured vehicles and gave time for the 20th Guards Brigade to deploy in a thin cordon around the city, which temporarily slowed the German advance. However, the 2. Panzer-Division attacked in full force on 23 May, threatening to overrun both British battalions. Initially, a signal from the British War Office instructed Fox-Pitt to 'stand fast' and 'fight it out', while British destroyers stood off the port and were ordered not to evacuate troops. By the afternoon, the Germans were clearly pushing into Boulogne and by 1800 hours Fox-Pitt was finally authorized to evacuate to avoid the destruction of his brigade. It was a near-run thing, with German tanks firing on the British destroyers entering the port, and the captain of HMS *Vimy* was killed by sniper fire. By 0240 hours on 24 May, the last British destroyers left Boulogne. Amazingly, two-thirds of the 20th Guards Brigade was saved, but 522 men were lost at Boulogne.[5] Two British battalions were badly mauled, each having lost one-third of their troops and many junior officers. Furthermore, the British did not notify the French garrison that they were evacuating their brigade from Boulogne, which elicited stinging criticisms from the French who were still fighting in Boulogne. Churchill was personally offended by the criticism of French generals who said that the British were being hypocritical and selfish, urging the French to stand and fight while evacuating their own troops.

While the action at Boulogne was developing, Churchill's War Cabinet ordered Brigadier Claude Nicholson's 30th Infantry Brigade (two regular and one TA infantry battalion, one tank regiment with 48 tanks) to proceed from Dover by ferry to stiffen the defence of Calais. Nicholson's brigade arrived on 22 May and had barely disembarked its combat echelons when the 10. Panzer-Division began attacking Calais from the south. Amazingly, Nicholson's brigade was able to hold off the 10. Panzer-Division for three days but, unlike Boulogne, Churchill ordered that the hard-pressed brigade would not be evacuated. He intended to demonstrate his cold-blooded resolve to his anxious French allies, vacillating members of his own War Cabinet, and the remorseless German enemy. Nicholson's brigade made its last stand on 26 May and was overrun; about 300 British troops were killed and 2,900 captured.[6] At the cost of an infantry brigade,

Churchill had made his point to all – he intended Great Britain to fight on no matter the cost.

Meanwhile, the headlong German advance was temporarily halted on the night of 23/24 May when German troops were within 9½ miles of Dunkirk. Generaloberst Gerd von Rundstedt, commander of Heeresgruppe A, had become nervous that his Panzer-Divisionen were over-extended and vulnerable to an Allied counterstroke, even though the trapped Allied armies were in fact conducting a fighting retreat to Dunkirk. Generaloberst Günter von Kluge, commander of 4. Armee, pressed hard to slow down the advance in order to let the infantry divisions catch up, and von Rundstedt agreed and ordered Guderian's Panzers to halt.[7] The next day, Hitler concurred and issued his own *Haltbefehl* (Halt Order), which was intended to conserve the Panzers for the next phase of operations in France.[8] It was not until 26 May that the Halt Order was rescinded, giving the BEF a vital 48-hour reprieve. Although some historians, such as B. H. Liddell Hart, have attempted to suggest that Hitler deliberately slowed the advance upon Dunkirk in order to allow part of the BEF to escape as a political gesture, this idea does not hold water.[9] First, the Halt Order occurred before Operation *Dynamo* had actually begun – Hitler had no way of knowing that the British could evacuate so many troops off the beaches. Second, Reichsmarschall Hermann Göring, head of the Luftwaffe, assured Hitler that his aircraft could prevent an evacuation and, on the morning of 27 May, 300 of his bombers demolished the port facilities in a massive raid. In German minds, the BEF was now trapped and not going anywhere. Hitler intended to annihilate the BEF, not allow it to escape.

British, French and Belgian troops fought desperately to maintain a defensive perimeter around Dunkirk while the Royal Navy began the evacuation using everything that could float. At first, Churchill and his War Cabinet believed that Operation *Dynamo* would rescue only about 50,000 troops before the Germans overran the perimeter, but the Herculean effort made by the Royal Navy greatly exceeded expectations. During the period 26 May to 4 June, a total of between

315,000 and 338,000 Allied troops were evacuated from Dunkirk, of which approximately 186,581 were British troops.[10] Another 35,000 British support troops had been evacuated prior to Operation *Dynamo* commencing. All five of the regular divisions were in poor condition after Dunkirk, but the evacuated TA divisions were in much worse shape. In order to pull off this miracle, the Royal Navy committed 40 of its destroyers, and these vessels suffered repeated enemy air and S-Boat torpedo attacks, resulting in six destroyers sunk and 23 damaged. Although many of the destroyers were stationary or heavily loaded with troops, Dunkirk made it clear that the Luftwaffe was a serious threat to the Royal Navy in the English Channel. Finally, the Royal Air Force also made an all-out effort to protect the evacuation, committing well over 200 fighters per day, but suffered the loss of 83 fighters (36 Spitfires and 47 Hurricanes). Operation *Dynamo* saved the bulk of a disarmed BEF at the cost of heavy losses of the ships and planes that would be most needed to defend Britain's shores from the threat of German invasion.

Even if re-equipped in Britain, the brief campaign in France and Belgium demonstrated that the British Army was fundamentally unprepared to conduct the kind of combined-arms warfare as practised by the Germans. Twice the BEF mounted large-scale tank attacks, both of which were costly failures. The first attack was conducted by 'Frankforce' – a jury-rigged team consisting of 4th and 7th Royal Tank Regiment (RTR) from the 1st Army Tank Brigade (88 tanks), two battalions of infantry and two artillery batteries – against the 7. Panzer-Division at Arras on 21 May. Although the 2½-hour long counter-attack gave the Germans a considerable fright, it ultimately failed and the British lost 53 out of 88 tanks engaged, including 14 of 16 Matilda II tanks. Both tank regiment commanders were killed and the 4th RTR was effectively destroyed. The second attack was launched by the 1st Armoured Division against the 2. Infanterie-Division (mot.) south of Abbeville on 27 May; the attack failed, with 65 British tanks knocked out and 55 inoperative due to mechanical faults.[11] Thus, the combat experience accumulated by the British Army during the brief campaign in France did little to add to the development of an effective doctrine for mobile warfare.

The dust had not even settled from the Dunkirk fiasco when Churchill decided to reinforce failure by organizing a second BEF to assist in the defence of France. Lieutenant General Alan Brooke, just rescued with his II Corps from Dunkirk, was ordered back to France to take charge of the 51st Infantry Division (TA) and 1st Armoured Division, which were south of the Somme River.[12] In addition, Churchill decided to send the 52nd Infantry Division (TA) and the 1st Canadian Infantry Division to join Brooke's command. Brooke had no chance to organize his scattered forces before the second phase of the German offensive vaulted over the Somme. Most of Major General Victor Fortune's 51st Infantry Division was cornered by German Panzers near St Valery on 12 June, resulting in the surrender of two brigades with 10,000 troops. Two days later, the first Canadian brigade arrived in Brest just as the Germans were marching into Paris. Brooke recognized that the situation was rapidly unravelling, which Churchill finally accepted and agreed to evacuate the second BEF from western French ports in Operation *Ariel*. The Canadian brigade landed at Brest was forced to evacuate after just 48 hours in France; although the Canadians saved their artillery, they abandoned all 216 of their vehicles (including brand-new Ford F15 CMP trucks) due to lack of transport.[13] It was a humiliating and costly debut, for no military gain.

British materiel losses in France were catastrophic. At Dunkirk alone, the British Army lost 2,347 artillery pieces (55 per cent of its total inventory), 509 2-pounder anti-tank guns (60 per cent of its total) and 615 tanks (47 per cent of its total). In addition, the British abandoned 63,879 vehicles, as well as 76,000 tons of ammunition and 165,000 tons of petrol.[14] Much of this materiel was incorporated into the German inventory for their own use. The loss of military trucks was particularly crippling since Britain only produced a total of 89,582 military trucks in 1940 and a similar amount in 1941; this meant that only a small portion of the British Army would be fully motorized for the next year. Some equipment was salvaged and returned to Britain – almost entirely from the second BEF – including 322 artillery pieces/anti-tank guns, 22 tanks and 4,739 vehicles.[15] The 5th Royal Tank Regiment of 1st Armoured Division was particularly fortunate and managed to ship 7 of its 52 tanks back to England.[16] Altogether, the British Army lost 722 tanks in France.[17] However, the important point here is that the only fully equipped divisions in the British Army had been in France and now they were virtually denuded of equipment. The TA units left in England were, at best, partly equipped and trained.

While Britain's production of aircraft was ramping up quickly in the summer of 1940, domestic production of weapons for the army was still so anaemic that it would take more than a year to re-equip the regular army and outfit the Territorials. The manufacture of tanks had not been a priority before Dunkirk and only 392 tanks were built in July–September 1942, of which 147 were Cruisers, 227 infantry tanks and 18 light tanks.[18] Regular units like the 5th Royal Tank Regiment were re-equipped with A-9 and A-13 cruiser tanks in July–August, but the Territorial armoured units had to make do with light tanks or armoured cars until 1941.[19] Manufacture of the Mk VI light tank ceased and the new Mark III Valentine entered serial production in September 1940. Artillery and anti-tank production was a particular shortfall, with not enough of the new 25-pounder Mk II guns to go around until mid-1941. Even rifles were a problem, with an average of just 8,600 completed at the Birmingham plant each month. However, production of small arms ammunition (over 40 million rounds per month) was adequate and 442 million rounds of .303 ammunition were available by September. Likewise, the stockpile of artillery ammunition was adequate. The supply of uniforms was adequate even to outfit much of the Home Guard within a few months, but the quantity and quality of some items was sub-standard. Amazingly, the same nation that was able to mass-produce Spitfires was unable to provide its soldiers with more than one pair of socks and they were of such poor quality that infantrymen found it difficult to march in them.

Table 1: British Production of Military Equipment, July–October 1940 [20]

Month	Tanks	25-pdr	3.7in AA	40mm AA	2-pdr AT	Army Motor Vehicles
July	129	60	183	128	200	9,624
August	126	72	136	124	148	8,779
September	122	78	148	116	150	8,444
October	144	108	104	138	211	8,154

In human terms, the British Army suffered about 17 per cent losses in France, comprising 4,206 killed, 52,165 missing and 16,815 wounded. A disproportionate share of these losses was in the infantry battalions, which had an authorized strength of 668 men (including 22 officers); altogether over 38,000 infantrymen – the equivalent of 57 battalions – were lost. The artillery also suffered 7,332 casualties, which left the British Army with very few trained artillerymen after Dunkirk. Likewise, the loss of almost 3,000 British officers severely impacted the ability of the British Army to train new recruits.

Dunkirk decimated the regular British Army and the few trained Territorial units. In the 2nd Infantry Division, a regular army formation, four of its infantry battalions were virtually destroyed; the 1st Battalion, Queen's Own Cameron Highlanders only had 79 survivors, the 1st Battalion, Royal Welch Fusiliers had about 150, and two of the battalions in the 4th Brigade about 200 each. In the 3rd Infantry Division, the 4th Royal Berkshires suffered over 50 per cent losses and in the 48th Infantry Division, the 2nd Battalion Royal Warwicks only had 137 survivors. The 51st (Highland) Infantry Division, a Territorial formation, lost six infantry battalions in toto. Once back in Britain, these divisions had to replace enormous gaps in their organizations, which often meant transferring support personnel into infantry billets. Replacing junior enlisted soldiers is one thing, but experienced NCOs and company commanders do not roll readily off assembly lines. Furthermore, the loss of so many regular soldiers in France meant that there were fewer skilled professionals to train the

TA divisions. Consequently, it would take even longer to bring the TA divisions up to the standard of combat readiness that would enable them to successfully fight German divisions.

British infantry units after Dunkirk were in poor shape for some time and particularly lacked tactical radios, mortars and transport. Some infantry battalions were given bicycles or civilian buses, but this did not solve the problem. In the 59th (Staffordshire) Infantry Division, a second-line Territorial formation assigned to protect the northern coast, the unit was provided with lorries from Newcastle breweries. Since the vehicles were only on loan to the army, they retained their commercial liveries and could not be painted as military vehicles.[21] In essence, much of the post-Dunkirk British infantry was like the static German divisions defending the French coast in 1942–44, bereft of first-line equipment and woefully short of experienced junior officers and NCOs. On top of this, Churchill made the decision – opposed by the Army leadership – to conscript another 324,000 men between June and August, but there was already a huge back-log in training the existing Territorial forces recruited in the first six months of the war. These new recruits were formed into 122 (Home Service or Holding) infantry battalions and provided with American-made rifles when they became available, but they were little better than Home Guard units.[22] It would have been better to use these new recruits in labour battalions to build coastal defences, freeing the regular army from such tasks, but Churchill preferred ersatz infantrymen. Thus, it is important to note that it was not just Dunkirk that hobbled the British Army, but the political decision to create the illusion of strength through numbers, which over-burdened the system of training and equipping new units.

Not all the British Army's regulars had been decimated by the French campaign. In mid-June, regular forces that had been deployed in India began returning to England. Five battalions of regular infantry were formed into the 29th and 31st Independent Infantry Brigades and provided with a battalion of new 25-pounder guns and Bren Gun carriers. While these two brigades were a godsend to the depleted regular forces, these troops required considerable re-training after years of distant colonial service. In addition, a number of cavalry regiments returned and, along with yeomanry regiments, they were formed into three Motor Machine Gun brigades; these formations were equipped with a motley mix of Bren Gun carriers, armoured cars and lightly armoured civilian vehicles known as 'beaverettes'. In June 1940, the Motor Machine Gun brigades were conceived as rapid reaction units but it quickly became apparent that they had negligible combat capability.

After Dunkirk, the British Army hastily put together a blue-ribbon commission under General Sir William H. Bartholomew to review doctrine, and in just two weeks it produced a report that acted as a doctrinal stop-gap for the next six months.[23] The hastily written Bartholomew Report drew a number of incorrect conclusions, such as the belief that the brigade group would be the basic fighting unit, not the division, and that the Bren Gun carrier could be used aggressively in the front line. British doctrine remained in a muddle after Dunkirk and it would not be sorted out until 1944. Troops that were regarded as 'trained' in 1940 often had little live-fire experience and much of their instruction was rote learning from outdated manuals.

In an odd footnote to Dunkirk, Hitler was interested in meeting some of the captured British prisoners and asked the OKH (Oberkommando des Heeres) to bring one officer and one NCO who could understand German to the Reich Chancellery in Berlin. It is likely that Hitler wanted to personally assess the morale of British soldiers. After talking with them for a while, Hitler said to them, 'well, boys, when you write home, you can write that this war is unnecessary'.[24]

Churchill Manoeuvres to Keep Britain in the War

Winston Churchill took over as prime minister on 10 May 1940 just as the German invasion of neutral Belgium and Holland was beginning. At the same time, a battalion of British Royal Marines invaded the neutral Kingdom of Iceland, a sovereign nation of 125,000 people. Churchill used the excuse that German U-Boats may have been violating Icelandic neutrality to seize Reykjavik, since it would greatly assist the Royal Navy in protecting the convoy routes. The Icelandic government protested, but then accepted British occupation.[25] Like his earlier recommendations to violate Norwegian waters to lay mines to interdict German shipping, Churchill was demonstrating his willingness to violate neutral territory.

Unlike his predecessors, Stanley Baldwin and Neville Chamberlain, Churchill was politically insecure (Chamberlain was still head of the Conservative Party, not Churchill) and he had no time to soberly consider preventative measures, but could only react to each succeeding crisis. In just six weeks, Churchill watched as France was beaten to its knees and defeated. Up to this point, all of Britain's strategy had been geared towards fighting a coalition war, with Britain focusing on naval and air operations against Germany while France and other allies conducted any ground campaigns. Yet not only did Britain lose its primary ally when France capitulated, but Italy joined the Axis side, thereby opening up a new theatre of operations in the Mediterranean and North Africa. By the end of June, Britain's strategic situation had markedly deteriorated and the only two game-changers – the United States and the Soviet Union – were waiting to see how events played out.

Six weeks before Hitler ordered preparations for an amphibious operation against Great Britain to begin, Churchill was speaking about the threat of enemy invasion in the House of Commons on 4 June. As Dunkirk was being overrun, Churchill famously stated that 'we shall defend our Island, whatever the cost may be, we shall fight on the beaches, we shall fight on the landing grounds, we shall fight in the fields and in the streets, we shall fight in the hills; we shall never surrender'. Yet not everyone in Britain's government was so confident. Josiah Clement Wedgwood, a Labour member of parliament for Newcastle-under-Lyme, had given a speech in the House of Commons on 7 May 1940, pointing out that if the Royal Navy could not stop a German invasion of Norway, it was possible that the navy might not prevent a landing in England, either.[26] Wedgwood was no wilting lily, but a veteran of the Boer War, Gallipoli and Siberia in 1918; like Churchill he ardently opposed Chamberlain's appeasement strategy and he was one of the first to join the Home Guard, though aged 68. If staunch defenders of the empire like Wedgwood doubted the war effort, Churchill's rhetoric would not be enough.

Churchill actually got on well with Wedgwood, who was cut from the same cloth as he was, but he could not afford doubt to be introduced into the British war effort. Instead, Churchill used his vaunted rhetoric as his primary weapon. He boldly proclaimed that 'we shall not be content with a defensive war', letting both Hitler and the British people know that he intended to wage real war, not merely hold out on an island fortress. However, Churchill had inherited a cabinet that included men deeply involved with pre-war appeasement policies, as well as Labour politicians who viewed him with innate hostility. Initially, Churchill had no real political allies in his coalition cabinet and the majority opinion among these men was psychologically at odds with Churchill's aggressive attitudes towards the war. Churchill also had to face the difficulty of waging protracted war in a modern democracy. The British population was infused with pacifist thinking, much like the French, and fearful of terror bombing; the civilian casualties caused by the Luftwaffe's attacks on the Spanish town of Guernica in April 1937 and the Dutch city of Rotterdam in May 1940 had left a particularly poignant impression. In early 1939, the British Ministry of Health estimated that there could be 1.8 million casualties in the first six months of enemy bombing; although these estimates were later proved to be wildly inaccurate, they seemed credible in July 1940.[27] On top of this, Chamberlain's government had failed to properly articulate British war aims or a path to victory, so it was difficult for the population to accept sacrifices when the objectives being sought were ambiguous. How long would conscription and rationing go on – and to what end? Thus Churchill was faced with steering Great Britain towards a commitment to all-out warfare, despite lack of political support within his own cabinet and an apprehensive, unmotivated population.

Churchill's inner War Cabinet consisted of himself, Neville Chamberlain, Lord Halifax, Clement Atlee and Arthur Greenwood; it is unlikely that there has ever been a group in charge of making strategic decisions whose members held more divergent viewpoints. The War Cabinet met at least once daily, sometimes twice. Churchill's only real allies were in the outer cabinet, which included Secretary of State for War Anthony Eden. Essentially, Churchill was the hawk who had long opposed Chamberlain's appeasement policies and urged rearmament; the fact that he had been proved right about Hitler's intentions did not create much political capital among his own Conservative Party peers. Churchill's reputation for reckless behaviour – highlighted by his connection to the 1915 Gallipoli fiasco – had stuck to him like glue throughout his career. While the Cabinet may have grudgingly admitted that Churchill had been more prescient than they had about the turn of events, that did not mean that he had a workable solution to lead them either to a military victory or an honourable peace.

Apparently on his own initiative, Lord Halifax met with the Italian ambassador in London, Giuseppe Bastianini, on 25 May. At this point, it looked as though much of the BEF would be lost in France. According to Halifax, Bastianini said that Italy was willing to broker peace negotiations between Germany and Great Britain, although the discussions were vague.[28] On 26 May, Halifax presented the idea to the War Cabinet of using the Italians to open peace negotiations with Germany – claiming that Mussolini could 'persuade Herr Hitler to take a more reasonable attitude' – but Churchill was adamantly opposed (at least in public) to negotiations with Hitler.[29] Although Churchill had spoken about the possibility of negotiations with the enemy in September 1939, he was disinclined to negotiate from a position of weakness brought about by the defeats in Norway and France. Halifax drafted a memo to the Italians that said that Great Britain would consider 'any proposal' that promised a 'secure and peaceful Europe' and argued within the Cabinet that Britain should try to get the best peace deal that it could, before the military situation grew worse.[30] Churchill insisted that Hitler could not be trusted to honour any agreements, while Halifax spoke of a 'European equilibrium'. For the next three days, the War Cabinet was plunged into crisis as Halifax aggressively pushed the other members to consider the possibility of a negotiated settlement and Chamberlain supported this proposal as well. There was also some support within Parliament for negotiations, particularly from the 77-year-old David Lloyd George and a group of 30 Labour MPs led by Richard Stokes. Churchill argued that resistance to German aggression was the only viable course since any settlement imposed as a result of a German military victory in France would inevitably result in 'the destruction of our independence'. In particular, Churchill stated that Hitler would force Britain to end its rearmament programmes, which would keep Great Britain in a position of military inferiority. To be fair to Halifax and Chamberlain, Churchill had no idea what terms Hitler might offer and provided no insight into how his policy of stubborn intransigence would lead Britain to a better situation, other than more sanguinary rhetoric about the conflict only ending when 'each one of us lies choking in his own blood upon the ground'. The outer cabinet applauded this speech, apparently thinking he was referring to someone else's blood.

The very idea of Great Britain considering a negotiated settlement with Hitler in 1940 remains something of a taboo subject even after 75 years, but Churchill's refusal to listen to Halifax and others in the Cabinet was a strategic mistake. As Cambridge historian David Reynolds has argued, Churchill based his decision to keep Britain in the war on two faulty assumptions – that Germany was near economic collapse and that the United States would soon enter the war. Yet there was not one hard shred of intelligence to suggest that either assumption was correct; Churchill simply wanted them to be correct.[31] Churchill made many mistakes during the course of the war and the outright rejection of negotiation would prove quite costly to Britain.[32] Churchill knew that Hitler was not likely to seek a punitive peace with Great Britain, but rather a quick end to hostilities so he could consolidate his conquests. Whether Churchill negotiated or not, German occupation of much of Europe was an irreversible fact that could not be changed with Britain's available resources. Yet opening covert negotiations – unrevealed to the British public – might have bought valuable time for the British Army and RAF to recover from Dunkirk, while also wasting Hitler's narrow window of opportunity to consider invasion. Even if the negotiations were broken off after a few months, this would have been a valuable victory for Great Britain.

It was only after nine cabinet meetings that Churchill was able to convince Attlee and Greenwood from Labour to side with him, which resulted in Halifax's isolation and his proposal for negotiations being voted down. Yet it was a close call and Churchill knew that his position was vulnerable until he could cleanse his cabinet of men who had little or no faith in victory. After this crisis was resolved, Churchill brought Lord Beaverbrook into the Cabinet to energize aircraft production and Duff Cooper as Minister of Information, while sending Chamberlain loyalist Samuel Hoare to Spain as ambassador. Chamberlain himself was diagnosed with cancer and resigned from the Cabinet in September. Eventually, Halifax would be sent as ambassador to the United States. By October 1940, Churchill's political position was stronger. Churchill also took this opportunity to do some house-cleaning in the military: he decided to replace the wooden-headed General Edmund Ironside, Chief of the Imperial General Staff (CIGS), with General John Dill. Ironside was kicked upstairs to take command of Home Forces but was soon replaced by Alan Brooke in mid-July and forced into retirement. Lord Gort was sent off on various overseas inspection junkets until made governor of Malta. Churchill brought Major General 'Pug' Ismay, a former Indian Army officer, to be his principal military advisor and Ismay remained in that position for the duration of the war. For the time being, Churchill had succeeded in keeping Great Britain committed to staying in the war.

However, doubt lingered even in Churchill's mind and on 12 June he told Ismay, 'You and I will be dead in three months' time.'[33] This unguarded remark, like his earlier speech about choking in one's own blood, indicated a fatalist streak in Churchill – which has now generally been white-washed from the Battle of Britain narrative.

Britain – Far From Alone – But Without a Strategy

When Churchill said on 14 July 1940 that 'we are fighting by ourselves alone…' he was of course overlooking the fact that Britain controlled an empire that directed one-fifth of the Earth's population. Britain's Commonwealth allies – Australia, Canada, New Zealand and South Africa – had already committed ground, naval and air forces to participate in the European war and were preparing substantial reinforcements. Yet even more vital in the long term was the Commonwealth partners' contributions to operating the Empire Air Training Scheme (EATS), which was expected to train up to 50,000 aircrew for the RAF per year. Prior to the war, the RAF relied upon small service schools to train pilots and aircrew, but this was insufficient for large-scale expansion in wartime. By April 1940, Australia and Canada were running basic flight training schools, which were invulnerable to enemy air attack and which opened a steady pipeline of trained aircrew for the RAF. Without the flight schools in Canada, the RAF's ability to replace combat losses and build up Bomber Command into an offensive force would have been severely curtailed.

Churchill also deliberately chose to ignore the fact that Great Britain still had one significant foreign ally – Poland. At the outset of the war in September 1939, the Polish Navy arrived in Scotland with the destroyers ORP *Burza* and *Błyskawica* and they were soon put to hard use in escorting Atlantic convoys. After the fall of France, General Władysław Sikorski brought about 30,000 Polish troops to Great Britain, enough to form two rifle brigades by late September to help defend the Scottish coast. General Dill reported to the British Cabinet that the Polish troops 'appeared to be of good quality' and would be re-equipped with surplus infantry weapons received from the United States.[34] The Polish Air Force also provided five squadrons for RAF

Fighter Command and four for Bomber Command; the Polish fighter pilots were a particularly valuable asset due to their previous combat experience against the Luftwaffe and they would play a major role in the Battle of Britain. In time, the Polish contribution to Great Britain's war effort would expand nearly ten-fold and participate in nearly all future campaigns. Yet while British political leaders gladly accepted Polish military assistance, they were annoyed by Polish hostility towards the Soviet Union. Chamberlain's government had gone to war to defend Poland against German aggression, but ignored similar Soviet aggression against Poland. Churchill wanted Polish military assistance for free, but was unwilling to provide more than empty promises about helping Poland to regain the land seized by the USSR.

On a smaller scale, Czechoslovakia would also contribute two fighter and one bomber squadron to the RAF when it needed them most. However, Dill was less impressed with the 3,000 Czech troops in Great Britain and stated that they 'were not of such high quality and would have to be carefully sorted out before re-arming'.[35] The Royal Netherlands Navy managed to bring four brand-new O-21 class submarines to England – which contributed to the British war effort in the North Sea – and 1,500 troops to form an infantry brigade. Enough Dutch pilots and aircrew reached Britain to form two squadrons in RAF Coastal Command. Of greater significance, the Norwegian merchant marine added 4 million tons of shipping (including 268 tankers) and 25,000 sailors to the Allied cause, which helped Britain's sea lanes to remain open.[36]

Nor was Churchill interested in Charles de Gaulle and his Free French forces. From his headquarters in London, de Gaulle was able to rally about 5,000 volunteers to the Free French standard in the summer of 1940, but less than 3 per cent of the French troops evacuated from France opted to join his cause. He had better luck with the undefeated French expeditionary force sent to Norway, many of whom chose to remain in the fight. By July, de Gaulle was able to form a brigade-size force (Corps expéditionnaire français libre) in England, comprising Foreign Legion troops, former Chasseurs Alpins, marines and sailors. While de Gaulle's forces were small in number, they were all-volunteer and often professional soldiers. Although Churchill publicly referred to de Gaulle as 'a man of destiny', in reality he refused to see the general or his regime as legitimate. Clement Attlee, now a key Churchill political ally, referred to de Gaulle as 'practically fascist' and the British military establishment viewed all Frenchmen as defeatist.[37] General Dill was reluctant to even give the French troops ammunition.[38] Without the fully fledged support of Churchill or the British military, de Gaulle found it extremely difficult to acquire materiel to re-equip his troops, but nevertheless he set in motion plans to form the 1st Free French Division as soon as possible. Within a year, he was able to expand his forces ten-fold.

Churchill, like many Englishmen (including King George VI), was relieved to be free from operating within the constraints of an alliance with France or other continental powers. Traditional Francophobia was exacerbated by the sudden collapse of the Third Republic and the creation of the Vichy regime, which caused Churchill and his War Cabinet to lose all objectivity in regard to France. Churchill openly referred to the French as 'traitors to the Allied cause' and within the British military there was widespread contempt for the failure of the French to fight harder. The ink was hardly dry on the capitulation document when Churchill suggested at the Cabinet meeting on 22 June that steps be taken to prevent the modern French battleships *Richelieu* and *Jean Bart* and the battlecruisers *Strasbourg* and *Dunkerque* from falling into German hands, even though all four were in North African ports. He ridiculously claimed that these four ships could 'determine the outcome of the war' and bluntly stated that rather than risking German seizure of these warships, 'we should have to fight and sink them'. Halifax suggested that diplomacy should be used to win over the French Navy in North Africa, but his voice carried little weight now.[39] Admiral François Darlan, commander of the French fleet, personally assured Churchill that no French warships would fall into German hands, but Churchill refused to accept this and began pressing the Cabinet for a military solution to neutralize all French warships. Another indicator that the War Cabinet was not making decisions based solely on direct threats to Great Britain was a suggestion by Admiral Sir Dudley Pound, First Sea Lord, that French oil facilities in the port of Marseille – in the Free Zone not controlled by the Germans – should be bombarded by the Royal Navy. On 23 June, the Cabinet ordered the Royal Navy to intercept the French cruiser *Émile Bertin*, which was carrying £60 million in gold to Martinique; Churchill cynically stated that 'we should keep the gold in trust for the French Empire, but that they must fight for it'.[40] However, the French gold safely reached Martinique.

In reality, the idea that the Germans could seize French warships in North Africa and provide them with trained crews to sail them out to do battle with the Royal Navy was preposterous and the Royal Navy leadership told Churchill that his hypothetical scenario was unrealistic. However, Churchill had no strategy after the fall of France, other than to hold on, but defensive war was not to his taste. Instead, he preferred aggressive actions to gain the strategic initiative, but often with little or no consideration for the consequences. Just six months before, as First Lord of the Admiralty, Churchill had advocated Operation *Catherine* – sending a good portion of the Home Fleet into the Baltic to raid German merchant shipping – completely ignoring the threat posed by the Luftwaffe, mines and U-Boats. The operation was cancelled. In late June 1940, the only viable offensive tool available to Churchill was the Royal Navy and he was intent on using it to demonstrate to all and sundry that Britain had the determination to fight on.

While the War Cabinet was considering what to do about the French fleet, another target of opportunity presented itself. A flotilla of four Swedish destroyers, purchased from Italy in March 1940, was near the Faroe Islands, which the British had occupied. Churchill suddenly presented the case that the destroyers could be seized by the Germans en route to Sweden and instead should be taken by the Royal Navy. With little thought for the diplomatic consequences, the four destroyers were cornered by three British destroyers on 21 June and their crews forcibly detained. There was dissent within the Cabinet about this action, which was a clear attack on a neutral nation, and eventually Churchill agreed to release the vessels on 30 June, but not before the weapons on all four destroyers were sabotaged. Relations with Sweden were severely strained, for no purpose.[41]

On 27 June, the War Cabinet met again to consider options for dealing with the French fleet and Churchill proposed an operation using Vice-Admiral Sir James Somerville's Force H from Gibraltar to neutralize the large French naval squadron at Mers-el-Kébir in Algeria.[42] Duff Cooper, Minister of Information and a close ally of Churchill, suggested that effective use of propaganda might win over the French fleet and some of the colonies, but that would take time. Churchill pressed the Cabinet for immediate action and they assented; the Admiralty was given just three days to plan Operation *Catapult*. No consideration was given to French neutrality or the effect on Franco-British relations. The essence of the plan was to present an ultimatum to each French naval squadron, with the choice of either handing their ships over to the Royal Navy, steaming to a neutral port or scuttling their ships. On 3 July, the Royal Navy commenced Operation *Catapult*. Only in Alexandria, Egypt, did the Royal Navy disarm the French squadron without any bloodshed; the French squadron in Portsmouth, England resisted and three lives were lost. However, these were sideshows – the stated intent of the operation was to disable the main French squadron at Mers-el-Kébir. After a failed attempt at negotiations, Somerville's Force H opened fire and sank the French battleship *Bretagne* and damaged the battlecruiser *Dunkerque*. A total of 1,297 French sailors were killed in the attack on Mers-el-Kébir, but the battlecruiser *Strasbourg* sortied past Force H and managed to reach Toulon. Three days later, Somerville launched an air strike which crippled the damaged *Dunkerque* in Mers-el-Kébir, inflicting further casualties. In the House of Commons, the attack on the French fleet at Mers-el- Kébir was cheered as if it was a battlefield triumph, instead of an unprovoked attack on a former ally.[43]

Vichy France promptly broke off relations with Great Britain – but not with Australia or Canada – and the French Navy retaliated for Mers-el-Kébir by launching several ineffectual bombing raids against

Gibraltar and ordering attacks on British shipping. Three British steamships totalling 15,801 tons were captured off Dakar and three other vessels were also seized. France and Great Britain were now in an undeclared quasi-war due to Churchill's rash actions and Operation *Catapult* had not even fully neutralized the four modern French capital ships, as intended. An air strike had managed to damage the battleship *Richelieu* in Dakar on 8 July, but she was repairable. Given the British attack, the Vichy leadership might have fulfilled Churchill's worst-case scenario by selling some of their warships to the Germans, but Darlan was unwilling to take that step. Admiral Somerville was ashamed by his role in the Mers-el-Kébir affair and called it the 'biggest political blunder of modern times'. However, Churchill took charge of the narrative and said that the attack was necessary for Britain's survival – which it was not – and that the attack further demonstrated British resolve. Yet taken together with the seizure of the Swedish destroyers and efforts to seize French gold, the Mers-el-Kébir attack amply demonstrates that Churchill was unable to formulate a real military strategy in July 1940 and was simply flailing about. Furthermore, the British actions against neutrals were clearly in violation of international law, handing a propaganda victory to Germany and greatly reducing de Gaulle's ability to recruit volunteers from French North Africa. Had Vichy France decided to ally with Germany as a result of this attack, the prospects for an enemy invasion of Great Britain would have been increased. Operation *Catapult* was an idiotic display of military force and represented the nadir of British strategy in the World War II.

Rather than impressing the Americans as he later rationalized, Churchill's primary benefit from Operation *Catapult* was making a clean break with France. In Cabinet meetings, Churchill stated that Britain 'was better off without France'.[44] After Mers-el-Kébir, Churchill could operate independently without having to consult with allies, which meant that, like Hitler, he could direct the war as he wished. However, after Mers-el-Kébir, Churchill's War Cabinet proved incapable of creating a realistic military strategy that could seriously challenge Hitler's hold on continental Europe. Churchill himself primarily viewed the war through tactical lenses, looking for opportunities to strike, but without any over-arching themes. He also had a tendency to micro-manage military operations, involving himself down to brigade-level at times. Churchill's close friend and scientific advisor, the physicist Frederick Lindemann, regularly attended War Cabinet meetings and Churchill relied heavily upon his statistical reports on everything from the bombing campaign to U-Boat losses.

Great Britain and France had not really developed a strategy since the beginning of the war, since neither the Chamberlain Government nor the French had wanted to mount a serious bombing campaign against Germany due to fear of retaliation. Instead, a vague strategy of economic strangulation was espoused, combined with a keen belief that internal fissures within the Nazi regime would tear it to pieces – which was just wishful thinking. Nor had the British Chiefs of Staff Committee (CSC) considered the possibility of enemy invasion, although bombing was expected.[45] Once France was out, it was obvious that the CSC needed to develop a new strategy and draft assessments were provided to the War Cabinet on 25 May. Amazingly, little had changed and Britain's service chiefs concluded, 'Germany might still be defeated by economic pressure, by a combination of air attack on economic objectives in Germany and on German morale and the creation of widespread revolt in her conquered territories.'[46]

Churchill was easily convinced by the fervent arguments of Air Chief Marshal Sir Cyril L. N. Newall that Bomber Command was capable of inflicting a 'knock-out' blow against the Germany economy. On 15 May, the Cabinet had approved a night-bombing campaign against the Ruhr and Newall claimed that Bomber Command could put 100 bombers a night over this region and destroy important targets like oil refineries and railroad marshalling yards.[47] Newall and the rest of the British service chiefs concluded that 'air attacks on Germany's oil centres will be an important contribution to the enemy's defeat...' and predicted that bombing would cause widespread shortages of food and oil in Germany by the winter of 1940–41, followed by a significant decline in industrial production by mid-1941. In other words, the RAF leadership was telling Churchill that as long as Britain could hold out against invasion, Bomber Command could bring the Third Reich to its knees within a year. At a Cabinet meeting on 20 June, Newall went so far as to state that 'our bomb raids were hitting Germany considerably harder than the German raids were hitting us'.[48] Professor Lindemann supported strategic bombing and advised Churchill that German will to resist could be broken through an air campaign. By 3 September, Churchill told the Cabinet that 'the bombers alone provide the means of victory'.[49] Unfortunately, this was an exaggeration of air power's potential to win wars without support of ground operations.

Churchill's strategic choices were shaped by faulty economic intelligence from the Air Ministry, an unimaginative CSC and exaggerated damage assessments by the RAF. Bomber Command had no ability to mount a 'knock-out' blow in the next 12 months because its numbers of aircraft were too few, its losses too high, its bombs too small and its navigation techniques completely inadequate for precision night-bombing of industrial-size targets. During July and August 1940 Bomber Command was incapable of sending more than 30–50 bombers against a single target and this number only increased to up to 130 bombers by the last quarter of the year. In contrast, the Luftwaffe was capable of sending 400 medium bombers against a single target. Priorities changed weekly – first oil, then armaments industries, then rail yards. In July, Bomber Command prepared Operation *Razzle* to try to burn German agricultural crops.[50] Lack of night navigational aids was the Achilles' heel of Bomber Command, although this was not fully realized until August 1941; then the Butt Report embarrassingly revealed that only 5 per cent of RAF night bombers dropped their bombs within 5 miles of their aim point. In fact, the British bombing efforts of 1940 inflicted hardly any damage on the German war economy at all and the CSC ignored the fact that Germany was importing 900,000 tons of oil per year from the USSR.

Nor were Bomber Command's Hampden and Whitley medium bombers up to the task of conducting a strategic bombing campaign, with losses amounting to 85 per cent and 53 per cent of production respectively. While the Wellington medium bomber was a decent aircraft, it was still being built in inadequate numbers and the RAF would not receive its first heavy bombers until February 1941.

Due to wishful thinking that the Nazi regime would suffer internal collapse – a rosy view held over from Chamberlain's Cabinet – Churchill became convinced that clandestine operations in occupied Europe could also contribute to victory. As often occurs when democracies look at authoritarian regimes, the British War Cabinet believed that the Third Reich was internally fragile and could be brought to collapse with the right external force. Clement Attlee went so far as to assert that Hitler 'had to win by the end of the year' before his economy and domestic support collapsed – which was more wishful thinking than sober assessment. Despite possession of some useful signals intelligence from Enigma, the British leadership at this time had very little solid information on the Germany economy or conditions in occupied Europe. The Special Operations Executive (SOE) was formed to support European resistance movements, although initially the SOE teams had very few resources and it was too soon for serious resistance movements to have arisen in Western Europe. Indeed, after Mers-el-Kébir few people in occupied France wanted to stick their necks out to work with the British, who were expected to be defeated soon. Collaboration with the enemy seemed a much safer bet for most, so SOE had little chance until Allied prospects for victory improved.

Churchill knew that Britain lacked the resources to conduct large-scale ground operations against Germany for some time, but hoped to employ the newly created Commando units to mount raids all along the coast of occupied Europe. Yet like the rest of the British Army after Dunkirk, the Commandos at this point were poorly equipped, poorly trained and incapable of mounting serious raids against the continent before 1941. Furthermore, the effort to create elite forces when the bulk of the regular field forces were short of junior officers and NCOs was recklessly irresponsible and driven by Churchill's intent to publicly demonstrate offensive spirit, not by military necessity. Thus without a real ability to hurt the Third Reich in the near term, the only viable offensive strategy aside from strategic bombing that Britain could pursue in 1940 was to concentrate its slim resources against Italy in the Mediterranean and Vichy France's overseas colonies, although even this could not lead to any real advantage in itself. Amazingly, during the Dunkirk evacuation the CSC was able to devote time to draft plans to send an expeditionary force to Crete.[51] Churchill would continue to favour these 'peripheral' operations for the rest of the war, all in an effort to evade the central truth – Great Britain lacked the resources to fight a major ground war in Europe on its own. Churchill's strategic formulations were ultimately based upon two assumptions – that Hitler would make a serious strategic mistake that Britain could exploit, and that the United States would fully support Great Britain and eventually join the conflict. Even the CSC concluded that 'without [the full economic and financial support of the United States] we do not think we could continue the war with any chance of success'.[52] In other words, Churchill's strategy was to pray for two separate miracles to occur, barring which, Great Britain had no chance of defeating the Third Reich.

Of course, most British strategy after Dunkirk was defensive in nature. The CSC assessed that 'there are three ways in which Germany might break down the resistance of the United Kingdom – unrestricted air attack aimed at breaking public morale, starvation of the country by attack on shipping and ports, and occupation by invasion'.[53] Oddly, Churchill did not initially believe that the Luftwaffe would attack civilian targets in England. At the Cabinet meeting on 18 May, Churchill stated that he 'thought the Germans would not adopt a policy of indiscriminate bombing' and would instead focus on attacking 'specific military targets'.[54] He was soon disabused of this optimistic view of German restraint. Nowhere was it more obvious that the War Cabinet was basing its decisions upon opinions rather than facts, than in the inordinate amount of time spent discussing measures to counter potential pro-German Fifth Columnists. Much of these discussions were based upon rumours from France and Holland, not proper intelligence assessments by Britain's security services like MI5. Indeed, Churchill sacked the long-time director of MI5, Vernon Kell, shortly after Dunkirk and then saddled the agency with rounding up and interning enemy aliens on the Isle of Man. Many of the German nationals were German Jews, who had no reason to cooperate with the Nazis and who could have contributed their language skills to the Allied war effort.[55] The Fifth Column and 'spy scare' wasted a great deal of the Cabinet's time during the summer of 1940.

Within the Cabinet, Churchill stated that he did not regard a German invasion as either likely or even feasible, even though the Royal Navy disagreed with his upbeat prognosis. It is not clear why Churchill would believe this, any more than he would believe that the Luftwaffe would not bomb civilian targets, but it was not based upon intelligence assessments. Yet in public, Churchill made frequent and lurid references to the threat of invasion, clearly in an effort to invigorate public opinion and to banish any considerations of negotiations with the enemy. It is likely that he believed a call to arms in the face of a national emergency would harden morale and get the British population accustomed to the idea of fighting and winning a war, rather than trying to find ways of getting out of it.

Victors' Choice: Hitler's Plethora of Strategic Options

On 9 October 1939, Hitler had spelled out his strategic intent for *Fall Gelb* (the campaign against France, Belgium and Holland) in Führer Directive No. 6, to 'win as much territory as possible in Holland, Belgium and Northern France to serve as a base for the successful prosecution of the air and sea war against England... .'[56] On 29 November 1939, Hitler further specified in Führer Directive No. 9 that, once the Allied armies were broken in the field, he intended to unleash the Luftwaffe and Kriegsmarine to 'deal an annihilating blow to the English economy'.[57] Hitler did not expect to overwhelm the Western Allies in a single campaign and made no plans for any operations beyond *Fall Gelb*. However, thanks to superior battlefield leadership and use of combined-arms tactics, the German Army (Heer) and Luftwaffe achieved an unexpectedly rapid victory over France, which offered Hitler a wide range of strategic options for follow-on operations. France was completely defeated and Britain – while still in the war – could not seriously threaten his hold on occupied Europe.

Although the Wehrmacht had not prepared for a war against Great Britain, military planners began to consider this possibility during the 1938 Munich Crisis. On 22 September 1938, General der Flieger Helmuth Felmy, commander of Luftflotte 2, wrote a memorandum for Generalfeldmarschall Hermann Göring, head of the Luftwaffe, on how a potential air campaign against Britain could be waged.[58] Felmy was pessimistic about the Luftwaffe's ability to conduct serious bombing attacks on England, but Göring was insulted by Felmy's report and suppressed it. In August 1939, Generalleutnant Hans Geisler, who worked on Felmy's staff in Luftflotte 2, took another look at the problem of attacking Great Britain from the air and concluded that the Luftwaffe's bomber force could not achieve decisive results on their own.[59] Geisler concluded that 'an air war against Britain in 1940 can only result in partial, though important, success, which could not have an effect, and threaten the British conduct of the war, before the second year of the war'. In short, Geisler stated that the Luftwaffe could only inflict significant damage upon Great Britain with a protracted air campaign over a period of at least two years.[60] Göring ignored Geisler as well and that officer was retired early.

In early 1939, Oberst Josef 'Beppo' Schmid, in charge of the Luftwaffe's 5th Branch (intelligence), ordered a study conducted on Great Britain. Schmid directed that not only Luftwaffe intelligence personnel, but civilian scientists, economists and other specialists, would contribute to the project – which was very atypical of German intelligence production. The results were published three months before the outbreak of war in a 94-page document known as *Studie Blau* (Blue Study). In modern parlance, this study would represent a Joint Intelligence Preparation of the Environment (JIPOE) product. Although some of the information used in the report was 4–5 years out of date – particularly about the British aircraft industry – it was a good baseline to assess Great Britain as an opponent. The study also incorporated imagery from the clandestine aerial reconnaissance effort over Great Britain that had begun in 1936 and then greatly expanded after the Munich Crisis. By mid-1939, the Luftwaffe had completely mapped Great Britain from the sky – the first aerial survey completed of Great Britain. Göring liked the report because it supported his notion that a strategic air campaign against Great Britain was feasible, which was a feather in Schmid's cap. However, *Studie Blau* was essentially a one-shot effort and Schmid did not have it updated after the war started.[61] By the time that *Studie Blau* was used by the Luftwaffe for planning in July 1940, it was well out of date.

Whereas the Luftwaffe was thinking about war with Great Britain, the Kriegsmarine was slow to consider anything beyond traditional U-Boat warfare against British trade. By the second month of the war, senior leadership within the Kriegsmarine decided to conduct a staff estimate to study possible options against Great Britain, including blockade and an amphibious landing. Vizeadmiral Otto Schniewind, the chief of staff of the Kriegsmarine's Seekriegsleitung (Skl), responsible for planning naval operations, formed a small group of planners under Korvettenkapitän Hans-Jürgen Reinicke, which spent five days assessing the requirements for a possible amphibious landing in England. Reinicke's *Studie Röt* (Red Study) was brief, only 12 pages, and emphasized the considerable difficulties of trying to mount any kind of landing operation unless the Royal Navy was neutralized. In essence, the study was done in a perfunctory manner and laden with an a priori bias against invasion. As Walter Ansel noted, the 'negative Navy attitude encouraged a tendency to fight the problem, instead of exploring what could be done'.[62] Reinicke's study regarded invasion as a very risky option in the face of opposition by the Royal Navy but concluded that it might be possible to land a small force on the eastern coast of England; he also recommended development of landing craft – just in case. The Reinicke study, submitted to the OKW (Oberkommando der Wehrmacht) on 1 December 1939, came down in favour of the blockade strategy as the best course of action against Great Britain. This conclusion was in line with the Kriegsmarine's existing capabilities and doctrine, since this force had primarily been structured to conduct anti-commerce operations against Great Britain, with U-Boats and a small number of powerful surface raiders. The Z-Plan, approved in March 1939, was intended to rectify the Kriegsmarine's inferiority versus the Royal Navy by constructing a balanced surface fleet, but Hitler cancelled this ambitious programme at the beginning of the war.

The other services in the OKW were asked to review the Reinicke study and the OKH decided to conduct its own staff study, led by Oberst Carl-Heinrich von Stülpnagel and Major Helmuth Stieff from the Operations Section.[63] At this point, von Stülpnagel was already a covert member of the anti-Nazi resistance and Stieff was also hostile to the regime; both men would be hanged in August 1944 for their role in the July 20th Plot. In any case, on 13 December 1939 the OKH study – designated *Nordwest* – assessed that a larger landing in East Anglia, consisting of 3–4 infantry divisions and supported by an airborne landing, was feasible. Like the OKH study, this also recommended a second echelon, consisting of two Panzer and one motorized division, as an exploitation force. Göring rejected the OKW assessment since it asked his service to do too much, and the Kriegsmarine remained unreceptive to the entire concept. Thus, the *Nordwest* study was shelved by Christmas 1939.

Hitler did not have a War Cabinet like Churchill, but he did not make his strategic choices in a vacuum. Instead he regularly attended Führer Conferences with his military advisors, but unlike Churchill these were not daily and he received much less input from civilians. Hitler sought professional military estimates from his services chiefs

(Generalfeldmarschall Walther Brauchitsch of the Heer, Göring of the Luftwaffe, Großadmiral Erich Raeder of the Kriegsmarine), and their respective staffs in the Oberkommando des Heeres (OKH, with Generaloberst Franz Halder as chief of staff), the Oberkommando der Luftwaffe (OKL, with General der Flieger Hans Jeschonnek as chief of staff) and the Oberkommando der Marine (OKM) and its planning group known as the Seekriegsleitung (Skl, headed by Vizeadmiral Otto Schniewind). Each of the services was supposed to coordinate through the OKW, headed by Generalfeldmarschall Wilhelm Keitel and his head of operations, General der Artillerie Alfred Jodl, but in reality inter-service cooperation was often poor and marked by rivalry. The OKW was created in 1938 to increase Hitler's control over the military, not to act as a joint headquarters. In terms of intelligence support in regard to Great Britain, Hitler was heavily dependent upon Admiral Wilhelm Canaris's Abwehr, which was subordinate to the OKW. Hitler also received input from his Foreign Minister, Joachim Ribbentrop, and his Minister of Propaganda, Josef Goebbels. Ribbentrop had served as ambassador in London before the war but his obnoxious behaviour made him a diplomatic flop and he had a burning hatred for England; Ribbentrop was one of the few German leaders opposed to negotiating a settlement with Britain.

While Churchill's War Cabinet often wasted time on secondary issues and made decisions based upon inaccurate information, Hitler had no real mechanism for formulating grand strategy. Instead, he consulted with the various service chiefs in order to determine what they could accomplish and then gave vague planning guidance, often encouraging competing planning efforts between the services. He then stuck his finger into the air and made his decision based on his personal inclinations. Despite the excellent traditions of the old *Großer Generalstab* (Great General Staff), German military men were not trained or encouraged to conduct strategic planning and generally shied away from economic, political and technological issues. Instead, these men were trained to conduct *Bewegungskrieg* (manoeuvre warfare) and they were honed to be the consummate crafters of operational-level campaign plans, but nothing higher. In particular, the quality of military planning in Halder's OKH was pedestrian and best suited to planning pincer-style offensives in a sterile way, without regard to weather or logistics.

When faced with an obdurate Great Britain, Hitler was uncertain how to proceed and he provided no real command guidance for several weeks after the French capitulation. Führer Directive No. 9 had spelled out a broad outline of attacking the British economy through air attacks on British ports, oil storage facilities and key war industries; mining of coastal waterways; and U-Boat, surface raider and aircraft attacks on shipping.[64] The mining and anti-shipping attacks had commenced from the outset of the war and by the end of June 1940 they had accounted for 469 merchant ships of 1.67 million tons (GRT); against this, the Kriegsmarine had lost the pocket-battleship *Admiral Graf Spee* and 19 U-Boats. However, Hitler had not yet authorized any serious bombing of ports or other ground targets. Great Britain's food imports were down about 10 per cent from pre-war totals – not entirely due to enemy action – but its economy had only been marginally impacted by Germany's anti-commerce operations. Clearly, something new was needed in order to push Britain toward negotiations to end the war, which was Hitler's desired end-state. Inside the OKW, the *Nordwest* study was dusted off and discussions were held as to what could be accomplished. Jodl drafted a memo on 30 June which outlined Germany's six strategic options:[65]

1. **Diplomacy:** Attempt to negotiate a settlement with Great Britain.
2. **Blockade/trade war (*Handelskrieg*):** Increase the pressure on Great Britain's economy by bombing commercial ports and critical facilities, sinking more shipping.
3. **Terror bombing:** Attempt to break British civilian morale by bombing all major cities.
4. **Invade:** Conduct an amphibious landing in England to force a capitulation.

5. **Indirect approach:** Conduct military operations against Great Britain's overseas territories in the Mediterranean region, in order to increase pressure on them and to secure resources and bases.

6. **Shift to a defensive strategy:** Ignore Great Britain and fortify Germany's position in occupied Europe. Demobilize some of the ground army and concentrate on strengthening the German economy and military technology, waiting for others to make mistakes.

In the heady days of late June to early July 1940, Hitler actually appeared willing to pursue all six strategic options, nearly simultaneously. He hoped to ease Great Britain out of the war without too great an expenditure of German lives and resources. Brauchitsch and most of the OKH believed that Great Britain was beaten after Dunkirk and that a diplomatic solution was within reach. Although Hitler's belief that peace was possible with Britain is often presented as wishful thinking, he did have some concrete evidence that there were influential British people who were sympathetic towards an accommodation with Germany.

Hitler's sudden and dramatic rise in Germany had attracted admirers in Britain as well. Unity Mitford was one of the first and most fanatical, who wormed her way into Hitler's inner circle and propagated the idea that Germany and Britain could cooperate against Communism. In 1932, Sir Oswald Mosley formed the British Union of Fascists (BUF) and one of his close associates was Major General (ret.) J. F. C. Fuller, the father of British tank forces in the World War I. In 1935, the Anglo-German Fellowship was founded based upon a suggestion by the Prince of Wales for a council to promote better relations with Germany; many influential Britons flocked to the council, including members of Churchill's own Conservative Party. Another member was Admiral Sir Barry Edward Domvile (retired 1936), a former head of British naval intelligence, who had fascist sympathies; in 1937 he founded another organization known as 'the Link', a pro-Nazi group that gained over 4,000 members. British fascists flocked to Hitler at the Nuremburg rallies and the 1936 Olympics – demonstrating to him that he did have ardent sympathizers in Great Britain. As far as Hitler could tell from these misguided Britons, an Anglo-German collaboration was feasible.

Yet Hitler was inconsistent with the diplomacy option, talking peace one moment, then devastation if he did not get what he wanted. Despite rambling table talk with his intimates about his admiration for the British Empire, he was unwilling to make even token efforts to further diplomacy. Stephen Bungay has claimed that on 22 June Hitler issued a month-long ban prohibiting the Luftwaffe from flying over Great Britain in order to tone down hostilities, but even if this occurred, it was not enforced.[66] He said that he wanted to demonstrate restraint in order to 'drive a wedge between the [British] people and their leaders'.[67] Yet British Cabinet records indicate a number of Luftwaffe night raids over Cardiff, Southampton, Bristol and Newcastle during this period, resulting in over 100 dead and 600 wounded.[68] If Hitler intended a halt to bombing as a gesture, the British clearly missed it.

Air actions over the English Channel were allowed as well as anti-commerce attacks. Hitler was truly baffled by the British rejection of negotiations, but was unwilling to spend much political capital to make a diplomatic solution work. He could have made offers to repatriate some of the wounded British prisoners captured in France or to evacuate the Channel Islands to jump-start negotiations, but it apparently never crossed his mind. He also could have suspended U-Boat attacks on British shipping, but he did not. German intelligence knew about Halifax's desire to open negotiations, but was unwilling to throw a bone to the pro-peace faction in Churchill's Cabinet. British historians have tended to downplay the possibilities for peace in 1940 because of Churchill's distrust of Hitler, but they ignore the precedent that Great Britain in similar circumstances negotiated the Treaty of Amiens in 1802 with another would-be European conqueror, Napoleon. While the treaty only resulted in a 14-month truce between England and France, it did demonstrate that a diplomatic solution was not completely far-fetched in a situation where England was left without continental allies.

Yet Hitler wanted a victor's peace, in which Britain's leaders acknowledged that they had lost the war and recognized Germany's conquests; in return, Germany would leave Great Britain and its empire alone. He lacked the flexibility of Napoleon, who was willing to make concessions to secure a peace treaty. After trying nothing and being out of ideas, Hitler's patience with a diplomatic solution ran out by mid-July and his final 'appeal to reason in England' in his speech in Berlin on 19 July was delivered in the language of war, not diplomacy. In his address, he stated that if Great Britain continued the war, then 'a great world empire will be destroyed'. In Hitler's mind, the British obviously needed another large dose of German military firepower before they would negotiate – a complete misread of the British mood at the time.

Großadmiral Raeder was the main proponent of the *Handelskrieg* (trade war) or Blockade strategy, because it was the least risky and costly for his service. However, in July 1940 the Kriegsmarine only had an average of about 15 operational U-Boats for Atlantic patrols, which was too few to seriously disrupt Britain's convoys. Thus, for the blockade strategy to work, the Luftwaffe also had to play a major role by attacking both shipping and British ports. Raeder urged an all-out bombing effort against Liverpool to disrupt British imports.[69] Yet Göring did not like cooperating with the Kriegsmarine since he was suspicious that Raeder wanted to build up a naval air arm which would undercut his own Luftwaffe fiefdom and he also believed that the blockade would take too long. Like Keitel and Jodl in the OKW, Göring optimistically believed that Britain was greatly weakened after Dunkirk and that one or two sharp blows would shatter its will to remain in the war. Thus Göring opposed the blockade strategy and ignored the invasion strategy, instead choosing to rely upon his Luftwaffe to impose a military solution upon Britain. While paying lip service to Hitler's alleged ban on combat operations over Britain, on 30 June Göring instructed his two primary operational commanders – Generalfeldmarschall Albert Kesselring with Luftflotte 2 and Generalfeldmarschall Hugo Sperrle with Luftflotte 3 – to begin efforts to lure the RAF's Fighter Command into air battles over the English Channel where it could be destroyed. Göring's initiative was strictly tactical, made without regard to strategic goals and it would shape how planning for *Seelöwe* unfolded over the next three months. Kesselring and Sperrle had only this vague guidance on which to proceed, but in early July they began attacking British coastal convoys in the English Channel in order to entice the Royal Air Force into battle. By 4 July, the *Kanalkampf* (Channel Battle) had begun in earnest and drew the Luftwaffe into a meaningless daily quest for local air superiority.

Göring was also a proponent of area bombing to terrorize the British population, in line with theories advocated by the Italian aviator Emilio Douhet in his influential book, *The Command of the Air* (1921). While Hitler had yet to authorize area bombing, Göring made it clear that his Luftwaffe had the resources to flatten London and other cities, as required. He wanted to get the lion's share of the credit for defeating Great Britain, which would increase his prestige in the Nazi hierarchy. However, the Kriegsmarine was opposed to area bombing because it wasted resources and instead wanted British ports bombed, while the OKW generally favoured attacks on industrial targets. Air power advocates could claim that bombing could win alone, but traditional army and navy officers had much less faith that civilian morale could be broken by bombing.

As to invasion, Raeder tried to talk Hitler out of it from the beginning but was forced to work on planning nonetheless. Due to Raeder's lack of enthusiasm for the project, the Kriegsmarine briefings at the Führer Conference in Berlin on 21 June left Hitler unimpressed; after the briefings he told his naval aide, 'How can we do an operation of this sort? It looks completely impossible to me. Losses will be heavy and no guarantee of success.'[70] Still, like all politicians, he wanted to keep his options open and on 2 July Hitler asked for further estimates from each of the services before he made a decision and stated that 'the plan to invade England has not taken any definite shape'. He did authorize some preparations 'for a possible operation' to begin.[71]

Both the Luftwaffe and Heer were keen to commit forces into the Mediterranean region or North Africa – either with or without Italian help – to threaten Great Britain's overseas possessions. The OKH was particularly interested in going after Gibraltar, which would require Spanish support, and Hitler agreed to this in principle. Diplomatic discussions with Spain were initiated while the OKH began a study that would result in *Unternehmen Felix*. However, at this point, the indirect approach did not seem to offer the potential to achieve decisive results, so it was placed on the back burner.

Surprisingly, Hitler did give some consideration to shifting to a defensive strategy and simply waiting until Great Britain's bankruptcy and military impotence led to a reconsideration of negotiations. On 18 June, Hitler announced his intent to reduce the army from 167 to 120 divisions and informed the German public that many troops would soon be de-mobilized.[72] This was not only a popular move but one which reduced the drain on German economic resources to maintain a large army that was now mostly unemployed. A week later, Hitler told his architect Albert Speer to prepare to initiate the hugely expensive project to reconstruct Berlin and Nürnberg (Nuremburg) into showcase cities.[73] Hitler the conqueror wanted to become Hitler the builder. At the same time, Hitler initiated a programme to begin constructing defensive fortifications on the eastern border with the USSR.[74] Eventually, the OKH was informed that the Heer would be reduced to just 62 divisions, half of which would be Panzer or motorized infantry.[75] Under this option, German industry would focus on increasing construction of U-Boats and bombers to escalate anti-commerce attacks, but the Luftwaffe would not bomb civilian targets in England and the war would drift back to the level of the 'Phoney War' in the winter of 1939/40, with limited casualties on both sides. Yet the Germans knew that Great Britain was seriously draining its foreign currency reserves to pay for American-made military equipment and that this debt was unsustainable. Eventually, even Churchill would recognize that Great Britain was losing more in human and financial terms than it was gaining by remaining at war.

Without an existential threat of invasion or a Luftwaffe Blitz, not only would it have been extremely difficult for Churchill to rally his countrymen to make sacrifices in order to remain in a lost war but assistance from the United States would have likely evaporated. By focusing on internal development, the Third Reich could have built itself up into an industrial powerhouse and had the resources to fully modernize a mid-size military force to keep the Soviet Union in check. Unable to conduct decisive ground operations on its own in Europe and with its economic strangulation strategy ineffective, eventually Great Britain would have been forced to concede to negotiations at some point in 1941–42. Of all the mistakes Hitler made in 1940–41, his decision not to stop while he was ahead was his gravest. Defensive warfare was not to Hitler's taste and patience was not his best suit, so instead he began to look for alternatives. Although the military was looking westward trying to figure out how to neutralize Great Britain, Hitler was flailing about, intent upon using his unemployed armies to smash his other 'enemies' in Europe.

He found one enemy in neutral Switzerland. Prior to the war, German Swiss relations were decent and Germany had sold 90 Bf-109D/E fighters to Switzerland. However, the Germans did not respect Swiss neutrality and during *Fall Gelb* the Luftwaffe repeatedly violated Swiss airspace in order to strike targets in central France. On 1–3 June, Swiss fighters intercepted several German flights through their airspace; one He-111 bomber and one Bf-110C fighter were shot down and another damaged bomber was forced to land in Switzerland. One Swiss Bf-109D fighter was lost in action. Göring decided to retaliate and on 8 June, II./ZG 1 made a sweep into Swiss airspace with 28 Bf-110C fighters and encountered 15 Swiss Bf-109E fighters. Two Swiss fighters were damaged but the Luftwaffe lost four Bf-110C fighters. Swiss radio further inflamed the situation by referring to their pilots as 'the Heroes of the Nation' and their 'victory' over the Luftwaffe.[76] Hitler was infuriated that the Swiss used German-built fighters to kill at least a dozen German aircrew and openly threatened retribution. The Swiss pulled all their air patrols back from the border and the incidents ceased, but once France was defeated Hitler ordered the OKH to begin a staff study on invading Switzerland. Later, he would describe the Swiss as 'disgusting and miserable people' and say that they were the 'mortal enemies of the new Germany'.[77] The OKH duly developed an invasion plan known as *Unternehmen Tannenbaum,* which it kept continually updated until the end of 1943, while 11 army divisions were aligned for this irrational mission. Hitler was incensed about Switzerland's 'armed neutrality' and losses inflicted upon the Luftwaffe, although his race-driven ideology compelled him to speak of the desirability of bringing these racially akin people into the Third Reich's orbit.

Likewise, Hitler was also reconsidering his relationship with erstwhile confederate, Josef Stalin. Through cunning diplomacy, Germany had neutralized the military threat posed by the Soviet Union with the 1939 Molotov-Ribbentrop Pact, which was renewed in February 1940. The economic clauses of the pact effectively negated the British blockade by providing Germany with large amounts of grain, oil, iron ore and manganese. In return, Germany was required to supply the USSR with military and industrial technology, which grated upon Hitler, who was ideologically opposed to Communism. In *Mein Kampf,* Hitler had written that 'when we speak of new territory in Europe today we must principally think of Russia and the border states subject to her'.[78] In time, this predilection turned into the doctrine of *Lebensraum* (living space), which Hitler advocated to be obtained at the expense of the Soviet Union. In the short run, the relationship with the Soviet Union provided the Third Reich with the material resources needed to wage war in the west and create a strategic stockpile, but in the long run it could make the Red Army into a more formidable opponent. Thus, Hitler was almost as ambivalent about the Soviet Union as he was about Great Britain, one minute wanting to ally with them, the next seeking to destroy them. On 4 June, Hitler authorized the German News Bureau to broadcast excerpts of captured French documents, which revealed Operation *Pike* – an Anglo-French plan to bomb the Soviet oil fields at Baku from bases in Iraq and

Syria.[79] British efforts to take military action against the Soviet Union during the brief Russo-Finnish War were already public knowledge, but Operation *Pike* added fuel to the fire and Hitler was hoping to entice Stalin into joint military action against the British in the Middle East. On other days, he wanted a preventative war with Stalin before the Soviet Union grew too powerful. Hitler began socializing his preventative war concept with senior military leaders even before the French campaign ended and by mid-July he had Brauchitsch, Halder and others echoing his rhetoric about the Bolshevik threat. Although Hitler was the driving force behind the idea of attacking the Soviet Union, many others within the Wehrmacht – including Halder – were receptive to this idea as well and suffered post-war amnesia at the Nuremburg Tribunals about their own culpability.[80] Yet Hitler's desire to attack Switzerland and the Soviet Union was driven more by irrational racial views and paranoia than sober strategic calculations. Hitler dived into these martial fantasies to avoid the hard work of making his three service chiefs work together to win the war at hand.

Meanwhile, both the Kriegsmarine and the Heer hastened to produce updated staff estimates on the invasion option. Großadmiral Raeder remained opposed to invasion but had Konteradmiral Kurt Fricke of the Skl working on a more detailed assessment, called *Studie England*. Fricke's assessment recommended a narrow-front landing on the southern coast of England as soon as possible, to take advantage of the poor condition of the British Army after Dunkirk. In contrast, Halder allowed the OKH staff to prepare a ridiculous plan premised on Jodl's characterization of the effort as a 'mighty river crossing' (*gewaltsamen Flussübergang*).[81] Jodl wrote, in an OKW memo on 12 July, that 'building a bridge, a fully secured sea transport lane must be created in the Straits of Dover'.[82] Meanwhile, the OKH developed their plan without regard to naval transport capabilities, tidal factors or the enemy and airily called for landing 40 divisions in eight separate landing areas on a 235-mile-wide 'broad front' between Ramsgate and Lyme Bay, including a landing on the Isle of Wight. According to this concept, the first wave would consist of 260,000 troops in 13 divisions and would be landed in two to three days while the follow-on waves would include six Panzer-Divisionen; in other words, the OKH expected the Kriegsmarine to transport one-quarter of the German field army across the English Channel. The OKH argued that a 'broad front' landing was essential for rapidly overwhelming the British ground defences. On 13 July, Brauchitsch and Halder presented the OKH 'broad front' plan to Hitler in a two-hour planning conference at the Berghof in Bavaria.[83]

Relaxing in his mountain retreat, Hitler accepted the absurd OKH recommendations as the basis for an invasion plan, even though it was done without input from the Kriegsmarine. He also still paid lip service to the Kriegsmarine's blockade strategy of wrecking Britain's economy by exerting all possible air–sea pressure on its trade routes, although he thought it would take a year or more to succeed. Furthermore, Hitler was willing to give Göring and his Luftwaffe the chance to demonstrate their ability to force Britain to the peace table, even though their efforts were not linked to either the invasion or blockade strategies. Thus, each of the services appeared to be offering him an alternative means of knocking Great Britain out of the war; rather than choosing, he decided to let all of them proceed. Consequently, on 16 July Hitler issued Führer Directive No. 16, which stated that 'since England, in spite of her hopeless military situation, shows no sign of being ready to come to an understanding, I have decided to prepare a landing operation against England, and, if necessary, to carry it out'. The operation was designated *Seelöwe* (*Sea Lion*) and all preparations were to be completed by mid-August.

Raeder Tries to Delay *Sea Lion*

Contrary to popular opinion, most German military planning during the World War II was fairly slipshod in nature, conducted by a handful of staff officers operating in single-service environments and armed with faulty intelligence assessments. Logistical factors were generally given little weight, which would lead to disaster later in the war. Germany's largest naval operation in the World War II – the invasion of Norway (*Unternehmen Weserübung*) – was planned by 15 officers from the OKW and Skl in just five weeks.[84] Operation *Barbarossa*, the largest land operation ever mounted, was planned by a handful of OKH officers in just a few months. Ignorance of enemy strength, dispositions and intentions was usually a major weakness in German military planning. Thus, it should come as no surprise that *Seelöwe* was also thrown together in a similar manner. Generalmajor Hans von Greiffenberg's operations department in the OKH was forced to work on multiple planning efforts aside from *Seelöwe*, including invasion plans for Switzerland and early staff work on the Soviet Union. Oberst Werner Pistorius was assigned a small section to write the detailed plans for *Seelöwe*.[85]

Likewise, German naval planning in the Skl for a potential invasion of England was continually hindered by extreme conservatism in the top leadership. Großadmiral Raeder was traumatized by the Kriegsmarine's bloody losses in the Norwegian campaign, particularly the sinking of the brand-new heavy cruiser *Blucher*, and was opposed from the outset to another risky operation that could lead to the destruction of his remaining surface fleet. Indeed, he seemed more concerned with protecting his surface warships than winning the war. Schniewind, in charge of planning in Skl, also favoured putting off *Seelöwe* until spring 1941.[86] Raeder was an old-style naval commander, focused on big-ship operations and not keen to participate in further joint adventures with the Heer and Luftwaffe. His relations with Göring were particularly bitter and detrimental to inter-service cooperation. Nor was Raeder interested in pulling together an invasion fleet from civilian barges and assorted pionier equipment. Indeed, Raeder was the wrong man to be commanding a guerrilla force like the Kriegsmarine in 1940, but Hitler did not recognize his unsuitability until 1942.

When he first saw the guidance for *Seelöwe*, Raeder was livid that Hitler had accepted the OKH's 'broad front' proposal without consulting the Kriegsmarine, and army–navy friction flared at the Führer Conference in Berlin on 21 July. Raeder pointed out that the

Kriegsmarine had nothing like the ability to transport 40 divisions to England and rapidly land troops and heavy equipment on beaches. Rather, it would take a week or more to land even a smaller force and the Kriegsmarine lacked the warships to protect invasion convoys against the Royal Navy for such an extended period. Consequently, Raeder asserted his belief that a landing would only be possible after the Luftwaffe had won air superiority over the English Channel, and this absolutist position became the official Kriegsmarine position. Yet the demand for complete air superiority as an operational prerequisite was absurd; the Germans had conducted *Fall Gelb* without complete air superiority, and the crossing of the Meuse at Sedan was conducted in spite of intense Anglo-French air attacks.

Jeschonnek attended the conference for the Luftwaffe and claimed that Kesselring and Sperrle's forces were already defeating RAF Fighter Command over the English Channel, although this was far from correct. Although Fighter Command had lost 41 fighters during the *Kanalkampf*, the Luftwaffe lost over 60 aircraft. Hitler was misinformed that the Luftwaffe was inflicting 3:1 losses upon the RAF, when in actuality the Germans were suffering an overall 3:2 loss ratio against the RAF. It was at this point that Hitler accepted the notion that air superiority over the English Channel was feasible and the sine qua non for *Seelöwe* to succeed. Hitler now ordered that assembling the invasion fleet for *Seelöwe* be given top priority and allocated enormous resources to make this happen. Having seemingly satisfied Raeder's complaints, Hitler ordered him to accomplish his mission. Yet Raeder was far from satisfied and a week later he informed the OKH that with available shipping it would take ten days to land just the first wave, which provoked Halder into accusing the Kriegsmarine of lying by suggesting that a landing 'was not possible at all'. Halder rejected Raeder's data on transport availability.

Another important point about *Seelöwe* that is often missed is that the inability of the Heer and Kriegsmarine to agree on the exact timing of the landing greatly reduced the window of opportunity in which to conduct the operation. The OKH demanded a dawn landing and would not budge, while Skl demanded a night crossing when there was at least 50 per cent illumination from the moon, which therefore reduced the available dates to only 3 or 4 days per month.[87] Late September was chosen as the estimated date for S-Tag (the first day of the invasion) not because of good weather in the Channel, but because of moon conditions – which were virtually irrelevant to the landing itself.

On 29 July, a three-day OKH/Skl planning conference began at the Berghof, but the Luftwaffe did not attend. At this point, the OKH was trying to transform *Seelöwe* into a practical operation, but Raeder was intent upon either delaying or cancelling what he regarded as a futile endeavour. He stated that sufficient amphibious shipping would not be ready prior to 15 September, which left only a narrow invasion window during 22–26 September which met both the OKH and Skl prerequisities. Raeder told the Heer that the Kriegsmarine could only provide the *Admiral Hipper*, four destroyers and three torpedo boats to escort the invasion force, which was less than truthful. The Heer continued to demand that the first wave land at dawn, but Raeder said that this was bad for the Kriegsmarine and now recommended landing two hours after high tide – in broad daylight. He also criticized the Heer's desire to land a force on the Isle of Wight, which he said was too close to the Royal Navy base at Portsmouth. Finally, he stated that weather conditions in the Channel would likely hinder a landing operation, although it was the Skl that had chosen this period. Instead, Raeder recommended that *Seelöwe* should be postponed until spring 1941 when the battleships *Bismarck* and *Tirpitz* would be ready and, in the meantime, the blockade strategy should become the primary means of pressuring Britain. Brauchitsch and Halder stated that 'the Kriegsmarine in all probability will not provide us this autumn with the means for a successful invasion of Britain'. Fed up with the Kriegsmarine's foot-dragging and pessimistic attitude, the OKH raised the possibility of shifting forces to attack Gibraltar or the Suez Canal while maintaining the blockade of British ports.

On 30 July, the subject of the Soviet Union was brought up, even though the conference was supposed to focus on *Seelöwe*. In his postwar diary, Halder stated that he recommended maintaining friendly ties with the Soviet Union to avoid a two-front war and he mentioned the presence of Generalmajor Erich Marcks 'on special assignment'.[88] In fact, on that day Halder assigned Marcks to develop an operational plan for an invasion of the Soviet Union.[89] Six days later, on 5 August, Marcks briefed Halder on his Draft Operational Plan East, which is often referred to as 'the Marcks Plan'. Keitel also decided that the OKW would develop a plan for action against the Soviet Union and assigned Oberstleutnant Bernhard von Lossberg to this task, although it was not ready until 15 September.[90] The fact that the OKH and OKW were both willing to devote planning resources to a contingency option while they were still struggling to complete an urgent operational requirement is simply amazing.

On the third day of this conference, on 31 July, with the Heer drifting into discussions of a Mediterranean strategy, Raeder suddenly proposed a limited cross-Channel invasion with ten regimental groups – about 30,000 troops – in May 1941. He said that by that time the battleships *Bismarck* and *Tirpitz* could be used in the operation.[91] The fact that this limited operation did not meet Hitler's intent of conducting a decisive action was not addressed by Raeder. At this point, with the Heer and Kriegsmarine leadership unable to agree on much, Hitler decided to bring up the Soviet Union. First, he stated his belief that the blockade strategy could take one or two years to achieve results. Then he lapsed into a monologue:

> Britain's hope lies in Russia and the United States… Russia is the factor upon which Britain is relying most… .With Russia smashed, Britain's last hope would be shattered. Germany will then be master of Europe and the Balkans. Decision: Russia's destruction must therefore be made a part of this struggle. The sooner Russia is crushed, the better. If we start in May 1941, we should have five months to finish the job.[92]

Hitler then discussed committing 120 divisions to the Eastern campaign.

As if reading from cue cards, Brauchitsch stated that 'if we cannot reach a decision against England, the danger remains that England will ally herself with Russia; the question then is whether we should carry on a war on two fronts, one of which would be Russia'. Generalmajor Walter Warlimont, representing the OKW at the conference, confirmed that Hitler stated he had decided to rid the world 'once and for all' of the danger of Bolshevism by a surprise attack on the USSR.[93]

At this point, many historians have made the mistake of assuming that Operation *Barbarossa*, the invasion of the Soviet Union, was now inevitable and had displaced *Seelöwe* and all other strategic options in Hitler's mind. However, Hitler did not yet have the results of either the OKH or OKW studies, and his early statements on his desired end-state were to occupy the Ukraine and the Baltic States, not to destroy the Soviet state in toto. Nor did Hitler even consider the impact of the loss of Soviet oil and grain upon his economy, which an invasion would surely precipitate. What Hitler was really stating at this conference was his frustration with his military chiefs to develop a workable plan to knock Great Britain out of the war, but he vented his anger toward his traditional enemy – Bolshevism. He made these declarations about attacking the Soviet Union bereft of any military, economic or intelligence data. In addition, it is important to note that Hitler had also recently asked for staff studies on the possibility of invading Switzerland (*Unternehmen Tannenbaum*), Iceland (*Unternehmen Ikarus*) and Ireland (*Unternehmen Grün*) – he was literally all over the place. Inconsistent, impulsive and irrational are the appropriate words to describe Hitler's strategic rationale at this point, not inevitable.

After announcing his intent to attack the Soviet Union, on 1 August Hitler reversed back to deal with his British problem and announced Führer Directive No. 17. This document ordered the intensification of air and sea attacks against Great Britain, in order to seek a decision. In conjunction with this directive, the OKL issued plan *Adlerangriff* (Eagle Attack), which specified massive attacks against Fighter Command's bases to destroy the RAF's fighter strength as well as ports and military-industrial targets to support the blockade strategy. In short, *Adlerangriff* was still primarily a tactical plan fixated on achieving local superiority, with only a partial effort devoted to wrecking the British economy and industrial base.

While the Luftwaffe moved forward with the execution of *Adlerangriff*, the OKH and the Kriegsmarine continued with the planning of *Seelöwe*, but they were working at cross-purposes. The OKH continued to press for as many landing sites as possible, while the Skl sought to land at only a few points. On 7 August, Halder met with the Skl leadership (Schniewind, Fricke, Reinicke) but failed to reach a compromise.[94] In particular, the Skl wanted to abandon the OKH's intention to land troops at Deal to help with securing the port of Dover and in Lyme Bay. Instead, the Skl wanted to concentrate on landings between Folkestone and Eastbourne, because this was all they felt that they might be able to protect with mine barriers. In frustration, Halder sent a memo of complaint to the OKW on 8 August, which stated that landings in these areas would be easy for the British Army to contain and 'even with the best preparation, the chances of success are extremely low'. It was in frustration at the cancellation of the Deal landing that Halder made his oft-quoted remark that being restricted to a narrow-front landing would be like 'putting the landing troops through a sausage machine'. Halder also stated that due to the Kriegsmarine's inability to unload the first and second echelons quickly, it would be impossible for German forces to mount a serious breakout effort from the beachheads until S-Tag plus 14.[95]

After much gnashing of teeth, Halder finally accepted that the Kriegsmarine had transport limitations and on 10 August the OKH submitted a reduced-scale plan that called for the landing of ten divisions within four days along a 100-mile-wide front. Raeder issued a counter-proposal for landing six divisions within six days along a 60-mile-wide front. After weeks of relative non-involvement, the OKW issued a directive on 18 August that called for only four landings between Folkestone and Brighton. The landings closer to Dover and in Lyme Bay were omitted. The OKH essentially ignored this version of the plan and continued to perfect its own plan. On 21 August, the OKH boldly proposed to conduct a preliminary airborne landing on the Isle of Wight to eliminate British coastal batteries and to neutralize the British naval base at Portsmouth, but the Luftwaffe failed to support this concept.[96]

After another week of bickering, on 26 August Hitler finally ordered the OKH to modify its plans to match the Kriegsmarine's transport capabilities and landing requirements. The result was the 'final' *Seelöwe* plan, issued on 30 August, which was planned for implementation on 15 September. Under the forced compromise, *Seelöwe* directed the landing of ten German divisions from the 9. Armee (AOK 9) and 16. Armee (AOK 16) in the first wave of the operation on S-Tag as follows:

- **Landing Zone B** (west of Folkestone): XIII Armeekorps with the 17. and 35. Infanterie-Divisionen, supported with an airborne landing by 7. Flieger-Division.
- **Landing Zone C** (Rye, east of Hastings): VII Armeekorps with 7. Infanterie-Division and 1. Gebirgs-Division.
- **Landing Zone D** (Bexhill/Eastbourne): XXXVII Armeekorps with 26. and 34. Infanterie-Divisionen.
- **Landing Zone E** (Brighton): VIII Armeekorps with 8. and 28. Infanterie-Divisionen and 6. Gebirgs-Division.

The second wave would consist of four Panzer-Divisionen (4, 7, 8, 10), two motorized infantry divisions (20, 29), two infantry divisions (12, 30), the Infanterie-Regiment (mot.) *Großdeutschland* and the brigade-size *Leibstandarte SS Adolf Hitler* (*LSSAH*). The third wave would consist of six infantry divisions (15, 24, 45, 58, 78, 164). Altogether, *Seelöwe* was expected to land the equivalent of 25 divisions in England within about 15 to 18 days. The 16. Armee would embark its forces from the ports of Rotterdam, Antwerp, Ostend, Dunkirk and Calais, while the 9. Armee would embark from Boulogne and Le Havre.[97] The Kriegsmarine was tasked with clearing British mines in the path of the invasion armada as well as laying protective minefields on both flanks in order to deter intervention by the Royal Navy. The Luftwaffe was tasked with gaining air superiority over the landing area and attacking any British warships that made it through the mine belt. Once ashore in strength, the Heer's mission was to 'defeat the British Army and to occupy the capital and further regions of England if the situation requires it'.

The Heer leadership, which had been leading the effort to turn *Seelöwe* into a reality, were crestfallen. Although the reduced frontage was a great concern, a real problem was that Folkestone would be the only port within easy reach of the landing force and it was far too small to sustain a ten-division force. Unlike the Allied leaders who planned the Normandy landings in 1944, the Kriegsmarine was determined to land well away from British ports due to their fear of the Royal Navy. If the Heer wanted Dover, Ramsgate and other ports, they would have to go take them themselves. The Heer also remained very annoyed about the Kriegsmarine's estimates of how long it would take to land the force, slowing the build-up to a crawl. Intervention by the Royal Navy was a certainty and having transports unloading for days offshore would provide juicy targets. Under these limitations, there was no hope of surprise and even a reduced-strength British Army would have plenty of time to gather its strength around the beachheads. The OKH anticipated bitter fighting for the beachheads, trusting to superior German tactical abilities to carry the day. Yet a successful breakout from such constricted beachheads, with poor logistical support, did not appear likely; the Heer leadership began to lose faith that *Seelöwe* would be successful.

No sooner had the OKH issued its operational order, than the Skl interjected that it would need an additional week to prepare to lay the barrier minefields. The Kriegsmarine also stated that it needed ten days of warning between the decision to conduct *Seelöwe* and actual mission execution. The OKW issued an order on 3 September, which established the updated timetable for *Seelöwe*; it agreed to the ten-day warning period and set S-Tag as 21 September.[98]

While preparing for the actual *Seelöwe,* both the OKH and Skl were busy planning diversionary and deception operations to confuse British intelligence. German forces in France intended to use *Fall Grün* to simulate a landing operation in Ireland with two corps, sailing from Bordeaux. Enough troops and ships were allocated to simulate loading operations to attract British attention, although the British CSC was more concerned about airborne landings. Due to British concerns about neutral Ireland's lack of coastal defences, the CSC prepared Plan W, which envisioned the 53rd Infantry Division (TA) moving from Belfast into Ireland to oppose any German landings – with or without Irish cooperation. At best, *Fall Grün* helped to divert one low-quality TA division and some planning resources, but the British knew that a landing in Ireland would be much more logistically difficult to sustain.

In August, the Skl put an incredible amount of effort into planning two diversionary actions: a cruiser raid and *Unternehmen Herbstreise* (Operation *Autumn Journey*), intended to simulate a major landing operation conducted from Norwegian and German ports against the northern coast of Britain. Raeder wanted to use the heavy cruiser *Admiral Hipper* and possibly the pocket-battleship *Admiral Scheer* to sail on S-Tag minus 6 to attack British cruiser patrols in the Denmark Straits, then attempt a breakout to raid Atlantic convoys. He believed that the Home Fleet might be tempted to send some of its capital ships to chase this red herring, although this seemed very unlikely. *Herbstreise* directed three convoys with a total of 11 merchantmen and 20 small escorts to depart from Norwegian ports with troops from three different divisions on S-Tag minus 3, sail into the North Sea and return to disembark their troops by S-Tag minus 2. An even more prominent convoy, including the 50,000-ton liners *Bremen* and *Europa* and the 18,000-ton liners *Gneisenau* and *Potsdam*, would depart from German ports escorted by the light cruiser *Emden*. The Skl was very impressed with *Herbstreise,* but the Heer – after weeks of hearing Kriegsmarine complaints about lack of transport – felt the navy was diverting precious merchantmen and warships away from the primary mission area. In particular, the Heer wanted every warship available protecting their convoys in the English Channel, not gallivanting around the Denmark Straits or North Sea. The amount of effort put into *Herbstreise* convinced many Heer leaders that the Kriegsmarine was not serious about conducting *Seelöwe*.

Many historians have attempted to use the 30 August OKH order and the 3 September OKW update for *Seelöwe* as the definitive version of the invasion plan, but in fact *Seelöwe* remained in constant flux, both before and after the target dates of 15–26 September 1940. Indeed, the OKH plan stressed that due to 'a large number of circumstances which cannot be determined in advance', the landing operations needed to be flexible and allow room for on-the-spot initiative of local commanders.[99] It is also important to note that German military operations in the World War II were not based on rigid plans. Instead, the Germans tended to develop a quick, loose scheme of manoeuvre, but actual operations were constantly tinkered with even during execution, as circumstances developed. In 1941, Hitler would invade the Soviet Union with the critical question of deep objectives and main effort still undecided. Similarly, *Case Blau* (the German summer offensive in Russia in 1942) was conducted with priorities shifting between Stalingrad and the Caucasus on a weekly basis. As a military commander, Hitler was both opportunistic and nervously undisciplined, frequently shifting objectives and apprehensive of enemy counter-moves. Thus, had *Seelöwe* been attempted, it is likely that local commanders, as well as Hitler, the OKH and the Skl would all have made significant modifications to the base plan as circumstances developed.

CHAPTER 2

Improvising an Invasion Force

Germany's Lack of Amphibious Shipping and Methods

At the start of the World War II, Japan was the only nation with any significant amphibious capabilities and doctrine to land troops on an opposed shore. During the 1930s, the Japanese developed the Special Naval Landing Forces (SNLF) and used them in multiple coastal operations in the Sino-Japanese War. By 1937, the Japanese had introduced the 21-ton Daihatsu-class landing craft with a bow-mounted ramp and the ability to land 70 troops or a light tank. By 1939–40, Japan had perfected its amphibious techniques in combat and had over 10,000 trained SNLF, as well as the ability to conduct brigade-size landings.

Britain, of course, had experience of amphibious operations, gained the hard way at Gallipoli in 1915. Churchill, as First Sea Lord at the time, had been one of the main advocates of a landing operation in the Dardanelles and received considerable opprobrium when the operation evolved into a costly failure. However, the mistakes made at Gallipoli contributed to British understanding of the practical difficulties of a landing operation. There was little interest in amphibious tactics in the immediate post-war period but this changed after the Munich Crisis in September 1938 revealed Hitler's aggressive intentions. Two months later, the Inter-Service Training Development Centre (ISTDC), which had been established to help foster joint operations between the three services, was tasked to begin developing both amphibious craft and amphibious doctrine, but this did not become an urgent priority until after Dunkirk. The two primary types available in 1940 were the 9-ton Landing Craft Assault (LCA), which could carry 36 troops or 0.4 tons of cargo, and the 21-ton LCM(1), capable of carrying one light tank, 100 troops or 15 tons of cargo. Only the LCM(1) was equipped with a bow ramp. During the Norwegian campaign, the Anglo-French used a handful of landing craft to conduct an opposed landing at Narvik on 12 May 1940, but all eight landing craft were lost when the Allies evacuated Norway in June. About a dozen landing craft were also used to assist the Dunkirk evacuation, but eight of these were lost as well. By July 1940, the Royal Navy had fewer than 50 landing craft (about 40 LCA and a few LCM(1)), sufficient to land a reinforced infantry battalion and a handful of light tanks. Churchill ordered the development of larger landing craft that could land several medium tanks on a beach – he was already thinking about sending British troops back to the continent. However, Britain had greater difficulty in refining amphibious doctrine, particularly when its landing craft were mostly being used for evacuations. The United States Marine Corps was also developing its own amphibious doctrine and landing craft, known as the Higgins boat. However, the first version of the 6.5-ton Higgins boat lacked a bow ramp and was fairly crude; it is little wonder that 50 of these inefficient craft were provided to Great Britain in October 1940 under Lend-Lease.

The German Kriegsmarine had put virtually no thought into amphibious operations prior to the war since it did not intend to fight Great Britain. Yet during the World War I the Kaiser's *Kaiserliche Marine* (Imperial Fleet) had conducted a single amphibious operation,

Operation *Albion*, in the Baltic in 1917. Unlike Gallipoli, Operation *Albion* succeeded in landing a reinforced army division on a hostile shore.[1] However, Operation *Albion* apparently left no lasting impression in the inter-war German Navy. Having lost all their capital ships due to the Treaty of Versailles, first the Reichsmarine (1919–35) and then the Kriegsmarine (1935–40) had to struggle to rebuild a surface fleet from scratch. German naval officers felt completely outclassed by the Royal Navy and sought ways to bypass British strengths, like the use of U-Boats and disguised raiders (*Hilfskreuzer*), not meet them head-on. As far as any landing operations in the Baltic, the Kriegsmarine leadership was willing to cede that mission to the Heer.

Thus, it was the engineers of the Heer who took the lead in experimenting with landing boats in the late 1930s. Pionier-Bataillon 2, stationed in Stettin, regularly used a handful of modified vessels to practise landing on coastal beaches and worked with Major Kurt Bräunig from *Waffenamt Prüfwesen 5* (Weapons Testing Department 5) in the *Heereswaffenamt* (Army Weapons Agency) to establish the requirements for future landing craft.[2] By the outbreak of the war, WaPrüf 5 had ordered the construction of a prototype, designated as the *Pionierlandungsboot 39* (PiLB 39). The 20-ton PiLB39 was a fairly sophisticated design, equipped with a bow ramp and able to land 100 troops or 20 tons of cargo (including vehicles) on a beach. However, WaPrüf 5 chose to build two prototypes and test them before initiating serial production. Since the first PiLB 39 was not completed until July 1940 and the second in mid-September 1940, serial production did not begin until after Hitler had postponed *Seelöwe*. Although only four PiLB 39s were built in 1940, a total of 55 were built in 1941. WaPrüf 5 continued to improve this handy vessel with upgraded models, but it was not available when needed most. It also meant that Germany had no purpose-built landing craft or proven amphibious techniques when Hitler ordered preparations for *Seelöwe* to commence.

Another item of landing equipment that WaPrüf 5 was trying to develop was an amphibious tractor known as the *Land-Wasser-Schlepper* (LWS). The 13-ton LWS was an amazing vehicle, capable of speeds of 6 knots in the water or 21mph on land; it could carry 20 troops or pull an amphibious trailer with a load of 20 tons of cargo. Although not armoured, the LWS was well suited to off-loading cargo from larger vessels directly onto a beach. Indeed, the LWS was a revolutionary advance in amphibious technique which would not be equalled until the American DUKW was introduced in 1942. However, the development process was very slow and only three prototypes of the LWS were available by the end of September 1940. The Heer was very impressed by the potential of the LWS and wanted to mass-produce it but the Kriegsmarine did not endorse it and only 21 of these vehicles were built during the entire war.[3]

Once saddled with the unwanted tasked of preparing an invasion flotilla, the Kriegsmarine repeated the procedure it used for Operation *Weserübung* against Norway: the OKM's Merchant Shipping Division (*Schiffahrtsabteilung*) was tasked with requisitioning suitable vessels in Germany and the occupied countries.[4] A total of 174 merchant ships were collected, ranging in size from small coastal freighters of 300–400 tons (GRT) up to passenger ships of 10,000 tons. Most were medium-size freighters in the 6–8,000 ton range. A few, like the German-built *Moltkefels* and *Niedenfels*, were modern cargo ships capable of up to 16 knots.[5] The *Schiffahrtsabteilung* took charge of modifying the vessels, including installing 2cm anti-aircraft guns and strengthening cargo areas; most of these transports were ready by 3 September. After hasty repairs, the captured French yards of Bordeaux, St Nazaire and Nantes were heavily involved in the conversion process. Typically, these modified merchantmen could be loaded with up to a battalion of troops, and the vessels equipped with heavy derricks could carry tanks, artillery and vehicles in their cargo holds. Even a small 3,648-ton steamer like the *Wolfram* could carry 857 troops and 30 trucks, as demonstrated during training exercises.[6] However, *Weserübung* was conducted very differently from the way that *Seelöwe* would have to be conducted; in Norway, poorly protected ports were captured by *coup de main* and then German cargo ships had been able to unload directly onto captured docks. This was not the case in Great Britain, where all the ports would be heavily guarded. Aside from four small captured Dutch ferries, modified to carry Pz II light tanks, none of the merchantmen were capable of disembarking directly onto a beach. Instead, the transports would have to remain offshore while some means was found to ferry troops and equipment from them to land on open beaches.

The initial assault landing units would be carried across the English Channel in minesweepers, R-Boats, motor fishing vessels and auxiliary coasters and trawlers, each of which was modified to carry about 75 troops. Once near the coast, the troops would off-load into powered *Sturmboote* (Type 39 Assault boats), each capable of carrying six infantrymen and a bow-mounted MG-34 machine gun. Other troops would debark in rubber dinghies and paddle ashore. While the infantrymen eliminated nearby British defensive positions, German Pioniere would begin clearing mines and beach obstacles. Tactically, the first moments of a German landing in England would have been conducted much like the assault crossing of the Meuse River in May.

Once the beaches were more or less cleared, the trans-shipment of men, horses and materiel from the offshore invasion fleet would begin. By late July, the OKM settled upon using powered and unpowered river barges (*Prähme*) for this task because they were flat-bottomed and readily at hand, not because they were well suited to the role. A total of 2,318 barges were collected, including 860 from Germany (mostly Rhine river barges), 1,200 from Holland and Belgium and 350 from France. About one-third of the collected barges were powered, the rest unpowered.[7] Yet even the powered barges were too slow to make it across the English Channel on their own and would require assistance.

Conversion work on barges began at Koblenz in Germany, as well as Amsterdam, Rotterdam, Antwerp and Ostend by 25 July. Initially, it was expected to gather and convert all 2,400 barges within just five weeks. Once in dockyard hands, the barges required a great amount of labour to refit them for use in the amphibious role, beginning with strengthening internal bracing to cope with heavy seas and installing a bow ramp to enable debarkation onto a beach. A number of barges were rejected as too old or unseaworthy. Barges that would carry tanks required concrete reinforcement under their decks. Some barges were equipped with concrete protection for the wheelhouse and troop areas. A number of barges were armed with light Flak guns and howitzers, requiring the construction of firing platforms. Altogether, outfitting the invasion fleet for *Seelöwe* required an enormous outlay of resources, including approximately 30,000 tons of iron and steel, 30,000 tons of lumber, 180,000 tons of concrete and 213,000 lifejackets.[8] Furthermore, over 7,000 German civilian workers and 15 Heer construction battalions participated in the barge conversion programme.[9] The barges also needed crews and these often came from the construction battalions – indicating that seamanship was not a requirement. Due to the redirection of so much dockyard labour to work on converting the invasion barges, construction on the battleship *Tirpitz* was delayed by four weeks. Although the conversion programme took until early September to complete, virtually all barges were ready by the time that the intended S-Tag date arrived.

The two primary barge types were the A1 (*péniche*) and the A2 (*kempenaar*). The A1 could carry 360 tons or three medium tanks, while the A2 could carry 620 tons or four medium tanks. Eighteen powered barges were modified as assault craft, by being reinforced with concrete protection on their sides and modified to carry and launch ten Sturmboote; these were designated as Type AS. In order to cross the Channel, the OKM assembled about 426 tug boats, each of which would tow one powered and one unpowered barge from the embarkation ports. Indeed, tug boats provided one of the critical capabilities for *Seelöwe* to even be feasible, but there were simply not enough. Instead, the Kriegsmarine substituted a variety of motor boats, many of which were clearly underpowered. Furthermore, the tows were supposed to cross the Channel at a speed of 6 knots in order to keep to any kind of schedule, but many of the substitute craft could not accomplish this. In desperation, some unpowered barges were lashed alongside powered barges, although they would have only been able to proceed at a crawl of 2–3 knots.

Since the Kriegsmarine was also averse to using any of its cruisers or destroyers for naval gunfire support, the Heer tried to arm as many of the barges and transports as possible, in order to provide some crude ability to engage targets on land. Five small coasters were converted into auxiliary gunboats, equipped with two 2cm or 3.7cm Flak guns and one 15cm or two 10.5cm howitzers, but these mini-warships were intended to help defend the transport fleet off the beachheads, rather than provide naval gunfire support.[10]

Despite the Kriegsmarine's lack of whole-hearted support, the assembling and conversion of an invasion force of this size was an amazing accomplishment by Germany. In just six weeks, Germany had created a large-scale – but short-range – amphibious capability where none had existed before. Jury-rigged it was, but the transports, barges and other craft were certainly adequate for their intended purpose. Germany had created an invasion fleet virtually out of thin air. Now the question was – how to use it?

Improvisation and Experimentation

While the Kriegsmarine leadership was reluctant to push ahead with *Seelöwe*, lower echelons in both the Heer and Luftwaffe showed amazing initiative in developing their own solutions to the problem of moving troops and equipment across the English Channel. Brauchitsch was concerned about Kriegsmarine foot-dragging and directed General der Pioniere Alfred Jacob from the OKH to order several pionier units in France to assist preparations for *Seelöwe* by constructing 'sea-going ferries' from pontoon bridge materiel. Brauchitsch wanted the Heer to have some amphibious capability of its own.[11] On the face of it, Jacob's directive seemed rather amateurish and even absurd, but this wild idea started a chain reaction that led to unexpectedly favourable results.

In Normandy, Pionier-Bataillon 47 launched into the task with gusto and began building unpowered rafts made of empty petrol tanks, wine barrels and kapock-filled floats. Although the initial versions were not very seaworthy, follow-on versions became more robust. Visiting a French aircraft plant in Amiens to look for aircraft pontoons to use in the next version of the rafts, officers from Pionier-Bataillon 47 ran into Major der Reserve Friedrich W. Siebel. Although just a reserve officer in the Luftwaffe, Siebel had the distinction of serving with Hermann Göring in the World War I and was a close friend; he was also tight with Generaloberst Ernst Udet, in charge of planning in the Air Ministry (*Reichsluftfahrtministerium* or RLM). Siebel had made a name for himself as aircraft designer and race pilot in the inter-war period and by the late 1930s he owned his own aircraft company. By July 1940, he was serving in the Luftwaffe and tasked with restoring French aircraft factories to support the German war effort. Upon hearing about the raft-building programme, he became interested in the preparations for *Seelöwe* and used his connections with Udet to stick his nose into the OKM's barge conversion programme. In the strict German military culture, these kinds of actions by a junior reserve officer were unheard of, but not only did Siebel gain access but he openly criticized the Kriegsmarine efforts as crude. He claimed that he could do better and again used his high-level contacts to get permission to form his own special unit, Sonderkommando Siebel.

Siebel first worked with Pionier-Bataillon 47, trying to improve their rafts, but he advocated larger, better-built powered ferries. He also reached out to several other units involved in building ad hoc landing craft and helped to coordinate their efforts. Again drawing upon favours, Siebel was able to receive a number of obsolescent BMW aircraft engines from a Luftwaffe parts depot and bridging materiel from Heer Pionier stocks. He quickly settled upon the concept of using a heavy pontoon bridge as the basis for a new powered catamaran-type design, which by late August was being tested as the Herbert ferry. The Herbert ferry proved to be quite good; in moderate seas it was able to transport a 40-ton load at a speed of up to 16 knots. Sonderkommando Siebel and Pionier-Bataillon 47 built a total of 22 Herbert ferries by mid-September, but the Kriegsmarine objected to this daring design. While the Skl was willing to use the Herbert ferries in *Seelöwe*, engineers from the OKM claimed that the design was too weak to withstand heavy seas and was dangerous.[12]

The OKM's criticism only stung Siebel into developing an even better design and he had the connections to make this happen. Operating outside normal channels, Siebel reached out to WaPrüf 5 (keeping in mind that Siebel was a Luftwaffe officer) seeking help to build a new ferry with better components. Somehow, he was able to place an order with Krupp-Rheinhausen to fabricate a steel framework, which could be covered with planking. For motive power, Siebel mounted four 75hp truck engines on the pontoons, although some were equipped with three 750hp aircraft engines. By 31 August, the first Siebel ferry was ready and tests revealed that it could move at up to 9mph. The prototype could carry 50 tons of cargo, but the improved production models could carry up to 100 tons. The Siebel ferry required a crew of 14. The large, flat deck of the Siebel ferry was sufficient to provide a stable firing platform for four 8.8cm Flak guns, as well as several 2cm Flak. Impressed with Siebel's design, the German Pioniere formed a special unit in Amsterdam to begin serial construction and were able to complete 25 Siebel ferries by the end of September 1940. As Peter Schenk noted, 'they were the only real landing craft in the Sea Lion fleet'.[13] However, higher authorities decided that the Siebel ferries would be assigned to Flakkorps I and II, which would mount several Flak batteries on them and use the armed ferries to protect the invasion convoys. Afterwards, the ferries would land the Flak guns onto the beachheads.

In addition to his heavy ferry project, Siebel also intruded into the OKM's barge programme and suggested motorizing some of the unpowered barges with old BMW 6U 600hp engines. At this point, Siebel gained support from the OKH – which was increasingly worried about the OKM's barge programme – and the OKM was pressured into accepting Siebel's help. He set about mounting two aircraft engines on several barges and tests indicated that they could move at 6 knots, although the engines were extremely noisy. Reluctantly, the

OKM allowed the conversions to begin and the new type barge was designated 'AF'. Altogether, about 100 AF barges were ready in time for the S-Tag date in late September and another 100 were converted in October.[14] The AF barge was not considered a major improvement, but it did slightly decrease the excess reliance on tugboats to tow unpowered barges.

Although the OKM resented Siebel's interference, it gradually came to realize that developing a better type of landing craft would in fact benefit the German war effort. Following the completion of the barge conversion programme in late September, the OKM authorized the creation of a brand-new type of powered landing craft, rather than a hasty conversion. Starting with Siebel's concept of using diesel truck engines to power a barge, the OKM spent the next six months developing the *Marinefährprahm* (MFP). The MFP was a shallow-draft powered barge, of riveted steel construction and equipped with a folding bow ramp, enabling it to land cargo directly onto a beach. The prototype, F-100, was not ready until 16 April 1941, but it was impressive; the initial MFP-A model was able to make 10 knots in heavy seas and could carry up to 105 tons, including three medium tanks. It was immediately apparent that the MFP was a major success and serial production began in July 1941, but too late for *Seelöwe*.

Meanwhile, the Heer tried to figure out how to actually load and unload troops and equipment onto a hostile shore. General der Panzertruppe Georg-Hans Reinhardt, commander of the XXXXI Armeekorps (mot.), was put in charge of an experimental staff that was supposed to examine the practical problems of amphibious landings.[15] Reinhardt conducted most of his experiments on Sylt, an island with nice, flat beaches off Schleswig-Holstein. Since Reinhardt's Panzers would be in the second wave of the landing, he had an incentive to succeed. One persistent problem that was identified was the clumsiness of existing bow ramps. While troops could disembark within minutes from a beached barge, getting tanks and other equipment onto beaches required a ramp that could be quickly lowered, was stable and had the weight capacity to carry 20-ton loads.

Initially, the Germans used a slow and unimaginative method of building a ramp by hand with timber once a barge was beached; this required a dozen men and about 20 minutes under ideal conditions. The second method was to use pre-made wooden ramps, but these still had to be extended and positioned by a squad of soldiers. In either case, if the stern of the vessel – still in the water – shifted, the ramp would shift, too. More complicated arrangements with booms and frames were tried – and rejected. By the time that S-Tag was at hand in September 1940, the Germans had still not perfected an efficient landing ramp, which meant that landing operations conducted under fire were going to be extremely difficult. Even after *Seelöwe* was postponed, the Kriegsmarine and Heer Pioniere units continued testing new and improved ramps well into 1941.[16] By spring 1941, the state of German ramps was much improved, enabling fairly rapid debarkation of tanks and motor vehicles.

Early problems with the landing ramps suggested that it was going to be difficult to get tanks ashore quickly on a defended beach, so the Heer began looking for alternatives. The Heer was adamant that it needed tanks to support the assault troops in the first wave, who would almost certainly have to engage bunkers and other prepared defences. Somewhere, someone got the idea of converting tanks to drive underwater so they could be dropped offshore and drive ashore under their own power. In late June 1940, the Heereswaffenamt (Army's Weapons Office) and the Kriegsmarine began testing the feasibility of developing deep diving tanks (Tauchpanzer) in order to land tanks in the first wave of the invasion force. The Tauchpanzers, or U-Panzers (*Unterwasser Panzer*, i.e. submersible tanks), were created by taking regular tanks, sealing all openings to make them watertight and equipping them with a flexible 60-foot-long snorkel for their engine exhaust. The early tests on Sylt – under ideal conditions – proved the idea was feasible. Once the concept was validated, the Heer ordered the formation of four Tauchpanzer-Abteilungen and their tanks would be modified for submerged use.

On 13 July, an experimental tank company was formed for

further testing of the concept. Meanwhile, the OKH directed the 1., 2., 3. and 5. Panzer-Divisionen to provide one company from each of their two Panzer-Regiments as cadre for the new Tauchpanzer-Abteilungen, designated A, B, C and D. Each Tauchpanzer-Abteilung received its third company from Heerestruppen (army-level personnel). By 24–27 July, all four Tauchpanzer-Abteilungen were formed and began training. Each battalion had 63 tanks (12 Pz II, 37 Pz IIIF/G/H, 12 Pz IVD and 2 Pz Bef III).[17] Some of these tanks included the latest Pz IIIH models, equipped with the 5cm KwK 38 L/42 gun, which represented a significant increase in anti-tank capability over the older Pz III models equipped with the 3.7cm gun. Thus altogether, over 250 tanks were allocated to support the first wave of *Seelöwe*. Reinhardt was not enthusiastic about the Tauchpanzer concept and delivered a report on 14 July that criticized the use of them in actual combat conditions.[18]

The Tauchpanzers required their own special barges, designated Type B, which had special pivoting ramps that allowed them to slide off the bow into the water. The concept was to launch the Tauchpanzer about 650 feet from shore, in water that was up to 50 feet deep. Then, the Tauchpanzers would drive along the seabed at up to 3.5mph until they emerged on the beach. It was a novel concept, but highly risky under combat conditions. For starters, if the barge crews (who were simply construction troops turned sailors) panicked under fire, they could easily disembark the tanks in water that was deeper than 50 feet – meaning that the snorkel would not reach the surface. Without air, the crew would quickly asphyxiate from carbon monoxide from engine fumes – as happened in one training event. With any kind of heavy seas, the tank might also capsize coming off the ramp, landing upside down under water. Assuming that the tank made it to the seabed upright and with an air connection, it was still blind and had to navigate strictly by its internal compass. If any kind of underwater obstacles were encountered, the tank could easily become mired or stuck. The Tauchpanzer had a maximum underwater endurance of 60 minutes, but carbon monoxide could become a problem after just 20 minutes. Tauchpanzer crews were provided with underwater escape training, but not under combat conditions. Essentially, the Tauchpanzer concept was highly risky to try for the first time on a contested beach, likely littered with obstacles, and losses would almost certainly have been heavy.

As a side effort, the Heereswaffenamt also decided to convert 52 standard Pz II light tanks into Schwimmpanzers, or swimming tanks. These much lighter tanks were fitted with box-type floats on both sides and a propeller was coupled to their final drive. The Schwimmpanzers would also be launched from Type B barges and could propel themselves at up to 3.5mph through the water. Although much less risky, the floats on the Schwimmpanzers were vulnerable to damage from machine-gun fire or shrapnel; if they lost buoyancy on one side they would sink like stones. If they made it ashore, the Schwimmpanzers could suppress enemy positions with their 2cm guns.

A Herculean Effort to Assemble the Armada

As the transports, barges, tugboats and other paraphernalia for invasion were converted or modified, it all needed to be moved to the embarkation ports on the Channel coast and crews found to man them. This required an enormous effort by the Wehrmacht to gather an estimated 20,000 able-bodied seamen for a variety of craft and then move them both along inland waterways and coastal shipping lanes. The Kriegsmarine provided 4,000 personnel from its own ranks and another 9,500 from naval reservists, but the rest were combed from the Heer and the Luftwaffe, who transferred anyone who had prior sailing experience.[19] Indeed, it was a mad scramble to get all these assets to the proper place in the short amount of time available before the autumn weather made an invasion impractical in 1940. *Seelöwe* had already missed one invasion window, the period 20–26 August, and it was not until late August that the armada really began to gather. While the British War Cabinet had been concerned about a sudden

German descent since early July, the Germans simply had no practical invasion capability staged before early September.

Although Raeder was against *Seelöwe*, many lower-level Kriegsmarine officers such as Kapitän zur See Heinz Degenhardt, chief of sea transport, worked miracles to meet the tight schedule. Most of the ports had suffered considerable damage during the *Fall Gelb* campaign and required extensive repairs.[20] After a slow start, German amphibious capability in the Channel ports increased dramatically in the last week of August and first week of September. At Amsterdam, for example, the number of barges climbed from 33 on 19 August to peak at 604 on 30 August. At Boulogne and Le Havre, the majority of their barges were in place by 19 September, although more kept trickling in until early October.[21] Likewise, most of the transports were staged in their embarkation ports by early September. Kapitän zur See Erich Bey brought seven of his destroyers from German ports to Brest and Cherbourg in early September, leaving the remaining three German destroyers refitting in dockyard. Minesweepers and minelayers also moved to the Channel ports in mid-September. During the build-up for *Seelöwe*, the only real problem was the assembly of motorized fishing coasters and trawlers, which were intended to carry the assault detachments to the landing areas. For a variety of reasons, many of these vessels were not actually ready and deployed until after the intended S-Tag had passed. In terms of gathering the fleet, the Germans achieved about an 85 per cent solution in time for the 24–26 September window and close to 100 per cent for the early October invasion window.

While the Kriegsmarine performed an almost superhuman effort in gathering so much transport shipping and converting it so quickly, naval logistics in the captured ports remained a major problem. Everything from engine lubricants, spare parts, fuel and drinking water for over 3,000 vessels was in very short supply. One of the biggest deficiencies was special distillate for the Kriegsmarine destroyers, which could only be produced in special evaporators at Kiel and Wilhelmshaven.[22] Without this special distillate, the finicky high pressure boilers on Bey's destroyers would quickly corrode and suffer breakdowns. Consequently, the Kriegsmarine was forced to rush special tanker cars by rail from Kiel to Brest and Cherbourg. The Kriegsmarine also had to move thousands of mines to the Channel ports in order to be able to lay the defensive minefields in support of *Seelöwe*.

Another major issue arose when the first transports and barges reached their respective embarkation harbours and the Heer demanded access to them to practise loading and then unloading on local beaches. The Kriegsmarine was not enthusiastic about army rehearsals, preferring to keep the invasion fleet nestled snug in harbours, rather than letting soldiers bash them about. Nevertheless, 16. Armee (AOK 16) conducted a regimental-size landing exercise on the beach at Le Touquet on 17 August, with Brauchitsch and Halder invited to watch.[23] A few more small trials were permitted in order to determine practical problems, but most of the German soldiers and the crews of the invasion fleet had very limited experience with basic loading and landing procedures by the time that S-Tag approached.

In order to prepare for the airborne component of *Seelöwe*, the Luftwaffe had to assemble the 7. Flieger-Division and its transport units near airfields in Holland and Belgium; both had taken heavy losses in the initial airborne landings in Holland in May 1940.[24] General der Flieger Kurt Student, the divisional commander, was still recovering from his wounds, although he was involved in planning for *Seelöwe*. Student's Fallschirmjäger were aggressive light infantrymen, lacking any significant heavy weapons and only trained for daylight parachute landings. The 7. Flieger-Division had few heavy weapons, but the new 7.5cm Leichtgeschütz 40, a recoilless rifle, would prove useful for direct fire support.

The 7. Flieger-Division had been hastily cobbled together and it was still not completely organized, but it could muster nine airborne battalions with about 6,000 assault troops by September 1940. In addition, the Luftlande-Sturm-Regiment was available, with three more airborne battalions. However, the air transport situation was marginal, since 250 Ju-52 transport planes had been lost in Holland, and on 17 August 1940 the Luftwaffe could only muster eight transport groups with 313 Ju-52 transports (193 operational). In addition, there were a few dozen DF-230 gliders available, each of which could carry nine Fallschirmjäger. Production of the Ju-52 was low priority, so only about 30 replacements were being received each month. Thus, by the time that the decision for *Seelöwe* arrived in mid-September, there were about 200 to 220 Ju-52 transports operational and maybe 40 to 50 gliders, which could theoretically move up to five airborne battalions in one lift. Without any appreciable reserves of Ju-52 transports or pilots, the Luftwaffe's airborne capability was still quite fragile.

CHAPTER 3

Diplomacy, Espionage and Intelligence

Churchill's Effort to Enlist US Help

Although impressions of Anglo-American relations today are influenced by the 'special relationship' of the Cold War era, Britain's efforts to solicit American military assistance in the first year of the World War II bore very little fruit. Even before the outbreak of the World War II, the British and French established the Anglo-French Purchasing Commission in New York City; the British delegation was headed by the Canadian businessman Arthur B. Purvis.[1] The purpose of the commission was to purchase American-made weaponry and other key material. Purvis had made his name in the munitions industry and during the World War I he had been sent to the United States to purchase all the stocks of acetone, needed for British ammunition production.[2] After France surrendered, the organization changed its name to the British Purchasing Commission (BPC). At the start of the war, the British were particularly interested in acquiring modern fighters and long-range bombers, both of which were in short supply. Sir Henry Self was the air representative who conducted aircraft purchase negotiations for the British.

Early on, the British commission was nonplussed by the unwillingness of the United States Government to extend war credits to the Allies to finance weapons purchases.[3] While President Franklin Roosevelt was sympathetic towards helping the Allies, one large sticking point was the 1934 Johnson Act, a US law that prohibited allowing credit to nations that had not repaid their debts from the World War I; Britain had stopped repaying its debt in 1932 and still owed the United States $4.4 billion.[4] In September 1939, Britain had $4.5 billion (£1.1 billion) invested in the United States and it began to sell some of these assets to provide the BPC with working capital. Canada also dutifully played its part for the mother country, eventually selling off over $7 billion (£1.9 billion) in investments and gold bullion.[5] Henry Morgenthau, Roosevelt's Treasury Secretary, made a list of British investments in the United States and carefully monitored Britain's cash flow.

In addition to financial constraints, Roosevelt had to deal with strong isolationist attitudes which opposed direct military involvement in a foreign war and regarded arms sales as the first step down a slippery slope. Indeed, arms sales in the World War I had led to U-Boat attacks on American merchant shipping. Nevertheless, Roosevelt demonstrated his willingness to provide arms to Great Britain by overturning the Neutrality Act with his 'Cash and Carry' scheme on 5 November 1939, which allowed American companies to sell arms to the Allies, as long as they were paid for in cash and delivered by Allied merchant ships; the law did not allow the US Government to directly sell weapons to the Allies. Many British politicians, including Churchill, were rankled both by the American failure to provide loans and the cumbersome procedures enacted to protect US neutrality, which caused lingering resentment throughout 1940.

Within this context, Purvis's BPC sought to buy American-built aircraft to enable the RAF to catch up with the Luftwaffe. Both the French Armée de l'Air and the RAF were particularly enamoured of the new Curtiss-Wright P-40B fighter, which was ready to begin mass-production at Buffalo, New York. On paper, the P-40B appeared to be similar in performance to the Spitfire Mk I, as well as having better range and being significantly less expensive.[6] The French were quick to place an order for over 200 P-40s in April 1940, but Sir Henry Self held off, hoping to purchase a licence for building the aircraft in Canada. Instead, he placed orders for the Bell P-39 fighter and the North American P-51 fighter, both still in development. The representatives were also very interested in the new four-engine bomber prototypes from Boeing and Consolidated since British designers would not be able to build such aircraft for another two years. Sir Henry Self knew that the British aircraft industry was focused on fighter and bomber production, so he sought to fill gaps in the British inventory, such as aircraft for the Royal Navy's Fleet Air Arm and patrol aircraft for the RAF's Coastal Command. However, due to the financial issues, the commission's efforts to purchase American weaponry were still in the negotiating phase when Germany began its *Fall Gelb* offensive. Shocked by heavy losses of men and materiel, the Anglo-French commission made a direct appeal to the US Government on 21 May for immediate shipments of a large amount of military equipment – in contravention of the provisions of the Cash and Carry law. The Allies presented a wish list that included aircraft, anti-aircraft, artillery, ammunition, small arms and destroyers. The next day, Churchill stated to his Cabinet that the United States, 'had given us practically no help in the war and now that they see how great was the danger, their attitude was that they wanted to keep everything which would help us for their own defence'.[7]

President Roosevelt could see that the military situation in France was desperate, but had to tread carefully. He decided to use subterfuge to evade legal restrictions, by asking the US military to examine its stockpiles and determine what was 'surplus' to American defence requirements. The US military was hostile to this Allied request; General George C. Marshall, US Army Chief of Staff, rejected the idea of selling any modern aircraft from the US Army Air Corps (USAAC) and did not like the idea of selling even obsolescent equipment from the World War I. Marshall pointed out that the US Army was woefully under-equipped itself and would not have any anti-aircraft ammunition for its own purposes until December 1940. Likewise, Admiral Harold Stark, US Navy Chief of Naval Operations, opposed the transfer of any destroyers, even 1918-vintage 'four-stackers' from the mothball fleets in Philadelphia and San Diego.[8] It took 12 days of pressure from Roosevelt before Marshall finally agreed to declare some of the older stocks as surplus, but the US Navy was adamantly opposed to any transfers. Finally, on 11 June the US War Department declared a large amount of equipment surplus and sold it as scrap to the firm US Steel for the sum of $37.6 million; the company then turned around and sold it to the Anglo-French purchasing commission. Over 600 train loads of equipment were sent to the port of Raritan, New Jersey, to where 12 British merchantmen were hurriedly dispatched.[9]

The first British merchantman, the SS *Eastern Prince*, sailed from New Jersey on 13 June with a load of 48 75mm field guns, 15,000 machine guns (mostly old Lewis Guns and Vickers), 12,000 Lee Enfield rifles and 28 million rounds of .30 cal ammunition.[10] The vessel sailed independently and arrived in Liverpool on 23 June. Altogether, the US emergency shipments delivered in June–July 1940 amounted to 895 75mm guns (M1917, M1897) with over one million rounds of ammunition, 300 3-inch Stokes mortars, 18,000 machine guns, 500,000 Lee Enfield rifles and 100 million rounds of .30 cal ammunition. The vast majority of this surplus equipment was obsolescent weapons that added very little to the British ground defence capability, aside from stiffening the TA divisions with some light artillery and providing rifle ammunition for training. Nevertheless, most of this American-provided equipment was handed over to the Home Guard as soon as Britain's domestic production was able to replace the losses in France. Later shipments included slightly more modern equipment, including Thompson sub-machine guns (eagerly adopted by the Commando units) and 25,000 Browning automatic rifles (BAR). Completely misreading the situation, Churchill confidently told his cabinet that American military intervention would occur within a matter of months.[11]

In fact, the US military and the Anglo-phobic US ambassador to London, Joe Kennedy, both predicted that Britain would not be able to withstand Hitler and advocated against further arms aid. Many Irish-Americans, like Kennedy, actually hoped that Germany would bring about the collapse of the British Empire.[12] Both General George C. Marshall and Brigadier General George V. Strong, in charge of War Plans, believed that Britain would either surrender or negotiate; Strong even made ridiculous predictions that Hitler would soon make aggressive moves against Panama or Brazil and pushed through a new war plan, RAINBOW 4, which envisaged the United States having to deal with a victorious Axis coalition after the fall of Britain.[13] Major General Henry H. 'Hap' Arnold, commander of the USAAC, was opposed to giving any of his modern aircraft to the British and was nearly relieved of command by Roosevelt. Arnold did succeed in preventing the British from getting the advanced Norden bombsight, which RAF Bomber Command eagerly sought. Deciding that the US military could not be trusted to see the larger picture, Roosevelt empowered Morgenthau to set up a special commission to determine which American military equipment could be provided to the British, thereby bypassing the War Department.

When France surrendered, Purvis was empowered to take over all existing French contracts in the United States, without regard to cost. With the stroke of a pen on 17 June, the BPC spent $500 million. Consequently, the RAF ended up with a large tranche of inferior aircraft that it never would have ordered itself, such as the Brewster Buffalo fighter and the DB-7 light bomber; one of the failings of the BPC was an over-emphasis on raw numbers, instead of quality.

Once the initial emergency shipment of surplus military equipment reached Liverpool, the BPC presented the US Government with another 'wish list' on 2 August, which included 96 destroyers, 25 motor torpedo boats, 50 maritime patrol bombers and 250,000 more Enfield rifles. Stark continued to resist any naval transfers, but was pressured into releasing 20 brand-new motor torpedo boats (MTB). However, since these brand-new vessels could not be rationalized as 'surplus', this ignited a political firestorm. The isolationist Senator David J. Walsh (D-Mass), a member of Roosevelt's own party, depicted the MTB sale as 'too dangerous' and threatened legislation to block all further arms sales. Roosevelt was forced to temporarily defer selling any new vessels to Britain but pressured Stark to re-think transfer of older destroyers. The Royal Navy was particularly hard pressed for destroyers, having lost 31 sunk since the start of the war and many more damaged, leaving too few for Atlantic convoy duties.[14] Many histories tend to depict the subsequent Destroyers-for-Bases deal as the liquidation of vessels that were merely rusting in mothballs, hence of little or no use to the US Navy. In fact, a number of these destroyers, such as the USS *Twiggs* and USS *Wickes*, were still fully operational warships in the US Atlantic Fleet. Finally, on 2 September Roosevelt authorized the transfer of 50 'four-stack' destroyers to the Royal Navy in return for basing rights on British territories in the Caribbean and Newfoundland; the first of these destroyers reached Northern Ireland in early November 1940 and they were soon employed as convoy escorts (six would be sunk by U-Boats during the war). The British Cabinet was incensed by the yielding of basing rights to a foreign power, but grudgingly assented when the alternative was no destroyers.

Meanwhile, Churchill's attitude veered from excessively optimistic predictions about what the Americans could do to help Britain to bitter frustration about how little they actually did. In addition to asking for more military aid, he requested that the US Navy deploy a squadron to Singapore to help with deterring the increasingly bold Japanese. When these actions did not occur, Churchill reacted as if another ally had betrayed him. In retaliation, he tried to delay the sharing of British advances in radar and ASDIC (i.e. sonar) technology with the Americans. A large part of the problem was that Churchill did not understand the American political system, preferring to think that President Roosevelt could simply steer the United States towards a declaration of war without bothering to gain the consent of Congress or the people. Nor did Churchill appreciate the fine line that Roosevelt had to walk due to the imminent national election coming in November 1940. Roosevelt's Republican opponent, Wendell Willkie, was already accusing Roosevelt of trying to drag the United States into the war and this had the potential to influence the election. The isolationist America First Committee, with aviator Charles Lindbergh as its prominent spokesman, accused Roosevelt of weakening the US military by sending too much military equipment to Great Britain. Consequently, Roosevelt tried to distance himself from the issue of arms aid, as well as the idea of eventual US entry into the war. On 30 October 1940, President Roosevelt emphatically told a rally in Boston that 'I have said this before, but I shall say it again and again and again; your boys are not going to be sent into any foreign wars'. This, of course, was a lie – Roosevelt knew that American entry was only a matter of time, but he refused to publicly acknowledge it.

After the election was won, Roosevelt quickly changed his tune and tried to manoeuvre Congress towards approving military aid to Britain where 'the dollar sign was eliminated', in his phraseology. By mid-August 1940, Britain's cash reserves were down to £490 million and three-quarters of it was already earmarked to pay for weapons contracts. At this rate, Britain would be out of gold by December 1940 and unable to purchase any more American-made materiel.[15] Recognizing Britain's approaching cash crisis, Roosevelt delivered his famous 'Arsenal of Democracy' speech on 29 December 1940 in which he stated:

> They [Britain] ask us for the implements of war, the planes, the tanks, the guns, the freighters which will enable them to fight for their liberty and for our security. Emphatically we must get these weapons to them, get them to them in sufficient volume and quickly enough, so that we and our children will be saved the agony and suffering of war which others have had to endure.[16]

Churchill also tried to influence the American public into supporting greater aid for Britain. In a speech directed to America in February 1941, he stated, 'give us the tools and we will finish the job'.

However, Roosevelt pointed out to Churchill that he could not get Congress to approve 'giving' any military aid unless it was obvious that Britain had expended its financial resources. Morgenthau advised Roosevelt to coerce Churchill into liquidating Britain's remaining investments in the United States, beginning with the synthetic fibre manufacturer American Viscose, which was worth well over $130 million. In December 1940, the company was sold to the US banking firm Morgan Stanley for only $54 million and was then re-sold for profit.[17] Churchill was incensed by this kind of extortion, propagated by Wall Street investors who could not care less about the Nazi threat, but he was in a weak bargaining position. In addition, Roosevelt sent the heavy cruiser USS *Louisville* to South Africa in January 1941 to collect £42 million worth of British gold bullion, so the BPC could continue to operate.

With these demonstrations of British financial sacrifice, Roosevelt was able to swing Congress towards large grants of military aid to Great Britain. Finally, on 11 March 1941 the Lend-Lease Act was signed into law and the next day Roosevelt asked Congress for $7 billion for the programme. The passage of Lend-Lease was the great game changer – far more than the fighter battles of September 1940 – which provided Britain with more armaments than it was able to purchase under Cash and Carry and paving the way for American industrial mobilization. In March 1941, over 400 US-built aircraft were shipped to England. Within a year, the shipment of Lend-Lease American-built Grant and Sherman tanks would provide the means for Britain to go on the offensive in North Africa. However, in financial terms, American military aid had come at a very heavy price that would negatively affect Britain's post-war economy.

Altogether, during 1939–40 the BPC placed orders for over 2,700 aircraft worth over $1 billion in the United States and yet barely 400 of these aircraft arrived before Lend-Lease was approved. Indeed, the

BPC's spending spree after May 1940 helped to push Britain towards bankruptcy – thereby contributing to Germany's strategic goals – while adding very little useful military capability in the short run. By the summer of 1940, the only American-built aircraft in significant numbers in RAF service was the Lockheed Hudson patrol plane; RAF Coastal Command had four operational squadrons with about 80–100 Hudsons. The Hudson was a decent aircraft and it proved useful in the effort to counter both U-Boats and the Fw-200 Condor long-range bombers, as well as to patrol England's southern coast.

However, efforts to boost Fighter Command with American-built fighters proved a complete bust. In July, 12 Brewster Buffalos and five Curtiss Mohawks arrived, followed by 49 Mohawks in August.[18] It was immediately apparent that both aircraft were inferior to the Bf-109E fighter and they were quickly assigned to RAF units stationed in Asia. In August 1940, the first Grumman F-4F naval fighters were received by the Fleet Air Arm but they were not adapted for carrier operations and instead the sole squadron was based in the Orkney Islands to help defend the fleet anchorage at Scapa Flow. Later, improved F-4F fighters would arrive in 1941 and be employed on Royal Navy escort aircraft carriers as the 'Martlet' naval fighter, which would contribute to defeating the Fw-200 Condor threat. The first P-40B fighter, re-designated in RAF service as the Tomahawk Mk I, arrived in England in September 1940, but was found to be unsuitable for combat. These aircraft were taken over from the French order and Curtiss had built them to French standard, without self-sealing fuel tanks or armour plating. The RAF assigned these fighters to local reconnaissance duties and resigned itself to wait for the improved Tomahawk Mk II in early 1941. Yet even these upgraded P-40s were regarded as inferior to the Spitfire and were sent to join the Desert Air Force in Libya. Otherwise, the bulk of the aircraft ordered by the BPC did not begin to arrive in the United Kingdom until mid-to-late 1941, well after the threat of *Seelöwe* had passed.

It is also remarkable that with British domestic aircraft production exceeding German aircraft production in 1940 by roughly a ratio of 3:2, the BPC's expenditure of so much British treasure was unnecessary. The Dunkirk disaster induced an air of panic and desperation in British aircraft purchases, rather than sober calculation. While purchases of American aircraft were generally a case of too little, too late as far as *Seelöwe* goes, this is not to say that they did not influence the air-sea duels between Britain and Germany. In addition to the F-4F fighter (Martlet) and Lockheed Hudson, the PBY Catalina flying boats would play a crucial role in hunting the German battleship *Bismarck* in May 1941 while the Consolidated B-24 long-range bombers would prove equally critical in closing the mid-Atlantic 'air gap' against the U-Boats in 1942–43. However, the RAF was disappointed by the P-39 Airacobra fighter-bomber and after brief service in a single squadron, most of them were pawned off as Lend-Lease to the Soviets. Likewise, the Boston and Maryland light bombers were mediocre designs that added little to British capabilities. Nor did the Boeing B-17 bomber or the P-51 Mustang fighter have successful careers in the RAF, even though they went on to play war-winning roles in the United States Army Air Force (USAAF) in 1944–45. One of the few positive results of the BPC spending spree was to infuse a large amount of British capital into the American aviation industry 18 months prior to Pearl Harbor, which helped to jump-start designs that otherwise might not have been ready until much later in the World War II.

In addition to weapons, the BPC also placed orders for freighters and tankers in American shipyards, to supplement production in Great Britain. The largest order was worth $100 million, placed on 19 December 1940 with Todd Shipyard for 60 Ocean-class freighters; the first of these freighters was completed in August 1941 and the last by October 1942.[19] These well-built freighters played an important role in the Battle of the Atlantic and no fewer than 18 of the 60 Ocean-class freighters were lost to enemy action.

In sum, Churchill failed to get the kind of American military assistance that he was seeking in June 1940 until well after the threat of *Seelöwe* had passed. Roosevelt was too cagey to be drawn into war by Churchill's rhetoric. In the long run, Lend-Lease provided critical support for the British war effort in 1941–44, but it came at the price of making the United States the dominant partner in the Allied camp. Churchill's quest for American aid weakened Great Britain financially and precipitated a slide towards second-tier status that was irreversible. In fear of losing Britain's independence to Hitler, Churchill instead surrendered it to Roosevelt, who was in no hurry to get into the war.

Table 2. British Major Purchases of American-made Aircraft 1939–40

US Aircraft	Order Placed	Number Ordered	Entered RAF/RN Service
Bell P-39 Fighter	13 April 1940	675	August 1941
Curtiss P-40 Fighter	Acquired from French Order	140	September 1940 (TOMAHAWK Mk I)
Curtiss P-36 Fighter	Acquired from French Order	120	July 1940 (MOHAWK)
Brewster Buffalo fighter	Acquired from Belgian Order	200	July 1940 (BUFFALO)
Grumman F-4F Wildcat fighter	Acquired from French Order	90+100	August 1940 (MARTLET)
North American P-51 fighter	24 April 1940	320+300	November 1941 (MUSTANG)
Boeing B-17C bomber	Early 1940	20	Early 1941
Consolidated B-24 bomber	September 1939 (by France)	26+139	March 1941 (LIBERATOR)
Douglas DB-7 light bomber	(by France)	200	Late 1941 (BOSTON)
Martin Model 167 bomber	(by France)	225	January 1941 (MARYLAND)
SB2 Vindicator dive bomber	(by France)	50	RN service in 1941
PBY Catalina flying boat	September 1939	50	Early 1941
Lockheed Hudson	1938	200	About 80–100 in Coastal Command in 1940

British Tactical Intelligence: Photographic Reconnaissance and Prisoner Interrogations

Britain's ability to evaluate the threat posed by *Seelöwe* was enhanced by its superior tactical intelligence capabilities, namely in aerial reconnaissance and prisoner interrogations. In addition, MI6 proved adept at document exploitation and the British scientific community assisted the military with technical exploitation of captured equipment.

In the late 1930s, Britain's MI6 became interested in the use of aerial photography to conduct clandestine reconnaissance missions over Germany. An Australian businessman and inventor, Sidney Cotton, was recruited into the effort due to his experience as a pilot in the World War I, his efforts to improve aerial photography and his business contacts in Germany. Working with Frederick Winterbotham, an RAF officer seconded to MI6, Cotton was provided with an American-built twin-engine Lockheed 12 passenger aircraft equipped with concealed vertical cameras in January 1939. In July–August 1939, Cotton flew on several trips into Germany and managed to covertly photograph military installations near Mannheim.[20] His experience in these clandestine missions led to the development of 'camoutint' paint, which made aircraft more difficult to spot in the sky, and improvements to prevent camera lenses from frosting over at altitudes over 20,000 feet. At the outbreak of war in September, the 45-year-old Cotton was brought into the RAF and charged with using his experience to create a high-altitude tactical aerial reconnaissance unit.

Initially, the RAF unit – dubbed 'Cotton's Circus' – was stationed at Heston airfield, 15 miles west of London, and equipped with Bristol Blenheim bombers. However, Cotton quickly recognized that the Blenheim was too slow to operate over enemy airspace and urged the use of modified Spitfire fighters for reconnaissance. Spitfires were in very short supply in 1939, but on 30 October Cotton's nascent unit was provided with two Spitfire PR Mk 1A fighters, each outfitted with two F24 vertical cameras. In February and March 1940, Cotton's unit was renamed the Photographic Development Unit (PDU) and received upgraded PR Mk 1B and C models, as well as the longer range PR Mk VI; these aircraft could fly reconnaissance missions and collect useful imagery at over 30,000 feet. Stripped of armament, the early Spitfire PR models had a slight edge in speed and altitude over the enemy's Bf-109E/F fighters, which meant that interception was difficult but not impossible. In May, the Spitfire PDU was the first to receive the new 100-octane fuel. In order to make them harder to spot, Cotton had his Spitfires painted a shade of blue that was soon dubbed 'PR Blue'. Under Cotton's command, Spitfire PRs flew successful missions over the German naval bases at Wilhelmshaven, Kiel and Emden. The PDU also suffered its first loss when a Spitfire PR Mk 1B was shot down by Bf-109E fighters near Arnhem on 22 March 1940. Eager to improve the images collected, Cotton began experimenting with oblique-angle photography and stereoscopic photography, which greatly enhanced the information that could be determined about a target.[21] Although Cotton was instrumental in creating this reconnaissance unit, he was too independent to suit the RAF leadership and was removed from command after Dunkirk. Instead, the RAF brought in a military professional, Wing Commander Geoffrey W. Tuttle, to head the unit, which on 18 June was re-designated as the Photographic Reconnaissance Unit (PRU) and placed under Coastal Command.[22]

Despite Cotton's success, the British Air Ministry was slow to recognize the importance of photographic reconnaissance and failed to provide supporting infrastructure. For photo interpretation of the imagery collected, Cotton turned to the Aircraft Operating Company, a commercial firm that had been involved in pre-war aerial mapping surveys in the Middle East. This company had two invaluable assets: Michael Spender, an experienced photo interpreter, and a Swiss-built stereo plotting machine (known as the Wild machine). Spender was on the cutting edge of developing photogrammetry, the ability to precisely plot and measure objects on images taken from great altitudes. In an experiment conducted by Cotton in December 1939, Spender was able to identify previously undetected German positions in the

West Wall. However, the Air Ministry was not initially interested in photogrammetry and regarded Cotton as something of a nuisance. Bomber Command already had its own reconnaissance capability and Cotton's PDU seemed redundant. It was not until late March 1940 – having been suitably embarrassed by Cotton's stunt of photographing the German battleship *Tirpitz* in Wilhelmshaven – that the Air Ministry reversed itself and decided to take over the Aircraft Operating Company and all its personnel.[23] Spender was brought into the RAF and the corporate facility at Wembley, in north-west London, became the Photographic Interpretation Unit (PIU).[24] With Spender's help, the RAF established a professional training programme and many of the PIU photo interpreters were female WAAFs (Women's Auxiliary Air Force). Procedures were established to enable first phase interpretation of imagery to be disseminated in report format within two hours of a Spitfire PR returning to base and hardcopy imagery within 12 hours. The PIU also developed a system for prioritizing imagery and disseminating it to the appropriate end-user. In contrast, the Luftwaffe's photo-interpretation capabilities were decentralized and rather slipshod.

During the period July–August 1940, Tuttle's PRU had a total of 11 operational Spitfire PRs, stationed at Heston and in Cornwall and Scotland. Eventually, the PRU would have 20 Spitfires in five flights, but the unit suffered some losses during the French campaign that were not yet made good. Furthermore, Bomber Command tried to task the unit to conduct reconnaissance against targets deep within Germany, which resulted in the loss of a Spitfire PR on 10 July, intercepted near Stuttgart by six Bf-109Fs. Despite such diversions, the PRU's primary mission at this time was to support Coastal Command by detecting signs of impending invasion and to provide imagery intelligence (IMINT) on German landing preparations in the Channel ports. Under Tuttle's leadership, the PRU flawlessly performed this task. The RAF's photographic reconnaissance collection effort was enhanced by the first-class photographic interpretation service provided by the PIU and its timely dissemination process. In all aspects of the intelligence cycle (direct-collect-analyse-disseminate) the RAF's IMINT capability greatly exceeded what the Luftwaffe could accomplish. Churchill and the Cabinet were provided with high-quality imagery that showed the steady build-up of the German invasion fleet in the Channel ports. Once the standardized Spitfire PR Mk IV arrived in October 1940, the RAF would have the ability to conduct high-speed, high-altitude aerial reconnaissance over most of Western Europe. On 29 October 1940, an improved Spitfire PR conducted a successful daylight 5½-hour reconnaissance flight to Stettin – an amazing accomplishment given the fact that Luftwaffe radars could track the flight.

In addition to rapidly developing aerial reconnaissance capabilities, the RAF was keen to develop its ability to exploit captured Luftwaffe prisoners and enemy equipment. However, the very first enemy prisoners were the 81 survivors from the sunken U-27 and U-39, captured by the Royal Navy between 14 and 20 September 1939. Prisoner interrogation was still a new field – rarely conducted during the World War I – but now Britain needed every advantage it could gain by learning about the enemy's tactics, intentions and equipment. By luck, captured members of the U-27 revealed some details about the use of magnetic mines off the British coast.[25] In October 1939, the Combined Services Detailed Interrogation Centre (CSDIC) was established at the Tower of London under the command of Colonel Thomas Kendrick from MI6; he had a total of just six officers (three army, one navy and two RAF). The purpose of CSDIC was to conduct professional interrogations of prisoners believed to have useful information. Since Kendrick had few prisoners to interrogate for the first six months of operation, he used the time to train his personnel. In spring 1940, the CSDIC was divided into three service teams: MI1(k) for the army, NID11 for the Royal Navy and A11(k) for the RAF.

While Kendrick was pulling together CSDIC, the British Army established two POW camps in Lancashire: No. 1 for officers and No. 2 for enlisted men. During the winter of 1939/40 a trickle of German prisoners were captured, including the first Luftwaffe aircrew.

Squadron-Leader Denys Felkin, chief interrogator for A11(k), was able to acquire indications about the existence of the Knickebein blind-bombing system from interrogation of several captured bomber crewmen from KG 4 and 27. Felkin also became expert at extracting useful order-of-battle information about Luftwaffe units from prisoners, which was unavailable from other sources. The standard approach focused on interrogating German junior officers and non-commissioned officers, who were expected to be less security-conscious, yet have potentially useful information. In July 1940, prisoner interrogation revealed that the Luftwaffe had introduced the 7.92mm PmK-v round, a steel-core round wrapped in phosphorus which ignited when fired.[26] Unlike the German stove-piped system (i.e. information was sent upward but not shared laterally with other organizations) of reporting, British prisoner interrogation reports were widely disseminated.

When the German invasion of France and the Low Countries began, the CSDIC received its first Heer prisoners, including 1,295 captured German troops from the 22. Infanterie-Division (Luftlande) and 7. Flieger-Division. Oberst Georg Friemel, commander of Infanterie-Regiment 65 and captured in Holland on 10 May 1940, was the highest ranking German prisoner of war in England.[27] Friemel and his troops were evacuated to Dover just before the Dutch capitulation. It would have been very useful to interrogate Friemel and his officers at length to learn more about German airborne tactics, particularly glider operations. However, due to the growing fear of German invasion, the War Cabinet decided to evacuate these prisoners to Canada on 21 June. Newer prisoners, captured in the air battles of July 1940, were the first to be interrogated at the recently established 'London Cage'.

While the PRU and the CSDIC were major steps forward for British tactical intelligence, the British Army's intelligence functions were in poor condition until well after Dunkirk. The main problem was that – like the German Heer – the British Army had very few dedicated intelligence professionals and tended to assign this function to whatever staff officers were available. In France and Belgium, the BEF lacked the ability to anticipate German actions due to inadequate intelligence support, and after Dunkirk army intelligence officers thought that Hitler would try to invade England right away, before he finished off France. General Ironside, as commander of Home Forces, used this off-the-cuff army assessment to develop a poorly conceived defence plan for Britain. However, defeat in Norway and France served as a catalyst for change and on 18 July the British Army created an Intelligence Corps, tasked with the collection, analysis and dissemination of military intelligence. Although it would be a long time before the Intelligence Corps had an experienced cadre of trained officers, this move would eventually help to improve British ground operations later in the war.

British Operational and Strategic Intelligence: Bletchley Park and *Seelöwe*

Since the disclosure of the wartime Enigma secret in 1974, there have been a number of lingering misconceptions about exactly what Allied code-breaking achieved and what its impact was upon the outcome of the war. Much of the problem derives from over-simplification – there was no single German Enigma code, but many different ciphers and procedures used by each of the Wehrmacht services. Older histories of the Battle of Britain omit any reference to Enigma and newer histories tend to swing between ignoring it or greatly exaggerating its role in 1940. Even an excellent history such as Stephen Bungay's *The Most Dangerous Enemy* (2000) got the story horribly wrong when it came to British code-breaking. In it, Bungay states that 'the British had scored a major intelligence coup early in the war by breaking the German's Enigma code, used for the transmission of high-level secret information, by using a device called "Ultra"'.[28] This one sentence has four major factual errors: (1) it was actually Polish code breakers who achieved this coup before the war; (2) the British only read Luftwaffe administrative traffic during the Battle of Britain; (3) Enigma was used for many non-secret transmissions, including weather reports; and (4) the device was Enigma, and 'Ultra' was the name of the Allied collection against it after 1942.

In 1926, the Reichsmarine (the predecessor of the Kriegsmarine) adopted a new enciphering machine for German naval communications, known as Enigma. Two years later, the Reichsheer also adopted Enigma and the Luftwaffe would adopt it when formed in 1935. Although the Enigma machine was based on commercially available technology, it was modified to be more secure for military communications and the Germans developed an almost religious faith in its security. However, German trust in the integrity of their communications was misplaced and they under-estimated the ingenuity of foreign code-breaking abilities. Enigma began to unravel in November 1931 when Hans Thilo Schmidt, a civilian official in the Ministry of the Reichswehr's cipher office, approached the French Deuxième Bureau (military intelligence) with the offer to sell them Enigma material. Hans Thilo Schmidt provided the French with manuals, standard operating procedures and settings for Enigma.[29] In addition to his knowledge of Enigma, Schmidt was also the brother of Rudolf Schmidt, who would rise to command a motorized corps under Guderian in May 1940. Oddly, the French Deuxième Bureau did not make a serious effort to break Enigma even with this information, but instead handed it off to their protégé, the Polish General Staff's Cipher Bureau (*Biuro Szyfrów*). Amazingly, a 27-year-old Polish mathematician in the bureau, Marian Rejewski, was able to use Schmidt's information to deduce the unknown wiring configurations within the Enigma rotors. Rejewski was also able to reverse-engineer and build an Enigma machine. By late December 1932, Rejewski had broken into Enigma and the Polish Cipher Bureau began reading encrypted German military communications.

It is not my intent to recount the entire effort to break Enigma, which has already been admirably told by a number of books such as Ronald Lewin's *Ultra Goes to War* (1978) and Hugh Sebag-Montefiore's

Enigma: The Battle for the Code (2000). Instead, I want to highlight the role of Enigma and British strategic-level intelligence in providing situational awareness to senior British decision-makers during the crisis period of 1940 and into early 1941. The Polish connection began on 25 July 1939, when the Polish General Staff invited representatives of the French and British cryptanalysis services to Warsaw, where they learned details of the Polish breakthrough into Enigma. Dilly Knox, Britain's leading cryptanalyst and a major player at MI6's GC&CS (Government Code and Cypher School) at Bletchley Park, was one of those invited to the two-day conference. Both the British and French delegations were presented with a copy of an Enigma machine, a mechanical 'bomba' that Rejewski had developed to assist in breaking the daily settings on Enigma and a host of other useful information. The Polish intelligence windfall jump-started the British code-breaking efforts at Bletchley Park, which had made no real progress against German pre-war Enigma communications. Alan Turing, the British mathematician, was tasked with exploiting the Polish information in order to break into the various Enigma ciphers.

Not only did the Poles provide Britain's intelligence services with the means to attack Enigma, but they also managed to preserve this secret when Poland was invaded and overrun in September 1939. Rejewski and his team of cryptanalysts were evacuated to France where they resumed their code-breaking efforts against wartime Enigma (which had additional security features). Turing, who was already working on an upgraded version of the 'bomba', visited France on 7 January 1940 to consult with Rejewski about the use of 'Zygalski sheets' used for manual decryption.[30] Thanks to Rejewski's help, two weeks later Bletchley Park was able to break the first GREEN cipher – used by the Heer for administrative purposes – although the information was three months old. When France was overrun in June 1940, Rejewski and his team were evacuated by the French first to North Africa, then back to Uzès (north-west of Marseille) in Vichy France. Although the British tried to get Rejewski and his 15-man team evacuated to England, the French were in no mood to cooperate after Mers-el-Kébir and they decided to keep Rejewski to assist Vichy France's communication intercept programme. It was not until after the demise of Vichy France that Rejewski and some of his associates were able to reach Great Britain in 1943, but they were not allowed to work at Bletchley Park and excluded from efforts to target Enigma. While the Germans made a great many mistakes during the World War II, the Allied failure to properly utilize Rejewski's talents in 1940–41 must be noted as a senseless and unnecessary failure.

Without Rejewski, the British codebreakers at Bletchley made slow progress against Enigma during the winter of 1939/40. It is important to note that each German service used one or more different Enigma ciphers, with different numbers or rotors and settings used, so the British were faced with multiple target sets. The primary sets that interested Bletchley Park's codebreakers were the Luftwaffe RED cipher and the Kriegsmarine's DOLPHIN cipher, but traffic from nearly a dozen other Enigma ciphers was being collected. In addition to the Polish assistance, the British codebreakers enjoyed several lucky breaks in early 1940. On 12 February, three Kriegsmarine Enigma rotors were captured from the U-33 sunk off Scotland and on 26 April more material (including decoded cipher text) was captured from a German trawler off Norway. Armed with this additional information, Turing's Hut 8 team were able to begin reading a small amount of Kriegsmarine Enigma traffic on 11 May. However, at this point the British were only able to read this Enigma cipher sporadically and often with a two-week delay, which greatly reduced its operational value.

The two main analytic units at Bletchley Park in 1940 were Hut 6, headed by Gordon Welchman, which analysed Heer and Luftwaffe traffic and Hut 8, headed by Turing, which analysed Kriegsmarine traffic. Analysis was initially done by hand and relied heavily upon looking for German operator errors and standardized formatting procedures – which precluded near-real-time code-breaking. Turing had convinced the GC&CS to invest £100,000 into developing his 'bombe', which was a mechanical decryption device that improved upon the Polish 'bomba'. The first 'bombe' mechanical device –

dubbed 'Victory' – was built in March 1940 but this early model was problematic and it was not until an improved model (Agnes) became operational on 8 August 1940 that Bletchley Park could attack Enigma in earnest. Once operational, the bombe enabled rapid computations which made it possible to break into German Enigma traffic at a much greater speed than heretofore possible. Whereas previous decryption required several weeks or more, with good clues on Enigma settings, a bombe could enable codebreakers to read a message within about 24 hours of it being received. Collection of the actual raw Enigma traffic was accomplished by numerous Y-Stations, which sent paper transcripts to Bletchley Park. The collection, analysis and dissemination of Enigma-derived intelligence was placed under the code name BONIFACE, which limited dissemination to senior military and political leaders.[31]

Welchman's team in Hut 6 was making good progress against the Luftwaffe's RED cipher because of poor operator procedures in that service. However, the Germans introduced new security procedures for Enigma on 1 May 1940, just before the opening of *Fall Gelb*, which temporarily blinded Bletchley Park. Yet the German mitigation effort was only briefly effective and on 22 May Welchman's team broke into RED and began decrypting Luftwaffe Enigma traffic within 48 hours. At this point, British code-breaking efforts began to have some operational impact, although too late to alter the catastrophic situation in France. Furthermore, the entire concept of communications intelligence from Enigma decryption was radical and encountered considerable scepticism from senior leaders in 1940, who often doubted its veracity. Moreover, Bletchley Park translated the decrypted messages, but added little or no analytic content to describe the importance of the message, which could leave end-users uncertain as to the significance of the special intelligence.

Indeed, it usually took someone outside the Enigma production chain to evaluate its content. For example, in June 1940, the Y-Stations began to intercept references to 'Knickebein' on RED traffic, but this meant nothing to the code breakers at Bletchley Park. This situation highlights one of the limitations of Enigma in the early days – dependence upon technical analysts to interpret data on German military technology. Fortuitously, the 28-year-old physicist Reginald V. Jones, who worked for the intelligence staff at the Air Ministry, was read into BONIFACE and was well aware of the German pre-war commercial Lorenz blind-landing system. Based upon information provided by CSDIC prisoner interrogations and the COMINT (Communications Intelligence) from Bletchley Park, Jones suspected that the Luftwaffe was adapting the system for blind-bombing at night, but this proved a hard-sell to senior leadership. Since the RAF's Bomber Command had rejected the use of radio navigation aids as unnecessary, there was considerable opposition to Jones's conclusion that the Luftwaffe had such a system. No less than Sir Henry Tizzard, senior scientific advisor to the Air Ministry and one of the primary advocates of radar, rejected Jones's conclusion. It was only with Churchill's direct support that Jones was allowed to test his theory and prove that the Luftwaffe was, in fact, using radio navigation for blind-bombing. Throughout July, analysis of RED traffic revealed that the Luftwaffe was installing Knickebein stations near Cherbourg and Brest, as well as a new system dubbed 'Wotan'. Bletchley Park's analysts also learned that KG 54 was one unit being equipped to use the blind-bombing technique and would be able to conduct precision night-bombing by August.[32]

Even with the help of the improved bombe, with more under construction, Bletchley Park was only able to decrypt 178 Enigma messages between March and December 1940, giving just occasional snapshots of German activity and mostly from the Luftwaffe's perspective. Thanks to BONIFACE, the Royal Air Force had an excellent idea about the Luftwaffe's order of battle in July and learned about *Adlerangriff* within a week of Göring issuing this order. Over time, decrypted messages gave further insight into the Luftwaffe's operational intent and some mission-specific information. Air Chief Marshal Sir Hugh Dowding, head of RAF Fighter Command, was a recipient of BONIFACE intelligence and this provided him with reliable forewarning about RAF airfields that were to be attacked.[33] It is important to emphasize, however, that BONIFACE's impact on the struggle between Fighter Command and the Luftwaffe was not in itself decisive and that code-breaking formed only one part of British intelligence collection in 1940.

Exploitation of RED traffic did provide Churchill with warning of German invasion planning, when details of Führer Directive No. 16 appeared in Luftwaffe signals in late July, but the operation's name was unknown until after *Seelöwe* was postponed. Instead, British intelligence referred to the German invasion plan as 'SMITH'. Surprisingly, Churchill did not accept outright the idea that Hitler was actually moving forward with invasion planning because initial invasion fears had proven incorrect. On 1 July, the Joint Intelligence Sub-Committee (JIC), which reported to the War Cabinet on all intelligence related to German intentions, stated that it could not determine the enemy's likely course of action, but that 'Germany's Military Superiority is such as to enable her to move in any direction she pleases with little or no warning'. Three days later, the JIC pointed to enemy invasion preparations and stated that an invasion was possible by 15 July.[34] The JIC was the senior organization in the British intelligence pyramid and served as a data fusion centre for COMINT, HUMINT (human intelligence) and IMINT.[35] When this invasion date passed, Churchill grew sceptical in regard to intelligence about SMITH. Although BONIFACE provided further information about SMITH, including the alerting of 7. Flieger-Division for a possible airborne mission and Siebel's ferry-building efforts, it was imagery confirmation by the PRU of barge concentrations in the Channel ports that convinced Churchill that SMITH was real. Thus another important point about BONIFACE that often gets lost in the mix is that operational use of Enigma-derived intelligence was multiplied through fusion with other intelligence collection efforts.

Meanwhile, Turing's Hut 8 enjoyed much less success against the Kriegsmarine's DOLPHIN cipher and only managed to break six messages throughout 1940, none in anything close to real time. This failure to penetrate Kriegsmarine communications had a detrimental impact upon the British ability to anticipate how *Seelöwe* might be conducted as well as to counter the on-going German U-Boat, *Hilfskreuzer*, and surface raider attacks on British commerce. Without much to go on, the JIC initially concluded that the main landing of *Seelöwe* was likely to be conducted against the east coast in Lincolnshire, Norfolk or Suffolk, with a possible two-division-size raid conducted from Norway against northern England or Scotland.[36] The JIC was aware of the assembling of barges in the Channel ports but seems to have regarded this as a feint and thought the main attempt would come across the North Sea. Consequently, the British Army deployed strong forces in the east and the Royal Navy planned to position a battle squadron at Rosyth to counter any German threat from Norway, as well as reinforcing Nore Command. It was not until the RAF's PRU continued to deliver reams of photographs of the unmistakable build-up in the Channel ports that the JIC began to reverse itself in early September and declared the main threat to be against the southern coast. Nevertheless, the British remained uncertain about where the Germans might attempt to invade and much of Britain's defences remained oriented toward the non-existent threat from across the North Sea.

It is important to distinguish that during the period from August to December 1940, the British code breakers read a significant amount of Luftwaffe RED traffic, but they barely scratched the surface of Kriegsmarine signal traffic. Both the Heer's operational Enigma network and the Abwehr's more secure network (Enigma-G) were impenetrable at this time. The Kriegsmarine's DOLPHIN cipher was not reliably broken until June 1941 and the Heer and Abwehr ciphers remained secure until October 1941. Consequently, the kind of strategic intelligence that Churchill and the CSC received was far more narrowly defined than is often suggested. For example, Churchill knew the essence of SMITH/*Seelöwe* from BONIFACE, but he did not know the exact landing areas the Germans had chosen, the size of the assault force or the enemy's operational timeline. The information derived from RED was probably most useful to RAF Fighter Command because it gave an indication of enemy target emphasis, but it did little for the Royal Navy and nothing for the British Army. Churchill was apparently frustrated with what BONIFACE could not tell him and looked to the PRU's photographic intelligence to fill in some of the gaps.

On 7 September 1940, at 2007 hours, the GHQ Home Forces issued the code word 'CROMWELL' to the Southern and Eastern Commands, indicating that invasion was imminent, probably within the next 12 hours. This alert was issued based upon the JIC's assessment of available intelligence from BONIFACE, photographic evidence of the build-up of German barges in the Channel ports and the increased tempo of the Luftwaffe air offensive over London. Yet the alert was based on faulty analysis of the available bits and pieces, which were not enough. British intelligence could not see what was going on inside the OKW, OKH or Skl, and jumped to hasty conclusions. The fact that the CROMWELL alert went to the Eastern Command indicates that the JIC still believed that an invasion of East Anglia was possible. CROMWELL was quickly rescinded the next morning, even though Hitler had not actually made his decision on whether to launch *Seelöwe* or not. The key point the CROMWELL alert brings out is that Bletchley Park's efforts to break Enigma were not yet capable of reliably answering the priority intelligence requirements (e.g. what is the enemy going to do next?) of Churchill's War Cabinet and the CSC.

The JIC did have one other source of intelligence at this point – a Polish-run espionage network in occupied France known as Interallié. When France fell, a good number of Polish military personnel were left behind and they had made no peace with the Germans. Polish Air Force Captain Roman Czerniawski established Interallié and recruited about 100 Polish and French operatives to report on German military activities in France. Czerniawski was able to regularly exfiltrate reports to Colonel Stefan Mayer, the former head of the Polish Cipher Bureau, now in London. In late 1940 and early 1941, the reports from the

Polish-run Interallié network provided the only reliable information coming out of occupied France and did indicate large-scale preparation and training for invasion.

Table 3. German Enigma Codes Attacked by British Codebreakers in 1940–41

German Name	British Code Name	Service	User	Date of Compromise
Heimisch	DOLPHIN	Kriegsmarine	U-Boats everywhere and surface warships in home waters	June 1941
Ausserheimisch	Pike	Kriegsmarine	*Hilfskreuzer* and surface raiders	Never broken
	RED	Luftwaffe		22 May 1940, with 2 day-delay
	GREEN	Heer	Used by units in home Wehrkreis (military districts)	October 1941
		Abwehr		October 1941

The Utter Failure of the German Abwehr versus Britain's MI5

On the other side of the Channel, the men planning *Seelöwe* had very little idea about the state of British defences or intentions. German efforts to conduct espionage or HUMINT operations in Great Britain were a complete failure due to a combination of the Abwehr's amateurish approach and the vigilance of British counter-intelligence efforts led by MI5. Nikolaus Ritter, an Abwehr officer in the Hamburg office, was responsible for recruiting agents for Britain even before the war. Initially, Ritter tried to develop professional spies who could be used for an extended period. He was able to recruit one useful agent, Walter Simon, who conducted two successful espionage operations in England in 1938, then returned with information about RAF airfields and industrial facilities that benefitted Luftwaffe targeteers back in

Berlin. However, a slip-up led to Simon's arrest by MI5 in February 1939, and he was deported. Ritter also recruited a Welshman by the name of Arthur Owens on the Abwehr payroll before the war, although he produced little of value.[37] Yet even with this limited pre-war espionage, the Abwehr still managed to learn about the construction of the Chain Home radar sites and several new RAF air bases.

The Abwehr missed two great opportunities to set up spy networks in Great Britain. Given that there were a significant number of Nazi sympathizers in Britain during the 1930s, it is amazing that the Abwehr made no effort to reach out to Oswald Mosley's British Union of Fascists (BUF) or other pro-German politicians.[38] Although the British Government enacted Defence Regulation 18B at the start of the war, which included provisions to incarcerate enemy sympathizers, it was not enforced under Chamberlain's government. During the period from September 1939 until May 1940, many pro-German sympathizers were still at liberty and some might have worked with the Abwehr – the advantage of using English-speaking natives who could not easily be detected is obvious. Yet this window of opportunity closed when Churchill became prime minister because he decided to enforce 18B to its maximum extent, ordering the arrest not only of Mosley and his BUF associates, but even men like Admiral Sir Barry Domvile. Retired Major General J. F. C. Fuller was investigated for his ties to Fascism and Hitler, but not arrested. Despite much talk of potential Fifth Column activities in Britain, the Abwehr's apathy and Churchill's eagerness to arrest pro-German sympathizers quickly snuffed out the pool of potential local recruits.

After nine months of indolence, the Abwehr was suddenly tasked to gather information from inside England to facilitate the forthcoming air-sea campaign. In desperation, Ritter put his best agent, Simon, back into play even though he was already known to MI5. Landing in southern Ireland via U-38 on 12 June 1940, Simon was spotted coming ashore and arrested the same day.[39] Soon thereafter, Ritter was tasked with running Operation *Lena*, to insert more agents into Britain to gather information useful for *Seelöwe*. He began a recruiting drive in Hamburg, assembling a collection of pro-Nazi Danes, Dutch and Finns, who were given only minimal training before being sent across the English Channel. Another Abwehr official, Kurt Mirow in Cologne, set up a duplicate recruiting effort, without informing or coordinating with Ritter. Mirow's operation was exceedingly amateurish and he dispatched four poorly trained agents to the south coast of England in a fishing boat on 3 September. One group of two agents landed near Dungeness, in between *Seelöwe*'s intended landing zones B and C. Before being caught, agent Jose Waldberg managed to send two radio messages back to the Abwehr, including one that reported, 'No mines, few soldiers, unfinished blockhouse'.[40] This brief message was the only legitimate HUMINT report ever received by the Abwehr from an agent in England during the war. All four agents were soon arrested and Waldberg was executed in December 1940.

Meanwhile, Ritter tried to establish a more robust system of delivering agents into England by working with Hauptmann Karl-Edmund Gartenfeld from the Aufklärungsgruppe OBdL, a specialized reconnaissance group. Gartenfeld, a highly experienced pilot, flew an He-111 bomber that was painted matte black, and specialized in clandestine parachute drops over enemy territory. On 6 September, Gartenfeld took off from Brussels and flew low over the Channel, then successfully dropped the Danish agent Gösta Caroli near Northampton; Caroli employed negligible tradecraft and was quickly arrested. However, Gartenfeld demonstrated that the Abwehr had the ability to covertly deliver agents into England; the problem was the men sent were hopelessly inept at their jobs. Ritter recruited more agents, including Karl Grosse, an English-speaking German who had joined the Abwehr's Bataillon *Brandenburg* infiltration unit.

However, Ritter made the crucial mistake of using Arthur Owens – whom he believed to still be a reliable agent-in-place – to be the primary contact for most of the new Abwehr agents parachuted into England. In fact, Owens had revealed his involvement with the Abwehr to MI5 in 1938 and he had been turned into a double-agent, designated 'Snow'. By using Owens, who was allowed to contact Ritter via radio, MI5 was able to learn the identity of many of the Abwehr-recruited agents and arrest them as soon as they arrived in England. This did not occur in every instance and Karl Grosse was parachuted into England by Gartenfeld on 3 October 1940. Despite his affiliation with the *Brandenburgers*, Grosse proved to be a very poor agent and was almost immediately captured by a farmer and handed over to the police. MI5's Double Cross Committee became extremely adept at turning each captured agent and then used them to funnel useless or misleading information to the Abwehr. As David Kahn noted, 'not a single German spy in Great Britain was legitimate'. Every one of the Abwehr's operatives was a double-agent, run by MI5's Double Cross Committee.[41]

The failure of Ritter or anyone else in the Abwehr to detect MI5's Double Cross operations defies common sense and suggests something more than routine incompetence. The German historian Monika Siedentopf has argued that members of the Abwehr group in Hamburg, such as Herbert Wichmann, had ties to the anti-Nazi resistance and may have deliberately sabotaged Operation *Lena*. Given the verified complicity of Admiral Canaris and other members of the Abwehr in the resistance, this is a distinct – but unconfirmed – possibility.[42] On the other hand, the equally glaring failure to detect Enigma compromises suggests an organizational close-minded approach to intelligence operations, which invites disaster. In any case, it is also noticeable that Operation *Lena* was not conducted in a way that was likely to return much useful information even if MI5 had not immediately scooped up its agents. Landing agents in the central English countryside would not answer the priority intelligence requirements for *Seelöwe* about British coastal defences in Kent and Sussex. Nor were any of the agents provided with reliable means of covert communications or cover stories to evade even cursory inspection. Operation *Lena* was doomed to failure by incompetent planning and execution.

In addition to frustrating the Abwehr's ability to conduct espionage in England, the counter-intelligence vigilance of MI5 also detected possible treachery within the US embassy in London. Tyler Kent, an American cipher clerk with possible anti-communist or isolationist sympathies, was observed trying to pass secret cables to the Abwehr. These cables apparently included communications between First Sea Lord Winston Churchill and President Franklin D. Roosevelt concerning possible naval cooperation or aid. As prime minister, Churchill directed MI5 to arrest Kent on 20 May and the United States waived his diplomatic immunity. A raid on Kent's apartment revealed nearly 2,000 stolen US State Department cables. While it does appear that some of these purloined cables may have reached the Abwehr, they had little value other than to point out that Churchill was counting on American military assistance.[43]

Incompetence and Treason Deny Germany Reliable Intelligence

In order to conduct *Seelöwe* with any chance of success, Hitler desperately needed accurate intelligence about British military capabilities and conditions in England, but the general incompetence of the Wehrmacht's various intelligence services failed to supply this vital ingredient. Even Germany's ability to conduct its blockade strategy against Great Britain was severely undermined by its inability to assess enemy production and losses, denying the Wehrmacht a reliable measure of the effectiveness of its air-sea operations. Adding insult to injury, the Wehrmacht's intelligence services were riddled with men who opposed Hitler's policies and deliberately leaked information to the enemy.

Intelligence was not a strong suit in the German military tradition and the structures employed by the Third Reich were ripe with inefficiencies that barred effective collaboration between the services. German intelligence collection was 'stove-piped', i.e. information went up but was not shared laterally with other organizations; inter-service collaboration was effectively nil. The best men went into operations, not intelligence. In theory, the OKW's Cipher Department, known as OKW/Chi (Oberkommando der Wehrmacht Chiffrierabteilung), headed by Oberstleutnant Fritz Boetzel, was one of the premier collection organizations and focused on collecting enemy and neutral diplomatic communications, as well as foreign radio broadcasts. The OKW/Chi had two main collection sites near Berlin and Nürnberg, as well as sub-stations in the occupied territories; its analysts attempted to break encoded traffic and, if successful, it was translated and the final product disseminated as a *Verlässliche Nachrichten* (Reliable Message or VN). Most of the VNs dealt with mundane diplomatic activities and press reports; however, there were occasionally useful items about shortages in England or Lend-Lease shipments.[44]

Although the Germans had captured a partially intact British Typex cipher machine (based on commercial Enigma) at Dunkirk and a cipher code book in Norway, Boetzel's OKW/Chi enjoyed very little success against British communications.[45] Nor did the OKW have any mechanism to coordinate or fuse information collected by the three services, which meant that it was very difficult for Hitler and his key subordinates to develop a clear picture of enemy capabilities and intentions. Instead, the OKW/Chi produced a great deal of innocuous information. Reichsmarschall Hermann Göring regarded the OKW/Chi with such contempt that he simply decided to establish his own communications intelligence organization, known as the *Forschungsamt* (Research Bureau or FA), which created a wasteful duplication of effort.[46]

Prior to the war, the Germans achieved a significant intelligence coup by conducting a large-scale clandestine imagery collection effort over England. Most of the imagery was quite good but, by 1940, some of it was five years old. Furthermore, the collection effort was not matched by an equally competent exploitation effort, which noted the construction of the Chain Home radar sites but attached no great importance to them. Inadequate photo interpretation was a perennial weakness of the Luftwaffe.

While the Germans had some insight into British communications, it was unrecognized at the time that the OKW's secure communications were highly vulnerable to 'insider threats' from anti-Nazi officers. General Erich Fellgiebel, head of OKW communications, and his deputy Generalleutnant Fritz Thiele, were not only deeply involved with the anti-Hitler conspiracy but they were passing classified information to the 'Lucy' spy ring in Switzerland. It is likely that some of this information was passed on to Britain's MI6. Boetzel and his deputy Major Andrea from the OKW/Chi were both involved in passing classified information to outsiders. Because the covert activities of all these officers were not revealed until 1944, resulting in their executions, it undoubtedly impacted Germany's ability to develop reliable intelligence to support military operations against Great Britain. Many of these officers were worried that a successful *Seelöwe*, coming on the heels of his success over France, would make Hitler's control over Germany incontestable and hence sought to thwart this operation.

Admiral Wilhelm Canaris headed the Abwehr, the OKW's intelligence agency. Canaris was enigmatic, having started as a vocal supporter of Hitler but then shifted to covertly work against the regime by 1938. Although still unconfirmed, Canaris may have been in secret communications with Britain's MI6 and there is little doubt that he acted to sabotage Hitler's effort to bring Spain in on the Axis side. Anti-regime treason, combined with organizational lassitude and toleration for widespread mediocrity and incompetence, led to the Abwehr's generally abysmal performance as an intelligence organization. Amazingly, the Abwehr – which was mainly focused on espionage operations – had no real analytic section in 1940, which meant that the OKW could not actually conduct the entire collection cycle.[47]

Nor was the insider threat confined to the Wehrmacht. In early November 1939, the German physicist Hans Ferdinand Mayer, director of research at Siemens in Berlin, covertly supplied the British embassy in Norway with technical data on a variety of new military programmes including radar and radio navigation. This information, dubbed the Oslo report, was forwarded to MI6 and reviewed by various intelligence officials, including Reginald V. Jones, who was researching German developments in radar. The sum total of covert leaks from military and civilian sources seriously undermined the German war effort and gave vital clues to assist British military research and development; this trend would continue throughout the war.

Each of the German service branches had their own intelligence organizations. The most effective was the Kriegsmarine's B-Dienst (*Beobachtungs-Dienst*, Observation Service), a branch within the Skl that was responsible for intercepting and analysing enemy naval communications (COMINT, in modern terms). This branch, headed by Kapitän zur See Heinz Bonatz, was also tasked with breaking enemy naval ciphers through cryptanalysis. Wilhelm Tranow, a civilian cryptographer, was in charge of B-Dienst, Section IIIF, which collected and analysed the Royal Navy's encrypted and unencrypted communications. Under Tranow, Section IIIF succeeded in breaking the British Naval Cipher No. 1 and auxiliary codes before the war, which allowed them to track the movements of the Royal Navy. On 28 December 1939, B-Dienst was able to intercept and decode signals from the battleship HMS *Barham*, confirming that it had been hit by a torpedo from U-30.[48] By early 1940, B-Dienst was reading up to 50 per cent of the Royal Navy's communications traffic and could track most of the capital ships. However, intelligence advantages are often transitory and the British suddenly changed their naval codes on 20 August 1940, effectively blinding B-Dienst one month prior to *Seelöwe*'s intended S-Tag. Although Tranow's Section IIIF was able to make progress against the new British naval codes by early October, by then *Seelöwe* had been postponed. By spring 1941, B-Dienst had recovered and was able to decrypt a good portion of British naval communications.[49]

B-Dienst also had great success against the British and Allied Merchant Ships (BAMS) code in 1940, which allowed them to track convoy movements to some extent. Indeed, B-Dienst's ability to read merchant ship communications traffic was just as much a force multiplier for the Kriegsmarine's limited U-Boat force as radar was for the RAF's fighters. However, the Kriegsmarine's other senior intelligence office, Kapitän zur See Gottfried Krüger's 3/Skl (Foreign Navies Branch) was more of a hindrance. It produced intelligence estimates, relying on B-Dienst VNs, and was responsible for determining the amount of merchant shipping being built by Great Britain and its Allies, as well as ascertaining the amount of Allied tonnage sunk each month. Generally, 3/Skl's estimates tended to be inaccurate since Germany lacked reliable data on foreign merchant vessel construction.[50]

The situation in the Luftwaffe was even worse, because intelligence functions were spread over several organizations that did not cooperate well. Oberst Josef 'Beppo' Schmid, heading the OKL's 5th Branch, was the senior Luftwaffe intelligence officer and reported directly to Göring. Schmid was another example of how cronyism undermined the performance of the Wehrmacht: he was not only a close friend of Göring, but had participated in Hitler's failed 1923 Munich putsch, which marked him as a stalwart Nazi. Consequently, Schmid had very high standing in both Hitler's and Göring's estimation. However, Schmid knew little about intelligence work, and aside from *Studie Blau* his branch produced volumes of useless or incorrect information. Schmid's overt pro-Nazi bias affected his assessments and he tended to tell his superiors what they wanted to hear. Throughout 1939–40, Schmid kept telling Göring that Germany was out-producing Britain in aircraft and that the RAF would run out of fighters. He argued that the RAF could be defeated in a 2–4 week campaign and was exaggerating RAF losses in August 1940 by more than 300 per cent.[51] Among Schmid's most egregious errors, he inaccurately assessed that the Bf-110 was superior in dog-fighting capability to British fighters, which led to its misuse against the RAF in July and August 1940.[52] On 16 July, Schmid issued his first assessment of the RAF's strength, which was only off by 3 per cent, but his estimate of British monthly fighter production was off by 40 per cent.[53] Much of Schmid's estimate of enemy aircraft production was based upon reports from one of the Abwehr agents in England, who was actually a double-agent. By early September, Schmid reported that Fighter Command was essentially destroyed. Schmid's failure to conduct a proper intelligence assessment of the RAF's capabilities played a major role in shaping the poor German operational decision-making evident in September 1940 and influenced the postponement of *Seelöwe*.[54]

Although the Luftwaffe had some knowledge of British radar developments, Schmid failed to include any information about Chain Home capabilities in his 16 July estimate. Generalleutnant Wolfgang Martini, the Luftwaffe's chief signal officer, who was responsible for German radar developments, tried to warn Göring about British radar but was ignored. Martini also ran the Luftwaffe's Cipher Office, which collected COMINT on RAF communications, but this information was not integrated into Schmid's assessments.[55] On 7 August, Schmid did mention British radar in an updated assessment, but incorrectly believed that it would prevent the RAF from massing its fighters in any one sector. While Martini had plenty of radar experts, Schmid failed to draw upon their expertise to analyse British radar capabilities. Martini also directed the radio-intercept units that supported each Luftflotte.

The most accurate information about the RAF's order of battle actually came from the III./Luftnachrichten-Regiment 2, which supported Kesselring's Luftflotte 2; this battalion had a radio-intercept station established at Wissant, south of Calais. The one real drawback of the RAF's GCI (Ground Control Intercept) system was that it required a tremendous amount of radio traffic, which the Wissant intercept site collected and analysed. Consequently, Martini's *Funkhorchdienst* organization was able to develop a comprehensive order of battle for the RAF, including the ground radio stations that supported each group in Fighter Command. From Wissant, Martini's signalmen could track British convoys in the Channel and they knew where and when Fighter Command had its fighters deployed on a daily basis. Apparently, very little of this information reached Schmid's 5th Branch, or it was ignored.[56]

Schmid was also tied to the outdated *Studie Blau* as his primary reference for target development due to the lack of reliable imagery intelligence collection over the interior of Great Britain. In wartime, Luftwaffe reconnaissance units relied mostly on Do-17P and He-111 aircraft to collect aerial photographs over England, which were highly vulnerable to fighter interception. Photographing targets on the coast continued in 1939–40, but inland cities were more difficult to reach in daylight without interception. Furthermore, the Luftwaffe used low-resolution mapping cameras best suited for survey work, not point target analysis. Unlike the RAF, the Luftwaffe did not use stereoscopic imagery and lacked a central imagery interpretation centre, so many important targets were missed or incorrectly identified. Once the British starting camouflaging targets and dispersing their aircraft production facilities, the target guides in *Studie Blau* became outdated. While the Luftwaffe did have a few unarmed Bf-109E-5 fighters modified to carry cameras, they lacked the range of the Spitfire PR aircraft and were restricted to tactical targets. Due to Fighter Command's efficient intercept system, Luftwaffe reconnaissance aircraft were obliged to fly at extreme altitudes to avoid destruction, which reduced the quality of imagery collected.

Of all the services, the Heer was the most ignorant about what awaited them on the other side of the Channel. The Heer relied upon the OKH's 3rd Branch (Foreign Armies West or FHW), headed by Oberstleutnant Ulrich Liss, for information about the British Army and coastal defences. Although Liss spoke fluent English and had visited Great Britain before the war, none of his subordinates had any intelligence training and most were reservists, including former bankers. The Heer's primary collection capabilities rested upon tactical-level COMINT, prisoner interrogations and document exploitation (DOCEX), none of which were practical across the intervening English Channel. Furthermore, Liss's branch focused on enemy order of battle, but made no effort to assess enemy capabilities or intentions.[57] Nor was the FHW very good at order-of-battle analysis in regard to Britain, since it vastly over-estimated the number of divisions available in September 1940 and their level of equipment and manning. The Germans estimated that Britain had 37 infantry and two armoured divisions available, of which half were at full strength; thus, FHW expected the enemy to have 20 combat-ready divisions.[58] In fact, the British Army could barely field 13 combat-ready divisions out of the 29 they had and only four or five were fully equipped. In modern terms, the FHW contributed very little to German intelligence preparation of the battlefield (IPB) and the exaggeration of enemy ground strength only reinforced the hesitation of Hitler to proceed with *Seelöwe*.

The inability of the German intelligence services to provide reliable assessments prevented the Wehrmacht from accurately gauging its relative effectiveness in air-sea operations against Great Britain. Without accurate knowledge of the enemy's dispositions or key vulnerabilities, neither the Luftwaffe nor Kriegsmarine could inflict a decisive blow. Nor could the Germans hope to conduct *Seelöwe* with any hope of success when they could not locate the Royal Navy's capital ships or properly estimate Britain's ability to resist invasion. Uncertainty fed Hitler's fears, but if German intelligence could have revealed the weakness of Britain's defences he might well have regarded *Seelöwe* as a risk worth taking.

Hitler's Effort to Enlist Spanish Help

On 14 June, 1940, 4,000 Spanish troops marched into the city of Tangier, a neutral city of 60,000 guaranteed by a 1924 treaty between Britain, France and Spain. With Paris occupied, General Francisco Franco moved quickly to take advantage of the situation – which caused great consternation to the new British ambassador in Madrid, Sir Samuel Hoare. Two days prior to the occupation of Tangier, the 47-year-old Franco, fascist dictator of Spain since his victory in the Spanish Civil War in April 1939, switched Spain's status from 'neutral' to 'non-belligerent'. Although the civil war had inflicted great devastation on Spain, including over 500,000 dead and a devastated economy, Hoare believed that Franco's declaration of 'non-belligerence' and occupation of Tangier signalled a shift that could bring Spain into the Axis camp at any time. The British were aware of Spanish designs upon the British naval base at Gibraltar and rampant Anglophobia in Franco's regime. Soon thereafter, Hoare provided an assessment along these lines to the Foreign Office in London and recommended active measures to prevent Spain from joining the Axis.

Churchill decided to use a carrot and stick approach to keeping Spain out of the war. First, through Hoare he advised Franco that Great Britain would abide by the terms of the War Trade Agreement signed in March 1940 and promised that 100,000 tons of wheat from Canada and several shipments of oil would arrive later in the summer of 1940. After three years of civil war, Spain's agricultural sector was badly damaged and one-quarter of the population was near starvation levels. Spain's entire gold reserves had been shipped to the Soviet Union by the Republicans and then appropriated by Stalin, so Franco had no foreign currency reserves. Britain was Spain's only viable source of oil. Aware of Spanish distress, Hoare dangled the possibility of a £4 million loan, which Spain could use to import vital commodities.[59] However, if Spain joined the Axis, the Royal Navy would be in a position to throttle Spain's imports and attack its vulnerable coastline.

In order to hedge his bets, Churchill decided to employ Hoare's suggestion to bribe select Spanish generals to convince Franco to remain neutral. Captain Alan Hillgarth, the Royal Navy's attaché in Madrid, had connections to MI6; he approached Juan March, an influential Spanish banker to facilitate the bribery scheme.[60] March had worked as a double-agent for MI6 during the World War I and was well placed to reach out to senior officials in the Franco regime. Both Hoare and Hillgarth believed that there was widespread corruption in the Spanish military and that bribery would be an effective means of buying influence in the regime. Recently revealed documents indicate that MI6 spent over $10 million on bribes in Spain and that multiple Spanish officials were compromised.[61]

However, it appears that MI6 wasted its money. Many of the persons listed as recipients of bribes were not in a position to influence Franco or were outright political opponents. Franco's brother Nicolás took British bribes, but as Spanish ambassador in Portugal he was far from the centre of decision-making. Generals Kindelàn, de Llano and Orgaz also took bribes but they had already been relieved of their commands or shuffled off to remote postings. The only officer with any real influence that British money bought was General Antonio Aranda, an engineer, but he was later accused of working with the British and arrested. On the whole, the offer of British wheat appears to have purchased more Spanish goodwill than MI6's bribes.

Franco's primary decision-making group in regard to military strategy was the *Junta de Defensa Nacional*, comprising himself, General Juan Vigón as the head of the Supreme General Staff (*Alto Estado Mayor*) and the heads of the three services: Lieutenant General José Varela, minister of the army; Admiral Francisco Moreno, minister of the navy; and General Juan Yagüe, minister of the Spanish Air Force. All four were loyal to Franco, but did not agree on entering the war on Germany's side. Yagüe was the strongest advocate of joining the Axis and had close ties with Göring and the Luftwaffe, but both Moreno and Varela were Anglophiles. Franco's foreign minister, Colonel Juan Beigbeder, was also an Anglophile with an English mistress and was on close terms with Hoare.[62] Internally, Franco's regime was far from secure and was undermined by dissent and intrigue from ultra-right Falangists and pro-monarchists. Yet despite a multitude of domestic problems, Franco was well aware that Hitler had changed the balance of power in Europe by defeating France and that a moment of great opportunity had arrived. At the same time, Franco and much of the Spanish military were obsessed with expanding south into Africa and regarded Vichy France's territories in Morocco and Algeria as ripe for the picking. Franco and his confederates were essentially colonial officers who had made their names in Morocco during the Rif War and afterwards, so that was their primary focus – not defeating Britain. With German help, Spain could potentially enlarge its sphere of influence at the expense of the defeated Allies.

Franco was also keenly mindful that German Ju-52 transports had carried his troops to Spain in 1936, ultimately facilitating his rise to power. During the Spanish Civil War, Germany assisted Franco with over $200 million in military aid, including air support from Legion Condor. Franco was committed to repaying his war debt to Germany with exports of iron ore and wolfram (tungsten), both vital for the German war effort. In mid-June, Franco also activated a plan to covertly assist German U-Boat operations. Prior to the war, the German merchant marine had deliberately interned over 50 of its vessels in Spanish ports; loaded with naval stores and fuel, these ships were intended to act as resupply ships for U-Boats. Franco agreed to allow U-Boats to enter the Spanish ports of Vigo and El Ferrol; the first, U-43, arrived on 19 June and three more arrived in the next two weeks. Amazingly, the Spanish businessman Juan March assisted the Germans in moving naval supplies through Spain to support their U-Boat operations, while simultaneously working with MI6 to bribe Franco's generals.

Since Hitler initially saw no need to involve Spain directly in the war – expecting a British peace offer – covert U-Boat bases seemed sufficient. Franco expected a British capitulation as well and like Mussolini he wanted to jump on the bandwagon in the hour of victory. Thus, Franco decided to make the first move to joining the Axis by sending one of his few trusted confederates, General Juan Vigón, to Germany on 11 June to meet with Hitler. Vigón presented Hitler with a letter from Franco that stated, 'I would be deeply gratified to render you at any time, such services as you might consider most valuable.' Vigón also delivered a Spanish request for German military assistance and, once fulfilled, Spain would enter the war. In terms of military objectives, Vigón declared Franco's intent to seize Gibraltar, all of Morocco and part of north-west Algeria. With no obvious benefit for Germany, Hitler ignored these outlandish requests.[63] On 27 June, German troops reached the Spanish frontier and some officers, such as Generaloberst Heinz Guderian, wanted to continue into Spain to immediately attack Gibraltar. On the same day, General Yagüe was relieved of command after being accused of working with the Germans against Franco. While it is unclear if these charges were true, the removal of the most pro-Axis member of the junta was not auspicious for Spanish-German cooperation.

It was not until the practical difficulties with *Seelöwe* became apparent in July 1940, that Hitler became more interested in using Spain to seize Gibraltar and as a stepping stone into North Africa. On 22 July, Hitler sent Admiral Canaris and a small delegation to Madrid to sound out Franco on joining the Axis. Although Canaris's role in the covert anti-Hitler conspiracy is a fact, the nature of his interactions with Franco is unclear. Did Canaris dissuade Franco from joining the Axis? While some Germans later suspected this, there is no factual account to confirm it. Nor is it likely that Canaris would have been foolish enough to blurt out something to Franco or other Spanish leaders such as a prediction that Germany would lose the war; this has been alleged, but without any confirmation.[64] There were many pro-Nazi members within Franco's junta and it is likely that someone would have revealed outright treason by Canaris if it had occurred to the nearest Gestapo representative. Instead, it is likely that Canaris contributed to friction in the German efforts to bring Spain into the war by simply accentuating negative factors, such as Germany's inability to provide Spain with any appreciable amount of military equipment or raw materials (which was true) as well as emphasizing Hitler's disinterest in Spanish claims in North Africa. Canaris also apprised Franco of problems with implementing *Seelöwe* and the Spanish dictator apparently thought it best to delay Spain's entry into the war until after German troops had successfully landed in England.

Despite Canaris's lack of enthusiasm, Franco continued to express his enthusiasm for the Axis cause, his hatred of Britain and willingness to lend a hand, but he also pointed out to Canaris that the Spanish economy could not survive a British blockade without German help. His diplomats provided Canaris with a list of vital aid needed before Spain could enter the war, including 344,000 tons of petroleum products, 500,000 tons of coal, 200,000 tons of wheat, 100,000 tons of cotton and 25,000 tons of crude rubber.[65] Franco's material requirements greatly exceeded the amount of food and fuel that Churchill was offering and suggests that he was trying to play off both sides in order to get the maximum aid for Spain. At the same time, Franco continued to bargain with Hoare for Canadian wheat and British loans. Hoare also pressed the Americans for Red Cross shipments of food to Spain. In order to satisfy Franco, Hitler and Ribbentrop vaguely promised him that economic aid would be forthcoming and pressed to seal the deal. By 27 August, a draft treaty was prepared, outlining the terms for Spanish entry into the war and an attack on Gibraltar. Halder's OKH was already preparing a plan known as Operation *Felix* to attack Gibraltar and Raeder showed far more enthusiasm for it than he did for *Seelöwe*.

By the beginning of September 1940, it seemed that British efforts had failed and that Spanish entry into the war on the Axis side was imminent. Spain's military was not ready for war against Britain, but it was eager to pounce upon Vichy French territory in North Africa. Franco's *Junta de Defensa Nacional* had begun planning for possible military action against Gibraltar in late 1939 and had decided to increase the army from 250,000 to 450,000.[66] However, Spanish military capabilities were modest, barely adequate for defence. In July 1940, the 340,000-man Spanish Army consisted of ten corps headquarters with 24 infantry divisions, as well as five independent tank regiments with 200 light tanks, but most of its equipment was worn out. About 30,000 troops were stationed in the Spanish Protectorate in Morocco, 10,000 in the Balearic Islands and 6,000 in the Canary Islands. On paper, the Spanish Air Force seemed powerful with over 600 aircraft, including 264 fighters and 360 bombers, but it was actually a potpourri of left-over Italian, German and Soviet aircraft.[67] Three-quarters of Spain's fighters were obsolescent I-15, CR.32 or He-51 biplanes – no match for Spitfires or even Hurricanes. As a military alliance with Germany beckoned, Franco betrayed his true intentions by sending four more divisions to the Spanish Protectorate in Morocco in order to invade French Morocco and more troops to defend the Canary Islands against a British invasion.[68]

Thus, the real disconnect between Germany and Spain came about because Hitler and Franco were working at strategic cross-purposes and each wanted to use the other for objectives that only suited themselves. Franco wanted German aid so he could essentially fight a localized colonial war in North Africa, whereas Hitler wanted Spain in order to inflict a body-blow upon the British position in the Western Mediterranean and improve the Kriegsmarine's ability to interdict British convoys moving north along the west coast of Africa. U-Boats and Fw-200 Condors based in Spain could also seriously threaten British lines of communication to the Middle East, which would assist Mussolini. Hitler was also influenced by the Destroyer-for-Bases deal announced on 3 September, which suggested to him that intervention by the United States was now possible. In that event, Raeder claimed that Germany would need advance bases in the Atlantic, such as Spain's Canary Islands or in North Africa, to interdict any US naval operations in the eastern Atlantic.

Expecting Germany to meet his material demands, Franco sent his brother-in-law Serrano Suñer to Berlin on 16 September as a special envoy to negotiate the final details of Spanish intervention. Suñer was enthusiastically pro-German and a leading advocate of Spain joining the Axis. However, Suñer told Ribbentrop that Spain immediately needed at least 400,000 tons of grain as well as an allotment of 56,000 tons of petroleum products per month for its military needs. Although Hitler agreed to Franco's territorial demands 'in principle', Ribbentrop brusquely presented Suñer with a demand for an advance base in the Canary Islands and two in Morocco, once it was occupied by Spanish troops.[69] Ribbentrop made a clumsy reference to German intervention in Spain, with or without Franco's cooperation. It was also apparent to Suñer that Hitler was considering aggression against Vichy France by overrunning Morocco and possibly Algeria, in addition to seizing British Gibraltar. These German intentions upset Franco – particularly the idea of permanent German bases on Spanish soil – and caused him to begin reconsidering the idea of entering the war. Franco also learned about the postponement of *Seelöwe*, which made it apparent that Britain was far from beaten. After a month of foot-dragging, Franco removed Beigbeder and made Suñer his foreign minister, then arranged for a direct meeting with Hitler.

On 23 October, Hitler met Franco at the French border town of Hendaye. Hitler assured Franco that German forces could quickly capture Gibraltar and that *Seelöwe* would be conducted in 1941. Franco stated that Spanish troops would have to lead the attack on Gibraltar and rejected the OKH's plan for Operation *Felix* as an affront to Spanish honour. The meeting lasted three hours and left Hitler unsettled because it was clear that Franco was not on board with his strategic plans and only obsessed with gaining Morocco and as much economic aid as possible. Nevertheless, Suñer signed a protocol on 6 November which stated, 'Spain will intervene in the present war of the Axis Powers against England after they have provided it with the military support necessary for its preparedness, at a time to be set by common agreement of the three powers...'[70] According to the protocol, Germany was pledged to provide Spain with food and raw materials for its war effort.[71] Six days later, Hitler signed Führer Directive No. 18, which authorized Operation *Felix* once Spain entered the war and stipulated that these operations would drive the British out of the western Mediterranean. It was expected that Spain would enter the war in January 1941 and that Operation *Felix* would complete the capture of Gibraltar by late February 1941. Thus, Hitler would then have the option of mounting *Seelöwe* against England in spring 1941 or mopping up the British position in the Mediterranean. Serious consideration was also given to sending a motorized corps into Morocco, to ensure the rapid capture of Atlantic naval bases for the Kriegsmarine.[72] All three German service chiefs, Göring, Raeder and Brauchitsch, supported the latter concept as the least risky and most rewarding. Had Franco agreed, the Wehrmacht would have been drawn to the south in 1941, not the east.

Despite what appeared to be a done deal, Franco had a change of heart. He was uncertain that Hitler would honour his promises of aid or recognize Spanish claims in North Africa. Franco was also concerned about becoming a minor Axis satellite; German officers had scoffed at Spanish preparations to attack Gibraltar as amateurish and said that it could only be accomplished by German forces with the Spanish acting in a supporting role. Operation *Felix* required two German corps with 65,000 troops to enter Spain to attack Gibraltar and this was unsettling – it could even turn into a de facto occupation. In addition, the Luftwaffe wanted to move 800 aircraft into Spain to support *Felix*, with thousands of personnel, while Hitler kept mentioning building air bases in Spain and the Canary Islands; altogether this commitment suggested a semi-permanent presence. On 8 December, Franco informed Canaris that German troops would not be allowed to enter Spain and thus a chagrined Hitler was forced to postpone Operation *Felix*. However, Franco was aware that he could not completely defy Hitler without serious consequences, so he left the door open to future Spanish military participation. Six months later, Franco allowed over 18,000 Spanish volunteers to form the 'Blue Division' to join Operation *Barbarossa* against the Soviet Union, thereby allowing Spain a limited form of intervention on the Axis side. Later, five Spanish aviation squadrons rotated to the Eastern Front, serving in turn as the 'Blue Squadron'.

Hitler's intent to use Spain as a springboard for a peripheral strategy against Britain in the western Mediterranean was frustrated by Franco's own parochial designs and unwillingness to take any real risks. British bribes and Canaris's maladroit diplomacy likely played a part, but not a decisive one. Indeed, Franco only wanted to come into the war once it was obvious that Britain was defeated and no longer able to harm Spain. Without Spain to put additional pressure on Britain in the Mediterranean, any effort to mount *Seelöwe* in spring 1941 seemed no more promising than it had been in September 1940.

Had Franco acceded to Hitler's demands, Operation *Felix* would have proceeded and probably captured Gibraltar by February 1941. The British garrison of four infantry battalions would have put up very tough resistance, but the lack of RAF fighter defences would have enabled the Luftwaffe's Ju-87 Stukas to gradually pound the base into rubble. With the skies around Gibraltar controlled by the Luftwaffe, the Royal Navy's Force H would have had to withdraw from the region and evacuation of the Gibraltar garrison would have been impossible. The British planned to attack the Canary Islands with a sizeable force (Operation *Puma*) of about 8,000 troops in the event that Gibraltar was attacked, but the seizure of these islands would not have yielded any real benefit. The loss of Gibraltar and the provision of air bases in Spain would have greatly enhanced Raeder's *Handelskrieg* strategy against British trade routes, which would have put additional pressure on the British economy. With Gibraltar in Axis hands, Hitler would also have been more likely to keep *Seelöwe* as an active option for spring 1941. Furthermore, Axis control of the Straits of Gibraltar might have enabled an Italian surface warfare group to operate in the Atlantic and potentially reach Brest to support *Seelöwe*. While the British would attempt to blockade Spanish ports, the loss of Gibraltar would have complicated this effort and in 1940–41 the Royal Navy could not spare many warships for this purpose; most likely, the Royal Navy would have relied upon its submarines to interdict Spanish mercantile trade.

One aspect of Spain's possible military intervention that has not been addressed in existing literature is the potential sale of Spanish warships to the Kriegsmarine to improve the odds of success for *Seelöwe* in 1940 or 1941. For all of Churchill's exaggerated concern about the Germans acquiring French warships, he apparently gave no thought to the more realistic possibility of Germany simply purchasing surface warships from Spain. While the Spanish Navy in 1940 was in poor condition due to lack of fuel and spare parts, it could still field one heavy cruiser, three light cruisers and 18 destroyers. Had Germany tried to purchase some of these naval units and sail them from Vigo to Brest, this would have been a far more credible threat than the idea of capturing French capital ships in North Africa. The Spanish heavy cruiser *Canarias*, completed in 1936, was a modern 8-inch gun cruiser based on the British Kent-class, while the Churruca-class destroyers were similar to the British G-class destroyers. As for crews, Franco could have allowed naval volunteers to provide the bulk of manpower, as he later did with the Blue Division and Blue Legion. If Britain could purchase destroyers from a neutral United States, surely Germany could purchase warships from a neutral Spain.

The creation of a 'Blue Flotilla' consisting of the *Canarias* and a flotilla of five Churruca-class destroyers could have provided the Kriegsmarine with some surface warfare capability that was lacking in September 1940, but this was apparently not considered. The most likely reason is that the Spanish Navy had grand plans to rebuild itself with German assistance and was unwilling to sell off its few effective units.[73] Yet Spain was in desperate straits for food in mid-1940 and an immediate German shipment of grain might have made such a deal more palatable. Hitler might also have agreed to forgive part of Spain's financial debt in return for warships. Later in the war, Germany did in fact purchase trawlers and freighters from Spain for clandestine resupply operations. Nevertheless, even the suggestion of such a naval purchase in July 1940 might have provoked a British naval attack on Spanish naval units, thereby bringing Spain into the war on the Axis side.

The general outline of Operation *Sea Lion* was determined in a three-day planning conference at the Berghof, beginning on 29 July 1940. Here, a relaxed Hitler discusses the invasion concept with Großadmiral Erich Raeder, who recommended postponing the invasion until May 1941. In the wings, Generalfeldmarschall Walter von Brauchitsch, Alfred Jodl and Wilhelm Keitel represent the army's point of view. The Luftwaffe was noticeably absent from this important planning conference and sent no representative. (IWM HU 75542)

Prime Minister Winston Churchill made a point of personally inspecting coastal defences, in order to gauge morale and infuse war-fighting spirit into front-line troops. Here, he observes enemy air activity over the Channel from Dover Castle on 28 August 1940. Although Churchill used the threat of invasion to rally the nation, he did not believe that the threat was real until he was shown photographic evidence of large numbers of barges massing on the opposite shores. (IWM H3499)

The German Type IX submarine U-37 dry-docked in Lorient in early August 1940. The acquisition of naval bases in France effectively doubled the mission effectiveness of Admiral Dönitz's small U-Boat force by reducing time spent in transit. From Lorient British convoys off West Africa were also far more accessible. (Bundesarchiv, Fotograf: Mannewitz)

A British merchant ship sinks in flames after a U-Boat attack. By December 1940, Britain and her allies had lost 4.5 million tons of merchant shipping to U-Boats, mines, aircraft and surface raiders. Dönitz's U-Boats managed to sink over 200,000 tons of shipping each month. While the Kriegsmarine lacked the numbers to achieve decisive success, they were doing fairly well in the battle of attrition. (Bundesarchiv, Fotograf: o. Ang.)

The beach at Sandgate, near Folkestone, on 10 July 1940. At this point, the beach defences only consisted of a few rolls of concertina wire. Gradually mines, Admiralty Scaffolding and a few bunkers were added, but the defences remained thin until mid-1941. On S-Tag, the German 17. Infanterie-Division would have landed near here. (IWM H 2187)

British Home Guard troops patrol along cliff paths near Dover in March 1941. The Home Guard was quickly armed and equipped as a light infantry force that was capable of guarding parts of the coastline or other fixed points, but it lacked the junior leadership and firepower to stand up to regular enemy infantry. (IWM H 8111)

German troops in a motorized fishing cutter with a pneumatic raft in tow, training on the French coast in late June 1940. Hitler had not even begun to consider invading England at this point, but local commanders were already leaning forward for the anticipated landing in England. Across the Channel, the British leadership was worried that the Germans would mount a hasty invasion before the British army could be re-equipped after Dunkirk. (Bundesarchiv, Fotograf: Bernhard Borghorst)

Preparations for *Seelöwe* continue in the small French port of Fécamp, 9 October 1940. Despite postponement, units continued to practise loading and unloading procedures in anticipation of an invasion sometime in early 1941. These motorized fishing boats could each carry about 30 Gebirgsjäger and could cross the Channel in about ten hours. Troops would disembark into speed boats or rafts and head to the beach. (Bundesarchiv, Fotograf: Hecht)

The German Type 1934A destroyer *Friedrich Ihn* (Z-14) in pre-war markings. In September 1940, *Ihn* was one of Kapitän zur See Erich Bey's seven destroyers based at Brest and they would have been the largest Kriegsmarine warships directly involved in *Seelöwe*. The Type 1934A class destroyers were faster and better armed than most of the British destroyers deployed in the English Channel, but they were heavily outnumbered. (Bundesarchiv, Fotograf: o. Ang.)

The German M35-class minesweeper M8 was in the 1. Minensuchflottille, which would escort Transport Fleet C from Calais to the beaches near Rye in East Sussex. The M35 class minesweepers were credible escorts, armed with two 10.5cm guns, two 3.7cm and two 2.2cm dual-purpose Flak guns. The Royal Navy referred to this type as 'Channel destroyers' and could not simply disregard them and go after the German invasion convoys. The M35 class was also well suited to minesweeping and anti-submarine work. (Bundesarchiv, Fotograf: o. Ang.)

The German R-Boats (Räumboote) were designed as coastal minesweepers but were often used as escort vessels. In *Seelöwe*, the Räumboote would have to sweep the routes ahead of the invasion convoys and then screen the flanks against British interference. The R18 was part of the 1. R-Bootsflottille, which had eight R-Boats, and which was assigned to lead the advance detachment of VIII Armeekorps to land east of Brighton. The R18 was a 115-ton vessel capable of 20 knots and armed with a 3.7cm and two 2cm guns, but no torpedo tubes. The R-Boats were also capable of laying smoke to shield convoys. (Bundesarchiv, Fotograf: o. Ang.)

A German S-Boat (Schnellboote) moving rapidly across the waves; the diesel engines were capable of 37–39 knots. A total of 21 S-Boats were to be involved in *Seelöwe* and they were capable of lethal hit-and-run attacks with their twin torpedo tubes and 2cm Flak guns. The older S-Boats, like this one, were built in 1936–39. (Bundesarchiv, Fotograf: Dreyer)

The Kriegsmarine employed large numbers of converted fishing vessels as coastal escorts; most vessels were 350–700 tons. Over 50 Vorpostenboote were assigned to escort the invasion convoys for *Seelöwe*. Armament varied considerably and included captured French weapons. This example, off Norway in 1940, is armed with a bow-mounted 8.8cm gun and a 2cm Flak on the stern. The crew usually consisted of naval reservists. (Bundesarchiv, Fotograf: o. Ang.)

Another Vorpostenboot in 1940. While these auxiliaries could not stand up to a British destroyer, the British would have to deal with them before moving on to attack slow-moving barge convoys. In a night action, sinking even a couple of Vorpostenboote would take time, enabling the convoy to disperse. The same dynamic occurred in Atlantic convoy battles where British armed merchant cruisers were able to resist heavily armed German surface raiders long enough for most merchant ships to escape. (Bundesarchiv, Fotograf: o. Ang.)

An aggressive campaign of mine-laying in British coastal waters began in 1939 and continued throughout the first several years of the Second World War. The Germans employed an increasingly sophisticated arsenal of contact and influence mines that inflicted considerable losses and strained the Royal Navy's ability to keep vital waterways open for shipping. Although mine barriers would not have prevented the Royal Navy from attacking the invasion convoys, they would likely have exacted a toll. (Bundesarchiv, Fotograf: o. Ang.)

The crew of a concealed 15cm-gun battery on the *Hilfskreuzer Widder* swings into action, mid-Atlantic, September 1940. The Royal Navy was caught by surprise when half a dozen disguised German surface raiders began attacking commerce in the Atlantic, Indian and Pacific oceans in 1940. The Kriegsmarine's *Hilfskreuzer* campaign was economical on resources and had destroyed over 600,000 tons of shipping by late 1941. Furthermore, the Royal Navy was forced to spread its cruisers across the globe in search of these elusive raiders, yet failed to find any until May 1941. (Bundesarchiv, Fotograf: o. Ang.)

A 6-inch-gun coastal battery at Sheerness in a training exercise. The British began the construction of emergency coastal batteries along the south and east coasts in July 1940, but only a small number were ready by September. Due to the limited training and ammunition and rudimentary fire control, the 6-inch-gun batteries were instructed to withhold fire until enemy shipping was within 3,000 yards. The gun crew is exposed, making the battery vulnerable to air or ground attack. (IWM H119)

Großadmiral Erich Raeder, commander-in-chief of the Kriegsmarine. More than any other man in the German decision-making process, it was Raeder who ensured that there would be no attempt to execute *Seelöwe* in 1940. Raeder was driven by a bureaucratic mindset, with his twin goals of acquiring more resources for the Kriegsmarine while keeping losses of men and ships to a minimum. The heavy losses in Norway shocked him and increased his aversion to further risk, particularly for his beloved big ships. Consequently, he advocated the siege strategy rather than invasion. It is not clear whether Raeder believed that the invasion fleet could actually succeed in landing troops in England, but he evidently found it unacceptable that such a landing risked losing many of the Kriegsmarine's remaining surface units. (Bundesarchiv, Fotograf: o. Ang.)

Gunners rush to their positions at the Culver Point Battery on the Isle of Wight, 24 August 1940. This battery, which protected the east side of the island, consisted of two 9.2-inch guns in open positions, which were vulnerable to air attack. In the event of a landing on the Isle of Wight, the Germans would likely have conducted a glider assault to neutralize this position. It was not until 1941 that the British began providing their coastal batteries with adequate anti-aircraft defences. (IWM H 3233)

A platoon from the 1st Battalion, Royal Scots Fusiliers (29th Infantry Brigade) marches along a beach on the coast of England, 19 July 1940. This is a glamour shot, intended to show cheerful, well-equipped troops ready to defend England's shores; marching in column along a beach serves no useful training or tactical purpose. In addition, note the absence of beach defences and the platoon leader – the British Army was extremely short of junior infantry officers after Dunkirk and relied upon the professional NCO corps to provide front-line leadership. (IWM H 2351)

Another glamour photo. Troops from the 6th Battalion Black Watch training in July 1940. Even after the disastrous French campaign, British infantry training was still outdated and taught trench-style tactics from the First World War. Failure to inculcate modern, combined-arms tactics in the infantry led to frequently poor battlefield performances in 1941–42. Simply put, even the British regular troops were hardly able to conduct successful offensive operations in September 1940 against a skilled opponent. (Author)

A 4.5-inch howitzer from the 87th Field Regiment, assigned to the 55th (West Lancashire) Infantry Division, dug in and camouflaged on 16 July 1940. This weapon was actually introduced before the First World War and several hundred were still in front-line service in 1940–41. The 4.5-inch howitzer had a maximum range of 4 miles, which meant it was out-ranged by German division-level artillery. British artillery after Dunkirk could not win a firepower duel with Germany's more modern artillery. (IWM H 2243)

HMS *Intrepid*, based in Dover, was likely to be one of the first British destroyers to make contact with the German invasion fleet. HMS *Intrepid* was commissioned in 1937 and carried four 4.7-inch guns in single mounts and was capable of 36 knots. However, she had no radar or 20mm dual-purpose guns at this point, which limited her ability to successfully attack multiple small targets in a night action. (IWM A 7871)

The British battleship HMS *Rodney* was stationed at Scapa Flow in mid-September 1940. The *Rodney* was the very symbol of British naval superiority but she and her sister ship HMS *Nelson* were virtually irrelevant to stopping *Sea Lion*, since the Home Fleet commander had no intention of exposing them to enemy air attacks in the English Channel. (Bundesarchiv, Fotograf: o. Ang.)

Bomber Command's ability to achieve decisive results with strategic bombing in 1940–41 was hampered by too few aircraft and the limited range and payload of their twin-engine bombers. Here, Handley Page Hampden bombers from No. 49 Squadron are being loaded with 250-GP bombs which had very limited blast effect in cities. Both bombers in this photo were lost on operational sorties between 17 August and 4 September 1940. (IWM CH 262)

A Blenheim Mk 1F night fighter from No. 25 Squadron, 25 July 1940. The RAF's first purpose-designed night fighter was equipped with the AI Mk III radar, which was adequate to get the fighter in the general area of an enemy bomber, but insufficient to assist an actual terminal intercept. Consequently, RAF night fighters only achieved a handful of kills in 1940 and it was not until March 1941 that the situation changed.By spring 1941, RAF night fighters were beginning to achieve regular kills against enemy night raids, but too late to prevent heavy civilian loss of life in the Blitz. (IWM HU 104651)

The German Heer experimented with building some of its own unpowered rafts, made of wine and oil barrels with decking laid over them. Here, officers watch a test at the beach of Carteret on the Cotentin Peninsula in late August 1940, where a 10.5cm howitzer has been loaded. Off to the right is a Herbert ferry, which was a catamaran-type design. These rafts proved seaworthy, but were far from ideal for a cross-Channel invasion. (Bundesarchiv, Fotograf: o. Ang.)

Modified river barges assembled in Wilhelmshaven for *Seelöwe*. Note that the bows have been redesigned with assault ramps. The Kriegsmarine's decision to employ modified civilian barges for the invasion has been much criticized, but the primary purpose of these vessels was to trans-load equipment from steam ships anchored offshore to the beach. Given the tight time constraints imposed upon *Seelöwe*, the modification and assembling of this ersatz invasion force was an amazing example of wartime improvisation. (Bundesarchiv, Fotograf: Bernhard Schwarz)

CHAPTER 4

Kriegsmarine and Luftwaffe Capabilities against England, 1940–41

Daylight, Medium-Level Bombing: Doomed From the Start

In the 1930s, the bomber was widely regarded with a mix of horror and admiration – here was a weapon its advocates, like Douhet, Trenchard and Mitchell, argued would transform future warfare by inflicting utter devastation upon an opponent.[1] In 1932, British Prime Minister Stanley Baldwin had made his famous statement that 'the bomber would always get through', which became axiomatic. Less obvious was the corollary that 'the reconnaissance plane did not always get through', and without accurate intelligence, bombing was far less effective. All nations went into the World War II with a Doomsday impression of strategic bombing and tried to prepare for the worst.

Surprisingly, there were no bombing raids against either sides' capitals during the first ten months of the war, but the aerial devastation of Warsaw and Rotterdam provided previews. It was not until July 1940 that this paradigm changed, as Hitler opted to demonstrate his military power to Britain's leaders and people, in order to frighten them into offering peace negotiations.

Throughout the aerial campaigns of 1940–41, the Luftwaffe's twin-engine, medium bomber force was the primary threat to Britain's cities and war industries. At the operational level, Göring, Jeschonnek and the OKL were faced with three options in employing their bomber force against Britain:

1. **Counter-force.** The most obvious method was to attack the enemy's primary military defences: command and control (C^2) centres, radar sites, airfields and key military facilities as a prelude to follow-on military operations, such as *Seelöwe*.

2. **Centre of gravity.** A more focused method was instead to focus bombing on targets that were crucial to the enemy's war industries: electrical power, fuel production and storage, transportation and armaments manufacture. By destroying critical industrial targets, the defender would quickly lose the ability to resist and the attacker would gain a clear superiority.

3. **Counter-value.** A third option was to attack the civilian population with area bombing in order to level large swathes of cities or set them alight; this had yet to be attempted on a large scale and was initially forbidden by Führer Directive No. 17 on 1 August. An additional twist on the counter-value approach that the Luftwaffe learned in Spain was the use of delayed-action bombs, which could deny areas to the enemy for up to several days, like a minefield. Pre-war theories exaggerated the effects of 'terror bombing' on civilian morale and both the Luftwaffe and Bomber Command were uncertain how much of an enemy's civilian workforce needed to be killed, injured or 'de-housed' before that nation's

economy faced collapse. It quickly became apparent, however, that the 'counter-value' approach of attacking population centres took a great deal more time and bombs than anyone imagined in mid-1940.

Once operational priorities were decided, the attacker had several tactical choices on how to deliver their bombs: during daylight hours or at night, at medium altitudes or at low altitudes. In July 1940, the Luftwaffe's preference was to conduct medium-level daylight bombing over England against the RAF's defensive infrastructure in order to gain air superiority over southern England; i.e. Göring chose a counter-force strategy because it seemed expedient. He judged that the centre of gravity approach would take too long and he could not yet attack London, so going after the RAF seemed logical. He did not expect the bombers themselves to achieve decisive results, but their strikes would bring up RAF Fighter Command, which would then be defeated by the Luftwaffe's fighters. Göring's *Adlerangriff* was premised on the arrogant idea of just rushing in and overwhelming the RAF with brute force methods and assumed that the enemy would act in an uncharacteristically passive fashion, allowing itself to be blown to bits on the ground or mown down by the Bf-109 Jagdflieger. Yet among the many problems with *Adlerangriff*, foremost was that the Luftwaffe's tools were inadequate for the task, both in terms of operational strength and technical capability.

Despite the fact that *Fall Gelb* had led to rapid victory in the Western campaign, the Luftwaffe suffered painful losses of men and equipment that could not immediately be replaced. Altogether, the Luftwaffe lost 521 medium bombers in May to June 1940 (30 per cent of its strength) and 203 more were damaged.[2] Losses in *Fall Gelb* were equivalent to more than two months of bomber production, which was then averaging 310–340 bombers per month.[3] While these losses could be replaced by early September, the push to start operations against England gave the bomber units little respite between campaigns to refill their ranks. About 2,000 bomber crewmen were killed or wounded in the six-week Western campaign, including over 400 pilots. Since the Luftwaffe had no appreciable reserves of trained pilots or aircrew, the personnel losses in France, followed by the losses over England, began a steady drain that could not be reversed without an operational pause. One of the lessons that both the Luftwaffe and RAF Bomber Command would learn the hard way in 1940–41 was that one could not embark upon a protracted bomber offensive without adequate reserves, or the bomber force would soon be reduced to a state of exhausted impotence. Göring and Jeschonnek approached the campaign against England with blissful disregard for the condition of their bomber units because they erroneously assumed only a short-term effort would be required.

Due to the urgent need to replenish his depleted medium bomber force, Göring was not in a position to launch an all-out offensive against England until August. A number of historians have criticized Göring's failure to employ a coherent strategy during the Battle of Britain, but he was constrained to mount limited operations in July due to the poor state of his bomber units, as well as the inadequate stockpile of bombs and fuel in the airfields near the Channel. Even the small-scale *Kanalkampf* in July and early August still cost Luftflotten 2 and 3 at least 41 bombers (13 Ju-88, 16 He-111 and 12 Do-17) over the Channel as well as a dozen bombers being used in reconnaissance roles.

Nevertheless, Göring started the aerial campaign against England with the largest and most powerful bomber force extant in the world at that time. On 6 July 1940, the Luftwaffe had a total of 1,437 twin-engine medium bombers, of which 993 were operational (69 per cent); most of these bombers were deployed in Luftflotten 2 and 3.[4] These formations consisted of 16 Gruppen of He-111H, eight Gruppen of Do-17Z and seven Gruppen of Ju-88A. The He-111H was the proven workhorse of the fleet, with the Ju-88A promising but still in need of further refinements. Nearly one-third of Göring's front-line bomber strength consisted of the obsolescent Do-17Z, which was clearly inadequate for any strategic bombing campaign, being far too slow, too short-ranged and unable to carry a decent bomb load. The

Do-17Z was already being phased out in favour of the Ju-88A and production would cease in December 1940. An additional four Gruppen with 124 medium bombers were deployed with Luftflotte 5 in Norway, but due to the lack of long-range fighter escorts they only played a minor role in the 1940 campaign.

Table 4. Luftwaffe Bombers and Fighter-Bombers, 1940

Type	Cruising Speed (mph)	Max Speed (mph)	Range (miles)	Ceiling (feet)	Bomb Load (kg)
Ju-88A-5	235	285	1,500	30,000	1,400
He-111H-3	235	270	750	28,000	2,000
Do-17Z-2	230	265	680	26,700	1,000
Bf-110C-4	250	350	540	31,800	500

Like all bombers designed in the mid-1930s, the Luftwaffe's twin-engine bombers were not designed to deliver a particularly large payload. The He-111H could carry a 2,000kg bomb load (typically 8x SC250 or 32x SC50 internally) but versions without the external bomb racks could not carry any bomb bigger than the SC250. Newer versions of the He-111H were provided with external bomb racks that enabled them to carry one of the larger SC1000 or SC1800 bombs.[5] The Ju-88A-5 could only carry a 1,400kg bomb load (typically 2x SC500 or 4x SC250 externally and 10x SC50 internally). The Do-17Z-2 was the least effective bomber, only capable of delivering a 1,000kg bomb load (4x SC250 or 20x SC50). During daylight operations, bombers typically flew in *Staffelkolonne* (three 3-plane Ketten flying in column) or *Staffelwinkel* (three 3-plane Ketten flying in 'V' formation); the former was better for point targets and the latter for area targets. Altitudes between Ketten varied up to 500 feet, giving the formation a staggered appearance.

While the point has often been made that the Luftwaffe was trying to mount a strategic bombing campaign against England with tactical bombers – and without a four-engine heavy bomber – these are specious arguments because the Luftwaffe did not have adequate bombs or bombsights. Furthermore, RAF Bomber Command was concurrently conducting a strategic bomber campaign against Germany with similar twin-engine bombers, which is typically not mentioned. For the Luftwaffe's campaign over Britain, range was not an issue since the existing He-111 and Ju-88 bombers could reach targets as far north as Scotland and as far west as Belfast; there was no part of Great Britain that the Luftwaffe could not bomb with its existing twin-engine bombers. Rather, the lack of a fighter that could escort bombers north of London made long-range daylight bombing range problematic. The frequently noted 'mistake' by the Luftwaffe not to build large numbers of four-engine heavy bombers like either the Do-19 or Ju-89 ignores the fact that both prototypes actually had less payload and range than the He-111.[6] Nor would larger 'bomb trucks' in 1940 have made much difference if the bombs they delivered were not that accurate or powerful. The Luftwaffe started the war with the Lotfernrohr 3 and BZG-2 bombsights which were not fully stabilized and tended to allow errors in drift.[7] Under ideal daylight bombing conditions, a level bomber at 15,000 feet might drop half of its bombs within 820 feet of its intended aim point (i.e. its circular error probability or CEP).[8] However, combat experience over England, with partial cloud cover and an active defence, often resulted in a CEP of one-quarter of a mile or more, which was inadequate for seriously damaging point targets like airfields or factories. In order to lessen the effectiveness of British anti-aircraft guns, the Luftwaffe soon shifted to daylight raids at 18–20,000 feet, which further decreased accuracy. The Ju-88 was designed to attack in a steep dive and release at much lower altitudes, which could increase accuracy a bit, but this also greatly increased the risk from enemy anti-aircraft guns and barrage balloons.[9] In the attack on Ventnor radar station on 12 August, 15 Ju-88s from KG 51 dived on their target and scored 15 hits of 74 bombs dropped – some of the best German daylight bombing of the campaign.[10] Another issue that degraded German bombing accuracy was the oddly configured internal bomb bay in the He-111H, which held the bombs nose-up and then dropped them in a clumsy tumbling procedure.

Furthermore, the Luftwaffe's existing stockpile of bombs was primarily composed of the lightweight 50kg SC50 and 250kg SC250 bombs; the SC50 had an explosive filler of 25kg of cast TNT, while the SC250 had 130kg of Amatol/TNT. Steel was in particularly short supply in the German war economy and relatively little was going for bomb production, so the Luftwaffe leadership opted for larger numbers of small bombs, rather than heavier types. Only about 5 per cent of German bombs were 500kg or heavier. As an expedient blast weapon, the Luftwaffe began using naval parachute mines (Luftminen) on 16 September 1940; these mines were filled with 2,000lb of Hexanite, a very powerful explosive similar to RDX. When used against cities, the Luftminen could inflict great damage for up to 2,000 feet. However, the Luftminen had a very high 'dud' rate when used on land and only a few hundred were available for the bombing campaign.[11] The Luftwaffe's heaviest bombs, the SC1000 'Herman', SC1400 and SC1800 'Satan' were not introduced until November 1940 and then only in small numbers. The main German incendiary bomb was the 1kg B1 BL, which had a thermite filling. Incendiaries were dropped in an AB36 or a BSK36 container that held 36 bomblets, which were scattered by time fuse above the target. Although the Luftwaffe employed considerable numbers of incendiaries, it never achieved the kind of success that Anglo-American bombers did with creating 'fire storms' in urban areas. Thus, even if the Luftwaffe had been able to field a heavy bomber in September 1940 – which would have come at the cost of fewer medium bombers – they would still have been forced to drop mostly small bombs without any great accuracy.

Even in a well-aimed 'stick' of bombs, usually only a few would be on or near the target. Airbases were particularly difficult targets because of the passive defensive measures employed by RAF Fighter Command to protect its fighters on the ground: reinforced 'blast pens' to protect its fighters against bomb blast and wide dispersal patterns of parked aircraft. Since RAF fighters took off from grass strips, cratering had little effect on operations. Most of the sensitive facilities – operations room, fuel and communications, were buried underground. Industrial facilities were not as well protected, but often required large bombs to do real damage, particularly to machine tools. As RAF Bomber Command would later discover, factories could still function even without roofs.

Although the Luftwaffe had begun to field advanced radio navigation systems for accurate bombing at night, Luftwaffe daylight navigation was not always up to par. In one particularly egregious incident, on 10 May 1940 three He-111s from KG 51 accidentally bombed the town of Freiburg thinking it was Dijon, resulting in the deaths of 57 German civilians.[12] Although warned to stay away from London, German bombers repeatedly dropped bombs near the city in August 1940, which led to the escalation of attacks against civilians by both sides. Instead of bigger bombers, the Luftwaffe needed better bombsights, better navigation and bigger bombs. German bombers also accidentally dropped bombs in the Republic of Ireland in late August 1940, and Dublin was bombed by mistake in January and May 1941. All it took was some low-hanging clouds or hazy weather to send the Luftwaffe's daylight bombers off course.

It was also evident well before the Battle of Britain that the ability of the Luftwaffe's Bf-109 and Bf-110 fighters to defend its bomber formations in daylight against enemy fighter attack was inadequate. German bombers had relatively weak defensive armament and could not operate effectively in enemy air space without strong fighter escort, which meant that daylight raids north of London were not practical. In September 1939, Polish fighters had managed to shoot down 50 German medium bombers (about 4 per cent of those engaged), despite a German 4:1 numerical superiority in the air.[13] In the Western campaign, even without radar, French fighters still managed to shoot down significant numbers of German bombers, including 15 of KG 4's He-111s on 19 May 1940.[14] As a general rule of thumb, anything above a 3 per cent loss rate (i.e. losses divided by sorties) in a protracted air campaign tends to result in the offensive culminating before it has achieved its objectives. The Germans knew this but had succeeded in Poland and France because enemy fighter bases had been overrun by the Heer before Luftwaffe bomber losses became crippling. Against England, with its efficient Radar GCI system, Luftwaffe medium bombers even with fighter escort suffered losses of more than 5 per cent in August 1940, which eventually compelled them to abandon daylight bombing. Nevertheless, this British success had no effect on overall Luftwaffe bomber sortie rates, which actually increased from 4,779 sorties in August, to 7,260 sorties in September and 9,911 sorties in October; as Stanley Baldwin predicted, the bombers did get through.[15]

Table 5. Luftwaffe Bomber Losses, 1 July–15 September 1940

Period	Do-17 Losses	He-111 Losses	Ju-88 Losses	Total Bomber Losses	Sortie Loss Rate	Bomber Crew KIA/MIA
1–31 July 1940	39	32	39	110	2.2%	360
1–31 August 1940	75	98	104	277	5.7%	792
1–30 September 1940	61	101	87	249	2.2%	c.800+
TOTAL	**175**	**231**	**230**	**636**	**3.7%**	**c.2,000+**

Despite fierce resistance from Fighter Command and heavy losses, the Luftwaffe bomber sortie rate grew significantly between August and October, totalling 21,950 bomber sorties in that period. In contrast, RAF Bomber Command during the same period made only 8,983 sorties and lost 190 bombers (a 2.1 per cent loss rate), but most of the missions were at night. Furthermore, Luftwaffe bomber raids caused the deaths of 14,363 British civilians in three months, whereas Bomber Command killed fewer than 50 German civilians in this period. While Luftwaffe bombing did not achieve decisive results, it was achieving far more than Bomber Command was achieving.

Technologically, the Bf-109E fighter was designed as a fast interceptor and was not well suited to bomber escort duty due to its limited range and endurance, but equally important was the psychological dimension – German fighter pilots were trained to be aggressive hunters, not passive shepherds of slow-moving bomber formations. When they were able to focus on offensive counter-air missions, as in July, the Bf-109 fighters could knock down plenty of enemy fighters, particularly Hurricanes, at a cost of only 18 of their own. However, when tied to protected bomber squadrons over England, they became far less effective and they could not reliably protect their bomber formations from well-directed enemy fighter attacks and keep losses to an acceptable level. In August, 125 Bf-109s were lost and another 234 in September. The Luftwaffe's single-engine fighter force nearly broke itself trying to protect the bombers, but this was entirely unnecessary since at night the bombers could fly wherever they pleased over Great Britain without escort.

Of course, the RAF did have radar, which made daylight bombing over England prohibitively expensive for the Luftwaffe. Nineteen Chain Home (CH) radar stations were deployed along the southern and eastern coast of England, with the ability to detect enemy aircraft formations at medium altitude out to 120–125 miles and provide up to 30 minutes' early warning of raids. Radar's detection capabilities deprived the Luftwaffe of the ability to achieve surprise attacks with its main bomber force. Chain Home did have its limitations: each station could only cover a fixed 60° arc looking out to sea and could not detect targets below 1,500 feet in altitude. Once enemy aircraft flew inland, Chain Home could not turn to track them. Nor could Chain Home signals determine target altitude, only bearing. Furthermore, with a wavelength of 40 feet, Chain Home was best suited to identifying large aircraft formations at medium-high altitudes, but was inadequate for spotting a handful of aircraft. In order to redress these deficiencies, in early 1940 the RAF began to install Chain Home Low (CHL), which could turn to look in any direction out to 25 miles and provided low-level detection down to 500 feet. Luftwaffe intelligence did not learn about the existence of the Chain Home sites until June and then failed to appreciate that the RAF had developed an integrated GCI system that relied very heavily upon radar. With Chain Home, RAF Fighter Command had developed GCI tactics that were the perfect counter against daylight raids by medium-altitude bombers.

Low-Level Bombing, Delayed-Action Bombs and Night-Bombing

Despite the inherent technological limitations of his medium bomber force, Göring did have a few tricks up his sleeve that could inflict real damage on Britain's war effort. Although Luftwaffe intelligence under-estimated the value of British radar in mid-1940, there was an understanding that the current methods of medium-level bombing lacked the accuracy to attack point targets. Consequently, in July 1940 the Luftwaffe formed an experimental fighter-bomber unit known as Erprobungsgruppe 210 (Erp. Gr. 210), under the command of Hauptmann Walter Rubensdörffer. This unit, which was formed from ordinary pilots from three other units, was equipped with two Staffeln of Bf-110C and Bf-110D and one Staffel of Bf-109E-4B fighter-bombers and specifically trained to conduct low-level, precision attacks. Typically, Erp. Gr. 210 attacked in small groups of just four aircraft at 1,000 feet or less, coming in at 310mph, which made it very difficult for Chain Home radar stations to detect. Even if CHL detected an Erp. Gr. 210 attack group, warning time would be reduced to less than four minutes – insufficient for Fighter Command to get its fighters into action against them. Each of Rubensdörffer's raiders could deliver a pair of 250kg or 500kg bombs, then use their speed to escape the target before Fighter Command arrived. The RAF was not expecting low-level attacks and was caught unprepared when they were suddenly introduced in July.

Aside from Erp. Gr. 210, the only other Luftwaffe unit trained for low-level attacks was Hauptmann Joachim Roth's 9./KG 76 equipped with nine Do-17Z bombers. This unit was capable of flying under the detection capability of CHL radar and bombing targets from 100 feet or less; at this altitude, accuracy was not an issue, but bomber survivability was. Altogether, the 40 aircraft of Erp. Gr. 210 and 9./KG 76 provided Luftflotte 2 with a limited ability to mount surprise, low-level precision attacks. RAF intelligence was unaware that the Luftwaffe had developed specialist low-level attack units, but relied upon the RAF Observer Corps to spot any intruders that flew below the radar. Aside from a limited number of 40mm Bofors anti-aircraft guns and some elderly Lewis Guns, the only other defence against low-level attack was barrage balloons and a new system, known as Parachute and Cable (PAC).[16]

These two low-level units proved their worth during the early stages of the Luftwaffe offensive against Great Britain. On the opening day of *Adlerangriff*, Rubensdörffer's Erp. Gr. 210 attacked four Chain Home radar stations and damaged three of them at no loss to his unit. Briefly deprived of early warning, RAF Fighter Command was unable to make any interceptions over southern England for the next two hours.[17] Rubensdörffer was killed three days later in a low-level attack on RAF Kenley, but Erp. Gr. 210 continued to achieve remarkable – if costly – successes with low-level attacks throughout October 1940. Roth's 9./KG 76 was committed to a low-level attack against RAF Kenley on 18 August and his nine Do-17Z bombers came across the Channel at a height of only 70 feet. Undetected by Chain Home, Roth's bombers were spotted by the Royal Observer Corps which alerted Fighter Command. Roth succeeded in bombing Kenley and inflicting considerable damage – three hangars and eight Hurricane fighters destroyed on the ground. However, one Do-17 was downed by a PAC rocket and three more were shot down by fighters after the attack, including Roth, who was killed. Low-level attacks also proved successful against British aircraft factories, but losses were heavy for these specialist units. Other than increasing anti-aircraft and barrage balloon defences around key targets, the British had no real answer to prevent low-level daylight attacks in 1940.

Another development that caught the British by surprise was the German introduction of delayed-action bombs equipped with a completely new type of electrical fuse (*zünder*). In 1932, Herbert Rühlemann, a German engineer at Rheinmetall, perfected a revolutionary type of electrical fuse. Although Göring has often been described as anti-technology, he was quick to recognize the importance of Rühlemann's breakthrough and in 1935 directed the Luftwaffe to place an order with Rheinmetall for 200,000 of the new electrical fuses to be used on bombs. Four years later, Göring ordered the construction of a new factory near Breslau at a cost of RM 38 million, in order to begin mass-production of the electrical fuses.[18] At the start of the air campaign against England, the Luftwaffe was using the Type 15 impact fuse on most of its bombs and was getting ready to introduce the Type 17 fuse on the SC 250 in August. The Type 17 fuse could be deployed as either the 'mV' (*mit Verzögerung*, with short delay action) or as the 'LZZ' (*LangZeitZünder*, long time delay) versions. The SC 250 LZZ was dangerous for up to 96 hours and might explode if moved – but the British did not know that.

On the other side of the hill, the British were only vaguely aware the delayed-action bombs might be a problem. In early June 1940, the first Bomb Disposal Units (BDU) were formed but the personnel were essentially untrained and lacked any kind of equipment beyond shovels. Knowledge of German bomb fuses was virtually nil. It was also unclear who would command the BDUs and they started out as neglected auxiliaries. Based upon experience from the French campaign, the British initially assumed that the Luftwaffe would use impact fuses and BDUs would only deal with duds. This lackadaisical attitude toward bomb disposal continued until early August, when Luftwaffe raids on English soil began in earnest.

On 13 August, *Adler Tag*, the Luftwaffe first used the Type 17 fuse on SC 250 bombs dropped on RAF airfields. The BDU teams were totally unprepared to deal with such a sophisticated device and for several weeks there was no counter to this German innovation. Five days later, one BDU team attempted to deal with an unexploded

Type 17 by trial and error and only succeeded in blowing itself to bits.[19] After this, the BDU soldiers were more circumspect about Type 17s, meaning that many were just left in place as Unexploded Bombs (UXB) until proper defusing techniques were developed. By late August, there were 62 UXBs at Biggin Hill alone and the number was mounting daily.[20] More than anything else, the Type 17 fuse threatened Fighter Command's ability to use its airfields in Kent and Sussex. Before the end of August, the Luftwaffe further complicated matters by introducing the Type 50 (*Sonderzünder* or special fuse), which was equipped with special trembler switches that detonated the bomb if it was moved. Delayed-action bombs were now fitted with both Type 17 and Type 50 fuses, making life very difficult for the BDUs.

Churchill had a sense for when things were going against Britain and quickly realized that the new German electrical bomb fuses were a real menace. On 25 August, he sent a memo to the War Office which addressed the problem of delayed-action bombs and directed that the defeat of the Type 17 fuse be given top priority. Major General Brian Taylor was made Director of Bomb Disposal and the BDUs were greatly expanded and better equipped. By September, 1,500 personnel were assigned to the BDUs. Churchill also ensured that some of the best scientific talent was put on the task of developing counters to the new German fuses. In true British fashion, the solution was found in a committee. Herbert J. Gough, an engineer who was Director of Scientific Research (DSR) in the War Office, was made chairman of the Unexploded Bomb Committee. Gough had already developed a simple fuse extractor in May and his committee was soon well on its way to developing a fuse discharger to defeat the electrical fuse.

However, the Germans kept up the pressure. By early September, the BDUs had discovered 724 UXBs with Type 17 fuses.[21] Then on 2 September, the Luftwaffe introduced the Zus 40 (*Zussatzünder*, auxiliary fuse), an anti-tampering device designed to explode if the Type 17 fuse was removed. Just as Gough's committee was closing in on solving the Type 17 problem, the Zus 40 proved another tactical victory for the Luftwaffe. By early October, there were 3,000 UXBs reported and by December the number had risen to 15,000. For a time, the BDUs were nearly overwhelmed by the number of UXBs and while they succeeded in neutralizing 80 per cent of the bombs, it came at the cost of 87 killed in action and over 100 wounded.[22] It was not until spring 1941 that the BDUs had the means to neutralize the latest German bomb fuses. Post-war statistics later revealed that 8.5 per cent of German bombs dropped were UXBs.[23] However, the BDUs missed many of the UXBs and they continue to be regularly found in England even 75 years after the war; on 10 August 2015, an unexploded SC 500 was discovered in east London, the third found that year.[24]

Göring's final trump card was precision night-bombing. The Luftwaffe and RAF Bomber Command took diametrically opposed approaches to the concept of night-bombing. Bomber Command endorsed night-bombing from the beginning of the war and trained its crews for night navigation, but initially made no effort to develop electronic navigational aids to assist them. In contrast, Göring and many other senior Luftwaffe leaders saw little need for night-bombing, but authorized the *Reichsluftfahrtministerium* (RLM, or Air Ministry) to invest in developing electronic navigational aids based on the commercial Lorenz radio navigation system. By early 1940, an early developmental system known as Knickebein was introduced, which transmitted on 31.5 MHz and enabled fairly precise night navigation – but only at tactical ranges.[25] By June, the British had created an aerial electronic intelligence (ELINT) unit equipped with three Avro Ansons, which detected the Knickebein signals and confirmed their frequency. Using available commercial Lorenz transmitters, Dr Reginald V. Jones from the Air Ministry staff was able to develop a jamming system known as 'Aspirin' which seriously interfered with the ability of Luftwaffe pilots to hear the Knickebein signals. Since the Germans did not begin using Knickebein for night raids until August, the British counter-measures were in place in time.

Even as it became apparent that Knickebein was compromised, the Luftwaffe introduced the more sophisticated X-Gerät system, operating on 60 MHz. The primary transmitter array was installed near Cherbourg and could send a narrow navigational beam 125 miles over England. A special pathfinder unit, Hauptmann Kurt Aschenbrenner's KGr 100 equipped with 30 He-111H bombers, had been established in June 1940 and just completed two months' training to use the X-Gerät system. When outfitted with special receivers, KGr 100 bombers could reduce their CEP to just 110–130 yards. On 9 August, KGr 100 moved into Vannes airbase in Brittany and prepared to participate in *Adlerangriff*. On 13 August, *Adler Tag*, KGr 100 conducted the first night attack with X-Gerät, targeting the Spitfire factory at Castle Bromwich, near Birmingham. Twenty He-111's were guided directly to the target and X-Gerät told the autopilot when to drop the bombs; amazingly, 11 bombs hit the factory and inflicted 48 casualties. Göring now had a pathfinder bomber unit that could lead precision strikes over England. Over the next three months, KGr 100 mounted 40 raids using X-Gerät before the RAF could counter the system.

The most successful demonstration of X-Gerät occurred on the night of 14/15 November 1940 with Operation *Moonlight Sonata* – the bombing of Coventry. Pathfinders from KGr 100 used X-Gerät to accurately mark the centre of the city which was then bombed by 363 bombers from Luftflotte 3. The centre of Coventry was devastated by between 446 and 552 tons of bombs, the vast majority of which were 50kg bombs or 1kg incendiaries; a total of eight SC 1800, 11 SC 1400, 26 SC 1000, 78 SC 500 and 430 SC 250 were also used. Civilian casualties totalled 568 killed and 863 seriously injured – a result still well beyond what RAF Bomber Command could achieve against German cities. British defences were ineffective – only a single Do-17Z bomber was shot down by anti-aircraft fire, even though Coventry's 40 anti-aircraft guns fired 6,700 rounds. The RAF Fighter Command mounted 49 night-fighter sorties, resulting in 11 sightings, which led to two engagements – but no kills. *Moonlight Sonata* demonstrated that the RAF's putative air superiority could not prevent the Luftwaffe from destroying British cities at night.[26]

Dr Jones and the Air Ministry staff worked quickly to counter the new German system, but could only deduce its characteristics. The

RAF referred to X-Gerät as 'Ruffian'. Jones incorrectly guessed 'Ruffian's' operational frequency and the Air Ministry's ELINT Ansons could not detect the signals. Existing jammers were ineffective. It was not until 6 November that Jones got a lucky break when a KGr 100 He-111H made a forced landing on the beach near Bridport; the X-Gerät receiver was recovered and examination revealed the actual operating frequency. In less than two weeks, the RAF had four jammers known as 'Bromide' operational and interfering with X-Gerät signals. However, each jammer could only protect a small area and KGr 100 was still able to use X-Gerät against other targets, such as Southampton and Sheffield.[27] British jamming on the night of 14/15 November 1940 was ineffective and failed to protect Coventry. Jones also recommended that the RAF bomb the X-Gerät transmitters near Cherbourg, which may have had some effect later during the Blitz.

Even though the British could claim some success in electronic warfare by early 1941, the fact remained that British defences against night-bombing were minimal in 1940. Even without precision accuracy, German night-bombing remained a very real threat and British civilian casualties remained high throughout the 'Blitz' (see Table 6). Britain's night air defences were much less effective than its daylight defences. British anti-aircraft units employed a fixed azimuth system that mistakenly assumed that enemy aircraft would fly at constant speeds and altitudes. In reality, British anti-aircraft fire was mostly ineffective against Luftwaffe night raids. On one particularly good night, British anti-aircraft guns fired 8,326 rounds and managed to shoot down 2 out of 235 attacking enemy bombers. Nor were RAF night fighters much use at this time. On paper, the RAF night-fighter force seemed impressive: 10½ night-fighter squadrons equipped with over 100 aircraft (65 Blenheims, 21 Defiants and 16 Hurricanes). At the start of the war the British made a crash effort to develop and deploy a small aerial intercept radar on aircraft and by July 1940, all of the Blenheim 1F night fighters were equipped with the AI Mk III radar. On the night of 22/23 July 1940, a Blenheim succeeded in intercepting and shooting down a Do-17Z bomber – the first AI intercept in history.

Table 6: British Civilian Casualties, July–December 1940[28]

Month	Killed	Injured	Total Casualties
July	258	321	579
August	1,075	1,262	2,337
September	6,954	10,615	17,569
October	6,334	8,695	15,029
November	4,588	6,202	10,790
December	3,793	5,044	8,837
TOTAL	23,002	32,139	55,141

Unfortunately, the British night-fighter system was not really practical in 1940 for a number of reasons. The AI Mk III radar had a range of just 4 miles, so the aircraft had to be cued on to the target by ground-based radar, but Chain Home did not look inland. The British relied upon the Observer Corps to track aircraft over Britain in daylight, but this system did not work at night. In consequence, Blenheims were assigned to patrol areas along likely enemy approach routes and simply tried to detect passing bombers. Nor was the AI Mk III radar very reliable and it could not detect targets hidden in ground clutter, although the improved AI Mk IV improved detection capabilities a bit. Even if radar contact was established, the Luftwaffe had re-painted most of their bombers black, which made them extremely difficult to spot unless the night fighter was very close. Furthermore, the Blenheim was simply too slow to catch German bombers except in the most favourable circumstances. Altogether, the Blenheim night fighters scored only a handful of victories in July–December 1940. By November, only 38 Blenheim night fighters were still serviceable and only a handful of Beaufighters were available, so sortie rates were too low. In desperation, Fighter Command assigned three squadrons (85,

87 and 151) of Hurricane fighters to night-fighter duty, even though they lacked radar; the concept was to institute standing patrols around cities like London and hope to spot enemy aircraft in search light arcs. A Hurricane from No. 85 Squadron succeeded in shooting down an He-111 bomber on 27 October, but this was a rare event.

Once again, a committee approach solved these problems in due course. The new Beaufighter, armed with four 20mm cannons and the new AI Mk III radar, began entering service in small numbers in October 1940. The Beaufighter had the speed to catch German bombers and a powerful armament, but still lacked an effective cueing mechanism to put it onto the target. Flight Lieutenant John Cunningham of No. 604 Squadron succeeded in shooting down a Ju-88 in November, then one of KGr 100's He-111 bombers in December, but this was a drop in the ocean against over 7,000 German night bomber sorties conducted over England in this period.[29] It was not until the introduction of the Type 7 GCI radar in January 1941 that a solution was found; using the CHL radar as the starting concept, the new radar could scan in a 360° arc, which meant that it could track German bombers across Britain. With this new radar and more Beaufighters in service, British night fighters were able to score three victories in January and four in February, against over 1,500 enemy sorties. By March, about one in every 150 German night bomber sorties was falling victim to an RAF night fighter and this climbed to one out of every 80 by April. In April 1941, Flight Lieutenant Cunningham shot down five He-111 bombers with his Beaufighter, becoming the first night-fighter ace. The new radar also improved the ability to vector Hurricane fighters into enemy bomber streams; Flight Lieutenant Richard Stevens claimed two victories in January 1941, then five in April and three more in May. By the time that the main Luftwaffe offensive against Great Britain ended in mid-May 1941, the RAF finally had a means to inflict appreciable losses upon the German night bombers.

Finally, the Luftwaffe did make some effort to develop jamming tactics against Chain Home, which could have influenced the conduct of *Seelöwe*. In July, a team from the German Laboratory for Aviation (*Deutsche Versuchsanstalt für Luftfahrt* or DVL) built a simple jamming station in France which had some effect against CH; then a second, more sophisticated jamming station was built in September, which interfered with Chain Home's bi-static signals. Generalleutnant Martini's *Funkhorchdienst* was able to collect a great deal of information on British radar systems and began to develop jamming techniques that would later be put to good use in supporting the 'Channel Dash' in February 1942. At that time, Martini's efforts assisted the battleships *Scharnhorst* and *Gneisenau* to sortie from Brest and remain undetected in the English Channel for over 13 hours.[30] Martini pioneered the use of aerial jamming aircraft and electronic counter-measures which, while not available in September 1940, might have been available to support a *Seelöwe* conducted in May 1941. The ability to blind or deceive the British early warning networks would also have paid great dividends in the German air offensive against England and greatly reduced the effectiveness of Fighter Command.

Luftwaffe: Operational Choice of Targets

In order to defeat Great Britain or at least suppress its defences, the Germans had to employ their limited Luftwaffe and Kriegsmarine resources against the most critical targets. However, due to the lack of accurate intelligence assessments and a fickle mindset in the Luftwaffe leadership, Germany was slow to prosecute the most valuable British targets until the window of opportunity for *Seelöwe* had passed. Constant switching of targets prevented decisive results from being achieved, but that does not mean that they were not achievable.

Starting with the pre-war *Studie Blau*, the Luftwaffe assigned each target in Great Britain an alpha-numeric designator, beginning with the prefix 'GB'. The targets were broken down into specific groups, which included military airfields, gas works, water works, power plants, electrical sub-stations, munitions plants, aircraft engine manufacturers and factories

THE BLITZ, 1940–41

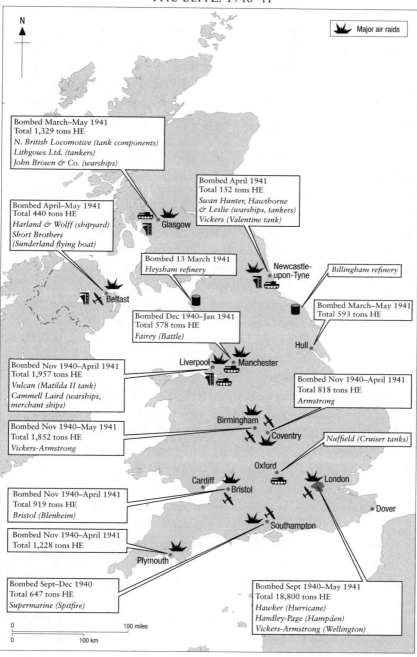

N

Major air raids

Bombed March–May 1941
Total 1,329 tons HE
N. British Locomotive (tank components)
Lithgows Ltd. (tankers)
John Brown & Co. (warships)

Bombed April 1941
Total 152 tons HE
Swan Hunter, Hawthorne
& Leslie (warships, tankers)
Vickers (Valentine tank)

Bombed April–May 1941
Total 440 tons HE
Harland & Wolff (shipyard)
Short Brothers
(Sunderland flying boat)

Glasgow

Billingham refinery

Newcastle-
upon-Tyne

Bombed 13 March 1941
Heysham refinery

Bombed March–May 1941
Total 593 tons HE

Belfast

Bombed Dec 1940–Jan 1941
Total 578 tons HE
Fairey (Battle)

Hull

Liverpool   Manchester

Bombed Nov 1940–April 1941
Total 1,957 tons HE
Vulcan (Matilda II tank)
Cammell Laird (warships,
merchant ships)

Bombed Nov 1940–April 1941
Total 818 tons HE
Armstrong

Bombed Nov 1940–May 1941
Total 1,852 tons HE
Vickers-Armstrong

Birmingham

Coventry

Nuffield (Cruiser tanks)

Oxford

London

Cardiff

Bristol

Bombed Nov 1940–April 1941
Total 919 tons HE
Bristol (Blenheim)

Dover

Southampton

Bombed Nov 1940–April 1941
Total 1,228 tons HE

Plymouth

Bombed Sept–Dec 1940
Total 647 tons HE
Supermarine (Spitfire)

Bombed Sept 1940–May 1941
Total 18,800 tons HE
Hawker (Hurricane)
Handley-Page (Hampden)
Vickers-Armstrong (Wellington)

0   100 miles

0   100 km

producing tanks and other military equipment. For example, the Standard Motor Company plant in Coventry, which manufactured engines for the Blenheim light bomber, was designated by the Germans as target GB737.[31] Yet despite the available aerial imagery on these targets, the Luftwaffe had little or no other information available to inform them about current levels of activity in these targets or what they were doing for the British war effort.

Within the Luftwaffe hierarchy, Schmid's 5th Branch, Group III (Ic/III) was responsible for selecting targets in Great Britain, but it failed to conduct a real assessment of the enemy's centre of gravity (COG).[32] Given that Prussian military theorist Carl von Clausewitz laid out the principles of analysing an enemy's strategic centre of gravity in his 1832 book *Vom Kriege*, it is amazing that over a century later the Wehrmacht was incapable of utilizing these principles to fight wars more efficiently. Instead, Group III simply provided Schmid with a list of about 50 industrial targets in Great Britain, ranging from aircraft factories, to power plants, ports, steel plants and even food manufacturing centres. Schmid then briefed Göring and Jeschonnek on these possible targets, who then selected targets for attack based on no particular criteria; this method of target selection helps to explain why the Luftwaffe did not concentrate its bombing efforts against one key system, like the Allied bombing offensive would later attempt against ball bearings or oil. In essence, the failure of Schmid's 5th Branch to provide a real intelligence assessment of how to cripple Britain's war effort allowed Göring and Jeschonnek to scatter the Luftwaffe's bombing campaign across too many targets.

Both Göring and Jeschonnek initially favoured bombing RAF Fighter Command's airfields, but these were not critical targets for three reasons: (1) there were too many airfields to neutralize with the available resources, (2) early warning from radar prevented the Luftwaffe from catching significant numbers of RAF fighters on the ground and (3) fighter squadrons did not need fixed bases from which to operate. Apparently, the Luftwaffe leadership forgot that Fighter Command proved its ability in France to operate from grass strips with pilots sleeping in tents and mechanics servicing aircraft in the open. The Luftwaffe Jagdflieger would do the same in Russia in 1941–42. Fixed bases were nice, but not a necessity for this generation of fighters. Events quickly demonstrated that the temporary loss of Kenley or Biggin Hill really made no difference to Fighter Command's ability to resist daylight air raids.

Britain's defence against *Seelöwe* rested on two primary factors: RAF Fighter Command and the Royal Navy's Home Fleet – these were the two relevant operational centres of gravity. Fighter Command provided the critical capability of destroying enemy bombers and depended upon five critical requirements: (1) Chain Home for early warning, (2) Group and Sector headquarters for Command and Control, (3) the training units for pilot replacements, (4) the RAF aircraft repair and maintenance units and (5) fighter production factories to replace losses. If the Germans could damage any of these five critical requirements, Fighter Command's ability to destroy enemy bombers would be reduced. The Royal Navy's critical capability was to sink enemy shipping in or near British waters, which depended upon four critical requirements: (1) RAF Coastal Command to detect and identify enemy invasion forces, (2) superior surface warfare units to overwhelm enemy invasion escorts, (3) minesweeping units to clear enemy mine belts in the Channel and (4) functional bases to provide fuel and repair services. These factors of COG Analysis are depicted in Table 7.

Table 7: British Operational-level Centres of Gravity, September 1940

COG	Critical Capability	Critical Requirement	Critical Vulnerability
RAF Fighter Command	Destroy enemy bombers over Great Britain	Early warning (Chain Home) C^2 (Group/Sector HQ) Pilot training Maintenance units Fighter production factories	Enemy precision night-bombing tactics
Royal Navy Home Fleet	Destroy enemy shipping in home waters	Reconnaissance (RAF Coastal Command) Surface warfare Minesweeping Functional bases	Enemy acoustic, magnetic and influence mines

During the campaign of July–September 1940, the British operational-level COGs had two critical vulnerabilities: RAF Fighter Command was nearly useless against German precision night-bombing tactics and the Royal Navy had difficulty clearing German acoustic, magnetic and influence mines. Either of these vulnerabilities – if properly exploited – could marginalize Britain's two greatest strengths.

Although dismissive of Martini's warning about British radar, Göring did authorize major attacks against Chain Home in the opening move of *Adlerangriff* in August. These attacks did succeed in temporarily neutralizing four Chain Home stations, but the Germans were apparently disappointed that the sites were not destroyed. While the 360-foot-tall transmitting towers, made of open girder steel construction, were relatively impervious to blast, the 240-foot-tall receiver towers made of wood were not. At several damaged sites, the British continued to transmit – even though the receiver towers were down – which fooled Martini's intercept teams into thinking the sites were still active. In fact, the initial Luftwaffe strikes on Chain Home were fairly successful and if continued, might have deprived Fighter Command of much of its early warning. However, Göring did not see it that way and concluded, 'It is doubtful whether there is any point in continuing the attacks on radar sites, in view of the fact that not one of those attacked has so far been put out of action.'[33]

While a few sector headquarters were damaged by air raids, No. 11 Group headquarters at Uxbridge was barely scratched and the Luftwaffe made no concerted effort against Fighter Command's C^2 nodes. Nor were RAF training or maintenance units seriously affected by enemy operations. Attacks on British aircraft factories began in mid-August but were sporadic and successes were not followed up; rather than ruthlessly pounding a critical target to annihilation, the Luftwaffe was content to drop a few bombs on a factory and call it a day. Spitfire production was affected by the raid of 26 September on the plants near Southampton, but this came too late to influence the daylight battles over England in August–September 1940.[34] Only modest effort was made to attack Hurricane factories, even though this aircraft was the backbone of

Fighter Command. Jeschonnek in particular was opposed to 'wasting' effort against industrial targets and issued an order on 2 September that only small numbers of aircraft would be committed to such raids.[35] Instead, he and Göring came to believe – based upon Schmid's inflated damage reports – that the raids on Fighter Command's airfields had destroyed its main strength and that attacks upon London would draw out the remaining British fighters.

Aside from the *Kanalkampf* in July, the Luftwaffe virtually ignored the Royal Navy for the next ten months. A few raids were mounted against Royal Navy bases, but were sporadic. A raid on Scapa Flow on 16 March by Ju-88s put the heavy cruiser HMS *Norfolk* out of action for three months and a raid on Glasgow on 18 September severely damaged the heavy cruiser HMS *Sussex*, but there was no sustained effort to destroy the Royal Navy's heavy units in port. In contrast, the RAF made repeated attacks against Kriegsmarine surface units in port, whereas the Luftwaffe put only a half-hearted effort into reducing the Home Fleet's surface warfare capabilities – although they clearly had the ability to bomb all the major naval bases within range of the potential *Seelöwe* invasion beaches. Göring was not interested in *Seelöwe* or bombing naval bases, or even mundane factories, but rather sought to impress Hitler – and the British – by wrecking London and Britain's other major urban areas. Like 'Bomber' Harris's later obsession with de-housing the German workforce, Göring's choice of targets was a departure from any kind of strategic rationale.

In terms of Great Britain's strategic centre of gravity, it was essentially its industrial-economic base, with which it could mass-produce the tools of war and provide a base for the future prosecution of war against Germany. Britain's two strategic-level critical requirements were the ability to import raw materials and the ability to manufacture military equipment and merchant shipping. High-value targets associated with these requirements included petroleum production and storage, aluminium fabrication, electrical power plants, major ports and shipyards. For the most part, Luftwaffe attacks against these types of strategic targets were sporadic and opportunistic, mostly occurring during the Blitz. Ironically, the first real damage inflicted on a critical industrial target in Britain was by an RAF Blenheim bomber, not a German bomber; on 14 July a Blenheim returning from an aborted raid accidently dropped a bomb on the High Duty Alloys Ltd plant in Slough. This company cast aluminium alloy pistons for the Rolls-Royce engines that powered the Spitfire. The accidental bombing scored a direct hit on the plant and inflicted 45 casualties. Britain only had two hydrogenation plants (Heysham and Billingham) and four small refineries, but no concerted effort was made to smash them. Liverpool was the only place where the Luftwaffe made a real effort to attack the British strategic centre of gravity. Großadmiral Raeder had been urging attacks against the city since late 1939 and he stated that a major air campaign against Liverpool could cripple British imports. Although Göring was reluctant to support any idea suggested by Raeder, he did authorize four nights of raids from 28 to 31 August, with 629 bomber sorties dropping 455 tons of explosives on the city. However, the Luftwaffe did not return to Liverpool in force until 28 November and thereafter conducted sporadic raids on the city until 7 May. Altogether, the Luftwaffe conducted 12 major raids against Liverpool with more than 2,500 bomber sorties, dropping over 2,400 tons of bombs and inflicting considerable damage, but the effort was insufficient to seriously disrupt British imports. Indeed, Liverpool received only one-tenth the amount of bomb tonnage that London received, even though the latter was more of a political target.

Nor was the construction of warships for the Royal Navy or domestic merchant ships singled out for attack. In September 1940, there were five aircraft carriers, five battleships, 15 light cruisers and over 50 destroyers under construction in British yards, two-thirds of them in Glasgow or Newcastle.[36] Amazingly, the Luftwaffe did not mount any serious raids against Glasgow or Newcastle until March 1941, causing only minor disruption. Nor were these targets particularly well protected; the Luftwaffe sent 439 bombers to attack Glasgow on 13–14 March 1941 and lost only two to anti-aircraft.

Losses of warships, particularly new destroyers, would have had a ripple effect upon the Royal Navy's ability to defend convoys against U-Boat attacks, but the Luftwaffe leadership failed to see this.

The main point here is that the Luftwaffe made only sporadic and inconsistent efforts to disrupt either the British operational or strategic centres of gravity. Instead of focusing on a few targets and blasting them to kingdom come, the Luftwaffe spread its bombing effort across too many targets, thereby dissipating its efforts. However, the Luftwaffe clearly had the ability to attack the critical requirements supporting Britain's COGs and a powerful and sustained effort against one or more critical requirements would almost certainly have impaired Britain's ability to resist and may have been enough to set the conditions for *Seelöwe* to be executed in late September 1940.

Minenkrieg: The Close-in Threat to Britain's Maritime Commerce

On 22 September 1938, General der Flieger Helmuth Felmy wrote a memorandum for Göring on how an air campaign against England could be waged. Presciently, Felmy wrote that an air campaign against land targets with the He-111 bomber could not be decisive. Instead, he identified the Royal Navy, enemy merchant shipping and ports as the key targets and recommended the use of large-scale aerial mine-laying to block British ports. He also recommended the creation of a division of heavy, long-range bombers under Kriegsmarine control to conduct anti-shipping operations.[37] Göring rejected Felmy's memorandum, but authorized the development of aerial-delivered mines.

Göring fought the idea of a separate naval air force tooth and nail, but in 1936 he had agreed to form seven Küstenfliegergruppen to support the Kriegsmarine. It was agreed in the inter-service memo authorizing their formation that the primary function of these units was maritime reconnaissance, but aerial mine-laying was also possible. Actually, since the Küstenfliegergruppen were equipped with a heterogeneous collection of He-59, He-60 and He-115 floatplanes and Do-18 flying boats, Göring had no use for these aircraft anyway. The He-115 was the only modern aircraft with the range and payload to be useful for combat. At the start of the war, all these groups fell under the command of Generalleutnant Joachim Coeler, a former naval aviator who transferred to the Luftwaffe in 1933. All the coastal aircraft would eventually be formed into the 9. Flieger-Division, under Coeler's direct command. However, based upon Felmy's and Geisler's earlier memoranda, Raeder was able to successfully lobby Hitler for the Luftwaffe to provide medium bomber units to conduct anti-shipping operations. Reluctantly, Göring transferred first the I./KG 26 and then II./KG 26 with He-111 bombers, followed by I./KG 30 with Ju-88 bombers to fall under a new formation, designated as the X. Fliegerkorps. Geisler was assigned to command this formation and he was tasked with developing a maritime strike capability, while Coeler focused on reconnaissance and mine-laying.

Germany deployed a great number of 'secret weapons' during the World War II – some effective, some not – but one of the first ones introduced was the magnetic influence mine, which could be dropped from aircraft, or deployed by U-Boats or surface vessels. The basic concept was that the mine was outfitted with a sensor that could detect the magnetic field generated by a ship's steel hull; when a ship approached, the sensor would detect the magnetic field and detonate the mine. In theory, the explosion would create an underwater gas bubble that could break a ship's keel. Unlike conventional mines that a ship had to strike, the magnetic mine acted as an 'area denial weapon' and was perfect for Raeder's anti-commerce strategy. However, the mines were expensive compared to conventional contact mines and Germany had not yet amassed a large stockpile of magnetic mines before the war. In September 1939, the Kriegsmarine had about 1,500 magnetic mines and 20,000 contact mines, while the Luftwaffe had 250 magnetic mines.[38, 39] The Kriegsmarine had ambitious plans to manufacture 50,000 of the aerial-delivered mines, but the production rate was only 100 magnetic mines per month in November 1939; it was hoped to have 2,800 LMA- and

LMB-type magnetic mines by 1 September 1940.[40]

It would have been prudent to wait until sufficient magnetic mines had been produced before committing them into combat, but Raeder refused to wait. The day after Britain declared war on Germany, Raeder commenced mining operations off the English coast with four small Type IIA U-Boats laying a small number of TMA mines; these were moored magnetic influence mines with a 215kg warhead.[41] The other available type, the TMB magnetic mine, had a 580kg warhead and rested on the bottom in 85–100 feet of water. On the afternoon of 10 September, the British 8,641-ton cargo ship *Magdapur* struck one of the TMA mines off the east coast of England and broke its back, becoming the first victim of Germany's mine campaign. However, both the Type II and Type VII U-Boats typically carried 12 TMA or TMB mines which only enabled them to lay a relatively small linear minefield. Thus, the initial small-scale use of magnetic mines resulted in the sinking of only six ships totalling barely 16,000 tons in September 1939. Nevertheless, Raeder was adamant about the use of magnetic mines and wanted the campaign expanded as quickly as possible. He believed that *Minenkrieg* (mine warfare), would form an important component of his *Handelskrieg* strategy.

Kommodore Karl Dönitz, in charge of the Kriegsmarine's U-Boats, was not in favour of utilizing U-Boats to lay mines since it was extremely hazardous and less certain than torpedo attacks on shipping.[42] Personally, he distrusted mines as unreliable. He wanted to off-load this mission on the surface navy or on the Küstenfliegergruppen, in order to get his U-Boats back to attacking convoys. Nevertheless, Raeder ordered Dönitz to continue to lay mines off the eastern coast of England and Scotland with Type II boats and to begin using Type VII boats against the western coasts. The Kriegsmarine also ordered production of the TMC mine with a larger 1,000kg warhead, for use against warships.

While getting off to a slow start, the mines soon proved their lethality. Dönitz's U-Boats laid 21 minefields and sank 30 ships of 104,400 tons between September and December 1940. Another subtle benefit of the

German mine offensive was that it discouraged neutral merchant ships – particularly American – from sailing into British waters, which meant that the British merchant marine had to fill in for neutral shipping that 'opted out'. Although hazardous, only one Type II submarine, U-16, was lost on a mine-laying operation.[43] The embarrassment to the Royal Navy was considerable: on 21 November, the brand-new cruiser HMS *Belfast* had its keel broken by a magnetic mine laid by U-21 in the Firth of Forth. On 4 December, HMS *Nelson*, the flagship of the Home Fleet, was also badly damaged by a magnetic mine laid by U-31 in Loch Ewe, in north-west Scotland. The Royal Navy was unwilling to move the damaged battleship until all the mines had been swept from the loch entrance, which required a month of sweeping and cost two trawlers sunk. Finally, HMS *Nelson* was moved out of her imprisonment and spent five months under repair.

In conjunction with the U-Boat mine-laying effort, Raeder ordered his destroyer squadrons to conduct offensive mining operations off the English coast, beginning on 17 October 1939. Unlike the U-Boats, each destroyer could deliver 60 mines and a squadron-size operation could create a much larger minefield. The German destroyermen laid over 1,100 mines by the end of December, which sank 47 ships totalling 165,000 tons, as well as the destroyers HMS *Blanche* and *Gipsy*. About half the destroyer-laid mines were magnetic mines; the rest were contact mines (EMC, EMD), which also proved effective. Lord Mountbatten's destroyer, HMS *Kelly*, was disabled by a contact mine off the River Tyne. Amazingly, the Royal Navy did not detect any of these sorties – including one that laid mines off Newcastle – and believed the mines had been placed by U-Boats.[44]

The Royal Navy was well aware of the threat posed by the magnetic influence mine because it had developed its own version of this weapon in 1918, but it had not devoted any effort to creating counter-measures. Instead, the Royal Navy started the war with 21 Halcyon-class minesweepers, which were designed to counter conventional contact mines by snagging and cutting their cables. A large number of trawlers were taken into service as auxiliary minesweepers at the beginning of the war, for coast minesweeping duties. Standard sweeping tactics with paravanes sufficed against the Kriegsmarine's EMA/EMC-type moored contact mines, but were useless against the magnetic influence mines since there were no mooring lines to snag. Efforts to clear the German minefields off the River Tyne were a complete failure. In Portsmouth, the Mine Experimental Department at HMS *Vernon* was tasked with countering the German magnetic mines.

Meanwhile, Coeler had been champing at the bit to get his 9. Flieger-Division into action against British shipping, but daylight operations in English waters had already proven costly when RAF Fighter Command shot down four of his He-115s in October. It took a while to work out the procedures for aerial mine-laying at night, but by mid-November Coeler was ready to begin his part of the *Minenkrieg* effort. The two types of aerial-delivered magnetic mines (Luftminen) available were the Luftmine A (LMA) with a 300kg charge and the Luftmine B (LMB) with a 705kg charge; a parachute was used to retard the weapons' descent and an impact fuse was supposed to detonate the warhead if it accidently dropped on land. On 20 November 1939, four He-59 floatplanes from 3./Küstenfliegergruppe 906 dropped six Luftminen into the Thames Estuary on the first night and the group delivered 26 more over the next two nights, including some dropped in the Humber Estuary and near Harwich.[45] Follow-up missions on 6–7 December delivered 28 LMB-type magnetic mines.[46]

The magnetic mining operation by 9. Flieger-Division was a complete disaster and it was immediately apparent that the coastal pilots were untrained in night operations since they lost eight aircraft in crashes.[47] The greatest damage inflicted by this operation occurred when one pilot idiotically crashed his He-115 into one of the Chain Home radar antennas at RAF West Beckham. Otherwise, these 61 air-delivered magnetic mines achieved nothing. Adding insult to injury, two of the LMA-type Luftminen dropped by the Luftwaffe landed on mud flats in the Thames Estuary and failed to self-detonate, as designed. This was a lucky break for the British because the mines were spotted on 22 November and a team from HMS *Vernon*, led by Lieutenant Commander

John G. D. Ouvry, was able to disarm both of the mines. Through rapid technical exploitation of the captured mines, several potential counter-measures were developed.[48] Over the next two months, trying a variety of methods, the RAF was able to perfect a method of detonating the magnetic mines from the air using modified Wellington bombers.

Meanwhile, the Kriegsmarine greatly increased their delivery of magnetic mines by U-Boat in December to January. On 6 January, U-30 laid 12 TMB mines off Liverpool and these eventually succeeded in sinking a tanker and three freighters. Had the Germans continued this kind of effort, mercantile traffic into Britain's largest port could have been seriously disrupted. On 19 January, the U-34 laid its magnetic mines inside Falmouth Bay, which quickly sank a 7,800-ton tanker. In response, the Royal Navy employed an expedient approach using towed skids with electrified cables that succeeded in detonating eight of U-34's remaining magnetic mines.[49] In February, Raeder wanted to extend mine warfare to Canadian waters, requesting to send two U-Boats to lay mines off Halifax, but Hitler rejected the recommendation 'in view of the psychological effect on the United States'.[50]

By February, the Royal Navy began using the more effective 'Double-L' sweep method to clear magnetic mines and succeeded in neutralizing 300 mines by June.[51] A more permanent solution was degaussing ships to reduce their magnetic fields – a prodigious task – and although most warships had gone through the process by August, most merchant ships had not. Nevertheless, at that time Churchill informed Parliament that the mine threat had been 'effectively mastered'. Yet in reality, the British had only defeated the first generation of German magnetic mines.

Indeed, the use of U-Boats to deliver magnetic mines remained a serious hazard to British coastal shipping until the Norwegian campaign diverted most of the available U-Boats to support that effort. Dönitz kept trying to persuade Raeder to drop the mine-laying campaign, arguing that it was taking U-Boats away from convoy attacks. Indeed, Dönitz aggressively pushed his authority and after the Norwegian campaign no more U-Boats were sent on mine-laying operations in

1940. It was not the Royal Navy counter-measures which defeated the Kriegsmarine's mine campaign, but Dönitz's tactical small-mindedness, which was obsessed with the *Tonnageschlacht* (tonnage battle); he simply could not accept that interfering with traffic in and out of Liverpool was more important than sinking random ships in the Atlantic. Instead, Raeder increasingly relied on his destroyers to lay mines and in five missions in January to February they laid 782 more mines (including 280 magnetic) off the English coast, which sank 19 ships of 73,000 tons, including the destroyer HMS *Grenville*.

After the loss of so many destroyers in the Norwegian campaign, Raeder pulled the destroyers off the mine-laying mission, which left Coeler's 9. Flieger-Division as the only game in town. During April to May, the 9. Flieger-Division began using He-111 bombers in aerial mine-laying off the British coast, dropping 188 magnetic mines, which sank 14,564 tons of shipping. With the fall of France, the 9. Flieger-Division gained a small number of Fw-200C Condors of I./KG 40, which were assigned to fly 12 night mine-laying missions between 15 and 27 July, which resulted in the loss of two Condors. This was a complete misuse of these precious long-range aircraft and Luftwaffe pilots came to loathe aerial mine-laying since it required aircraft to fly low and slow.

Amazingly, the Germans learned in March 1940 from the open press that the British had recovered a magnetic mine and developed counter-measures – which was confirmed by B-Dienst.[52] Raeder ordered the immediate development of upgraded mines in order to make them harder to sweep. Next-generation magnetic mines included ship counters, delayed-activation mechanisms and a clock system that could turn the arming mechanism off for part of each day; these measures – which the British were not fully aware of until 1941 – continued to make the magnetic mine a threat to shipping in coastal waters. In mid-December 1940, 9. Flieger-Division dropped 300 mines into the Thames Estuary, which sank 12 ships.[53]

Even as the British were getting a handle on curbing the magnetic mines, the Germans introduced an acoustic mine on 28 August; this weapon could be detonated by the sound of a ship's engines, not its magnetic field. By the time that the Kriegsmarine began planning *Seelöwe,* the acoustic mine was ready for use in quantity and the Royal Navy did not yet have counter-measures in place for this new type.[54] Events demonstrated that both the conventional EMC/EMD-type mines and the new magnetic mines were lethal early on 1 September, when a squadron of five British destroyers on an offensive patrol off the Dutch coast unexpectedly encountered an enemy minefield. The destroyers HMS *Esk* and *Ivanhoe* were sunk and HMS *Express* was badly damaged. During *Seelöwe,* the Kriegsmarine expected to lay thousands of mines on the flanks of the invasion flotillas and, given their effectiveness off the Dutch coast, it is likely that they would have proved a hazard to Royal Navy destroyers trying to intercept the invasion. From 14 September to 30 October, 9. Flieger-Division dropped over 1,000 mines into British waters, although British counter-measures were able to prevent this from closing any ports. In another stroke of good fortune, the British retrieved an acoustic mine on 30 October, but B-Dienst reported this information and the Kriegsmarine soon fielded a new combined magnetic/acoustic fuse for its mines.

In short, the *Minenkrieg* campaign had the potential to make a major contribution towards interdicting Britain's overseas trade and restricting the operations of the Royal Navy in coastal waters. However, the premature disclosure of the magnetic mine seriously undermined this effort, as did the poor inter-service coordination between the Luftwaffe and Kriegsmarine on mining operations. Another key tactical deficiency was that the Germans spread the mines across too many targets and failed to regularly re-seed important minefields, like outside Liverpool. While British adaptive counter-measures played a major role in preventing the Germans from achieving decisive success with mine warfare, the loss of 500,000 tons of shipping and half-a-dozen warships in the first six months provides a glimpse of what might have transpired if the Kriegsmarine had waited to begin large-scale *Minenkrieg* in preparation for *Seelöwe.* In short, Germany failed to fully exploit its initial advantage in mine warfare at a time when it could have proved decisive.

Above and Below the Water: Bombs and Torpedoes

In addition to mines, British warships and merchant vessels in the waters around Great Britain faced serious threats from enemy motor torpedo boats, specially trained Luftwaffe anti-shipping units and U-Boats. Unlike the mine threat, the Royal Navy was far from finding a reliable defence against any of these heterogeneous threats and they constituted serious impediments to the British ability to interfere with German invasion flotillas attempting to cross the English Channel.

At the start of *Fall Gelb*, the Kriegsmarine committed the 1. and 2. S-Bootsflottillen into coastal operations in the North Sea. In their first encounter with the Royal Navy, four S-Boats (*Schnellboote,* German motor torpedo boats, known to the British as E-Boats) intercepted Lord Louis Mountbatten's 5th Destroyer Flotilla on 9 May and torpedoed his flagship HMS *Kelly.* Although the Kriegsmarine never had more than 21 operational S-Boats deployed in the North Sea and English Channel in 1940, the Royal Navy was shocked that one of its most modern destroyers could be crippled by enemy light surface craft. The S-Boats were night hunters and very difficult to spot, particularly when the Royal Navy did not yet have surface search radar on its destroyers. Using ambush tactics, the S-Boats came in fast, launched their two 21-inch G7a torpedoes and then sped off at 40 knots behind a smokescreen – the Royal Navy was not accustomed to this kind of hit-and-run surface threat. During the Dunkirk evacuation, S-Boats again demonstrated their lethal night tactics in a series of slashing attacks which sank the British destroyer HMS *Wakeful* and two French destroyers. Once France capitulated, Kapitänleutnant Heinz Birnbacher's 1. S-Bootsflottille moved into Cherbourg and Korvettenkapitän Rudolf Petersen's 2. S-Bootsflottille moved into Ostend. The Royal Navy was now faced with countering an S-Boat threat that could strike across the Channel with little or no warning.

Prior to the war, the Royal Navy had built 18 small motor torpedo boats (MTB) of its own, but they were considerably smaller and less well armed than the German *Schnellboote*. Furthermore, the German

S-Boats were trained for surface night action, whereas the Royal Navy's coastal forces were primarily focused on anti-submarine and coastal escort functions. Soon after encountering S-Boats in the North Sea, the Admiralty ordered the development of a new type of motor gunboat (MGB) to counter them, but none of these would be available before the end of 1940. In the meantime, the Royal Navy was forced to use destroyers and its lightly armed coastal forces to try to contain S-Boat raids. On 19 June, the S-Boats began operating off Dungeness, which would soon be designated as one of the landing areas for *Seelöwe*; sinking first a freighter, then a tanker.[55]

In July, the S-Boats began attacking convoys in the English Channel and there was little that the Royal Navy could do to stop the raids. The S-Boats also began laying mines in the Thames Estuary; each boat could carry six EMC contact mines.[56] Between July and mid-September, the S-Boats sank 13 merchant ships in the Channel, although the total tonnage was only about 29,000 GRT. Four British MTBs, patrolling for the S-Boats, were lost on mines, while three S-Boats were lost, all on mines. RAF Coastal Command bombed S-Boat bases in France, but failed to achieve any major success. By the time S-Tag approached, the Kriegsmarine had two veteran S-Bootsflottillen ready to protect the eastern flank of the invasion armada against Royal Navy destroyers. Should the Royal Navy attempt to move against the invasion convoys at night, they would undoubtedly encounter S-Boats lurking in ambush; engagements between destroyers and S-Boats in 1940–42 usually ended up badly for the destroyers. Indeed, the S-Boats would remain a problem for the Royal Navy long past *Seelöwe* and these night hunters were still able to achieve significant victories in the English Channel as late as April 1944, when they inflicted massive losses on Exercise Tiger in Lyme Bay.

The Royal Navy also had to worry about Geisler's X. Fliegerkorps, which was tasked with attacking British surface units and merchant shipping in the North Sea and English Channel. Geisler's premier unit was I./KG 30 equipped with the new Ju-88 bomber, which was capable of making steep dive-bombing attacks on ships. His operations officer was Major Martin Harlinghausen, another former sailor, who developed a plan to attack the battlecruiser HMS *Repulse* at Rosyth. Hitler approved the plan – the first air raid on Britain – but issued restrictions that no warships in the dockyard area could be bombed, in order to avoid civilian casualties. On 16 October 1939, nine Ju-88s from Sylt flew undetected across the North Sea and appeared suddenly over Rosyth. HMS *Repulse* was in dry-dock so the bombers switched to attack warships in the Firth of Forth. Dropping their bombs from just 500 feet, Ju-88s hit the light cruiser HMS *Southampton* with a 500kg bomb and damaged the cruiser HMS *Edinburgh* and destroyer *Mohawk* with near-misses. Two Ju-88s were shot down by Spitfires as they tried to escape, but the raid managed to inflict 16 dead and 44 wounded upon the anchored warships. The next day, X. Fliegerkorps mounted a raid on the Home Fleet at Scapa Flow and more raids in January and March. On 16 March 1940, a Ju-88 scored a hit on the anchored heavy cruiser HMS *Norfolk*, which suffered four dead and seven wounded. Meanwhile, X. Fliegerkorps turned out its He-111 bombers from KG 26 against merchant shipping in the North Sea in January 1940 and managed to sink 12 ships of 23,944 tons. In February, a Ju-88 scored a direct bomb hit on the minesweeper HMS *Sphinx* off the Scottish coast, sinking it. A total of seven German bombers were lost on maritime strike missions in the first six months of the war, five lost to fighters and two to anti-aircraft fire. German bombing accuracy at sea was steadily increasing.

The Norwegian campaign proved to be a real eye-opener for the Royal Navy in regard to the Luftwaffe's anti-ship capabilities. Admiral Sir Charles Forbes, commander of the Home Fleet, led a task force consisting of his flagship, the battleship HMS *Rodney*, two other capital ships and over 30 cruisers and destroyers. On 9 April, Forbes's fleet was attacked by X. Fliegerkorps off Norway: HMS *Rodney* was hit by a 500kg bomb and the destroyer HMS *Ghurka* was sunk; two cruisers were lightly damaged. Although four Ju-88s were shot down by British anti-aircraft fire, Forbes was shocked by the ability of enemy aircraft to penetrate his defensive screen.[57] A week later, Forbes tried to send the heavy cruiser HMS *Suffolk* and four destroyers to bombard a German-held airfield near Stavenger, but X. Fliegerkorps swarmed all over the British task force and crippled HMS *Suffolk* with two bomb hits (inflicting 32 dead and 43 wounded). It is noteworthy that these successes off Norway were achieved under marginal weather conditions and against warships that were manoeuvring at full speed and shooting back.

Three more British cruisers and two destroyers were damaged by German air attacks off Norway by the end of April. On 19 April, Oberleutnant Werner Baumbach, a Ju-88 pilot in KG 30, attacked the French light cruiser *Émile Bertin* off Namsos and struck it with a 500kg bomb; this action began Baumbach's rise as one of the best anti-shipping pilots in the Luftwaffe.[58] In May, the cruiser HMS *Curlew* – one of the few ships in the Royal Navy equipped with air search radar – was sunk by Ju-88 bombers. By the end of the Norwegian campaign, the Home Fleet had suffered considerable punishment at the hands of X. Fliegerkorps and the German aircrews were becoming increasingly proficient at bombing warships. Forbes returned to Scapa Flow with the conviction to avoid further risking his capital ships in areas where the Luftwaffe had strong forces.

Soon thereafter, the Luftwaffe was quick to move air units into captured bases in Denmark and Norway, which increased the air threat to British shipping off Scotland. On 23 August, four He-115s from 3./Ku.Fl.Gr. 506 based in Norway attacked the convoy OA 203 off northern Scotland; the 5,053-ton freighter *Llianishen* was torpedoed and sunk, while a 6,677-ton freighter was sunk by bombs. The He-115s had been modified for torpedo attack since March, but this was their first successful aerial torpedo attack. Three days later, a group of four He-115s and eight Ju-88s attacked convoy HX 65 off Scotland; one 5,057-ton freighter was sunk by bombing, and torpedoes finished off the 11,445-ton passenger ship *Remuera*. The Kriegsmarine had funded the development of the aerial-delivered F5a torpedo against the Luftwaffe's objections and the weapon had an extended development period due to its quirky characteristics. By spring 1940, the Küstenfliegergruppen had 135 F5a torpedoes, but monthly production was kept at a pathetic rate of ten torpedoes and Göring was trying to kill the programme.[59] A number of He-111 bombers in X. Fliegerkorps were provided with launching gear, but Göring refused to allow these aircraft to drop torpedoes – yet. Although the Kriegsmarine had validated its aerial torpedo capability, inter-service rivalry derailed the programme when Germany needed it most. By September 1940, the Küstenfliegergruppen had just 38 F5a torpedoes in stock, but the improved F5b was being developed and would enter service in 1941.

In addition to enemy mines, bombers and torpedo-carrying floatplanes, Royal Navy units deployed to oppose *Seelöwe* also had to consider the threat of U-Boat attack in home waters. The Kriegsmarine started the World War II with the G7a steam-driven torpedo and the G7e/T2 electric-driven torpedo, which could be equipped with magnetic or contact detonators. Early on, U-Boat commanders realized that the magnetic detonator was worthless and switched to reliance on contact detonators, although these were far from fully reliable either. The sinking of the aircraft carrier HMS *Courageous* by U-29 on 17 September 1939 and the battleship HMS *Royal Oak* by U-47 on 14 October 1939 were both serious psychological shocks to the Royal Navy and the death of 1,352 sailors in these two attacks provided a grim taste of what surprise submarine attacks could achieve. After the loss of the *Royal Oak*, the Home Fleet temporarily withdrew to Loch Ewe, but on the morning of 30 October, the Type IIC U-56 found the Home Fleet sailing in formation west of the Orkneys: HMS *Nelson*, *Rodney* and *Hood* escorted by four destroyers. The U-56 evaded the destroyers and struck HMS *Nelson* with three G7e/T2 torpedoes, using contact detonators – which failed to explode. Soon, the Kriegsmarine would realize that it had gone to war with unreliable torpedoes and that up to one-third of all attacks were spoiled by technical malfunctions. Much of the problem was unique to U-Boat operations, since the G7a torpedo performed fairly well when launched by Kriegsmarine destroyers and S-Boats.

Nevertheless, the U-Boats continued to attack Royal Navy warships when favourable conditions appeared. In January 1940, the destroyer HMS *Exmouth* was sunk off northern Scotland by a Type IIB U-22 with the loss of her entire crew of 198 sailors, followed by the loss of HMS *Daring* to U-23 in February, with only five survivors from her crew. In both cases, these destroyers had been attacked and sunk in surprise night attacks, despite manoeuvring. The commander of the U-23 was Kapitänleutnant Otto Kretschmer, one of the Kriegsmarine's best U-Boat commanders. On the other hand, Royal Navy destroyers had sunk a number of U-Boats in 1939–40, thanks to ASDIC, but without surface search radar they had difficulty spotting U-Boats on the surface at night. After the Norwegian campaign, Dönitz conducted a thorough review of the poor torpedo performance, which gradually resulted in improved torpedo effectiveness. By the time that *Seelöwe* became a possibility, the Royal Navy knew that it remained vulnerable to U-Boat attacks, particularly at night, but it was unaware that the Kriegsmarine U-Boats still had torpedoes that were not fully reliable.

Handelskrieg: The Distant Threat to Britain's Maritime Commerce

Britain's economic well-being and ability to remain in the war depended upon imports of oil, raw materials and foodstuffs from overseas. In 1940, Britain's key imports included 19.3 million tons of food (including 5.8 million tons of wheat and 2.1 million tons of maize), 11.2 million tons of oil, 4.5 million tons of iron ore, 3.6 million tons of steel, 112,000 tons of bauxite for aluminium, 87,600 tons of chrome, 13,400 tons of wolfram ore (tungsten), 2,400 tons of Molybdenum and 200,000 tons of raw rubber. For example, the Rolls-Royce Merlin engine, which powered both the Spitfire and Hurricane fighters, depended upon imports of Molybdenum from the Climax mine in Colorado, bauxite ore (to make aluminium) from British Guiana and nickel ore from Ontario, Canada.[60] Germany victories on the continent did deny Great Britain access to important resources including 90 per cent of its iron ore imports from French North Africa and Scandinavia, foodstuffs from Denmark and Holland and timber from the Baltic.[61] Britain was able to increase domestic production of food, coal, timber and iron ore in order to reduce some of its import needs, but it would take until 1942 before shortages were alleviated. In the meantime, the Royal Navy's primary mission was to ensure that the economic lifelines – particularly to Halifax, the Caribbean and South Africa – remained capable of maintaining the flow of raw materials and food.

At the start of the war, Britain and the Commonwealth had the largest merchant marine in the world, comprising 2,965 vessels of 17.52 million GRT, including 445 tankers. Despite the loss of over 3 million GRT of shipping in the first 12 months of the war, the Commonwealth still had 3,053 vessels of 17.59 million GRT as well as 704 foreign vessels of 3.7 million GRT at the end of September 1940.[62] Under Churchill's emergency construction programme, British yards in Glasgow, Liverpool, Belfast and Newcastle were expected to build up to 1.2 million GRT of new shipping per year; in fact, only 780,000 tons were built in 1940. The difference was made up by contracting to build 439,000 tons in the United States. The addition of Dutch, Norwegian and Polish merchant shipping also helped to alleviate shortfalls in domestic construction.

The essence of Raeder's *Handelskrieg* (trade war) strategy was to interdict Britain's overseas commerce by neutralizing its ports and sinking enough of its merchant shipping in order to constrict Britain's imports to catastrophic levels. Without enough oil, raw materials or food, Britain would be forced to seek terms – that was Hitler's reasoning in the summer of 1940. However, Hitler was reluctant to authorize unrestricted submarine warfare in order to avoid provoking the United States and he limited where U-Boats and surface raiders could operate. Even within the Kriegsmarine, Raeder and Dönitz disagreed on the best means to conduct *Handelskrieg*; Raeder wanted to use a mix of forces, including U-Boats, mines, surface raiders and long-range aircraft to interdict British trade. In contrast, Dönitz believed that his U-Boats alone could sever Britain's overseas trade.[63] Extrapolating from data on the U-Boat campaign in the World War I, Dönitz argued that a force of 300 medium-size U-Boats, with 100 at sea at any one time, could sink 1 million GRT per month, which would destroy Britain's commerce in an 18-month campaign. Dönitz's numbers were overly optimistic and Raeder did not accept them. Instead, Raeder short-changed Dönitz's U-Boat arm in the lead-up to war in 1938–39 and did not build enough of the Type VII U-Boats that Dönitz insisted were critical to winning *Handelskrieg*.[64] Nor did Dönitz want the larger Type IX U-Boats that the OKM forced upon him. Dönitz believed that the best way to win *Handelskrieg* was to sink as many enemy merchant ships as possible and he developed a philosophy of *Tonnageschlacht* (tonnage battle) that focused on simple metrics rather than insightful strategic analysis. He did not care what kinds of ships were sunk, as long as there were plenty of them. Consequently, Dönitz did not favour distant U-Boat operations because submarines would waste too much time in transit, nor did he favour mine-laying. Instead, he wanted to fight the decisive battle in British waters, close to friendly ports, so that U-Boats could go out, attack whatever shipping they found and return as soon as possible for more torpedoes. Dönitz's *Tonnageschlacht* was a narrow-minded approach to anti-commerce operations that would greatly undermine the ability of the U-Boat force to deliver a real knock-out blow.

At the start of the war, Dönitz had only 57 operational U-Boats of which just 27 were ocean-going U-Boats.[65] In 1939–40, Dönitz had to conduct U-Boat operations within the context of Raeder's concept of how to conduct *Handelskrieg,* which meant diverting U-Boats to participate in the mine-laying campaign and then the Norwegian campaign. Like the RAF's Chain Home GCI system, Dönitz had worked out a system to maximize the tactical effectiveness of his limited U-Boat force: *Rudeltaktik* (Wolfpack tactics). He believed that by using land-based communications he could deploy scouting lines of submarines that would relay sighting reports to his headquarters;

when a convoy was spotted, he would vector all available U-Boats against it. Dönitz even managed to practise *Rudeltaktik* with 15 U-Boats in the Atlantic in May 1939.[66] Furthermore, he wanted the U-Boats to attack on the surface at night, to nullify the Royal Navy's ASDIC capabilities. In theory, massed U-Boat attacks at night on the surface could maul even a well-escorted convoy. However, several efforts to employ *Rudeltaktik* in the first six months of the war failed because there were too few U-Boats available. Indeed, there were not enough U-Boats at sea to even form decent scouting lines, so most convoys were never detected. Instead, the U-Boats mostly attacked ships sailing independently or stragglers from convoys – a tactical method akin to scavenging.

Although Dönitz's U-Boats managed to sink 261 ships totalling 946,570 GRT by mine, torpedo and gunfire in the period September 1939 to May 1940, this inflicted no real disruption to Britain's imports. Hitler had confined the U-Boat campaign to the Western Approaches and very few convoys were attacked. On the critical Halifax-Liverpool route, of the first 46 convoys – which totalled 1,613 ships – the only losses to enemy action were five ships sunk and three damaged.[67] This is an important point to make that often gets lost in most narratives but the fact is that prior to the fall of France, British convoys in the Atlantic were more at risk from storms than they were from enemy action. Thus, Britain's economic strength had not been seriously impacted by the first phase of Dönitz's U-Boat campaign, which gave Churchill the confidence that he could fight a protracted war. However, his confidence would be shaken by *Rudeltaktik,* when it did appear.[68]

Amazingly, Germany put very little effort into U-Boat construction until after the fall of France and new construction did not keep up with losses. In the first nine months of the war, Dönitz lost 24 submarines (eleven Type VII, six Type IX, seven Type II) and received only nine new submarines (three Type VII, two Type IX, four Type II). The work-horse Type VII U-Boat was in very low-rate production and none were commissioned from December 1939 until the end of September 1940. While the improved Type VIIC was ordered in

September 1939, none would be commissioned until November 1940. The larger Type IXB U-Boat was just starting serial production, with one or two built per month, but these boats tended to be easier to detect. Instead of focusing on medium submarines, the OKM wasted resources building 16 Type IID coastal submarines in the second half of 1940, which were of negligible use for *Handelskrieg*. Consequently, at the start of the campaign against the English coast in July 1940, Dönitz had just 15 operational ocean-going submarines (one Type IA, ten Type VII and four Type IX), plus 18 Type IIB/C coastal submarines. Furthermore, the diversion of workers and materiel for *Seelöwe's* barge modification programme negatively impacted U-Boat construction in Hamburg, which delayed the introduction of the new Type VIIC U-Boat.[69] New U-Boat construction did not begin to rise above losses until autumn 1940 and Dönitz could still rarely deploy more than a dozen U-Boats into the Atlantic even by May 1941. As a stop-gap solution, the Italians agreed to transfer some of their submarines to operate in the Atlantic.

Table 8: German U-Boats Commissioned, June 1940–May 1941

Month	Type IID	Type VIIB	Type VIIC	Type IXB	Type IXC	TOTAL
June 1940	2			1		3
July 1940	1			1		2
August 1940	2			1		3
September 1940	2	1		2		5
October 1940	3	1		2		6
November 1940	2		2	1		5
December 1940	2	1	1	2		6
January 1941	2		2		2	6
February 1941		1	1		1	3
March 1941			1		2	3
April 1941		1	2		1	4
May 1941			1		2	3
TOTAL	16	5	10	10	8	49

Given these circumstances, the ability of the U-Boats to make any serious contribution to forcing Britain to its knees in 1940 or 1941 appeared negligible. At the current rate of loss, it was Dönitz's U-Boat arm that would break, not the British merchant marine. However, the situation began to change in mid-June, as the Royal Navy was distracted by evacuations from Norway and France and Dönitz was able to briefly surge 18 U-Boats out to sea. By this point, German torpedo defects had also been partly rectified. On 15 June, U-38 attacked convoy HX 47 in the Western Approaches and sank a tanker and a cargo ship. On 20–22 June, Dönitz was able to bring four Type VII U-Boats to bear against convoy HX 49, which was only escorted by two elderly sloops; although the attack was not fully coordinated, these U-Boats sank four ships, including two tankers.[70] While the loss of four out of 50 merchantmen was hardly catastrophic, it was an indicator that convoys would soon be attacked in force. Dönitz tried to form a five-boat Wolfpack to intercept the *Queen Mary* off Spain, but they failed to spot her. Nevertheless, Dönitz's operational surge in June resulted in the sinking of 355,000 tons of shipping, which was double what had been achieved in any previous month. On the down side, only four U-Boat sorties could be mounted in July.

In early July, the U-30 (Type VII) was the first U-Boat to arrive in Lorient and was soon followed by three more.[71] Dönitz was determined to use the captured French naval bases to increase the operational tempo of his limited U-Boat force but initially the limited amount of support facilities in situ led to a slow build-up. The first U-Boat patrol from Lorient did not begin until 13 July and it had to be aborted due to engine defects. On 25 July, Kapitänleutnant Otto Kretschmer sortied from Lorient in U-99 and boldly attacked convoy OB 191, sinking a freighter and damaging three tankers. Another factor in the U-Boat's changing fortunes was a growing stable of aggressive, competent skippers, with men like Günther Prien in U-47, Kretschmer in U-99 and Joachim Schepke in U-100 leading the charge. Whereas 39 per cent of the U-Boat patrols in the first nine months of the war sank no Allied shipping, this failure rate dropped to 6 per cent in the rest of 1940.

Thus, Dönitz had fewer U-Boats, but much better trained veteran crews and the so-called 'Happy Time' was about to begin. By August, Dönitz had ten of his U-Boats operating from Lorient, which greatly reduced the transit time to attack shipping in the Western Approaches. On top of this, the Italians agreed to transfer six of their submarines to operate in the Atlantic from Bordeaux; the first, the *Alessandro Malaspina*, sank an 8,406-ton British tanker from Convoy OB 193, then reached Bordeaux on 4 September. Seven more Italian submarines would arrive in October and they were assigned to operate off Portugal.

While Dönitz banked on his U-Boats to defeat Great Britain, Raeder still believed that surface warships and long-range aircraft could strike hard blows against British trade. During the period 1929–36, the German Navy made an exorbitant RM 252 million investment in building the three large Deutschland-class cruisers known as Panzerschiffe or 'pocket battleships'.[72] These vessels were specifically designed to conduct *Handelskrieg* and with a range of 10,000 nautical miles they could strike shipping as far distant as the Indian Ocean. Equipped with six 11-inch guns and diesel engines capable of 28 knots, the Deutschland-class cruisers were optimized for surface raiding. The *Admiral Graf Spee* conducted its sole war cruise in the South Atlantic in September to December 1939, sinking nine ships of 50,089 tons before it was found by the Royal Navy and engaged in the battle of the River Platte. Despite besting three smaller British cruisers, *Graf Spee's* captain opted to scuttle his vessel on 18 December 1939.[73] None of the cargo intercepted by *Graf Spee* – maize, frozen meat, dairy products, wool, zinc and lead – was worth the loss of such a fine, expensive warship. Meanwhile, her sister ship *Deutschland* prowled the North Atlantic for two months and sank only two freighters of 10,000 tons before returning to Germany.

Admiral Scheer, which suffered from a variety of maladies with its powerplant, spent the first year of the war leisurely refitting in Germany and did not conduct her first war patrol until October 1940. On 5 November 1940, the *Scheer* intercepted convoy HX 84 (Halifax–Liverpool) south-west of Liverpool and quickly sank the escort, the armed merchant cruiser HMS *Jervis Bay*. However, the convoy scattered quickly and *Scheer* was only able to sink six of the 38 merchant ships. Although the loss of 33,331 tons of shipping and 379 sailors was a serious blow, most of the convoy made it to England. Indeed, even though *Scheer* badly damaged the tanker *San Demetrio*, carrying 11,200 tons of aviation fuel from Texas, the tanker slipped away. *Admiral Scheer* then sailed south and eventually reached the Indian Ocean, before returning to Germany in April 1941. *Scheer's* six-month cruise eliminated 17 ships of 113,000 tons, and succeeded in capturing one British tanker as a prize.

The Hipper-class heavy cruisers were intended for general fleet duty but were pressed into the surface raiding role as part of the deception effort for *Seelöwe, Unternehmen Herbstreise*. However, the *Blucher* had been sunk in the Norwegian campaign in March 1940 and the *Prinz Eugen* was still involved in sea trials in the Baltic. The *Seydlitz* was 95 per cent complete in September 1939 but construction had been halted. In late 1940, only the *Admiral Hipper* was ready for operational employment. In December, the *Hipper* made a sortie into the Atlantic and at dawn on Christmas Day engaged the troop convoy WS-5A north of the Azores, but discovered it was escorted by two aircraft carriers, three cruisers and six destroyers. Nevertheless, *Hipper* engaged the heavy cruiser HMS *Berwick* in a 35-minute action and scored four 8-inch hits (a 2 per cent hit rate), disabling one turret and causing flooding. Before retiring, the *Hipper* also badly damaged the 13,994-ton transport *Empire Trooper*, which had 2,400 troops aboard. Amazingly, the British convoy scattered and *Empire Trooper*, which was dead in the water, was left behind without escort. It was only with the greatest luck that this transport staggered into Gibraltar ten days later.[74] On her second sortie in February 1941, the *Hipper* had more luck and encountered the dispersed and unescorted British convoy SLS 64 near the Azores; it was a massacre, resulting in the sinking of seven of 19 merchantmen in the convoy, totalling 32,806 tons. In these two raids, *Hipper* sank a total of nine ships of 40,218 tons; most victims were carrying general cargo, ranging from iron ore to oranges.[75]

The two Scharnhorst-class battleships were general-purpose warships that could be used for *Handelskrieg* or for conventional naval operations. Due to battle damage suffered off Norway in June, neither the *Scharnhorst* nor *Gneisenau* was available to support *Seelöwe* in September 1940. Once repaired, the two battleships were employed in Operation *Berlin*, a 60-day raid into the North Atlantic in January to March 1941. Hitler issued specific instructions that the battleships were to avoid engaging any convoy escorted by British battleships; yet as soon as British intelligence learned of the German sortie, they reinforced the escorts on the Halifax–Liverpool (HX) and Freetown–Liverpool (SL) convoy routes. On 8 February 1941, *Scharnhorst* and *Gneisenau* found convoy HX 106 but broke off when they spotted the battleship HMS *Ramillies*. On 8 March, they found convoy SL 67, which was escorted by the battleship HMS *Malaya*. Finally, on 15 March, the two German battleships encountered vessels from the dispersed convoy OB 294 and sank or captured six tankers sailing independently. The next day, *Scharnhorst* and *Gneisenau* bagged nine more ships from the dispersed convoy before the battleship HMS *Rodney* appeared and they had to break off the action. In all three encounters between the *Scharnhorst* and *Gneisenau* and British battleships, they were able to use their 30-knot speed to break off the action and escape from their much slower opponents. Altogether, the two German battleships sank or captured 22 ships of 113,690 tons during Operation *Berlin*, including seven tankers of 46,185 tons. Although the presence of British battleships prevented attacks on two convoys, the Royal Navy was forced to commit seven of the Home Fleet's nine available capital ships to convoy defence during March 1941 and this still failed to inflict any damage on the surface raiders.

In order to conduct patrols of more than a few weeks, the Kriegsmarine perfected the technique of refuelling at sea, which was a procedure that the Royal Navy – which had plenty of fixed bases worldwide – did not master until 1945. With an adequate support network of tankers to keep them refuelled and supply ships to provide re-victualling, warships like the *Scharnhorst* and *Gneisenau* could remain at sea for several months. In time, the Royal Navy would learn that the way to counter the surface raiders was to identify and take out their clandestine support ships.

Raeder was eager to employ the Kriegsmarine's largest warships, the 41,700-ton battleships *Bismarck* and *Tirpitz*, in raids into the Atlantic even though these vessels were not well suited for the *Handelskrieg* strategy. These large battleships, equipped with 38cm guns and heavily armoured, were designed to engage enemy warships, not unarmoured freighters. The Bismarck-class battleships also required a great deal more support to conduct long-range raids than the Deutschland-class cruisers, which increased the logistical 'footprint' that was required to support operations in the Atlantic. Raeder hoped that the *Bismarck* or *Tirpitz*, if teamed up with other surface raiders, would enable the Kriegsmarine to attack the better escorted HX-series convoys, which were far more important to the British war effort than convoys from Freetown. However, he did little to rush these fine warships into service and *Bismarck* was not operational until March 1941 and *Tirpitz* not until January 1942. In contrast to the leisurely 7–11 months required to conduct final trials and crew training for their surface warships, the Royal Navy was able to compress the time required to ready its new King George V-class battleships after commissioning to just 3–4 months.

Altogether, six raids by German surface raiders between September 1939 and March 1941 resulted in the sinking or capture of 59 merchantmen of 327,000 tons, including eight tankers. Four convoys were attacked, but only two (SLS 64 and OB 294) dispersed and unescorted ones were badly mauled. Tactically, surface raiders could not destroy convoys because they scattered in all directions when attacked. The British only succeeded in cornering and eliminating one raider, but failed to damage any of the others. It was clear that Royal Navy battleships were too slow to intercept these fast raiders and the battlecruisers HMS *Hood*, *Renown* and *Repulse*, which had the speed, were never in the right place. Furthermore, the inability of Bletchley Park to break into naval Enigma codes in 1940 deprived the Royal Navy of advance warning of raider activity; instead, the navy relied upon 'RRR' (Raider warning) sighting reports from merchantmen under attack. On the other hand, the Kriegsmarine had a very low sortie generation rate for its raiders and only *Admiral Hipper* made more than one raid in the first 18 months of the war. No raiders were at sea during the period July to September 1940 to divert Royal Navy warships away from *Seelöwe*. Furthermore, the surface raiders never attacked a convoy that had more than a token escort, despite superior speed.

As the Germans moved into their newly acquired bases in France, Geisler's X. Fliegerkorps also revealed a novel long-range maritime strike capability. Back in mid-September 1939, Hitler had approved the conversion of eight Fw-200 Condor airliners into maritime patrol aircraft for the Luftwaffe and, once ready, these aircraft were provided to Hauptmann Edgar Petersen's 1./KG 40 in February 1940. In March, the Luftwaffe began low-rate production of the Fw-200C, at a rate of four aircraft per month. Initially, the Fw-200 Condors were used in a variety of roles, including maritime reconnaissance and mine-laying, but Peterson pushed hard to use them against enemy merchant shipping. In July 1940, Geisler's X. Fliegerkorps began attacks against British shipping in the Irish Sea, but the limited range of his He-111 and Ju-88 bombers meant that all of these anti-shipping operations were vulnerable to intercept by land-based RAF fighters. On 2 August, Petersen's 1./KG 40 moved into Bordeaux-Merignac airfield with nine Fw-200 Condors and he received authorization to begin attacking enemy shipping in mid-August. The four-engine Fw-200C Condor had a typical operational range of 930 miles, with three hours on station and could carry a 1,000kg bomb load (usually four SC250 or twelve SD50 bombs).[76] It was the only aircraft that could attack shipping west of Ireland, well beyond range of British air cover.

It took some time to work out the best tactics for these jury-rigged bombers and Petersen only had three or four Fw-200s operational on any given day. Lacking a proper bombsight, the Fw-200 Condors employed *Tiefangriff* (low-level attacks), coming in just 50 yards off the water – which made them difficult to spot. Initial attacks in August to September only sank three ships and damaged nine more, but by October the Fw-200 began to attack convoys west of Ireland and inflict significant losses. The British merchant marine had very little defence against low-level air attacks, so the Fw-200 Condors found only feeble resistance. RAF Coastal Command was tasked to counter the Fw-200 raids, but they lacked the long-range aircraft to provide air cover over all convoys. By Christmas 1940, with just a handful of aircraft, Petersen was able to sink 100,000 tons of shipping and damage another 180,000 tons – he was off to a promising start. Recognizing that the Royal Navy had been caught by surprise by the sudden emergence of the Fw-200 Condor – which Churchill dubbed 'the scourge of the Atlantic' – the Admiralty ordered a crash programme to develop counter-measures, but this would not bear fruit until mid-1941.

During June 1940, it also became apparent to the Royal Navy that Raeder had another ace up his sleeve – disguised merchant raiders known as *Hilfskreuzer* (auxiliary cruisers). During the World War I, the Kaiser's navy had used *Hilfskreuzer* to sink or capture over 350,000 tons of Allied shipping and Raeder intended to utilize 'false-flag' tactics as well. However, for Raeder the *Hilfskreuzer* were not auxiliary units but, in fact, one of the premier strike elements in his *Handelskrieg* strategy because they would be used to strike at Britain's worldwide trade network and disperse the Royal Navy's strength in trade protection. Unlike the U-Boats and Condors which were currently only engaging British shipping in the Western Approaches, Raeder intended to use the *Hilfskreuzer* in all the oceans, thereby depriving the British of any 'safe areas'.

In September 1939, the Kriegsmarine began converting the first *Hilfskreuzer* and five were ready by Christmas 1939. In March, the *Atlantis* (HSK-2) sailed, followed by five more in the next several months. Employing 'false-flag' tactics, the *Hilfskreuzer* sailed past the British cruiser patrols in the Denmark Strait disguised as Soviet freighters. Each was armed with six 15cm guns, a mix of 2cm and 3.7cm Flak guns, 21-inch torpedoes, mines and a floatplane; in essence, these vessels had the firepower equivalent to a light cruiser, but without the speed or armoured protection. Designed for endurance, the *Hilfskreuzer* could go up to eight months without refuelling, although the Skl had developed a sophisticated clandestine resupply network known as the *Etappendienst*. Under this system, other disguised resupply ships and tankers could allow the *Hilfskreuzer* to remain at sea for a year or more. During May to June 1940, six of the *Hilfskreuzer* passed undetected through British patrols and reached their operational zones.

On the night of 13/14 June, the *Hilfskreuzer Orion* (HSK-1) covertly laid 228 EMC moored contact mines in New Zealand waters, north of Auckland. Less than a week later, the 13,400-ton liner RMS *Niagara* was sunk by one of the mines; this was a particularly painful blow, since the vessel was carrying 8 tons of South African gold (worth £2.4 million) intended to pay for American military equipment. The Royal Navy was shocked by the appearance of a large minefield in distant New Zealand waters, as well as a sudden rash of 'missing ships' in the Pacific and Indian Ocean. By September, Raeder had the *Widder* operating in the North Atlantic, the *Thor* in the South Atlantic, the *Atlantis* and *Pinguin* in the Indian Ocean and the *Orion* and *Komet* in the Pacific. In June, the *Hilfskreuzer* sank or captured eight ships of 48,427 tons, followed by 11 ships of 67,494 tons in July. The toll continued every month, averaging more than 60,000 tons of shipping disappearing. Often, the *Hilfskreuzer* were able to select the most valuable targets, such as large tankers, and unlike the surface raiders their victims did not scatter.

The Royal Navy approach to countering disguised merchant raiders – based upon experience in the World War I – was to deploy a large number of cruisers on the main trade routes and wait for a merchantman under attack to radio an 'RRR' report. However, only one-third of *Hilfskreuzer* victims managed to radio a report before they were sunk or captured. Nor could *Hilfskreuzer* be found by radio Direction-Finding since they typically employed radio listening silence. In order to increase the Royal Navy's presence on distant trade routes, the

Admiralty converted 54 civilian vessels into Armed Merchant Cruisers (AMC), armed with left-over 6-inch guns. However, it soon became apparent that the AMC were no match for the *Hilfskreuzer* when the *Thor* engaged the AMC *Alcantra* off Brazil on 28 July and out-fought it. By September, the Royal Navy had seven heavy cruisers, 18 light cruisers and 15 AMC deployed on distant trade protection from the South Atlantic to the Pacific, but had not spotted a single *Hilfskreuzer*. These six former merchantmen were able to significantly disperse the Royal Navy's strength away from more critical areas and to strike globally, without warning.

In sum, Raeder's plans for long-range anti-commerce operations were just coming to fruition at the start of the Luftwaffe's campaign against Great Britain and the Royal Navy was stretched too thinly to protect all of the worldwide trade networks. Lack of surface search radar, long-range maritime aircraft and reliable intelligence about enemy activities made countering any of these threats unlikely before mid-1941. Nor did the Royal Navy fully appreciate that its defences against U-Boat attack were still rudimentary. Indeed, the Royal Navy in September 1940 was poorly deployed to defend against *Rudeltaktik*, combined with unexpected attacks by Condors and *Hilfskreuzer* – for the first time, Britain's overseas trade was going to come under serious, sustained attack.

Kriegsmarine: Operational Choice of Targets

Inside the Kriegsmarine's Skl, the consensus was that sinking large amounts of enemy shipping would eventually cause critical shortages that would cripple Britain's economy and undermine national morale. Counting tonnage sunk was fairly simple and, like the 'body count' method used by the United States in the Vietnam War or 'Bomber' Harris's bomb tonnage figures, provided an easily comprehensible metric to assess the results of operations. However, the system was undermined by wilful inflation of tonnage claims by Dönitz and others, in order to claim greater success for the Kriegsmarine. Yet the greatest weakness of the Kriegsmarine's approach to anti-commerce operations was a failure to connect damage inflicted to desired strategic goals. Unlike the Luftwaffe, the Kriegsmarine was slow to conduct any real analysis of Britain's wartime economy and figure out where it was most vulnerable. Instead, the Kriegsmarine simply attacked the entire British trade infrastructure, hoping for a victory through cumulative attrition. However, the information was readily available – without any need for Abwehr agents – to determine where the British trade network could be broken.

Using the methodology discussed earlier, Britain had two strategic centres of gravity in 1940 that gave it the strength to remain in the war: its industrial base and its national morale. Both of these COGs depended on imported goods. The Luftwaffe could try to attack both of these through bombing, but the only way to stop the imports was for the Kriegsmarine to interdict Britain's overseas trade infrastructure; these imports could be attacked en route or at the source. Attempting to deprive Britain of key resources – oil, bauxite and iron ores – was a more straightforward proposition than attempting to interdict food supplies, since the former originated from only a handful of ports. However, even temporary disruptions in the food supply – resulting in tighter rationing in Britain – could move the Germans closer towards the goal of weakening British resolve.

Table 9: British Strategic-level Centres of Gravity, September 1940

COG	Critical Capability	Critical Requirement	Critical Vulnerability
Britain's industrial base	Manufacture aircraft, ships and other equipment to sustain war effort	Oil Bauxite (Aluminium) Iron ores	Source of key raw materials is distant and vulnerable to interdiction
Britain's national morale	Provides support for continuing the war effort	Food imports	Relatively small number of refrigerator (reefer) ships to deliver meat

Kapitän zur See Gottfried Krüger's 3/Skl (Foreign Navies Branch) was not unaware of the importance of oil to the British Empire and, early on, the Kriegsmarine identified enemy tankers as a high-priority target. Yet the Kriegsmarine made no special effort to attack oil delivery as a system during the first year of the war and only sank 10 per cent of the pre-war tanker fleet – which was quickly replaced. Random tanker sinkings were not going to deprive England of oil and even Dönitz's *Rudeltaktik* system, when instituted, was a recipe for tactical, not strategic, success. Deploying small numbers of U-Boats across wide swathes of ocean to search for convoys was like looking for needles in a haystack and too many convoys were never sighted. Driven by his *Tonnageschlacht* metric, Dönitz preferred to sink vessels based on their gross tonnage, not what they were carrying. U-Boat 'aces' were recognized by most tonnage sunk, not most valuable cargoes eliminated. In war, when killing and destruction are disassociated from logical end goals that could lead to victory, the activity becomes random and meaningless.

In fact, the British oil infrastructure was highly vulnerable to attack by the Kriegsmarine. In 1940, 40 per cent of Britain's oil came from the refineries on the Dutch island of Aruba, one refinery on Dutch-owned Curacao and one refinery on British-owned Trinidad.[77] Britain usually imported refined fuel products and small amounts of crude oil, since it only had a handful of domestic refineries. Indeed, most of the RAF Fighter Command's limited supply of 100-octane fuel came from Aruba.[78] RAF Fighter Command had only begun to receive small quantities of 100-octane fuel in July but it was so rare that only Spitfire units received 100-octane fuel at this time. Although tanker losses were not significant in the first nine months of the war, the need to convoy greatly increased the amount of time required to move tankers across the Atlantic; instead of going directly from the Caribbean to Liverpool as they had before the war, they now had to proceed to Halifax to form into convoys. Consequently, delays reduced British monthly fuel imports by 25 per cent in late 1940 – irrespective of German attacks. Britain did get a considerable amount of fuel from Iraq, Burma and the Dutch East Indies, but the transit times were even longer and efforts were made to reduce this dependence.[79]

Literally, it was Caribbean oil keeping Britain in the war.

On 23 September 1939, President Roosevelt announced a Maritime Security Zone in the Western Hemisphere and declared that the United States Navy would mount a Neutrality Patrol to report on the movement of ships belonging to belligerents out to 300 miles from shore. Two US Navy heavy cruisers and four destroyers were assigned to patrol the Eastern Caribbean, but the security zone did not include foreign possessions or colonies. In substance, the American Neutrality Patrol was not serious and German merchant shipping was able to slip through it to try to return home. However, it had an impact on Hitler's thinking and he directed Raeder not to conduct any operations in this zone in order to avoid antagonizing the United States. Thus, by a simple executive decision, Britain's oil supply from the Caribbean was declared off-limits to the Kriegsmarine.

Raeder continued to press Hitler to authorize attacks on Britain's distant oil network. With the capitulation of Holland, Britain sent small numbers of troops into Dutch Aruba and Curacao to protect the refineries. On 21 May, Raeder asked Hitler for permission to attack the oil refinery on Aruba, but Hitler curtly dismissed this idea for the time being with the off-hand remark that 'the oil centres belong to Standard Oil, which is an American corporation'.[80] On 11 July, Raeder informed Hitler that six *Hilfskreuzer* were at sea and that 'their crews might be used to effect the occupation of the [Allied] colonies'.[81] Throughout the autumn of 1940 and the spring of 1941, Raeder continued to bring up the need to mine Halifax and attack targets in the Caribbean and argued that since the United States was not really acting like a neutral, Germany should not respect its Maritime Exclusion Zone. Hitler deferred and did not change his mind until December 1941.

The refineries on Aruba, Curacao and Trinidad were virtually unprotected in September 1940. Britain rushed the 4th Battalion, Queen's Own Cameron Highlanders from Scotland to Aruba, but only 520 lightly armed territorial troops arrived by 3 September (one company was sent to Bermuda). In addition, Aruba was guarded by

GREAT BRITAIN UNDER SIEGE, SEPTEMBER 1940–MAY 1941

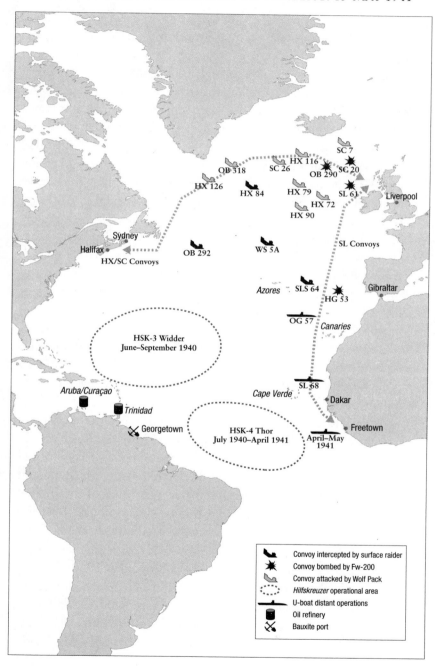

SC 7

HX 116

SC 26   OB 290   SC 20

OB 318

HX 126   HX 84   HX 79   SL 61

HX 72   Liverpool

HX 90

Sydney

Halifax   OB 292   WS 5A   SL Convoys

HX/SC Convoys

Azores   SLS 64   HG 53   Gibraltar

OG 57   Canaries

HSK-3 Widder
June–September 1940

Aruba/Curaçao   SL 68   Cape Verde   Dakar

Trinidad

Georgetown   HSK-4 Thor
July 1940–April 1941   Freetown

April–May
1941

	Convoy intercepted by surface raider
	Convoy bombed by Fw-200
	Convoy attacked by Wolf Pack
	Hilfskreuzer operational area
	U-boat distant operations
	Oil refinery
	Bauxite port

about 200 Dutch marines, a coastal battery with 7.5-inch guns and a few coastguard vessels. The large refineries on Trinidad and Curacao were only protected by small numbers of local militiamen. The Royal Navy had a single cruiser patrolling the entire Caribbean and a handful of obsolete aircraft in the area. The Santa Anna refinery on Curacao was particularly vulnerable since tankers had to transit through a narrow, 130-yard-wide channel known as the Shottegat to enter Willemstad harbour. The islands were not even under blackout, which would greatly aid an attacker at night. However, the Germans did nothing to interfere with the oil traffic until the United States entered the war. Then, on 17 January 1942, the Skl issued Operation Order No. 51 'West Indies', which authorized attacks on all three islands. Raeder emphasized that the refineries were the main targets and they were to be shelled. Operation *Neuland*, a joint effort by five German Type IX U-Boats and five Italian submarines, was set in motion and a coordinated attack against oil targets on Aruba and Curacao commenced on the night of 16 February 1942. Although a number of tankers were sunk or damaged, Dönitz disobeyed orders and told his U-Boat commanders to focus on torpedoing tankers instead of shelling the refineries. Nor was any effort made to mine the harbours. Thus, the Kriegsmarine targeting of Britain's oil lifeline proved to be too little and far too late.[82]

Despite Hitler's reluctance to risk antagonizing Roosevelt, the oil refineries were clearly located on belligerent territory and Raeder could have invested the effort to persuade Hitler that German attacks would not provoke a serious reaction from the United States. He also could have pointed out that the disruption of a large chunk of Britain's oil supplies, in conjunction with an invasion threat, could drive the British to consider a diplomatic solution. It is unlikely that Dönitz could have mounted an attack on the islands with his handful of Type IX U-Boats from Lorient before early September 1940. Nor is it likely that a U-Boat, equipped with a single 10.5cm deck gun, could inflict catastrophic damage on a large refinery. Mines could have disrupted tanker traffic for a few weeks, but thereafter the local defences would improve. However, several *Hilfskreuzer* were already operating off the South American coast by July 1940 and numerous German covert supply ships of the *Etappendienst* were able to sail across the Atlantic without detection, demonstrating that the Royal Navy was spread too thinly to stop disguised warships.

Germany had the potential in August 1940 to mount a decisive raid against the Dutch West Indies using converted merchant ships, sailing from French ports, disguised as Soviet freighters (a practice already in effect). Given that plenty of merchantmen were being modified for troop transport in *Seelöwe* as well as diversionary operations, the diversion of three to participate in a special operation of this importance was feasible. Three ships, each carrying 300 troops and landing boats, would have been sufficient to mount 'false-flag' raids against Aruba, Curacao and Trinidad, with the intent of capturing the refineries long enough for Pioniere troops to place explosive charges in the key facilities and destroy them. If the well heads could be damaged – as the Soviets did at the Maikop refinery in 1942 – the refineries could be rendered non-operational for six months or more. Afterwards, German raiding troops could either attempt to return home or seek internment in nearby neutral Colombia. Such a raid, even if only partially successful, could have cut off nearly half of Britain's oil supply for a period of many months and forced Britain to send precious military resources to defend the Caribbean. As it was, even without any German attacks on the West Indies, Britain was faced with serious oil shortages during the winter of 1940/41, and 'by the end of May 1941, oil stocks in the United Kingdom had fallen below the level that had been declared to be the absolute minimum for safety'.[83]

Likewise, Britain's supply of bauxite for aluminium production was also vulnerable to attack since all 302,000 tons imported came from British Guiana. Like the West Indies, British defences in Guiana were negligible.[84] As part of Operation *Neuland*, U-Boats attacked ore carriers coming from Guiana and sank a number carrying bauxite ore, but it was again far too late. German mining operations in the Caribbean in 1940–41 would have been far more productive than sinking random ships off Scotland.

As for attacks on food supplies, it was the British who actively tried to fire-bomb the German wheat crop in 1940 and experimented with aerial-delivered anthrax sub-munitions in 1942. Even if Germany had possessed a stockpile of biological agents to use to contaminate British food sources, Hitler was unlikely to authorize use due to fear of retaliation. Most of Britain's supply of meat came from Argentina and New Zealand, both of which required refrigerated merchant ships for trans-shipment. Greater efforts could have been made to single out these vessels, but the Kriegsmarine leadership was more interested in sinking large amounts of tonnage rather than the specific cargo they contained.

In sum, the Kriegsmarine had the resources to potentially do more to impair Britain's war effort in August to September 1940, but operations were not focused against the enemy's strategic centre of gravity. Instead, the Kriegsmarine was only inflicting random damage that did not cause any part of the British economy to collapse.

CHAPTER 5

Countdown to *Sea Lion*

Churchill's Bad Calls: Nellie, Z-Batteries, Apology, Menace

Throughout his career, Churchill was prone to making impulsive decisions about military affairs based on personal 'hunches', rather than on sober analysis. Sometimes Churchill's decisions were inspired, including his creation of the Landship Committee in 1915, which led to the development of the tank in the World War I. On some occasions, his decisions represented sound concepts but were undone by poor execution – Churchill's support for the expedition to Gallipoli in 1915 was the classic example of this type of decision-making. Churchill received considerable public opprobrium for the Gallipoli disaster and for other mistakes in his political career, but his decision-making as leader of Great Britain in the World War II has generally not been viewed too critically since the Allies achieved victory, as he predicted. However, Churchill did make a number of very poor military decisions in 1939–40 which seriously undermined the British war effort but most historians have ignored these decisions and chosen to focus on supporting the Battle of Britain mythology.

As First Lord of the Admiralty in 1915, Churchill supported the development of the tank, but he also became enamoured of motorized trench-digging machines to help break the trench stalemate. The tank was a good idea which worked, but Churchill's mechanical 'moles' were not and the scheme was eventually rejected. At the start of the World War II, Churchill was once again appointed First Lord of the Admiralty and he wasted no time resurrecting his 'mole' concept. With Churchill's full backing and £1 million from the Admiralty's research and development budget, a top secret programme was begun in October 1939 to develop a new motorized 'mole' to dig trenches across a 'No Man's Land' that did not exist. Although the Anglo-French had no plans to mount any offensives on the Western Front and thus his 'mole' did not meet any doctrinal or operational requirement, he did not care. A full-scale working model of the 'mole' was constructed by December 1939 and Churchill was impressed by its digging ability and managed to get more funding for the project. By this point, the 'mole' – which underwent many name changes to avoid revealing its purpose – emerged as a 130-ton tracked vehicle that was five times larger than a Matilda II, Britain's largest tank. In order to build the 240 'moles' envisioned by Churchill, British industry would need to supply 20,000 tons of steel and 200 Rolls-Royce Merlin engines. Churchill connived to get top priority for his top secret project and kept the British Army – which had not asked for the 'mole' – in the dark. The fact that the 'mole' project threatened to divert precious resources away from vital aircraft and tank production did not deter Churchill, nor did the rising cost of the project, which reached £8 million by March 1940.

Amazingly, Churchill maintained his commitment to the 'mole' project even after France capitulated and there was no Western Front. While he did concede to reducing the number of projected 'moles' from 240 to 33, he used his new position as prime minister to ensure that the project continued to receive a high priority. Throughout the period that German invasion threatened, considerable resources were being poured into perfecting a machine that served no useful military purpose. Engineers who could have been helping to advance the design of British tanks were wasted on the 'mole' effort. The British Army desperately needed anti-personnel mines (it had none), 3-inch mortars and more automatic weapons, not trench-digging machines. Finally, a prototype dubbed 'Nellie' was ready by May 1941 and Churchill approved production several months later. After all this effort, the 'mole' project produced just four machines in 1943, which were set aside and never used in combat.[1] Churchill failed to appreciate that the nature of warfare in the World War II was radically different from the World War I and that mechanized trench-digging machines were irrelevant. Yet Churchill's support for 'Nellie' was every bit as ridiculous as Hitler's love affair with gargantuan 100-ton tanks and just as inimical to the war effort.

Churchill backed other militarily questionable projects as well, such as anti-aircraft rockets (referred to as 'unrotated projectiles'), with his son-in-law Duncan Sandys and his science advisor Frederick Lindemann playing major roles.[2] By August 1940, a large percentage of Britain's cordite and steel was going into developing 'Z-batteries' of rockets to defend air bases and merchant shipping from German air attacks.[3] In short, the rockets were inaccurate and of negligible value and the effort would have been better placed on accelerating the development of night fighters and improved conventional anti-aircraft for ships, such as the reliable 20mm and 40mm guns. There were a number of things that the RAF and the Royal Navy desperately needed in September 1940, but rockets was not one of them. Churchill also allowed his friend Lord Beaverbrook, minister of aircraft production, to divert more resources towards the production of ad hoc armoured cars known as 'Beaverettes'. General Alan Brooke opposed the diversion of armour plate and weaponry to equip these silly vehicles instead of increasing tank production, but was ignored.[4]

Aside from his passion for every wild technical idea that came along, Churchill also made operational and strategic decisions based upon outdated imperialistic criteria, as if Great Britain was not in a life or death struggle with the Third Reich. As soon as Italy declared war on Great Britain and France capitulated in June 1940, Churchill oriented British strategy towards attacking the overseas colonies of both. In the Middle East, General Sir Archibald Wavell had 86,000 British and Commonwealth troops, including the 7th Armoured Division. Although Italy had over 200,000 troops in Libya and 150,000 in East Africa, additional reinforcements from Australia, India and South Africa were en route to Wavell and his forces were adequate to hold Egypt for some time. Yet when Italian forces invaded British Somaliland on 3 August and quickly overran the tiny British garrison, Churchill became apoplectic with Wavell since this was the first British colony that had been lost. Losing all perspective that British Somaliland was a small, backward colony of no great economic value, Churchill began pressing Wavell to switch from a defensive strategy to an offensive strategy in both Egypt and East Africa. Of course, an offensive strategy meant sending large reinforcements to Wavell.

On 13 August 1940, Churchill informed the Cabinet that 'now that we were so much stronger, he thought that we could spare an armoured brigade from this country'.[5] Given that the British Army was still recovering from Dunkirk and faced with invasion, Churchill's statement appears to fly in the face of any kind of military logic. General Dill opposed the idea, but Churchill simply ignored him. Consequently, three tank regiments – the 7th RTR equipped with Matilda IIs, the 2nd RTR equipped with A9/10/13 Cruiser tanks and the 3rd Hussars equipped with Mk VI light tanks – were designated for immediate transfer to the Middle East. In addition, 48 anti-tank guns and 48 25-pounder guns would go to reinforce Wavell. At Churchill's instigation, Operation *Apology* began a series of convoys from England, around the Cape of Good Hope, to reinforce Wavell's forces in the Middle East. The first vessel left Liverpool on 22 August 1940 and the main convoy (AP 3) left with the tanks and artillery on 10 September and arrived in Suez on 22 October. All these vital assets were sent away from England just as the threat of invasion was approaching its peak. Operation *Apology* gave Wavell the equipment to mount a powerful counteroffensive in December 1940 known as Operation *Compass*, which inflicted a severe defeat upon the Italian 10th Army.

Furthermore, the AP-series convoys were only the beginning, as Churchill began to send more units to support expeditionary warfare in Africa and the Mediterranean with little thought given to the possibility of enemy responses. Shortly after *Seelöwe* was postponed, Churchill decided to send the entire 2nd Armoured Division and two squadrons of Hurricane fighters to reinforce Wavell's command. While *Apology* led to a short-term victory in Libya, the addition of more forces only encouraged Churchill to recklessly send a 58,000-man expeditionary force to Greece in March 1941; this force was promptly defeated when the Germans invaded and it lost most of its equipment. Indeed, Churchill was dumbfounded when German forces appeared in Egypt, then Greece, then Crete, and swept Wavell's over-extended forces aside. Churchill's decision to send so much armour to the Middle East when the threat of the invasion of England was very real is rarely mentioned in Battle of Britain histories because it was highly reckless and decreased the ability of the British Army to defeat a German invasion should it occur.

However, in the catalogue of Churchill's poor decisions, his authorization of an expedition to occupy the port of Dakar in West Africa tops the list of frivolous objectives. Dakar was held by Vichy French forces and Churchill was keenly aware of the presence of the 35,000-ton battleship *Richelieu* sheltering there. As with Mers-el-Kébir, Churchill was obsessed with eliminating any potential French capital ships that could be used against the Royal Navy and used suspect intelligence to bolster his case that the Germans were interested in the *Richelieu*.[6] De Gaulle had convinced the War Cabinet that a landing at Dakar would be unopposed and that the colony would quickly rally to the Free French, but was wary of Churchill's intentions.[7] However, since Churchill held de Gaulle and his Free French in low regard, the idea of acquiring more Free French was no inducement.

Initially designated as Operation *Scipio* (later changed to *Catapult*), the War Cabinet approved the expedition to Dakar on 5 August.[8] Churchill pushed the Admiralty to commit substantial resources from the Home Fleet to Operation *Catapult*, despite the risk of German invasion. Forbes was ordered to detach the battleship HMS *Barham*, the cruisers *Fiji* and *Devonshire* and four destroyers from the Home Fleet to participate in Operation *Menace*, while Force H in Gibraltar was also ordered to contribute forces. Five battalions of Royal Marines, totalling 4,200 troops, were also committed to the operation, leaving just one battalion in England. It is particularly galling that while Churchill was telling Roosevelt about his dire need for destroyers to protect convoys and Great Britain, he could spare a dozen for the non-urgent Dakar operation.

On 30 August, HMS *Barham* led the squadron from Scapa Flow and proceeded to Gibraltar, where they linked up with the battleship HMS *Resolution*, the aircraft carrier HMS *Ark Royal* and seven more destroyers. Designated as Force M, this fleet sailed on 6 September, linked up with four heavy cruisers en route and then arrived off Dakar on 23 September. Due to the earlier British attack at Mers-el-Kébir, the French were not interested in parley and immediately opened fire on Force M. Operation *Menace* was a disaster. French resistance prevented a landing and the battleship *Resolution* was badly damaged by a torpedo hit. HMS *Barham* was hit three times and several of the accompanying cruisers were also damaged. British gunnery also proved very poor; the two battleships fired over 400 rounds in daylight against the stationary *Richelieu* and failed to achieve any hits, but *Richelieu* scored a 15-inch hit on the *Barham*. After three days of poor gunnery, the Royal Navy aborted Operation *Menace* and sailed away. Churchill had committed a large proportion of the Royal Navy's strength to a side-show operation of no particular strategic value at a time of great national peril; the 12 destroyers committed to Dakar would have been better employed protecting convoys against U-Boats or reinforcing the anti-invasion patrols. Likewise, the presence of two more battleships and five cruisers in home waters in September 1940 would have rendered *Seelöwe* completely unfeasible. Amazingly, the historiography of the World War II almost completely ignores Operation *Menace*, particularly books about the Battle of Britain or Operation *Sea Lion*. However, Operation *Menace* was a foolish decision that weakened Britain's defences at a crucial moment and it was only due to Hitler's ambivalence toward *Seelöwe* that Britain did not pay a higher price than two damaged battleships for this mistake.

Despite Churchill's rhetoric about Britain's defences growing stronger throughout the summer of 1940, he was in fact cavalierly weakening Britain's defences by sending strong air, ground and naval reinforcements to conduct colonial-style expeditionary warfare overseas. Britain needed to consolidate its forces in late 1940, focusing on defeating the U-Boat threat, the night bomber threat and securing its coastal defences, instead of diverting forces to secondary areas. Yet the essential factor was that Churchill preferred an offensive, peripheral strategy and was not particularly interested in fighting the Germans head-on. Instead, he sought opportunities to fight the Italians and Vichy French, a strategic imperative that led to a year-long campaign in East Africa in 1941, the invasion of Syria in June 1941 and Madagascar in May 1942, then the 'Soft Underbelly' concept in 1943. All of these operations dissipated British strength and contributed nothing to the defeat of the Third Reich, while later exasperating the American allies he had so eagerly courted.

Where and When Will the Enemy Strike?

Many accounts of the D-Day landings emphasize the German inability to determine where and when the Allies would land in France in 1944, particularly the over-emphasis on the obvious landing site at the Pas-de-Calais area instead of the beaches of Normandy. Actually, the British did not do much better in September 1940 in trying to determine where *Seelöwe* might attempt to land. Throughout 1940, much of the British political and military leadership was more focused on the threat to East Anglia than the southern coast of England. Some of this fixation was due to precedent; in the World War I Admiral Franz von Hipper's battlecruisers conducted three raids on the coast of North Yorkshire and Norfolk in 1914–16. When the World War II started, Britain's home defences were naturally focused on the threat from across the North Sea, not along the English Channel. Most of the defensive preparations in the first nine months of the war were on the east coast and the expenditure of resources in that quarter helped to maintain a certain inertia even after the fall of France. It was not until enemy amphibious shipping began massing in Channel ports in late August 1940 that perceptions began to change. However, the critical point is that neither Churchill, his cabinet nor the British General Staff knew exactly where the enemy intended to land so they had to spread their limited resources across a very large amount of coastline. Furthermore, due to this uncertainty, the British had to develop multiple contingency plans to counter different courses of action; multiple contingency plans often lead to hesitation at key moments – i.e., are we executing the correct contingency plan or is this an enemy feint?

General Edmund Ironside had set the tone for the British defence in late June, by distributing forces to cover all possible enemy contingencies, rather than the most likely. Ironside committed the British Army to a relatively passive defence, beginning with a thin 'crust' defence on the coast and a fortified 'GHQ' Line to prevent further exploitation inland. While Brooke began making changes when he took over as commander of Home Forces on 19 July, they were only implemented in a gradual fashion. By late September, the British still had a thin defence on the coastline, but Brooke managed to assemble a small mobile reserve under GHQ control. Fortification work on the GHQ Line and other fixed defences continued. Nor did Brooke change Ironside's dispositions much, leaving four infantry divisions to cover East Anglia and strong forces in northern England and Scotland. Indeed, only three of the 26 available infantry divisions were allocated to the south coast, where the Germans actually intended to strike.

British expectations of a German landing began in earnest in July, leading to invasion alerts and false alarms throughout the summer and culminating in the CROMWELL alert of 7 September. Churchill was bombarded with rumours about enemy intentions, as well as a false alarm from President Roosevelt. On 8 September, Alan Brooke noted in his diary, 'everything pointing to Kent and East Anglia as the two main threatened points' – which indicated that he still regarded a landing attempt on the east coast as a distinct possibility.[9] Throughout the summer, the RAF and Royal Navy repeatedly sighted German barges and transports moving along the coast, which exacerbated invasion jitters. The British did know that the Germans had to invade by the end of September if they wanted to make an attempt in 1940, but that did not help much. By the time that Hitler was poised to decide on *Seelöwe*, the British military had been on high anti-invasion alert for weeks, which meant that their senses were becoming increasingly dulled. This is what happened to the Germans in 1944 – increasingly dulled by years of watching for Allied landings, they failed to properly evaluate the indicators that pointed to Normandy in June.

Nor were the British all that certain how a German invasion might be conducted. Churchill and others believed that the Germans would employ chemical weapons. The Admiralty thought that the Kriegsmarine had more warships available than it actually had and that the Germans might even use liners or fast merchantmen to land a force with little or no warning. Above all else, the British leadership was worried about enemy airborne landings and *coup de main* operations like the capture of Fort Eben Emael in Belgium. *Fall Gelb* had shocked the conservative senior British military leadership and, as a result, they tended to ascribe far greater power to *Sea Lion* than it merited. Due to the paranoid fear of German airborne landings, the British Army and Home Guard tried to defend too many points inland, rather than committing more forces to holding the coast.

In short, despite fairly good intelligence support the British senior leadership was unable to determine the enemy's most likely course of action, which would have seriously undermined their ability to effectively employ their anti-invasion capabilities, particularly in the opening stages of *Seelöwe*. British generals believed that East Anglia was 'good tank country' and, from that limited perspective, this represented the most dangerous enemy course of action. In contrast, the southern coast favoured the defence, so it was regarded as less vulnerable. On top of this, residual concerns about a German landing in Ireland kept substantial forces oriented westward, even though a landing in this area was well beyond German amphibious capabilities.

CHAPTER 6

British Anti-invasion Capabilities, 1940–41

Having attempted to outline every capability that the Third Reich could bring to bear against Britain in September 1940, it is now necessary to enumerate Britain's corresponding defensive capabilities. Churchill's War Cabinet discussed many possible last-ditch defensive options against invasion, including the use of flaming oil on the sea and the use of mustard gas; these ideas were ill considered at best, but provided much fodder for post-war writers. Far less attention has been given to Britain's actual military defences and how they were likely to be used to contest an invasion in September 1940. Indeed, except for Fighter Command, the status of Britain's defences in September 1940 has received scant attention in existing historiography.

The Royal Air Force

If Germany mounted *Seelöwe*, Britain's first line of defence would be

RAF Coastal Command, which was tasked with conducting maritime reconnaissance and anti-invasion strikes. In mid-September 1940, Coastal Command's No. 16 Group was primarily responsible for detecting the embarkation and departure of the invasion armada, then attacking it before it made landfall. At this point, it is important to note the difference between reconnaissance and surveillance: the first provides a brief snapshot of enemy activity, whereas the latter involves prolonged observation of a target. The first indication that the Germans were preparing to execute *Seelöwe* would likely come when No. 15 Group's Spitfire PRs photographed the invasion ports and loading activity was detected. However, this reconnaissance would only provide a glimpse of German loading activity, which could begin up to a week before the actual invasion commenced. Surveillance was the responsibility of No. 16 Group, which had just one patrol squadron, No. 206, equipped with 16 American-made Lockheed Hudson aircraft; this unit made regular patrols over the English Channel and was the most likely to spot the initial moves of an enemy invasion. In September, No. 206 Squadron flew one sortie per day, usually at dusk, to watch German activity near Cherbourg, Calais and Rotterdam; these sorties were designated 'Hatch', 'Dundee' and 'Hookos'. In addition, two nightly surveillance patrols known as 'Moon 1' and 'Moon 2' were flown in mid-Channel.[1] These were risky reconnaissance operations and losses were common.[2] However, since the Kriegsmarine intended to begin moving its invasion convoys out of their embarkation harbours during the afternoon of S-Tag minus 1, the invasion would actually be under way for a period of about six hours before Coastal Command was likely to spot it. It is also important to note that the bulk of Coastal Command's surveillance activity, over 30 sorties per day, was focused on watching the North Sea approaches, whereas only eight sorties were watching the English Channel.

Once loading preparations were detected, both RAF Coastal Command and Bomber Command would be alerted to begin bombing the embarkation ports. In July, the Air Ministry ordered Bomber Command to cooperate with Coastal Command in attacking enemy shipping in the ports, but initially the effort was half hearted; during July and August 1940 Bomber Command dropped only 66 tons of bombs on the ports (just 3 per cent of its total tonnage dropped for this period) and Coastal Command dropped less than 50 tons.[3] In September, once large numbers of barges were detected in the Channel ports, Bomber Command stepped up its efforts and dropped over 1,000 tons of bombs on these targets. Raids varied in size from ten up to 120 aircraft and although the effort was spread across eight ports, significant damage was inflicted. Between 15 and 21 September, Antwerp, Dunkirk and Le Havre were particularly hard hit. German defences against night raids were still rudimentary so British losses were just ten aircraft. Over a period of a week, Bomber Command was able to sink one torpedo boat, 12 transports, four tugs and 51 barges, which forced the Kriegsmarine to begin dispersing the invasion fleet in coastal waterways.[4] Against stationary invasion barges, tightly packed into ports, Bomber Command could inflict significant losses.

Once *Seelöwe* commenced, Luftflotte 2 and 3 would deploy large combat air patrols over each of the embarkation harbours to deny British reconnaissance patrols (between 23 and 26 September). Assuming that the No. 206 Squadron dusk patrols detected the emergence of convoys from the embarkation ports, it would probably be too late to launch substantial strikes against the enemy shipping in the Channel before the sun set at 1904 hours. Once the enemy was at sea, Bomber Command's level-bombers would have been of negligible value and the anti-invasion effort would have rested squarely upon the obsolescent Fairey Battles of No. 1 Group (six squadrons with about 90 Battles) and the Blenheim light bombers of Air Vice-Marshal Sir James Robb's No. 2 Group (11 squadrons with about 160 Blenheims). Both aircraft had already proven highly vulnerable to enemy fighter interception during the French campaign and their losses in battles over the Channel could easily reach 30–50 per cent. Neither aircraft was suited to strafing attacks since they carried only a single wing-mounted .303 calibre machine gun, and their bomb load, usually four 250-pound bombs, had to be delivered from altitudes under 110 yards to have any chance of hitting targets. German

Flak gunners on the convoys would have little problem hitting these slow bombers. Given that both Groups No. 1 and No. 2 were dispersed across nine different bases in Great Britain, the probability of Bomber Command mounting well coordinated multi-squadron attacks was very low and the Germans would probably be able to deal with sporadic squadron-size attacks before the sun set. Robb opposed sending his Blenheims on high-risk unescorted strikes and would be relieved four months later due to this issue. Yet once night fell on the eve of S-Tag, the invasion convoys would have been safe from air attack until the landing began the next morning at 0630 hours.

At dawn the next day, Coastal Command's No. 16 Group would likely mount anti-shipping strikes with its three Blenheim light bomber squadrons and three torpedo-bomber squadrons. As with Bomber Command, Coastal Command's aircraft would be condemned to daylight, low-level attacks into the teeth of enemy fighters and Flak. British torpedo bombers were best suited to attacking larger German transport ships rather than shallow-draft barges. Later experience gleaned from RAF efforts to stop the German 'Channel Dash' (Operation *Cerberus*) on 12 February 1942 demonstrates that Coastal Command was unprepared to mount large-scale anti-shipping attacks at a moment's notice and the attack they did conduct off Calais lost all six of six torpedo bombers committed without scoring a hit. Likewise, Bomber Command made 398 sorties against the German fleet and lost 17 bombers to enemy fighters without achieving anything.[5] The RAF's response to Operation *Cerberus* in 1942 indicated inadequate coordination between Fighter Command, Coastal Command and Bomber Command, which was likely to have been even more problematic in 1940. Thus, Coastal Command would likely have spotted the invasion convoys assembling and leaving port late on S-Tag minus 1, but it was unlikely to inflict significant damage upon them during the transit phase. Once Coastal Command began to attack enemy shipping on S-Tag, RAF losses of bombers were likely to be very heavy.

After the fact, Air Chief Marshal Sir Hugh Dowding aptly summed up RAF Fighter Command's mission by saying, 'mine was the purely defensive role of trying to stop the possibility of an invasion, and thus give this country a breathing spell ... it was Germany's objective to win the war by invasion, and it was my job to prevent such an invasion from taking place.' In mid-September 1940, Dowding had 19 fighter squadrons equipped with Spitfire Mk I and Mk II fighters and 31 fighter squadrons equipped with Hurricane fighters. Nine of these fighter squadrons were deployed with No. 13 Group in northern England and not immediately in range of the invasion area. During the period of 1 July to 23 September, Dowding lost a total of 576 fighters and 337 pilots in combat, yet on the morning of 24 September he still had 613 operational fighters (233 Spitfire and 380 Hurricane) and over 1,509 pilots.[6] Fighter Command was capable of generating up to 1,000 sorties per day in a surge effort or 500–600 sorties per day for a week. New construction during the same period totalled over 1,100 fighters, so Fighter Command could claim that it was getting stronger despite the Luftwaffe's onslaught. Although many RAF fighter bases had been bombed and five had been badly knocked about, the radar-based GCI system was still effective and Dowding had enough fighters left to contest most German daylight raids into British airspace. Indeed, Dowding's 50 fighter squadrons were the main factor preventing the Luftwaffe from achieving air superiority over southern England. Yet despite all these positive factors, Dowding's fighter squadrons would be of little use in defeating *Seelöwe* if it began.

Table 10. RAF Fighter Command Losses, 1 July–23 September 1940

Period	Spitfire Losses	Hurricane Losses	Total Fighter Losses	Fighter Pilots KIA/MIA
1–31 July 1940	33	47	80	74
1–31 August 1940	126	196	322	148
1–23 September 1940	57	117	174	115
TOTAL	**216**	**360**	**576**	**337**

On 14 September, the Air Ministry issued a memorandum to Fighter Command detailing its responsibilities in the event of enemy invasion. Whereas Fighter Command had heretofore only been responsible for daylight interception of enemy aircraft over Britain, the memorandum spelled out three primary missions: (1) providing air cover for Royal Navy units operating in the invasion area, (2) intercepting enemy airborne transports, and (3) providing escorts for Coastal Command and Bomber Command aircraft attacking the enemy invasion forces.[7] All of these missions implied operating over the Channel, where British pilot losses would increase dramatically and the short-ranged Bf-109s would not be at such a disadvantage as when operating near London. In pure fighter vs. fighter combat, the RAF's dog-fighting tactics were still inferior, leading to a slightly inferior kill ratio in favour of the Bf-109s.[8]

Indeed, rather than risking expensive battles of attrition over the Channel, Dowding decided that his fighters would not try to escort friendly strike aircraft all the way to target but only cover their assembly in British airspace and their return leg. Furthermore, Dowding's fighters would have to split their efforts across three missions and, instead of acting alone, they would now have to coordinate with the Royal Navy and other parts of the RAF – this had not been rehearsed. During the Norwegian campaign, the RAF had failed to protect Royal Navy warships off Norway and they would fail again in the Mediterranean in 1941. At Dunkirk, Fighter Command did provide some measure of air cover to shipping, but at a high cost. In the anti-invasion scenario, finding the right naval units at the right moment would be a serious challenge for Fighter Command. On 22 September, three Hurricanes from No. 85 Squadron on coastal patrol became disoriented due to heavy cloud cover and were forced to crash-land after exhausting their fuel. Dowding's pilots were simply not trained to navigate over water in variable weather and find vessels at sea and even if they could, limited endurance of his fighters meant that maintaining continuous air cover for warships in the Channel would require a large number of sorties. Just maintaining a single flight of six

Hurricanes over a destroyer squadron throughout S-Tag (over 13 hours of daylight) would require over 75 sorties. Maintaining a minimum level of air cover for two or more Royal Navy anti-invasion flotillas would require in the neighborhood of 150–200 sorties, or about 20 per cent of Dowding's daily sortie rate.

It is also important to note that while Fighter Command was keeping its numbers up, its pilot quality was steadily dropping, which would impact its ability to conduct complex missions over water. In order to keep up with pilot attrition, the RAF had been forced to reduce pilot training in June 1940 to just four weeks and omit training in aerial gunnery and navigation, which meant that many replacements appearing in August to September were essentially still novice pilots and completely unprepared to dogfight with enemy aircraft.[9] Heavy losses of Spitfires and Hurricanes in combat also meant that very few were available for training units, so most replacements had 15 hours or less in a Hurricane or Spitfire before they were assigned to an operational squadron (against new Bf-109 pilots who typically had at least 250 hours of flying experience). Although RAF Fighter Command would still have over 600 fighters operational at the start of *Seelöwe*, it was not in a position to engage in a protracted battle for air superiority over the Channel, raid enemy bases in France or provide the Royal Navy with extended air cover at sea. Thus, RAF Fighter Command in September 1940 was essentially a one-trick pony: very good at daylight GCI defensive tactics, but very little else.

Intercepting an enemy airborne landing would also be difficult. Based upon German experience in Holland and the available information on *Seelöwe*, the German airborne landings were expected to begin shortly after dawn, between 0600 and 0700 hours. Since the Luftwaffe typically did not mount large operations over England prior to 0930 hours during August and September, Fighter Command did not launch significant multi-squadron scrambles until the enemy's intentions were clear. The Luftwaffe did send large fighter groups across the Channel in the morning, which Fighter Command usually ignored as diversionary activity. Chain Home stations could detect enemy formations, but they could not tell the difference between aircraft types, so Fighter Command would have difficulty identifying that an airborne landing was in progress until it was spotted by the Observer Corps. Thus, a fighter sweep at dawn, followed by the first wave of Ju-52 transports, was not likely to provoke a large-scale response from Fighter Command. Rather than one single mass formation, the Luftwaffe Ju-52 transports would arrive in groups of 12 to 50 transports, spread out by time and distance. Unlike German bomber formations, the transport groups would not penetrate further than 5 miles into British airspace before dropping their loads, and they would fly at under 1,000 feet. German fighter escorts would be positioned well above them, looking out for the RAF. The Ju-52 transports would spend less than five minutes over England, so the first paratroopers would probably be jumping before the British fighters even arrived. Instead, Fighter Command would end up attacking the follow-on transport units and transports that were already on their return leg. Since the Ju-52s would drop their paratroops from low altitude, RAF Fighters would have to descend to a very low level to attack them, which would risk being 'bounced' by the Bf-109 escorts. In short, Fighter Command could intercept and destroy some of the Ju-52 transports, but not quickly enough to stop the airborne landing.

In short, the outlook for the RAF to stop *Seelöwe* in its tracks was negligible even under favourable conditions. Coastal Command could sink some shipping and Fighter Command could shoot down some transports, but the numbers were likely to be too small to stop a large-scale invasion. With some cloudy weather or mist thrown into the equation, the RAF's ability to interfere with *Seelöwe* may have been significantly less. However, the RAF would have much better chances to inflict damage upon the enemy once they arrived in their landing areas, where naval transports would be anchored offshore and barges would be beached – then bombers would have a fixed target that could be hit and strikes properly coordinated. Fighter Command would also likely do better shooting down the Luftwaffe's close air support aircraft attempting to eliminate beach defences, than frittering away its strength engaging in battles over the Channel. If the RAF had the discipline to hold back its main strength until after the invasion began, it would be better prepared to affect the long-term battle than launching a series of hasty, uncoordinated attacks at the outset.

The Royal Navy

Of all the misconceptions about *Seelöwe*, the ability and willingness of the Royal Navy to defeat an invasion attempt are often the most egregious. Typically, post-war histories have touted the overall strength of the Royal Navy as justification for claims that *Seelöwe* was doomed to failure and suggested that the Royal Navy would 'throw everything it had' at the enemy invasion fleet, but failed to make the effort to delve into the actual details required to intercept and destroy the invasion flotillas. Instead, assumption has often substituted for analysis. In the 1974 Sandhurst exercise simulating *Seelöwe*, it was assessed that the RAF and Royal Navy destroyed 25 per cent of the German invasion armada on S-Tag at the cost of three cruisers and three destroyers sunk. According to that exercise, by S-Tag plus 1 the Royal Navy committed 17 cruisers and 57 destroyers into the Channel battle and Mountbatten's 5th Destroyer Flotilla annihilated the German second wave, sinking 65 per cent of the barges.[10]

As S-Tag approached in late September 1940, only five of the Royal Navy's 14 capital ships were operational in home water; the rest were deployed overseas. Furthermore, Admiral Sir Charles Forbes, commander of the Home Fleet, was very wary of risking his capital ships in the English Channel where they could be bombed by the Luftwaffe and was content to rely primarily upon destroyers and light craft, supported by a few cruisers, to oppose any invasion. Forbes said that as long as the RAF was undefeated, the primary defence against invasion should be left to them and the army.[11] However on 13 September, the Admiralty informed Forbes that an enemy invasion was imminent and faulty intelligence suggested that the new battleship *Bismarck* and possibly the *Scharnhorst* or *Gneisenau* might participate in the effort – this may have been due to the German *Herbstreise* deception efforts. Forbes was directed to send a battlegroup consisting of HMS *Nelson* and *Hood* to Rosyth, where they could intervene if enemy capital ships appeared in the North Sea. The Admiralty also wanted the battleship HMS *Revenge* sent to Portsmouth to cover the south coast of England; this was the only British capital ship in a position to intervene against the first wave of a German invasion. Forbes complied only with the greatest reluctance and only after a direct order from Churchill. Thus, in terms of capital ships, the Royal Navy could only expect to employ a single elderly battleship against the first wave of a German invasion. Rosyth was 375 nautical miles from the actual German invasion areas (18–20 hours' sailing time for HMS *Nelson*) and Scapa Flow was 525 nautical miles distant (26–28 hours), but Forbes had no intention to risk sending them through the narrow Strait of Dover. Indeed, no British battleship sailed through the Strait of Dover until June 1944, by which time the Luftwaffe was no longer a threat to shipping. With Forbes' cautious mindset, the bulk of the Royal Navy's capital ships would have sat out the first phase of *Seelöwe*, leaving anti-invasion duties to less valuable warships.

Table 11: The Royal Navy's Operational Warships, 25 September 1940

Type	In Home Waters	Gibraltar	Mediterranean	Other Overseas Stations	TOTAL
Battleships	3		4	3	**10**
Battlecruisers	2	1			**3**
Aircraft Carriers	2	1	2	1	**6**
Heavy Cruisers	2		2	7	**11**
Light Cruisers	14		6	21	**41**
Destroyers	89	10	13	22	**134**
Destroyer-Escorts	7				**7**
Submarines	26		20		**46**

ROYAL NAVY DISPOSITIONS, 25 SEPTEMBER 1940

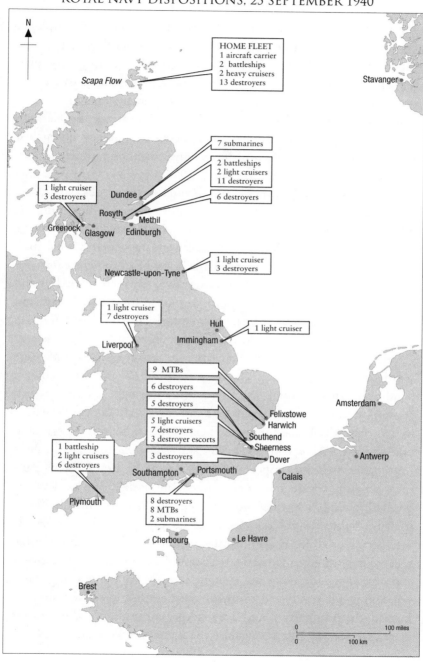

N

HOME FLEET
1 aircraft carrier
2 battleships
2 heavy cruisers
13 destroyers

Scapa Flow

Stavanger

7 submarines

2 battleships
2 light cruisers
11 destroyers

6 destroyers

1 light cruiser
3 destroyers

Dundee

Rosyth

Greenock   Methil

Glasgow   Edinburgh

1 light cruiser
3 destroyers

Newcastle-upon-Tyne

1 light cruiser
7 destroyers

Hull

1 light cruiser

Liverpool   Immingham

9 MTBs

6 destroyers

5 destroyers

Amsterdam

5 light cruisers
7 destroyers
3 destroyer escorts

Felixstowe
Harwich

Southend

1 battleship
2 light cruisers
6 destroyers

3 destroyers

Sheerness

Antwerp

Dover

Southampton   Portsmouth   Calais

Plymouth

8 destroyers
8 MTBs
2 submarines

Cherbourg   Le Havre

Brest

0   100 miles

0   100 km

Even without its capital ships, the Royal Navy could still employ a large force of cruisers and destroyers in the English Channel against the invasion fleets. The Admiralty developed a contingency plan known as 'Purge', which intended to use cruisers and destroyers to defeat the enemy invasion fleet. In his punchy analysis, Derek Robinson suggested that the Royal Navy could attack the German invasion fleets with four cruisers and 40 destroyers, split evenly against the east and west flanks of the enemy's invasion armada.[12] Leo McKinstry claimed that there were 70 destroyers in the Channel area.[13] In reality, in between Plymouth and the Thames Estuary (Nore Command), the Royal Navy had one battleship, seven light cruisers, 32 destroyers, six destroyer-escorts and 17 MTBs available to intervene against the first wave of *Seelöwe*. The Luftwaffe had scored a substantial but unrecognized victory by forcing the Royal Navy to reduce its naval forces at Dover to just one to three destroyers, which rotated in and out from Sheerness or Portsmouth. Yet aside from two J-class and three I-class destroyers, the threat of air attack caused the Admiralty to keep most of its modern destroyers at Scapa Flow and Rosyth. Instead, the majority of the destroyers assigned to anti-invasion duties were obsolescent V&W types, left over from 1918 and in mediocre condition. The situation was better with the light cruisers, which comprised three modern Town-class and two Arethusa-class vessels, as well as one older E-class and one C-class cruiser; the three Town-class cruisers (HMS *Manchester*, *Newcastle* and *Southampton*) were the most formidable. It is also important to note that the Royal Navy's anti-invasion forces were not concentrated but rather dispersed across seven different bases, which would make coordination difficult. Nor is it likely that the Royal Navy would execute Operation *Purge* as a single mass sortie of all its available anti-invasion forces based upon initial sighting reports from Coastal Command. Sending multiple destroyer and cruiser squadrons to sea at night to converge upon a single area was asking for trouble in terms of misidentification and fratricide. Instead, the Admiralty would likely keep some cruisers and destroyers in reserve for later strikes against the enemy's follow-on waves and much of the Nore Command was still focused on blocking any potential landings on the east coast from Norway.

During the period August to October 1940 there were a number of invasion alerts – often based upon sighting of German coastal traffic moving to the Channel embarkation ports – which caused the Royal Navy to conduct anti-invasion sorties. In such cases, Nore Command would send out a single squadron of five or six destroyers, supported by one or two light cruisers, to sweep the North Sea down to the Dutch coast. Due to the loss of HMS *Esk* and *Ivanhoe* to enemy mines on 31 August, Nore Command was unlikely to send a large force of destroyers close to enemy shores based on a single RAF surveillance report; too often destroyers had been sent charging after enemy sightings and found nothing. Given that the Admiralty was unlikely to receive solid reporting on German convoy movements until after dusk on S-Tag minus 1 and the destroyer squadrons were on two-hour alert, Nore Command would likely be capable of sending out a single destroyer squadron by about 2100 hours and contact with the enemy could be expected after 2300 hours. Under these circumstances, a destroyer squadron from Sheerness might encounter the tail-end of the German Invasion Fleet B just north-west of Calais around midnight. In order to get at Transport Fleet B, the British destroyers would have to risk crossing through the four CAESAR minefields (totalling 1,295 EMC/EMD mines) south-east of Dover, which the Kriegsmarine was expected to emplace in the week prior to S-Tag to block Nore Command's destroyers.[14] In the immediate area of the Strait of Dover, Dover Command would sortie its three destroyers and a flotilla of MTBs; these warships had the best chance of intercepting the vanguard of Invasion Fleet B after dusk and posed the greatest threat to this convoy.

Portsmouth Command would have to counter the enemy Invasion Fleets C, D and E on its own. Again, the normal practice for coastal sweeps was to send out a destroyer squadron from Portsmouth, but the light cruisers were based at Plymouth and HMS *Revenge* would have been kept back until the enemy invasion beaches were determined.

It is likely that the Luftwaffe would conduct additional raids against Dover, Portsmouth and Sheerness on S-Tag minus 1 in order to disrupt the Royal Navy's anti-invasion forces, which could somewhat impair the British response. Given the expectation that the Kriegsmarine would lay protective mine barrages to protect the flanks of the invasion convoys, Portsmouth Command developed Operation *J.E.* to use its minesweeper squadrons to identify new minefields in the Channel area instead of just blindly sailing at full speed towards the enemy. Thus, a sober assessment of the Royal Navy's ability to intercept the first wave of *Seelöwe* is that Nore and Dover Commands would try to intercept Invasion Fleet B south/south-east of Dover with one or two light cruisers and up to eight destroyers, while Portsmouth Command would initially sortie five destroyers (two B-class, one H-class, two V&W-class) against Invasion Fleets D or E. A follow-on force of one or two light cruisers and five destroyers from Plymouth may also have been sortied on the first night or kept in reserve until the German situation was clarified. In sum, on the eve of S-Tag the Royal Navy had the resources to intercept two of the four German invasion fleets with four small surface action groups, totalling two to four light cruisers and 13 to 18 destroyers.

Yet aside from the numbers, the odds of German convoys being successfully intercepted by British surface action groups was far from a foregone conclusion. In order to reduce the risk of losing warships to Luftwaffe attacks, the Royal Navy would almost certainly opt to conduct interceptions at night, but since few cruisers and no destroyers had radar as yet, finding vital targets in the dark and successfully attacking them would not be easy. Experience during the World War II indicates that, without radar, most night surface actions began at a range of 5–7,000 yards. On the night of 24/25 September, visibility in the English Channel was likely to be well under 5,000 yards. Under these conditions, medium-calibre naval guns typically have a 1 per cent or less hit probability; so for a destroyer equipped with a maximum of 600 rounds, this equates to six hits. While a single hit might sink a barge or tug, the larger transports could easily require ten hits or more to sink. In fact, the British destroyers of mid-1940 were poorly armed for night surface action; most had either four or five BL 4.7-inch (120mm) guns in open, single mounts or four 4-inch (102mm) Mk V guns; these could fire High Explosive (HE), Semi-Armour Piercing (SAP), Shrapnel or illumination rounds. Both guns used separate loading ammunition, which greatly reduced their rate of fire, and neither type had ammunition hoists. While the HE rounds would be useful against barges and transports, the SAP rounds were poorly suited due to their small bursting charges.[15] Obviously, shooting barges and transports with slow-firing, medium-calibre guns was not a good approach but the Royal Navy had little alternative, since virtually none of its destroyers were yet armed with 20mm and 40mm dual-purpose guns; these weapons did not appear in quantity until 1942.[16] The existing 2-pounder 'pom-pom' anti-aircraft guns were poorly suited for surface engagements. Destroyers could use their 21-inch torpedoes (four to six tubes per destroyer), but these happened to be in very short supply at the time and were unlikely to hit shallow-draft barges or the multitude of small craft. As for the light cruisers, they would probably be used to neutralize enemy escorts, but 6-inch guns were not much use against fast S-Boats.[17] Without radar, British destroyers would have to illuminate targets with star shells or searchlights. Since it was highly likely that the German convoy escorts would lay smokescreens to protect the transports, visibility in a night surface action would quickly deteriorate to point-blank range.

Another factor which was bound to reduce the impact of any British intervention would be the likelihood that the German invasion flotillas would become spread out as they crossed the Channel in the darkness; there would be no massed target for destruction, but rather a multitude of dispersed targets. Once under attack, invasion convoys would disperse even further. Derek Robinson suggested that British destroyers could simply swamp invasion barges with their bow waves, but this unrealistic tactic was unlikely since the British cruisers and destroyers would be forced to close in to point-blank range where the multitude of German defensive weapons would be more potent.

Contrary to the stereotypical notion of unarmed, unescorted barges crowded with helpless German troops, many of the barges and transports were armed with an assortment of 2cm and 3.7cm Flak guns whose high rate of fire could easily have raked the bridge and open gun mounts of any British destroyers that came too close. The larger transports were armed with 7.5cm and 10.5cm field guns. Furthermore, the invasion convoys would be escorted by far more substantial Kriegsmarine assets than is commonly understood. In addition to destroyers, torpedo boats and S-Boats, the Kriegsmarine was committing the bulk of its coastal forces to support *Seelöwe*, including about 20 M-35 minesweepers, 30–40 R-Boats (*Räumboote*, auxiliary minesweepers) and several dozen VP (*Vorposten*) auxiliary escorts. The 680-ton M-35-class minesweepers, which the British dubbed 'Channel destroyers', were well armed with two 10.5cm guns, two 3.7cm Flak and two 2cm Flak; at night they might easily be mistaken for destroyers. The R-Boats, although not equipped with torpedoes, did have two 2cm guns and were capable of 21–23 knots. Taken together, these light escorts had the numbers and firepower to prevent any intercepting British destroyers from focusing solely on the destruction of the invasion transports. Thus, given the forces and tactics employed by both sides, it is unlikely that any British intercept attempts could have destroyed more than small elements of the German invasion forces during the transit phase.

Later experience points to the inherent difficulties of the intercept scenario. The Royal Navy succeeded in intercepting German convoys several times during 1940–41 with less than spectacular results. On the night of 10/11 September 1940, the British destroyers HMS *Malcolm*, *Veteran* and *Wild Swan* intercepted a German coastal convoy off Ostend; they succeeded in sinking one VP boat and two trawlers towing a barge, but the rest escaped. On the night of 13/14 October 1940, Captain Philip Vian – certainly one of the Royal Navy's most aggressive front-line leaders – led four British Tribal-class destroyers to raid enemy shipping off the Norwegian coast. Vian encountered a German convoy consisting of four small freighters, escorted by three auxiliary minesweepers. HMS *Cossack* torpedoed and sank one freighter, while HMS *Ashanti* and *Maori* damaged another freighter and an escort with gunfire. Yet despite the disparity in firepower and speed, most of the convoy escaped Vian's destroyers.[18]

Seven months later, the Royal Navy's Mediterranean Fleet was tasked with intercepting German convoys attempting to reach Crete. Although some conditions were different, the fundamental problems of interception remained the same. On the night of 21/22 May 1941, Force D (three light cruisers and four destroyers) intercepted the German 1st Motor Sailing Flotilla (21 small steamers, trawlers and fishing boats) off Cape Spatha on the north-west tip of Crete. The convoy, which was crawling at a speed of just 2–3 knots, was carrying 2,331 troops from the 5. Gebirgs-Division and its only escort was the Italian torpedo boat *Lupo* (armed with three 100mm guns). Due to low clouds and limited illumination from the moon, visibility was limited to 2–4,000 yards. At 2229 hours, a British destroyer spotted the *Lupo* and its convoy; a brisk action ensued and the *Lupo* was hit 18 times, but only three shells exploded. The *Lupo* managed to rake the cruiser HMS *Dido* with 20mm fire at close range, inflicting 11 casualties. Despite suffering 28 casualties, the *Lupo* succeeded in breaking away at high speed. Force D then proceeded to sail into the midst of the convoy and spent two hours shooting it up. Yet even against a now undefended and slow-moving convoy, these seven British warships were only able to sink eight of 21 vessels before retiring. German troops on one transport noted that many of the British shells were fired too high, passing overhead. About 800 German troops went into the water but the damaged *Lupo* returned and saved all but 324. Just six hours after the action, the Royal Navy's Force C (four light cruisers and three destroyers) intercepted the German 2nd Motor Sailing Flotilla (30 small steamers and trawlers), which was carrying 4,000 troops, north of Crete. The convoy was escorted by the Italian torpedo boat *Sagittario*, which moved to delay the approaching British flotilla. Despite the lop-sided odds, *Sagittario* laid a smokescreen which concealed the convoy and boldly attacked the closest British destroyer, HMS *Kingston*. The *Kingston* was hit twice but British gunnery was very poor and both *Sagittario* and the convoy escaped northward. Force C contented itself with sinking two stragglers then retired due to the threat of enemy air attack.[19] These surface actions off Ostend and Crete do not reveal any ability by British cruiser-destroyer surface action groups to inflict massive casualties on enemy coastal shipping, even when the odds were dramatically in their favour.

Rather than surface interception, British minefields posed a far greater threat to the German first wave convoys since they could not be swept in advance without alerting the enemy. The Dover barrage, consisting of over 9,000 moored contact mines west of Folkestone, would almost certainly have inflicted casualties upon Invasion Fleets B and C. Although German minesweepers could clear a few corridors through the barrage, it would have been virtually impossible to manoeuvre unwieldy transports and barges through them in the dark. Consequently, a significant number of vessels in the first wave would be sunk or damaged by British mines, although this would effectively 'sweep' the approach corridors and reduce the threat to follow-on waves.

While the Royal Navy's destroyers would likely have difficulty interfering with *Seelöwe*'s opening moves, the same cannot be said for the following days and nights. Once the German invasion beaches were identified, the Royal Navy would commit its real strength to destroy the barges and transports anchored offshore and to interdict the German naval line of communications across the Channel. Inevitably, this would become a battle of attrition – not unlike the naval battles off Guadalcanal in 1942–43 – and victory would not be determined in a single night. The main British trump card – the battleship HMS *Revenge* and the remaining cruisers and destroyers from Portsmouth Command – would have to gain control of the sea against Bey's destroyers, a large force of torpedo boats, S-Boats and small craft. Although the Sandhurst study of 1974 made this seem a straightforward task, it would be just as difficult and frustrating for the Royal Navy to accomplish as it was for the Luftwaffe to achieve air superiority over England. In the face of incessant German air attacks, the weakness of British shipboard anti-aircraft defences suggests that the Royal Navy's surface warships in September 1940 could only achieve sea control in the Channel for brief periods of time, but could not permanently sever the invasion force's lines of communication. Simply put, the Royal Navy was capable of mounting 'Thunder Runs' through the Channel, shooting up assorted German shipping, but their warships could not remain there in daylight for very long. Consequently, the Germans were bound to shift most of their follow-on shipping to small convoys in daylight, with Luftwaffe air cover.

Nevertheless, the Royal Navy did have one trump card which is never mentioned in the usual literature about *Sea Lion* – its submarine force. In the long run, British and Dutch submarines could operate more freely in the Channel, attacking German supply convoys, day or night. British submarines had already enjoyed considerable success against the Kriegsmarine and German anti-submarine capabilities were modest. Indeed, in the long term, British and Dutch submarines were better able to interdict German shipping in the Channel and might well have been the main obstacle to the Germans getting their Panzer-Divisionen across the Channel in subsequent waves.

In a mark of desperation to disrupt German invasion preparations, the Royal Navy even resurrected the idea of using fireships. In July, the Admiralty began modifying three old tankers in Sheerness and developed a plan known as Operation *Lucid* to use them against the invasion barges assembled in Boulogne. Churchill approved of such aggressive measures and ensured that a proper naval hero was assigned to lead the enterprise – Captain Augustus W. S. Agar, who had been awarded a Victoria Cross for sinking a Russian cruiser in the Kronstadt raid in 1919. Nevertheless, Operation *Lucid* proved a useless diversion of resources and personnel.

In sum, the Royal Navy's ability to intercept the German invasion was undermined by the inability of Britain's intelligence services to determine the likely invasion areas, which led to excessive dispersion of available forces. Fear of the Luftwaffe, mines and U-Boats induced great caution in the Home Fleet's upper leadership, which made most of the capital ships irrelevant. British destroyers and light cruisers at the time were not equipped with search radar or dual-purpose automatic weapons necessary to conduct effective anti-invasion interceptions. Furthermore, Churchill's decision to conduct a secondary effort like Operation *Menace* further weakened the Home Fleet at a critical moment. As S-Tag approached, Churchill and his War Cabinet became increasingly nervous about the ability of the Royal Navy to stop a German invasion and he did not exactly give the Admiralty a ringing endorsement when he said, 'the Navy can lose us the war, but only the Air Force can win it'. By late September 1940, Churchill placed his faith in the RAF – not the Royal Navy – and simply hoped that the Germans would not try to mount an invasion.

British Army and Commonwealth Forces

If the Germans made it to English shores – which was likely if *Seelöwe* was attempted – then it would be up to the British and Commonwealth ground forces to contain and then defeat the invasion. Unfortunately, the British Army in September 1940 was little more than a 'cardboard force' that was not capable of sustained ground combat against a veteran and well trained opponent. Three months after Dunkirk, the British Army had 23 infantry and two armoured divisions in Great Britain plus four Commonwealth divisions, but only the 3rd and 43rd Infantry Divisions and 1st Canadian Division were at full strength in terms of personnel and equipment. Two more divisions – the 1st and 52nd Infantry – were close to full strength but the rest were still suffering from significant equipment shortfalls, particularly in terms of artillery, mortars, anti-tank guns, tactical radios and transport. Excluding the Home Guard, the British Army had over 1.3 million troops in uniform in Great Britain but this number was very deceptive since the actual amount of trained combat troops was fairly low and the bulk of the Territorial Army (TA) troops would take another year to train. Over 300,000 of these troops were support personnel (i.e. logistics, medical) and another 300,000 were anti-aircraft troops, coastal gunners or other secondary functions. In terms of combat infantrymen, tankers and field artillerymen, there were perhaps 100–120,000 available spread from Scotland to Land's End.

Military training is a subject that has been ignored in most of the *Sea Lion* literature and, when mentioned, is typically discussed in bean-counting fashion. In reality, the British Army's efforts to train its troops both before and after Dunkirk were hindered by a lack of relevant doctrine, inadequate resources and a didactic approach to instruction. The most recent manual on British infantry tactics had been written in 1937 and made little or no reference to combined-arms tactics, particularly cooperation with tanks.[20] British troops were well taught in the use of small arms and support weapons, but lacked the kind of realistic, small-unit combat training that German troops received. The training of initiative and aggression at platoon/company level, which was the crux of the Wehrmacht's battlefield success, was not encouraged in the British Army of 1940–41. Thus, even the regular and first-line Territorials had received insufficient realistic training and were not on a tactical par with their German opponents.

The German blow was destined to land on the coast of Kent and Sussex, defended by the troops of Lieutenant General Sir Guy Williams's Eastern Command. Williams was a 59-year-old engineer officer facing imminent retirement – hardly the model for energetic command. Lieutenant General Andrew 'Bulgy' Thorne's XII Corps held the coastline where the Germans planned to invade. Thorne was a Guards officer with wide experience, including a stint as military attaché in Berlin in 1932–35 and commanding the 48th Infantry Division in France; in Berlin, Thorne had got on quite well with Hitler due to having served in the same sector in the World War I. In September 1940, Thorne had two TA Infantry Divisions (1st London and 45th Wessex), one regular infantry brigade (29th Independent) and the 1st Motor-Machine Gun Brigade holding 150 miles of coastline. Relatively few troops were actually deployed on or near the beaches, in Forward Defence Localities (FDLs); for example, the 6th

Somerset Light Infantry of 135th Infantry Brigade had two of its four companies assigned to defend about 3,250 yards of beachfront around Dymchurch – where a regiment from the German 35. Infanterie-Division was supposed to land. In other sectors, the beachfront was held by platoon or section-size positions, reinforced with a few crude bunkers. The British Army had spent the past several months hurriedly building these bunkers, but these tall, angular structures were easy to spot and their 12-inch-thick, un-reinforced walls would not resist the fire of German 3.7cm Pak guns or 7.5cm infantry guns. Instead, British troops incorporated Napoleonic-era Martello Towers and other fortifications into their defensive plans. The Grand Redoubt located between Dymchurch and Hythe, in the middle of the German Landing Area B, was a particularly strong circular fort, complete with a moat and thick walls. However, the Germans knew the location of all these outdated coastal defences and could be expected to bomb them prior to the main landing.

The British fire support plan for the 'crust defence' on the beach was weak. The invading German troops were not going to be fighting British divisions, but rather British sections, platoons and companies deployed in linear defences. At the sharp point of the spear, a British infantry battalion in late 1940 was authorized 790 troops in one headquarters and four infantry companies; battalion firepower was based upon 40 Bren Guns, two 3-inch mortars and twelve 2-inch mortars. Each company consisted of 100 troops in three platoons, armed with a total of nine Brens and three 2-inch mortars. A 30-man infantry platoon, led by a subaltern, was armed with three Brens, one 2-inch mortar and 27 rifles. The magazine-fed Bren light machine gun was a good support weapon, but it had a much slower rate of fire than the belt-fed German MG-34 machine gun and only half the effective range. Some positions were also supplemented with American-made Browning machine guns or BARs or Vickers machine guns, which could make quite a difference. On the plus side, the ammunition shortages of June 1940 had been ameliorated and there was now plenty of small arms ammunition. For indirect fire support, the battalion mortar platoon was armed with just two 3-inch mortars, which were significantly out-ranged by the German 8cm battalion-level mortars. In contrast, an 820-man German infantry battalion was authorized 40 MG-34 machine guns and six 8cm mortars. Furthermore, a German infantry regiment could support the main effort with an infantry gun company armed with 7.5cm and 15cm infantry guns, for which British infantry brigades had no equivalent. Once ashore in strength, the firepower afforded by better German automatic weapons and mortars would enable German infantry units to quickly overwhelm their thinly spread Territorial opponents – it would not be much of a contest once the German troops got off the beaches.

Each British infantry battalion would typically deploy two of its companies to cover a 2-mile stretch of beach, while the other two companies were deployed further inland. British Army dispositions were heavily influenced by fear of enemy airborne attacks, particularly to seize airfields as the Germans had tried in Holland. Each infantry battalion was directed to form a mobile column, consisting of an infantry company mounted on whatever trucks, buses or motorcycles were available. Anti-invasion planning directed that the primary task of the mobile column was to counter-attack enemy parachute landings. At RAF Hawkinge, the 2nd London Infantry Brigade deployed two rifle companies and a mobile column with light artillery.[21] An infantry battalion commander would usually keep one infantry company in reserve, along with his carrier platoon, battalion mortars and sappers. Both the 1st London and 45th Wessex were extremely short on 2-pounder anti-tank guns and the 14.3mm Boys anti-tank rifles; the few that were available were deployed in 'anti-tank islands' inland. Thus, few if any reinforcements were expected to head towards the landing beaches.

Artillery support for the FDLs was very limited. Each division had three Royal Artillery field regiments for fire support. Although most field regiments had been re-equipped with new guns, they were often a mix of American 75mm guns, British 18/25-pounders, new 25-pounders and 4.5-inch howitzers, which complicated ammunition resupply. Since all British artillery regiments only had two batteries – a structural defect that was not remedied until 1941–42 – a battalion was fortunate to receive support from one 8-gun battery. In the Territorial units, this usually meant American-supplied 75mm guns or older 18/25-pounders, neither of which were a match for German division-level artillery. Lacking adequate tactical radios or signal gear, the Royal Artillery supporting the FDLs relied upon Battery Observation Posts (BOPs), linked to the guns by wire communications. The scale and timeliness of this artillery support was little different from 1914, and if the BOPs were overrun or the wire cut by shellfire, the artillery could not support the defence.

When invasion threatened, the Admiralty authorized the construction of over 40 emergency coast defence batteries along the southern and eastern coasts. Each battery consisted of two Mark VII or Mark XII 6-inch guns on single mounts, two searchlights, a Lewis Gun for air defence and a garrison of about 100 troops. Most of the 6-inch guns were positioned either on open concrete pads or within open-faced bunkers, which left them vulnerable to air attack, mortar fire or close assault. Since the gun crews were only able to fire a few rounds in training and fire control was rather basic, the batteries were instructed to only open fire when enemy ships approached to within 3 nautical miles of the coast. Several of these emergency batteries were within the German invasion area, including the St Mary's Bay battery, one in Eastbourne and another defending the minor port of Newhaven. The 56th Heavy Regiment also deployed two 6-inch gun batteries to cover either side of the Dungeness Peninsula.

At the water's edge, the British had erected 'Admiralty Scaffolding' along stretches of beach as obstacles, but this effort was incomplete in September 1940. The scaffolding was 9 feet high and consisted of steel tubes. Indeed, Britain poured enormous resources into producing the scaffolding – nearly 200 tons of steel was required to construct 1 mile of beach obstacles. Unfortunately, the scaffolding was not well anchored and tests proved that it could be shoved aside or pulled apart fairly easily.[22] In some areas, Royal Engineers had begun to construct concrete anti-tank cubes behind the scaffolding, but this effort was just beginning and would not cover wide stretches of beach until 1941. Some sections of beach were also bounded by a concrete sea wall that could be up to 2 feet high, but this would only present a minor obstacle to German tanks. German pioniers could either build ramps over the obstacle or blow holes in it with explosive charges. German infantrymen would actually find the sea wall as useful cover from British defensive fire on the beaches.

The British Army decided to mine likely landing beaches but were hindered by the lack of suitable mines. Unlike the Germans, with their excellent S-mine, the British Army had no anti-personnel mines in 1940 and had to improvise. Most of the mines were actually anti-tank weapons, which posed little threat to enemy infantrymen; the standard British Mk II anti-tank mine required 350 pounds of pressure to activate. While German U-Panzers might have been disabled by anti-tank mines on the beach, broken track was a straightforward matter to repair and since the minefields were not covered by anti-tank guns, they represented little more than a 'speed bump' to an invading force. In order to impede infantrymen, the Royal Engineers fabricated some wooden box mines but the main assistance came from the Admiralty, which provided Eastern Command with 74,160 Type C Naval Beach Mines, known as the 'Mushroom mine' for its appearance. The Mushroom mine was a very large weapon, weighing 50lb, including a 20lb Amatol charge – enormous compared to the 9lb German S-mine. In the XII Corps area, 12,345 Mushroom mines were laid, primarily around Newhaven and Cuckmere Haven in German Landing Area E. A typical British beach minefield consisted of two to three staggered rows of mines, surrounded by barbed wire to keep civilians out. However, the Mushroom mine proved far too sensitive and during the summer of 1940 inflicted numerous casualties on both British civilians and military personnel; between 20 and 22 September 1940, five British soldiers were killed by Mushroom mines in the Newhaven area. On 26 September, a German bomb that landed on a beach at Southwold caused a sympathetic detonation of 515 Mushroom mines, which damaged the British defences in this sector.[23] The mines were not entirely waterproof and they quickly deteriorated, while others were simply swept away by tidal action. In March 1941, Major General Clifford C. Malden, commander of the 47th Infantry Division, was killed by a Mushroom mine while inspecting coastal defences. Except for the Newhaven area, British mines would not have proven a serious obstacle to the Germans. Behind the mines, the Royal Engineers installed a few rows of Dannert wire (i.e. concertina wire), which was intended more to deter British civilians from walking onto mined beaches than delay enemy troops.

The 1st London Division, under Major General Claude F. Liardet, would bear the responsibility of stopping the German XIII Armeekorps from getting into Folkestone or Dover in the first day or two of the invasion. Liardet himself was a 59-year-old Territorial Army artilleryman who had been a manager at Lloyds of London before the war; he was bookish and out of touch with modern military methods. The Territorials also had their share of oddballs, such as Lieutenant-Colonel John R. J. Macnamara MP, who commanded the 1st London Irish Rifles on the coast near Margate. Macnamara was a key member of the pre-war Anglo-German Fellowship and he had travelled to Germany in the 1930s to attend Hitler Youth events. Openly sympathetic to the Nazis, Macnamara was not the sort of person that Churchill would have preferred to see guarding the coast against invasion. Brooke was trying to cull the unfit Territorial officers from key command positions, but this took time and it was not until mid-1941 that they could be replaced by more capable officers.

Once the Germans succeeded in overrunning the FDLs, they would need to quickly expand inland to link up with their airborne troops and to create a defensible beachhead, as well as to expand laterally to capture the ports of Folkestone and Dover. The German XIII Armeekorps would have to get across the Royal Military Canal, which was guarded only by the 18th Pioneer Battalion. The front-line brigades each had some companies deployed further back from the beaches, but they were dispersed to defend key towns, bridges and airfields. In the 136th Brigade sector, covering Invasion Area D, the brigade reserve consisted of just 15 Bren Gun carriers and about 100 motorcyclists located near Hailsham, about 5 miles north of the beaches. Clearly, a reserve this size could not be expected to retake much lost ground. North of Invasion Area B, the town of Ashford was a key position that was held by 1,300 Territorials and 700 Home Guard troops. Folkestone was defended by the 2nd London Brigade. Dover itself had a large but hodgepodge 8,000-man garrison under Brigadier Christopher Hugh Gotto, consisting of four recently raised battalions as well as several coast defence batteries. Brooke loathed Gotto and described him as 'a queer specimen'.[24] Behind its two divisions and one brigade on the coast, Thorne's XII Corps had deployed Major General Bernard Freyberg's 2 NZEF, which was provided with the 8th RTR (57 tanks). The New Zealanders were expected to mount immediate counter-attacks to counter German landings in the Dover-Folkestone sectors or to act as a second line of defence behind the Royal Military Canal. Freyberg created a battalion-size motorized rapid reaction unit known as Milforce, which was intended to respond to airborne landings or amphibious landings within two hours.[25] However, the two New Zealand brigades were supported by only a single artillery regiment and had very few 2-pounder anti-tank guns. Freyberg was a tough combat veteran and excellent leader, but he was sent to the Middle East just before the intended date for *Sea Lion*. Without Freyberg, the inadequately trained New Zealand troops would have difficulty mounting large-scale attacks. Given the profusion of missions, it is likely that 2 NZEF would have been committed into action piecemeal. Furthermore, even if successful, the New Zealand counter-attack would only affect the German forces in Invasion Area B. Thorne realized that he had insufficient forces within XII Corps to mount a serious counter-attack against more than one German landing site and he requested additional forces from Brooke. In London, Brooke was reluctant to detach forces from his GHQ Reserves but agreed to send Brigadier Oliver Leese's 29th Independent Infantry Brigade to provide Thorne with a larger reserve. Unfortunately, Leese's brigade did not arrive in sector until late September – after the likely date of S-Tag.

In order to crush the other German beachheads, Brooke maintained a large reserve under GHQ control, consisting of Lieutenant General Francis Nosworthy's IV Corps (2nd Armoured Division, 42nd and 43rd Infantry Divisions and 31st Infantry Brigade) and Lieutenant General Andrew McNaughton's VII Corps (1st Armoured Division, 1st Canadian Division, 1st and 21st Army Tank Brigades). Nosworthy's corps was deployed north of London and was intended to counter-attack any enemy landings in East Anglia, while McNaughton's corps was deployed south of London and expected to counter-attack enemy landings on the south coast. Although these two corps had most of Britain's available tanks, they had only a single medium regiment of artillery for support and the 42nd (East Lancashire) Division was a poorly equipped 2nd Line Territorial Division. The 43rd (Wessex) Division was a well-equipped 1st Line Territorial Division, but without much mobility. McNaughton, a 53-year-old Canadian artilleryman, would be in charge of leading the first large-scale response to the German invasion. Brooke disliked McNaughton, regarding him as unfit for large-scale command and was unsure that Nosworthy, an engineer, could manage to employ his armoured forces properly.[26] Nor was Brooke, who had an inflated sense of his own military talents, well suited to lead a desperate defence against a German invasion. Despite many post-war accolades about his soldierly qualities, Brooke's diary reveals that he was primarily a brooding paper-pusher and meeting participant, not in the same league as his potential German opponents. On top of this awkward command team, Churchill was also likely – in his self-assumed role as defence minister – to try to micro-manage the commitment of the GHQ Reserves.

Much of the conviction that the British Army could defeat a German invasion rests upon the notion that British armoured units would quickly launch powerful counter-attacks that would overwhelm the enemy beachheads before they were fully established. Unfortunately, this interpretation conveniently overlooks the technical and doctrinal defects which led to recurring defeats by British armoured forces in

1940–42. In bean-counting terms, Britain's armoured forces appeared to have partly recovered from Dunkirk, as the number of available tanks tripled from 250 in July to 762 by September 1940. On the eve of *Sea Lion*, Britain's Army had 265 infantry tanks (Matilda I and II), 179 Cruiser tanks (A-9/A-10/A-13), 318 light tanks (Mk VI) and about 50 'Dutchman' tanks on hand; the latter were Vickers light tanks ordered by Holland but taken over by the British Army after the Dutch surrender. Most of the real armoured strength lay in two independent units, the 1st and 21st Army Tank Brigades, which had almost all of the Matilda infantry tanks. The Matilda II, with up to 78mm of frontal armour on its glacis, had proved nearly impervious to the standard German 3.7cm Pak gun in France but the Germans had captured several Matilda IIs and were about to field the improved 5cm Pak gun with tungsten-core rounds. Furthermore, the Matilda II was a slow tank with limited range and prone to the kind of mechanical defects which plagued British tanks designed in the 1930s. Armed with a 2-pounder gun that had no HE round, the Matilda II only had a single coaxial machine gun to use against enemy infantry and anti-tank guns; British tankers were trained to use their coaxial machine gun at 450–650 yards' range.[27] Neither Army Tank Brigade had its own attached infantry or artillery and had not practised counter-attacking with other units. Even if infantry was available, British doctrine encouraged infantry tanks to advance in front, while infantry units followed at a distance of up to half a mile – this doctrine was not corrected until 1943.[28]

The two armoured divisions were a mixed bag and the British Army still had no experience using a complete armoured division in battle. The 1st Armoured Division had 125 Cruiser tanks and 23 light tanks in four armoured regiments, while the 2nd Armoured Division had 54 Cruiser tanks and 156 light tanks. The Cruiser-series tanks were fast, but very thinly armoured and highly vulnerable to the German 3.7cm Pak even at 550 yards. Like the Matilda II, the Cruiser tanks were all armed with the 2-pounder gun, while the Mk VI light tanks were all but useless. In France, one German 3.7cm Pak gun had knocked out 11 of 1st Armoured Division's Mk VI tanks. As Peter Beale noted in his study of British tank development, most British early war tanks were poorly designed and mechanically unreliable.[29] British tankers were trained to fight enemy tanks – not enemy infantry and concealed anti-tank guns.

The parlous state of British armoured doctrine also militated against a successful counter-attack by GHQ's Reserves against a German invasion. Brigade and regimental commanders retained a tank-pure mentality that French armoured units had already learned did not work against the German combined-arms team; regiments equipped with Cruiser and light tanks were trained to fight as cavalry, in massed charges. Attached motorized infantry, of which there was far too little in the British armoured divisions in 1940, followed the tanks to consolidate on the objective, but were not integrated at the company level. Nor was there adequate artillery support, since the single regiment of 24 25-pounders could provide only a single battery to support a tank brigade. Neither the 1st nor 2nd Armoured Divisions were trained to fight as combined-arms teams and regarded the armoured brigades as capable of attacking on their own. Despite heavy losses, these unsound tactics would persist until late 1942 and tank-infantry cooperation remained a critical deficiency for much of the war. At the squadron and regimental level there were some decent commanders, but above that level too many British armour commanders were either mediocre or incompetent. In the case of Major General Charles W. M. Norrie, commander of the 1st Armoured Division, he would perform poorly at the battle of Gazala in June 1942 and be relieved of command, which makes it doubtful he would have been any more successful in September 1940.

Later experience in the World War II indicates that German forces, even when expecting an amphibious landing, had difficulty quickly organizing large-scale armoured counter-attacks. At Salerno, it took the Germans four days to get their Panzers into action and at Anzio it was 12 days. It is highly unlikely that the inexperienced British armoured divisions could react more rapidly than the veteran Panzer-

BRITISH ARMY DISPOSITIONS, 25 SEPTEMBER 1940

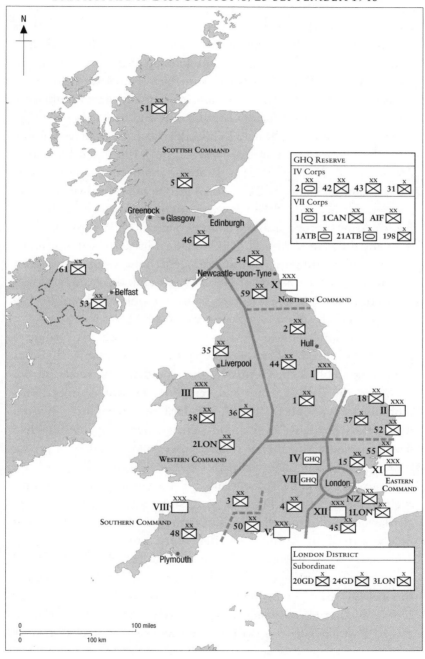

Divisionen of 1943–44. Even the best British commanders, such as Bernard Montgomery, were by-the-book and methodical when it came to offensive operations. Indeed, looking at the performance of the 8th Army in 1941–42 – Britain's premier combat-ready force – it is clear that the British Army was slow to assemble forces for offensive action and had great difficulty coordinating and executing offensives against German forces. Three actions in particular – Operation *Bacon* (15 July 1942), Operation *Splendour* (22 July 1942) and Operation *Manhood* (26–27 July 1942) – display a consistent litany of costly tactical failures, inadequate C^2 and an inability to coordinate infantry and armour in battle.[30] Nor is there any reason to believe that the British Army's response to *Sea Lion* in September 1940 would have been any different.[31] Attacking as individual brigades, without much air or artillery support, British armoured units would have great difficulty against even modest German anti-tank defences and losses would be heavy. Nor could Britain, which was only building 120–140 tanks per month, afford to replace heavy losses.

If the counter-attacks by the GHQ mobile Reserves came to grief, then Brooke would have to re-deploy as many infantry divisions as possible to block the Germans from any further advances inland. However, the British Army had very little tactical or operational mobility in September 1940. A standard British infantry division was supposed to have over 2,000 vehicles, but most divisions had been provided with a mix of civilian buses and cars in lieu of proper military transport; these civilian vehicles could not manoeuvre off road or pull field guns. By September, British units on the front line, such as the 8th Royal Fusiliers, were still equipped with a mix of civilian and military vehicles. Interestingly, when military lorries finally arrived in April 1941, they were American-built Dodge 1½-ton trucks with left-side steering, so drivers had to be re-trained how to use these strange vehicles. Lacking tactical mobility, much of the British Army in September 1940 was similar to the 'Static Divisions' that Hitler would raise to garrison the Atlantic Wall in 1944. It would take the British Army one or two weeks to move additional divisions into place around the enemy beachheads, giving the Germans time to consolidate. British artillery could bombard the German beachhead, but the Royal Artillery's arsenal in September 1940 lacked the range and firepower to be more than a nuisance, particularly once German troops entrenched themselves. The 4.5-inch (114mm) field gun was a good weapon that could hurl a 25kg HE shell up to 11.6 miles with Charge 3, but these weapons were only available in limited numbers, as were heavier 60-pounders (127mm) and 9.2-inch howitzers. British division-level artillery was dependent upon the new 25-pounder (87mm) and older 18-pounders (83mm) which could only fire relatively small HE shells out to a range of 6 miles. If German division-level artillery succeeded in getting ashore, with modern 10.5cm and 15cm howitzers, the Royal Artillery would be out-ranged and out-gunned.

Nor could the British Army expect to fare well in a protracted battle of attrition. At best, the British and Commonwealth forces might be able to deploy 40–50,000 trained combat troops against the invader in the first week, but there were very few trained reserves. The British Army had already suffered over 50,000 killed or captured in the first year of the war and would suffer another 80,000 killed or wounded during 1941–43; by 1943 the British Army no longer had the strength to keep all its divisions and disbanded three in 1943 and two more in 1944. By the Normandy campaign in mid-1944, the British Army was no longer in a position to replace infantry losses. Many of the Territorial divisions in 1940 were unprepared for any role beyond coastal defence and could not be fully trained or equipped before mid-1941. If committed to battle against an entrenched enemy, the bulk of the British Army's troops would have been little more than cannon fodder.

A number of historians have regarded the British Army as mediocre for much of the World War II, but its leadership gradually learned to balance tactical ineptitude with superior artillery and close air support by 1943–44. Unfortunately, neither the Royal Artillery nor the RAF had the ability in September 1940 to provide lavish fire support to the army, so it would be up to the infantry. Consequently, if the invader managed to get established ashore, the outlook for the British and Commonwealth forces was rather grim. Even if successful in a protracted battle to contain the German beachheads, British Army losses would likely have been so heavy as to preclude more than token participation in future Anglo-American offensives.

In sum, the British lacked adequate forces on the coastline to prevent an enemy landing, and counter-attack capabilities were undermined by inadequate mobility and firepower, poor tactics and insufficiently aggressive junior leadership. Too much of the British Army was deployed far from the landing areas and could not quickly reposition. Consequently, the British Army would be unable to effectively utilize its numerical superiority in the early stages of *Sea Lion* and would be unable to crush any German landings.

Home Guard

Many *Sea Lion* histories spend considerable time addressing the subject of the Home Guard, although the combat value of citizen militia against regular troops in the World War II was very low. Neither the Soviet People's Militia (*Opolcheniye*) or German Volksturm performed well in combat in 1941–45 and there is no reason to think that the Home Guard would have been any different. Typically the large number of Home Guard troops theoretically available – roughly 1.6 million in September 1940 – is used to suggest that this militia force would add considerable weight to Britain's defence.

Aside from minimal training and support weapons, the Home Guard was essentially tied to specific localities and had negligible transport to move elsewhere. In Sussex, there were 35,000 Home Guard troops in 20 battalions, including units in Brighton, Eastbourne, Hastings and Rye. In Kent, there were 45,000 Home Guard troops in 20 battalions, including units at Ashford and Dover. In addition to their American-supplied rifles, a typical Home Guard battalion was provided with four Browning machine guns, ten Lewis Guns and 23 BARs, but they had no mortars or anti-tank weapons. Each Home Guardsman was given 40–50 rounds of ammunition for his rifle. The main role of the Home Guard was patrolling and static defence of strongpoints, usually in villages. Although it has often been suggested that the Home Guard would be useful 'rounding up' dispersed German paratroopers, only three battalions were near the intended landing zones for the 7. Flieger-Division and Home Guard units took time to gather in their personnel. By the time that the Home Guard units were assembled, German paratroopers would already have formed up around their drop zones; militiamen were not trained to attack elite Fallschirmjäger armed with MG-34 machine guns and mortars. Thus, the German invasion forces would initially face no more than 80,000 Home Guardsmen in the landing areas and single battalions deployed in strongpoints would not represent much of a hindrance to a German combined-arms attack.

Recent studies indicate that half the Home Guard troops were under 27 and that more than one-quarter were only 17 or 18 years old. Rather than creating a large number of Home Guard battalions with limited combat capability, the War Office would have been wiser to cull the best personnel for active service and use others for labour battalions. Even during the height of the invasion scare in 1940 and continuing into 1941, British Army troops were seconded to assist with harvesting crops – a duty better left to the Home Guard. Like so many ideas pushed by the Cabinet in 1940, the Home Guard was an effort to spark a patriotic effort on the part of the population, but without adding much to real military capabilities.

British Chemical Weapons Capability, 1940

At the start of the World War II, Chamberlain's government quietly sent a diplomatic note to Germany through its embassy in Switzerland that said Britain would abide by the 1930 Geneva Protocol and refrain from using chemical weapons, if Germany agreed to similar restraint. Hitler agreed, since he intended to win without chemical weapons.[32] However, the British Government also decided to hedge its bets by preparing for chemical warfare in case Hitler reneged on this secret agreement. Britain had been testing and stockpiling small amounts of chemical weapons during the 1930s, but Chamberlain now authorized a significant expansion of the facilities involved in the production of mustard gas and phosgene. The Imperial Chemical Industry's (ICI) Randle Works, located near Runcorn in Cheshire, was already capable of manufacturing 350 tons of mustard and 45 tons of phosgene per week. Nevertheless, Chamberlain's War Cabinet allocated £546,000 to build a new chemical weapons plant in Rhydymwyn Valley, which would be operational by September 1940.[33]

When Churchill became prime minister in May 1940, Britain's stockpile of chemical munitions was growing fast; from only a few hundred tons at the start of the war, Britain's stockpile of chemical weapons would grow to almost 5,000 tons by the end of September.[34] The Randle Works was focused on producing two types of mustard agent, known as H.D. (Pyro) and H.T. (Runcol). Mustard is a blister agent that can be delivered as either a liquid or an aerosol, whereas phosgene (CG) is a choking agent that is stored as a liquid but is only delivered as an aerosol. The British also had small quantities of the blood agent hydrogen cyanide (JBR or VN) and vomiting agents such as chloropicrin (NC). In 1940, the primary British aerial delivery systems for chemical weapons were 65lb, 250lb and 500lb bombs held by Bomber Command and aerosol spray tanks; fill consisted of either mustard or phosgene. In contrast, the British Army had chemical ammunition for its 1918-vintage 6-inch howitzers (the shell contained 4.9kg of NC) and 60-pounder (127mm) guns, which had a chemical round filled with 1.5kg of VN. The modern 4.5-inch (114mm) gun had small quantities of chemical ammunition, filled with 1kg of CG or JBR. No recent training had been conducted by the RAF or British Army on planning to employ chemical weapons or the tactics of delivery.

Dunkirk was a severe shock to the British military and the sudden development of a possible invasion threat caused senior leadership to grasp at straws. Chemical weapons were grasped, because they were available. On 15 June, General Sir John Dill, CIGS, issued a memorandum entitled 'The Use of Gas in the Home Defence'. In it, Dill argued that Britain should consider using chemical weapons to disrupt a German invasion, noting that 'enemy forces crowded on the beaches … would present a splendid target'.[35] Churchill embraced this suggestion and Brooke went along with the idea, although no operational or technical analysis supported this flippant decision. The Air Ministry informed Churchill that RAF squadrons would require at least 24 hours' notice to prepare to employ chemical weapons – which meant that it was unlikely that they would be ready to use against the German first wave – but this was apparently ignored. In the decades since 1940, historians have blithely spoken of the British intent to use chemical weapons to stop *Sea Lion*, without making any effort to examine the factors that rendered this decision problematic.

While Britain in September 1940 possessed adequate stocks of chemical agents to use against the first wave of *Seelöwe*, the tactical employment of these agents would have been very difficult. Ideal conditions for chemical weapon usage is typically against a target area where the wind speeds are 5mph or less (essentially calm air), wind direction towards the enemy and a target zone that is roughly square in shape. Mustard gas requires fairly high concentrations to be lethal or seriously debilitating, between 10 and 100 million parts per million. Phosgene requires three times this amount to reach lethal density. However, the coastline from Folkestone to Brighton does not favour the use of chemical weapons because it is characterized by winds usually from the south-west and at the breezy speeds of 10–15mph; thus, any chemical agents dropped on or near the beaches would blow right back at the defending British troops and would quickly dissipate. Since the British objective in using chemical weapons would be area denial, to prevent egress from the beaches, the RAF and British artillery would have to deliver hundreds of chemical warheads in a long, thin rectangular box many miles long on each beach and maintain a lethal concentration for hours by continuing to deliver more warheads. Another factor weighing against the British use of chemical weapons was that bombs dropped in soft sand or water were less likely to detonate, so the 'dud' rate would have been significant. Aircraft using aerosol spray tanks would have been required to fly slowly, at altitudes under 1,000 feet over the invasion beaches, making them perfect targets for Flak.

Nor were the German troops involved in *Seelöwe* likely to be 'a splendid target' since they were well prepared for defence against chemical attacks. All troops were provided with a protective mask (either the GM30 or GM38) which could be donned in seconds and was proof against inhaled agents. In addition, troops were provided with Losantin tablets for skin decontamination, impermeable anti-gas capes to shield themselves from liquid agents and test kits to determine the agent being used against them. Thus, within minutes of the British initiating chemical warfare, most German troops would be masked, which would greatly diminish the effects of an attack. While unmasked troops might suffer 50 per cent casualties in a typical attack scenario, masked troops were expected to suffer losses of 2 per cent or less. Amazingly, neither Dill, Churchill nor post-war historians have grasped the obvious disqualification of chemical weapons to stop *Sea Lion*. As was well known in British pre-war chemical tests, even troops exposed to mustard gas do not usually display symptoms for four to 12 hours after exposure and the lethality rate is just 1–3 per cent. Thus, even if the RAF had dropped mustard gas bombs on the *Sea Lion* beaches, the effects would not have been much apparent until late on S-Tag, long after the German landing had commenced. Phosgene is a faster acting agent, with some casualties appearing in just 5 minutes, but the most pernicious effects do not appear for many hours.[36] When wind conditions, German anti-gas protective measures and the limitations of the two principal British chemical agents are examined holistically, it is apparent that chemical warfare would not have stopped *Sea Lion* and would likely have been little more than a localized nuisance.

Furthermore, German retaliation in kind would be almost certain to follow, with chemical munitions used against British troop concentrations and Fighter Command airfields. The German Nebelwerfer rocket launcher – of which the British were not aware – was specifically designed to inundate an opponent with large numbers of chemical rockets. Since British chemical defences were also quite effective, military gas casualties on both sides were likely to be low. As in the World War I, if Churchill had initiated chemical warfare against *Sea Lion* the results would almost certainly have been indecisive and only served to make operations more difficult for both sides.

CHAPTER 7

Feasibility of S-Tag, 25 September 1940

Seelöwe: The Movement Plan

There is no doubt that the Kriegsmarine's plan to move nine army divisions across the English Channel in four transport fleets and conduct an opposed landing on the south coast of England on the morning of S-Tag was overly complex. Over 2,600 vessels embarking troops from ten ports would have to be coordinated on a very tight schedule. Indeed, no one had ever attempted an amphibious landing on this scale before. Aside from the hazards of the sea and the enemy, the movement was likely to be continuously hampered by the inexperience of the naval crews involved. On the other hand, the weather during the period selected for *Seelöwe* to begin was favourable; the English Channel on 24–25 September was cloudy and hazy, with visibility 5 miles or less. The Channel had only light waves (Sea State 2/3) and the wind was westerly at 7–10 knots. At night, the moon provided almost 50 per cent illumination, which would assist the crossing. According to the operational plan, most vessels would not have to move more than 60 nautical miles during a period of relatively good weather. Although there would be mishaps, most of the crews and vessels were capable of achieving this objective. While Raeder and the OKM staff in Berlin undermined *Seelöwe* with their innate pessimism, the Kriegsmarine front-line leaders in the Channel ports were more upbeat about their ability to conduct the operation. Kapitän zur See Erich Lehmann, in charge of assembling invasion flotillas in Ostend, confidently said after the war, 'we would have gotten over'.[1]

Once Hitler approved the operation, the first order of business was for the Kriegsmarine to begin laying defensive minefields on the night of S-Tag minus 9 (16 September). The main effort would be to lay the ANTON and BRUNO barrier minefields totalling over 3,000 mines on either side of Transport Fleet E's route; this effort would involve Bey's destroyers escorting five minelayers and six minesweepers from Le Havre into the middle of the English Channel over the course of six nights from S-Tag minus 8 to minus 2. Five more German minelayers, escorted by torpedo boats and S-Boats, would lay the CAESAR minefields near Dover.[2] The DORA minefield, near Lyme Bay, was intended to interfere with British naval units from Portsmouth. The German minefields were laid in four rows, with the outer rows including booby traps to damage British sweeping devices. The Kriegsmarine was counting on these minefields to deter or delay any British effort to interfere with *Seelöwe's* movement plan – although there was a certain amount of prayer mixed in with this assessment.

Loading for *Seelöwe* was scheduled to begin on different days, depending on the port. At Antwerp, initial loading of vehicles would begin on S-9 (S-Tag minus 9) and in Dunkirk on S-8, but in Calais it would not begin until S-5. Stores were to be loaded first, then tanks, trucks and artillery, then horses and finally troops on S-2 or S-1. By S-2 (23 September), convoys from Amsterdam and Rotterdam would already be sailing down the Dutch coast to assemble off Ostend. After embarkation was complete on S-Tag minus 1, the loaded vessels would begin to move out of their embarkation harbours. At Calais, elements of Transport Fleet C were expected to sail at 1000 hours on S-1. There is little doubt that there would have been congestion and delays with so many vessels attempting to depart and the schedule for *Seelöwe* would likely not remain intact for long. Once the tows (each consisting of a tug and two barges), transports and other vessels left harbour, they would form up into columns and begin moving towards assembly areas just offshore. Escort units would link up with their charges at sea and proceed to the coastal assembly areas, with all vessels formed up by 1700 hours on S-1 (24 September). At approximately 1900–1930 hours on S-1, the actual crossing would begin with a flotilla of R-Boats or minesweepers moving ahead of each transport fleet to sweep for mines and lay lantern buoys to mark the route in the dark.

The first wave of *Seelöwe* was divided into three echelons: assault forces, combat support units and support units. About half the barges allocated to the operation were involved in transporting the assault echelon, while the second echelon mostly consisted of transports to carry artillery and heavy equipment. The rest of the barges and transports would carry the vehicles, horses and personnel of the division-level support services in the third echelon. Corps and division-level command and staff were inserted in the middle of the first echelon, so that they could land soon after the assault troops. There were four transport fleets (B, C, D and E) and each would travel along their own route from the French coast to the southern coast of England. The crossings for fleets B, C and D were expected to take about 10 hours (roughly from 2000 hours on 24 September to 0600 hours on 25 September) each at an average speed of 5 knots, although strong currents could reduce this to 3–4 knots, which would knock off the operational timetable by 2–4 hours.

Transport Fleet E from Le Havre and Cherbourg had a more flexible itinerary than the other three fleets, given the threat of Royal Navy forces from Portsmouth. Sailing time from either harbour was pegged to enemy activity and, if the risk was too great, the fleet would remain in harbour. If feasible, the two convoys would sortie and

GERMAN CONVOY ROUTES ACROSS THE ENGLISH CHANNEL FOR S-TAG

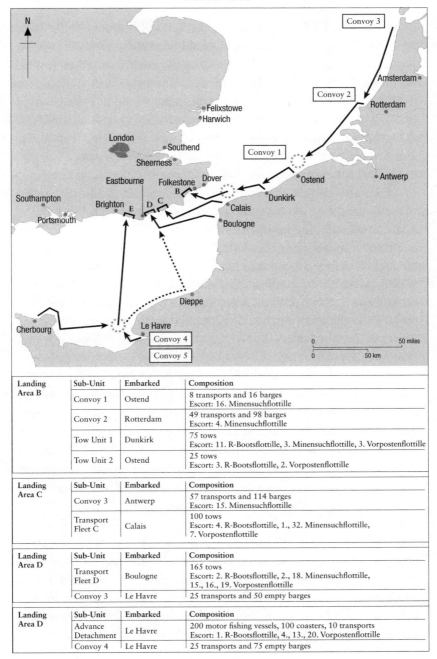

Landing Area B	Sub-Unit	Embarked	Composition
	Convoy 1	Ostend	8 transports and 16 barges Escort: 16. Minensuchflottille
	Convoy 2	Rotterdam	49 transports and 98 barges Escort: 4. Minensuchflottille
	Tow Unit 1	Dunkirk	75 tows Escort: 11. R-Bootsflottille, 3. Minensuchflottille, 3. Vorpostenflottille
	Tow Unit 2	Ostend	25 tows Escort: 3. R-Bootsflottille, 2. Vorpostenflottille

Landing Area C	Sub-Unit	Embarked	Composition
	Convoy 3	Antwerp	57 transports and 114 barges Escort: 15. Minensuchflottille
	Transport Fleet C	Calais	100 tows Escort: 4. R-Bootsflottille, 1., 32. Minensuchflottille, 7. Vorpostenflottille

Landing Area D	Sub-Unit	Embarked	Composition
	Transport Fleet D	Boulogne	165 tows Escort: 2. R-Bootsflottille, 2., 18. Minensuchflottille, 15., 16., 19. Vorpostenflottille
	Convoy 3	Le Havre	25 transports and 50 empty barges

Landing Area D	Sub-Unit	Embarked	Composition
	Advance Detachment	Le Havre	200 motor fishing vessels, 100 coasters, 10 transports Escort: 1. R-Bootsflottille, 4., 13., 20. Vorpostenflottille
	Convoy 4	Le Havre	25 transports and 75 empty barges

rendezvous off Le Havre around S-Tag minus 11 hours (1900 hours, 24 September); there, the decision would be made to proceed to either Landing Area D or E, depending upon the enemy situation. Unlike the other fleets, none of the barges in Transport Fleet E would be loaded with troops; instead, 175 empty barges would be towed behind 50 transports and 25 trawlers.[3] The advance guard of the VIII Armeekorps, consisting of over 8,000 troops in three regimental-size assault groups, would be carried across the English Channel in 300 motorized fishing vessels and coasters. Transport Fleet E was expected to make an 80-mile crossing of the Channel in about 11 hours, meaning that it would have to leave the assembly area off Le Havre by 1830 hours on S-Tag minus 1 – in daylight.

In the VII, XIII and XXXVIII Armeekorps, each infantry division formed a reinforced advance guard battalion (*Vorausabteilung*) to spearhead the initial landings; this was an 800–1,000-man force built around an infantry battalion, supplemented with pioniers, Panzerjägers and a close-support package. The Vorausabteilungen would be at the front of each invasion convoy and carried on fishing trawlers, minesweepers and Type AS reinforced barges. The four U-Panzer battalions would also be at the front of the line, carried in their special barges. Given the limited number of vessels in the Vorausabteilungen and the fact that they were in front of the convoys, these elements were likely to suffer the least in terms of delay and disruption. Only 30 minutes behind the Vorausabteilungen, the remainder of the assault echelon consisted of two infantry regiments, at least one artillery battalion, a reconnaissance battalion, motorized Panzerjägers, Flak troops, and more pioniers. All of this would be carried on 80–90 barges and two transports. The vanguard of the invasion fleet was expected to approach the British coast just before dawn and then pivot and sail parallel to the shore in order to deploy the transport columns for landing. Although the Kriegsmarine had flotilla commanders, communication between vessels was going to be poor and the transport fleets were likely to reach the British coast in a disordered gaggle, rather than orderly columns.

The second echelon would follow well behind the first echelon and most of the divisional artillery and vehicles were loaded aboard transports. A reinforced infantry battalion could be carried in six tows, consisting of six tugs and 12 barges.[4] Once these vessels reached their designated landing area, they would anchor offshore and wait for the barges used in the assault echelon to unload then move out to the transports; these barges would be used to trans-ship equipment from the transports to the beach. This trans-shipment was one of the weakest aspects of *Seelöwe*, since it required transports to use their on-board cranes to lift heavy equipment down into barges pulled alongside, while potentially under attack from British artillery, aircraft or warships. Tests indicate that trans-shipment would have been a very slow process. Once finished unloading the second echelon, the barges would re-cross the Channel to begin preparations to move the second wave across. The third echelon of *Seelöwe* would arrive in its own barges and thus avoid some of the trans-shipment problems. The Heer felt that this movement plan congregated too many vessels offshore during S-Tag and preferred to move the follow-on forces across in smaller, separate convoys – which would also represent smaller targets. Yet the Kriegsmarine rejected this sound advice due to their preference to concentrate all escort forces to protect four large transport fleets.

Although the movement planned did not intend to send empty transports and barges back to France until after the entire fleet was unloaded around S plus 2, this was unlikely to be conducted in actuality due to the growing intensity of British attacks. Consequently, once enough of the first-wave barges and transports had been unloaded, local commanders – unwilling to remain as sitting ducks – would likely return in small gaggle formations. When enough vessels returned to France, the loading of the second wave would begin. Many vessels would require repairs. The loading of complete Panzer-Divisionen aboard barges and transports would be very complex and time-consuming and the Kriegsmarine anticipated that the second wave was unlikely to cross until ten days after the initial landings (approximately 5 October). However, with losses and damage to the transport fleet and time lost in repairs and re-assembling the fleets, the Kriegsmarine would probably require two weeks to gather enough vessels to move even a few second-wave divisions across the Channel.

Seelöwe: The Escort Plan

One of the main criticisms of *Sea Lion* was that the Kriegsmarine lacked the surface warships to protect the transport fleets against the Royal Navy and, thus, the invasion would either be defeated during the crossing or have its naval lines of communications severed shortly thereafter. These off-the-cuff assessments are usually made with little effort to assess the Kriegsmarine's actual capabilities and through conventional lenses. The only major Kriegsmarine surface assets available – the heavy cruiser *Admiral Hipper* and the light cruisers *Köln* and *Nürnberg* – were assigned to cover the diversionary convoys in *Herbstreise*, not the actual convoys in *Seelöwe*. Halder and the OKH tried to insist on including these heavier forces in *Seelöwe*, but Raeder and the OKM refused. Hitler could have ordered it – this would have been an occasion where his style of micro-management might have actually helped the German war effort – but he remained aloof on *Seelöwe*'s tactical details. Instead, the Kriegsmarine intended only to employ its light forces to support *Seelöwe*.

The Kriegsmarine's light naval forces in September 1940 were far from insignificant in the context of naval combat in the tight confines of the English Channel. Bey had seven destroyers in Brest and Cherbourg, which would be used to protect *Seelöwe*'s western flank from interference by British units based in Portsmouth or Plymouth. Unlike the larger but mostly obsolescent collection of British destroyers, Bey had six modern Type 34A and one Type 36 destroyer, all of which were better armed and faster than their British opponents. In addition, the Kriegsmarine had 12 torpedo boats (five Type 35 built in 1939–40, three Type 24 built in 1928–29 and four Type 23 built in 1927) based at Le Havre and Cherbourg that would cooperate with

A ROYAL NAVY TASK FORCE ATTEMPTING TO INTERCEPT A GERMAN INVASION CONVOY ON THE EVE OF S-TAG

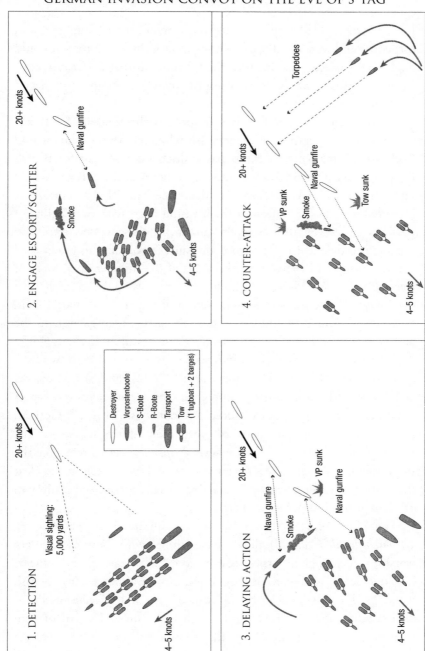

Bey's destroyers. The torpedo boats were armed with 10.5cm guns and torpedoes and were capable of 35 knots. Thus, the Kriegsmarine could deploy 19 surface warships into the Channel during *Seelöwe*, against an initial British reaction force of approximately 2–4 light cruisers and 18 destroyers.

Three German S-Boat flotillas, equipped with a total of 21 S-Boats, would also be operating in the English Channel. The S-Boats would likely lie in ambush near the barrier minefields and wait for British forces to appear. If British warships struck mines, the S-Boats would attack them as they tried to exit the minefield. The Kriegsmarine intended to clear the routes for the invasion fleets with five flotillas of R-Boats and seven minesweeper squadrons; these vessels were also expected to defend the fleet from any surface contacts and help land the advance guard battalions. About 20 of the minesweepers were of the 680-ton M-35-class, which the British dubbed 'Channel destroyers'. These modern vessels were well armed with two 10.5cm guns, two 3.7cm Flak and two 2cm Flak guns, which gave them the ability to engage in surface combat. Up front, about 30 R-Boats would lead the way; these auxiliary minesweepers were armed with two 2cm guns and would be useful against British MTBs and armed coastal auxiliaries. If British warships appeared, the German minesweepers would lay smoke screens to conceal the convoys. All in all, German minesweepers were going to be very busy during *Seelöwe*. The Kriegsmarine could also commit several *Sperrbrecher* to reinforce the minesweeping force; these large auxiliary vessels were designed to clear mines but were also heavily armed for surface action (typically two 10.5cm guns, four 3.7cm and eight 2cm).

For close escort, the Kriegsmarine intended to employ six *Vorpostenflottillen* (Patrol) squadrons, equipped with about 35 auxiliary warships. At first glance, these converted fishing steamers and trawlers did not seem to represent any hindrance to intercepting British warships. Each *Vorpostenboot* was armed with at least one medium-calibre gun (7.5cm or 8.8cm), a 3.7cm Flak gun and a pair of 2cm dual-purpose Flak guns. Given that few British destroyers were yet equipped with 20mm or 40mm dual-purpose guns, the Vorpostenboote were capable of offering significant resistance in a close-range night action. As noted earlier in the section on the Royal Navy's capabilities, the intercept of multiple naval convoys in the dark was a formidable challange for naval squadrons not equipped with radar. While a British destroyer squadron could overwhelm a pair of Vorpostenboote guarding the flank of a convoy, this would take time that would allow the transports to escape and lurking S-Boats to counter-attack.

Altogether, the Kriegsmarine would commit over 100 surface vessels to escort the four invasion fleets on S-Tag. Some would be superior to their British opponents in terms of firepower or speed, but the sheer numbers would seriously interfere with any intercepting Royal Navy units from coming to grips with the transports. The Royal Navy would likely pick off stragglers or damaged vessels, but the main convoys would be fairly difficult to overwhelm. Indeed, it was quite possible that the Royal Navy would be outnumbered in the initial night battles on S-Tag minus 1. Thus, the Kriegsmarine did have adequate escorts to protect the bulk of the transport fleets during the initial movement and landing phases. However, the German escorts would begin to suffer significant losses when they were asked to defend the anchorages in daylight hours and were exposed to air and sea attacks. The real question about *Seelöwe*'s viability is not whether the Germans could get across – they almost certainly could – but if there would be adequate escorts left to protect the second wave and subsequent supply convoys.

Most sources claim that the Kriegsmarine would also deploy 20 U-Boats to protect the flanks of the invasion fleet, and this is accepted at face value. However, Dönitz had a grand total of only 22 operational U-Boats on 24/25 September 1940 and no more than ten were in any position to participate in the opening moves of *Seelöwe*.[5] Three U-Boats were available to operate off the Thames Estuary to interfere with British naval movements from Sheerness and Harwich, while seven U-Boats could operate in the western end of the English Channel; half of these U-Boats were the short-range Type II type so time on station was limited. Five of Dönitz's best U-Boats, including Günther Prien's U-47, Otto Kretschmer's U-99 and Joachim Schepke's U-100, had just returned to Lorient and would not be ready to return to sea for at least 7–10 days. Furthermore, Dönitz was incensed with how his U-Boats had been appropriated in the Norwegian campaign and had a low opinion of *Seelöwe*. With a little foot-dragging on his part in terms of issuing new orders, only the five Type II boats might have been ready to support *Seelöwe* on S-Tag. Nevertheless, the Royal Navy was not aware of German U-Boat dispositions and would expect that most would be deployed to support *Seelöwe*.

Seelöwe: The Landing Plan

The Kriegsmarine designed the *Seelöwe* plan in order to begin the landing at high tide, just after dawn on S-Tag. At 0600 hours, the first airborne units would begin dropping north of Landing Area B and the first Vorausabteilungen would begin landing on the southern beaches. The Luftwaffe was expected to maintain fighter cover over the beaches during the day (which would require hundreds of sorties) and to provide on-call close air support as needed, although none of this had been properly rehearsed. The Germans would begin their invasion by landing relatively small, lightly equipped and dispersed forces across a wide swathe of southern England and hoping that they could hold the beachheads long enough to land their vehicles and heavy equipment. Like most German ground operations, *Seelöwe* was a gamble and depended upon the innate fighting ability of German small units and junior leadership to carry the day.

The OKH only had a vague idea where some British beach defences were located, but they knew that there would be beach obstacles and defensive strongpoints. Although Jodl's characterization of *Seelöwe* as a large river-crossing operation was nonsensical at the operational level, it did have some merit at the tactical level. In May 1940, the Heer demonstrated great ingenuity and pluck in crossing the River

BRITISH DISPOSITIONS IN KENT AND SUSSEX, 25 SEPTEMBER 1940

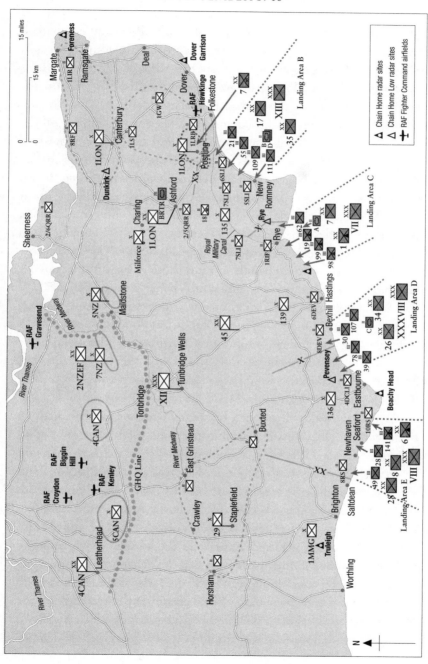

Meuse, despite formidable defences that included bunkers, barbed wire and stronger defences than the British had in Kent or Sussex. While the Meuse had been less than 110 yards wide, the Germans intended to use similar tactics to make the initial landings on the English coast, trusting to speed and audacity.

The lead elements of the Vorausabteilungen would appear off the coast just after dawn, embarked in R-Boats and armed fishing trawlers. As part of the plan, squadrons of Hs-126 aircraft were expected to drop smoke pots along the landing zones in order to reduce British visibility for several crucial minutes.[6] Offshore, the soldiers – most probably seasick after a night afloat – would climb into Sturmboote, carried in cradles on the side of vessels, and then launch. Each Sturmboot would carry six troops and an MG-34, racing towards the beach. Other men would paddle towards shore in large rubber rafts. A group of three light auxiliary gunboats – barges armed with a 7.5cm gun and some automatic Flak guns – would attempt to suppress any weapons firing from the shore. Off Dymchurch, barges loaded with U-Panzers would follow behind the Sturmboote. The tanks were supposed to launch offshore and crawl along the sea bottom, but under combat conditions the barge captains had permission to land them on the beach if necessary.

As a tactical example of one of the early landings, Vorausabteilung Bode from 35. Infanterie-Division expected to land 180 troops in 30 Sturmboote near Littlestone, about 1½ miles south of the 6-inch gun battery in St Mary's Bay. The beach here was sand and pebble, with absolutely no cover. This sector was held by a company from the 5th Battalion Somerset Light Infantry. While the 6-inch guns were not much of a threat to the speedboats, any British machine guns in this area could wreak real havoc. Easily half the assault troops could be killed or wounded in the first moments if the machine gunners ashore knew what they were doing, but with the help of some smoke and audacity, the survivors would likely create some breaches in the obstacle belt and begin to put fire on visible British beach positions. The initial moments of combat would be a sergeant's battle, much like it had been on the Meuse in May. Fifteen minutes later, the next assault group could also suffer heavy casualties coming in, but by 0700 hours Vorausabteilung Bode should have landed over 700 troops, of whom at least 300–400 were likely to be still effective. At that point, aggressive squad and platoon leaders were expected to carry the day and overwhelm one or more beach positions. Once the British crust defence was penetrated, the Germans would then roll up the other positions along the coast.

Several miles up the coast, the Germans would try to land two companies from Tauchpanzer-Abteilung D west of Dymchurch and all of Tauchpanzer-Abteilung B east of the town. This was a very nice stretch of beach, defended by B Company, 6th Battalion Somerset Light Infantry. Dymchurch was flanked by two Martello towers, No. 23 and 25, which had forward observers and machine guns. However, the British had no anti-tank guns in this sector. The 6-inch guns from the St Mary's battery would be presented with nice enfilade fire opportunities against the German barges carrying the Panzers and would likely inflict significant damage upon them. If the Panzers unloaded in deep water, doubtless quite a few of them would become mired but, nevertheless, the Germans were bound to get a number of Panzers onto the beach near Dymchurch. The real problem was that the U-Panzers lacked attached pioniers to clear mines and beach obstacles, so they would not be able to manoeuvre inland for up to an hour. Instead, the Panzers would remain at the water's edge, blasting any British targets that were visible.

Over in the 17. Infanterie-Division sector, Vorausabteilungen Schuler and Pannwitz were expected to overwhelm British forces near the Grand Redoubt, which was almost certainly to be the toughest point in the defence in Landing Area B. Just north of Hythe, four battalions of the 7. Flieger-Division would jump in the opening moments of the invasion. Gliders may have been used at Lympne airfield, a small emergency RAF base north of Hythe. Kampfgruppe Meindl and Stentzler, each consisting of two parachute battalions, would land north of the Royal Military Canal in an effort to assist

17. Infanterie-Division's push towards Folkestone. An hour later, four more parachute battalions would land, Oberst Alfred Sturm's Fallschirmjäger-Regiment 2 dropping right on top of the 2nd London Brigade's headquarters at Postling. By 0730, the German vanguard was expected to have fully landed and the main body would begin to land around 0800 hours. It should have taken the Germans 2 to 3 hours to mop up the British beach positions. By the time that low tide arrived at 1000 hours, the German main body should have landed some vehicles and artillery in each division sector and pioniers should have begun clearing the beach obstacles.

In Landing Area C, the VII Armeekorps was only likely to encounter heavy resistance near Rye and the mouth of the River Rother. The 1. Gebirgs-Division and Tauchpanzer-Abteilung A faced only light opposition in their sector. The XXXVIII Armeekorps landings in Pevensey Bay near Bexhill were likely to prove difficult. The 45th (Wessex) Infantry Division had two battalions defending this area and artillery in direct support. On the other hand, there were very few mines in this sector and no anti-tank guns, so the German Panzers might get inland fairly quickly here. Finally, the VIII Armeekorps landings in Area E would face difficult terrain and strong resistance. The 6. Gebirgs-Division was initially landing a regiment at Cuckmere Haven, which was defended by a machine-gun platoon, an infantry company and a pair of obsolete field guns. Landing Area E strongly favoured the defence, with cliffs along much of the beach and only two real exits at Seaford and Cuckmere Haven.

Altogether, each German division was expected to gain an initial lodgement in the first three hours of the invasion, then the mass of barges would beach themselves and begin disgorging equipment and heavy vehicles during the late morning and afternoon of S-Tag. The afternoon would be a particularly dangerous time for the Germans, as the RAF began to attack the anchored transport fleets offshore and Thorne's Eastern Command began to react to the landings. Although Milforce was likely to try to mount an operation against 7. Flieger-Division, the limited size of this force and its limited artillery support

THE LANDING OF THE 7. FLIEGER-DIVISION ON S-TAG

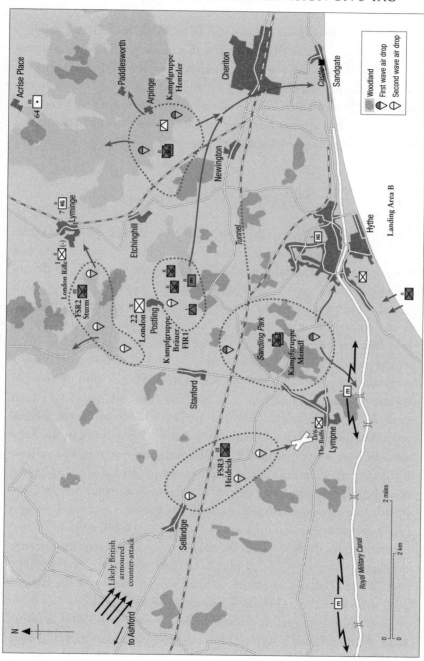

meant that any counter-attacks would be local. Indeed, the primary motivation of Thorne's command at this point would be to extricate any units in the outer crust that had become surrounded, rather than to threaten the beachheads. By late afternoon of S-Tag, the Germans would likely have over 40,000 troops ashore, including paratroopers, and as evening approached, the beached barges would refloat and return to the transports for more equipment.

Seelöwe: The Follow-Through

Once the Germans were ashore and began to establish control over the chaos on the beaches, the operational-level leadership would have two main priorities: (1) establish a coherent defensive perimeter to defend the beachheads and (2) establish lateral communications with neighboring units. Thanks to a combined-arms mentality that was firmly embedded in their tactical doctrine, the Germans intended to land Pioniers, Panzerjägers and Flak in the first wave and this capability would give them the ability to mount a credible defence very quickly – particularly against British troops who were not fluent with this type of combat. Even small numbers of 3.7cm Pak anti-tank guns could keep most British tanks at bay and they had been designed to manoeuvre around without vehicles. Likewise, the 2cm Flak gun could be used as a dual-purpose weapon against British bunkers and troops or against low-flying aircraft. German infantrymen were taught to dig in quickly when consolidating on a captured objective, and within a matter of hours, any British probes would encounter coordinated mortar and machine-gun fire. Again and again on the Eastern Front in 1941–43, even decimated German units demonstrated an ability to quickly establish effective defensive positions. By S-Tag plus 1, the Germans would have artillery and 8.8cm Flak guns ashore, which would make the beachhead perimeters virtually impregnable to local counter-attacks.

Establishing lateral communications between the four landing areas would require a serious effort on the Germans' part and may have taken several days to accomplish. The distance between the XIII Armeekorps at Dymchurch and the VII Armeekorps at Rye was 9 miles across the Dungeness Peninsula and Romney Marsh. Small patrols might have crossed this gap by the evening of S-Tag, but a British stand in the town of Lydd could delay a link-up until S-Tag plus 1. While the distance between the VII Armeekorps and XXXVIII Armeekorps was only 5 miles, establishing a link-up would require a pitched battle for the town of Hastings, which still had a population of 22,000 in September. The British 45th Division had a battalion-size force in Hastings and it would likely require 48–72 hours to root them out, even if attacked from both east and west. However, the British had no anti-aircraft defences in Hastings, which meant that Luftwaffe dive-bombers could be used to bomb resistance centres. The most difficult link-up would be by VIII Armeekorps from Landing Area E, which would require a difficult slog across 10 miles without any armour support. The best-case scenario was that most of the German beachheads could be linked up within 2–4 days, assuming that the British did not make a major effort to interfere and instead focused on building a second line of defence.

General Heinrich-Gottfried von Vietinghoff's XIII Armeekorps also had two other critical tasks that needed to be accomplished as soon as possible: link up with the 7. Flieger-Division and capture Folkestone harbour. After clearing the beach area around Hythe, the 17. Infanterie-Division would have to cross the 65-yard-wide Royal Military Canal, defended by British sappers and a few bunkers. The British were likely to blow up all the bridges over the canal as soon as the Germans landed, although it was possible that Fallschirmjäger from Kampfgruppe Meindl might capture one by *coup de main*. Crossing the Royal Military Canal would have required at least a reinforced battalion-size Kampfgruppe from Oberst Edmund Hoffmeister's Infanterie-Regiment 21 and then pioniers to establish a crossing site with rafts or rubber dinghies. On the Meuse, it had taken German pioniers 3½ hours to construct the first 16-ton bridge, but in Landing Area B, the bridges would first have to be unloaded from barges, moved inland to the canal through Hythe and deployed.[7] Given the chaos on the beaches, it is unlikely that German pioniers could have bridged the Royal Military Canal before mid-afternoon on S-Tag. Once across the canal, the German infantry would simply roll up the British sappers then advance to link up with the closest paratroopers, Kampfgruppe Meindl. During this time, at least until mid-afternoon on S-Tag, the Fallschirmjäger would have to hold off Milforce on their own and eliminate isolated British positions north of the canal.

After the link-up with 7. Flieger-Division was accomplished, von Vietinghoff was supposed to form Kampfgruppe Hoffmeister north of the canal. This battlegroup was to be built around Hoffmeister's Infanterie-Regiment 21 and augmented with tanks from Tauchpanzer-Abteilungen B, Brandenburg infiltration troops, a machine-gun battalion, artillery, motorized Panzerjägers, Pioniers and Flak troops.[8] Given the difficulty in getting equipment off the beach and across the Royal Military Canal, it is unlikely that Kampfgruppe Hoffmeister could be in a position to make a major push towards Folkestone until dusk on S-Tag. Most likely, the assault on Folkestone would have been deferred until dawn on S-Tag plus 1.

Despite plans to employ the 2nd New Zealand Expeditionary Force (2NZEF) to re-establish a defensive line along the Royal Military Canal, Thorne's XII Corps would have had its hands full just trying to salvage the forward elements of both 45th (Wessex) and 1st London divisions; both these units would suffer substantial losses on S-Tag. In London, Brooke would be reluctant to commit the GHQ Reserve in toto until he was certain that there would be no landings in East Anglia; consequently, he was likely to commit all or part of McNaughton's VII Corps to move towards the enemy beachheads and begin probing actions. However, given the limited amount of tactical transport, Brooke was unlikely to launch a major counter-attack before S-Tag plus 2 or 3, by which time the Germans would have in excess of 75,000 troops ashore.

For their part, the Germans had the resources to create these four lodgements and establish a cohesive front within about four days of landing. They would likely have the resources to conserve parts of their transport assets from British counterstrikes and establish both air and sea lines of communication between France and the beachheads in southern England. Once one or two airfields were repaired, wounded could be flown out and some supplies flown in. The Germans planned to bring in bulk supplies, like fuel and food, through captured ports, such as Folkestone and, eventually, Dover. However, it would take time to repair captured ports and airfields and the supply situation would be chaotic for some time, preventing the Germans from mounting large-scale operations. Instead, the Germans would have to focus on grinding towards key terrain, like Dover, with infantry and limited amounts of artillery. Even if elements of the second wave began to arrive on S-Tag plus 10, it would take another week to get these forces ashore and deployed. Thus, according to German planning, a proper breakout operation from the beachheads could not be mounted before about S-Tag plus 17/18 (12/13 October). Before that point, Brooke would be sure that no more major German landings were feasible in 1940 and he could concentrate all available forces in front of the German beachheads.

Seelöwe: An Assessment

It is not my intent to build a hypothetical scenario about *Sea Lion*'s likely outcome, as so many have attempted before. Instead, I have tried to dispassionately lay out the factors that would aid or hinder each side in the accomplishment of their operational goals. I would be remiss if I did not tally up those factors to try to draw some kind of conclusion. However, before getting into that assessment it is important to note a crucial factor that has often been overlooked in a rush to determine a winner in hypothetical *Sea Lion* scenarios. For lack of a better name, that factor is 'Luck'.

Throughout the first two years of the World War II, the Wehrmacht continued to win battles and campaigns that appeared to defy conventional logic. In *Weserübung*, the Royal Navy should have prevented the Germans from capturing distant Narvik, but they did not. In *Fall Gelb*, the French should easily have blocked Guderian from getting across the Meuse so quickly, but they did not. In North Africa, Rommel repeatedly defeated superior Commonwealth forces, and in Russia, the Germans never should have penetrated so deeply into that heavily defended country. Why did the Germans succeed against the odds so often in 1940–42? This is a difficult and controversial subject, one that is still virtually taboo in World War II historiography, but the answer is relatively simple. In essence, German commanders made their own luck by acting boldly and aggressively in ways that their opponents did not expect. To quote the Confederate General Nathan Bedford Forrest, all too often the Wehrmacht simply 'got there firstest, with the mostest'. By standard military logic, the Germans should not have attempted *Seelöwe* as long as the RAF and Royal Navy were intact, but it does not appear that the British were all that prepared if the Germans decided to defy logic. Indeed, the British defences in September 1940 were far less prepared than the French defences in May 1940, which had crumbled when hit hard. It is also important to note – however distasteful to some – that the British Army was defeated again and again in 1940–42 and its battlefield leadership compared to the Germans and Japanese was seriously deficient. In terms of numbers, the British had the edge in *Sea Lion*, but in terms of the intangible moral factors of war, the Germans had the edge. The British enjoyed their own form of luck, in terms of intelligence and technological breakthroughs, but these would only prove beneficial in the long run.

As discussed in the previous sections, neither the RAF nor the Royal Navy was likely to stop the first wave of *Seelöwe*. Any naval actions during the initial crossing would likely be indecisive and not inflict crippling losses upon the German invasion forces. On S-Tag, the Germans would establish four lodgements and link up with their paratroops, while the British beach defences would be overwhelmed in a matter of hours. RAF counter-attacks on the beachheads would inflict significant losses on the stationary transport fleet, but Luftwaffe fighters would cause Bomber Command and Coastal Command painful losses as well. On S-Tag, the British XII Corps would mount local counter-attacks against the 7. Flieger-Division, causing some losses. Overall, both sides were likely to suffer about 5 per cent casualties of engaged forces on S-Tag: roughly 3,000 British (mostly captured) and 4,000 Germans (800–1,000 dead).

After S-Tag, the likely sequence of events would be:

On S-Tag plus 1, the Germans begin to link up their beachheads and XIII Armeekorps begins its push towards Folkestone. Brooke commits the VII Corps to reinforce Thorne and to mount probing attacks towards Beach C. Naval actions occur in the Channel and large-scale air battles over the beachheads. The loss of British Chain Home radar stations at Rye and Pevensey degrade RAF Fighter Command's ability to detect incoming raids in the 11 Group sector.

On S-Tag plus 2, the British 1st Armoured Division makes a poorly planned counter-attack against the boundary of the German VII and XXXVIII Armeekorps in an effort to relieve the garrison in Hastings; the result is a fiasco with nearly 100 British tanks lost. Folkestone is captured.

On S-Tag plus 3, Hastings is captured. However, the Australian Imperial Force (AIF) would be committed to blocking the VIII Armeekorps from linking up with the XXXVIII Armeekorps. The 1st Canadian Division would be deployed to block the XIII Armeekorps. Brooke sends the 42nd (East Lancashire) to replenish the XII Corps defence near Dover. He also orders Southern Command to send the 4th Infantry Division to seal off the German lodgement at Beach E.

On S-Tag plus 4, three of the four German corps have linked up and established a coherent defensive front. The Germans weight their forces towards the XIII Armeekorps sector in an effort to push towards Dover. Brooke commits the 43rd (Wessex) Division to reinforce XII Corps.

By S-Tag plus 5, the German XIII Armeekorps is on the outskirts of Dover, but is stopped. German naval losses are becoming serious as the Royal Navy picks off vessels returning to France, but British destroyer losses are equally serious. Both the RAF and Luftwaffe are being worn down in heavy air battles over the beachheads.

Around S-Tag plus 7, the British V and VII Corps mount a major counter-attack against the isolated German VIII Armeekorps at Newhaven. For the first time, the British employ large numbers of tanks, artillery and infantry. The battleship HMS *Revenge* is brought in to shell the German positions and Bomber Command commits over 100 sorties. Although the German 28. Infanterie-Division is mauled, poor coordination weakens the British counteroffensive and VIII Armeekorps manages to hold on.

By S-Tag plus 8, both sides temporarily shift to the defensive and wait for reinforcements. The German forces in England have some supply difficulties, but are not in immediate danger. The Luftwaffe has an operational fighter base in England at the former RAF Hawkinge.

Around S-Tag plus 12, a medium-size convoy brings part of the XXXXI Armeekorps into Dover. British submarines sink several transports, but an armoured Kampfgruppe from 10. Panzer-Division is landed.

Around S-Tag plus 14, the Germans mount a major attack on the 43rd (Wessex) Division at Dover and shatter it with a brilliantly executed combined-arms attack. The British lack of anti-tank guns is now a liability and Brooke orders some of the more exposed positions abandoned. Dover is occupied by S+15 but is not operational for another week.

Around S-Tag plus 17, the Germans mount an attack on the Canadians at Ashford with 10. Panzer-Division. The Battle of Ashford lasts three days, but the Canadians hold. Meanwhile, a second British attempt to crush the isolated VIII Armeekorps, fails.

By S-Tag plus 20, the Germans have only succeeded in getting a small part of the second wave ashore due to limited port capacity at Folkestone and the declining number of operational transports. The Kriegsmarine informs Hitler that they can only sustain three beachheads and recommend evacuating the VIII Armeekorps from Newhaven to reinforce the lodgement around Eastbourne–Bexhill. On the British side, Brooke has committed all of the GHQ Reserve except the 2nd Armoured Division and now has ten divisions deployed around the enemy beachheads. He takes one division each from Western, Northern and Scottish commands to form a new reserve.

Given the German difficulties in shipping large mechanized units across the Channel with their declining transport assets, the descent into semi-static positional warfare akin to the later Anzio or Salerno beachheads is highly likely. The German first wave is a success, but the second wave is not. By mid-October, it is apparent that *Seelöwe* has become a 'beached whale'. Using their limited armour and skill at combined arms, the Germans can occasionally mount local attacks to gain key terrain, but they cannot breach the inland GHQ Line or mount a serious breakout attempt. The Kriegsmarine is able to maintain small-scale nightly resupply convoys across the Channel, which are usually able to evade British patrols. By S+20, both the Luftwaffe and the RAF are fought out and try to minimize their casualties in order to rebuild. The first month of fighting costs each side over 40,000 casualties.[9]

While the British have succeeded in preventing a German breakout, they cannot crush any of the lodgements and suffer heavy losses in the process. After three weeks, the British have committed most of their available troops and they cannot expect to mount another serious counteroffensive for some months. The Royal Navy has lost so many destroyers sunk or damaged that it can no longer mount regular patrols in the Channel. Instead, the Royal Navy decides to rely upon a new crop of

MTBs and motor gunboats (MGBs), as well as submarines, to interdict the German naval supply lines. After the Germans evacuate Beach E and use these troops to reinforce the forces in Beach D, Rundstedt reconfigures his forces for a winter battle along the GHQ Line. Although both sides mount local attacks in November, the campaign is essentially stabilized until the following spring. A German diplomatic overture seeking a Christmas armistice is rebuffed by Churchill.

At this point, the issue becomes how much longer either side could keep up a battle of attrition that is devouring its troops, ships and aircraft for no real strategic gain. Hitler had plenty of infantry to replace losses in England and could continue a battle of attrition for some time, as he would at Stalingrad in 1942. However, he would likely be running out of shipping after a few months of this and then his armies in England would become less and less capable. Given the resources of 1940, he would never get a large Panzer force across the Channel to capture London. Instead, his armies and fleets would bleed to hold onto obscure British towns, hoping for an armistice that became increasingly unlikely. While Churchill would likely remain upbeat no matter what, it was clear that the British Army could not sustain a battle of attrition into 1941. Unlike the North African campaign, where the majority of the casualties were Commonwealth troops, in Kent and Sussex they would mostly be British. In positional warfare of this type, a force of ten defending divisions could still expect to suffer about 45,000 casualties (including 10,000 dead) per month. By Christmas 1940, Brooke's forces would likely have suffered over 130,000 casualties, but there were no more Australian or New Zealand troops in the pipeline coming to Britain.[10] At best, the British might be able to train and equip sufficient replacements to mount a major counteroffensive in early 1941 but, if that failed, the only remaining option would be to hang on in the trenches. If fighting continued until May 1941, the British Army would be wrecked and unable to withstand any new German landings in East Anglia.

Continued British resistance might stop the German breakout from their beachheads, but it would also incur a cost for the empire overseas. With a major ground campaign on English soil, British forces in North Africa could not expect substantial reinforcements for some time. The British ability to hold Egypt would become more questionable, particularly if Hitler still sent Rommel's Afrika Korps to Libya in early 1941. Recognizing Britain's military weakness, Stalin might easily have been tempted to invade Persia in December 1940 in order to establish a base on the Persian Gulf. Likewise, the British position in India and the Far East would become even more vulnerable to Japanese aggression. British destroyer losses in the Channel battles would seriously weaken convoy defences at a critical time, allowing the U-Boats and Fw-200 Condors to increase their effectiveness against poorly protected shipping routes.

Over the winter of 1940/41, politics would shape the eventual outcome. Churchill would have made his point about resistance but, if continued into 1941, both the British Army and Royal Navy would be weakened to the point that Great Britain's stature as a world power would be seriously compromised. Without an intact army, Churchill could not play much of a role in his envisioned Anglo-American alliance. Indeed, the British failure to drive out the invaders would put the Lend-Lease Act in the US Congress at risk; American support would likely become increasingly tepid in expectation that Britain would eventually negotiate its way out of the war. Despite Churchill's strident rhetoric, it would become evident to most of his cabinet and the military that Britain could be fighting Germany, the Soviet Union and Japan singlehandedly before the end of 1941. The only remaining logic would be to achieve some kind of battlefield success, then negotiate. From Hitler's point of view, a draining, indecisive struggle in England would threaten to undermine domestic support in Germany for the war effort and present Stalin with an extended opportunity for mischief-making in Eastern Europe. Hitler would want to conclude *Seelöwe* while he could still claim a tactical, if not strategic, victory.

Thus, the likely end-game for the *Sea Lion* campaign would be an all-out British offensive to retake Dover in January or February 1941.

Around the same time, Hitler would be likely to order the Luftwaffe to resume large-scale night raids on London in order to demolish the British capital. Although neither side would be likely to achieve their military objectives, the stage would be set for a gradual acceptance that negotiations were the only way out of this self-defeating pit. Churchill would resist the idea, but Brooke's admission that the British Army would run out of infantry by mid-1941 and have to begin dismantling units would be the determining factor. Negotiating through Swiss intermediaries, Hitler would propose withdrawing all his forces from England in return for Churchill agreeing to an armistice. The likely result of *Seelöwe* would be an uneasy peace settling over Europe, while both Great Britain and Germany begin to rebuild their decimated forces for a future showdown under more favourable conditions.

Seelöwe: The Postponement

Of course, *Seelöwe* did not occur. If Hitler had intended to conduct *Seelöwe* on the most favourable days of 25 or 26 September, he would have had to give initial authorization on S-10, or 15/16 September. Instead, he hesitated, waiting to see if the Luftwaffe could succeed in crushing the RAF. By 13 September, Hitler was clearly wavering on making a decision about invasion. However, the results of aerial combat at 15 September were discouraging and made clear to Hitler that the RAF was not a defeated force. With Raeder and the OKM unwilling to take risks and Göring unconcerned with the planning or execution of an invasion, *Seelöwe* found itself without an advocate in Hitler's inner circle. Brauchitsch continued to argue for *Seelöwe*, but without strong conviction and Hitler had little respect for him. Raeder kept recommending postponing the invasion to spring 1941, while Göring suggested that the Luftwaffe could sever Britain's lifelines once Ju-88 bomber production increased. Without Kriegsmarine or Luftwaffe endorsement, *Seelöwe* appeared to be going nowhere and Hitler finally decided to move on to other things. On 17 September, he issued orders to the OKW that *Seelöwe* was 'postponed until further notice'.[11] Hitler's postponement of *Seelöwe* was due as much to inter-service bickering within the Wehrmacht as to Fighter Command's powers of resistance.

Yet Hitler refused to cancel the operation outright in order not to grant Churchill a propaganda victory or to dissuade Franco from joining the Axis. On 12 October, Hitler ordered that preparations would continue in order to put pressure on the British. He would decide whether or not to conduct *Seelöwe* in 1941, as Raeder had recommended all along. During October, serious preparations continued both in terms of improving the available amphibious craft and training the motley collection of crews. Hitler also ordered the Luftwaffe to increase its night-bombing of British cities and the Kriegsmarine to increase attacks on British convoys. His strategic intent was to maintain and increase the pressure on Great Britain, not walk away from a confrontation with Churchill. Contrary to interpretations that regard the postponement as cancellation, it is important to remember that Hitler postponed a number of important military operations, not just *Seelöwe*. Postponement did not mean abandonment; *Fall Gelb* had been postponed 19 times during the winter of 1939/40 and *Barbarossa* was postponed from May to June 1941. In 1943, he would postpone *Zitadelle* several times. In each case, *Fall Gelb*, *Seelöwe*, *Barbarossa* or *Zitadelle*, unfavourable circumstances prompted Hitler to delay an operation in hope of achieving a more favourable outcome at a later time.

As one indication that *Seelöwe* was not merely maintained as a deception operation, on 18 October the OKL instituted a priority programme to develop a new type of heavy glider that could lift a Pz IV medium tank across the Channel. Both Junkers and Messerschmitt built prototypes, but the Ju-322 Mammoth was an unflyable failure. The Messerschmitt Me-323 Gigant was more successful and first flew in February 1941. By June 1941, there were about 60 Me-323s available, enough to land a Panzer-Abteilung in England. The investment of RM 45 million in this programme indicates that the Wehrmacht was seriously planning for a bigger, better version of *Seelöwe* in 1941 or after the conquest of the Soviet Union.[12]

Typically, Hitler's intent to invade the Soviet Union is presented as an *idée fixe* that drove him to abandon *Seelöwe* post-haste and prevented him from logically assessing any strategic alternatives. However, this flies against the fact that Hitler gave full support to Operation *Felix*, the planned attack on Gibraltar, while concurrently directing the OKH to develop plans for Operation *Barbarossa*. Führer Directive No. 20, which outlined Operation *Marita* – the invasion of Greece – was delivered five days before Führer Directive No. 21 revealed Operation *Barbarossa*. Like any politician, Hitler was keeping his options open and planned for major operations in the Mediterranean against Great Britain, while also planning for war with the Soviet Union. When it became clear that Franco was not going to join the Axis, Hitler decided to put *Seelöwe* on the back burner. On 9 January 1941, Hitler ordered preparations for *Seelöwe* to cease, but this did not affect the Luftwaffe's Me-323 programme, nor Oberst Siebel's ferry programme, nor the Kriegsmarine's *Marinefährprahm* (MFP) programme, nor the Heer's development of *Pionierlandungsboote*. In other words, the inertia of *Seelöwe* preparations continued despite Hitler's edicts and, consequently, the creation of new air-landing and amphibious technology came to fruition in 1941. Britain was also held at risk by these new technologies, despite the Luftwaffe's failure to achieve a decision in 1940.

More than anything, the postponement of *Seelöwe* in September 1940 demonstrated how the German war effort against Britain was seriously compromised by personal agendas that Hitler allowed to pervert a rational military decision-making process. Just as Göring wanted to use his Luftwaffe to smash the RAF and gain personal glory, Raeder was more concerned with shielding the Kriegsmarine from potential public humiliation in the English Channel. Likewise, Dönitz's fixation on *Tonnageschlacht* diverted Germany's attention away from seeking to inflict crippling blows on Britain's economy.

September 1940 was the time for Hitler's famous willpower to kick in and demand that everyone fall in line behind a single objective – as he would do for *Barbarossa*. Instead, by tolerating these personal agendas, Hitler threw away any hope of achieving decisive results in regard to England. Hitler later complained in 1943 that he never should have let Raeder talk him out of conducting *Seelöwe*.[13]

CHAPTER 8

The Isle of Wight Gambit

During the planning of *Seelöwe*, both Hitler and the OKH had suggested preliminary operations or raids that might be conducted to put immediate pressure on Britain. On 13 July, Hitler was the first to suggest to Halder the possibility of a raid on the Isle of Wight.[1] Three days later, this idea was incorporated into Führer Directive No. 16, which allowed for 'limited operations' before the main invasion, such as the occupation of the Isle of Wight. Halder and the OKH favoured this idea as well, since it would not require a large force and could be conducted fairly quickly.

Both Hitler and Halder recognized that the Isle of Wight offered a potential offshore base to increase the pressure on Great Britain. The Abwehr did not know much about British defences, but it was unlikely that the island was held in great strength. Furthermore, since the Isle of Wight was separated from the mainland by the Solent (1–4 miles wide), the risk of strong British counter-attacks was small. Thus a relatively modest German force – perhaps two divisions – could be transported from Cherbourg and seize the Isle of Wight in a *coup de main*. Holding the Isle of Wight offered considerable advantages that could increase the feasibility of *Seelöwe*. First, German artillery deployed on the north side of the Isle of Wight could shell the mainland across the Solent and force the Royal Navy to withdraw its cruiser-destroyer forces from the naval base at Portsmouth. Second, capture of the island would provide the Luftwaffe with four civilian airfields that were much closer to England, thereby alleviating the problems caused by the limited range of the Bf-109 fighter and providing an emergency landing site for damaged aircraft.

The Isle of Wight fell under Lieutenant General Claude Auchinleck's Southern Command, which deployed Brigadier Daniel M. W. Beak's 12th Infantry Brigade from the 4th Infantry Division to defend the island.[2] Beak, a distinguished veteran who had been awarded the Victoria Cross in 1918, had three regular infantry battalions, a training battalion and five companies of Home Guard to defend an island that was 23 miles across. The main British concept for defending the Isle of Wight went back to the 19th century and focused on shielding Southampton and Portsmouth from enemy naval raids. Thus, the bulk of the defences on the Isle of Wight were traditionally focused at either end, around the towns of Bembridge in the east and Freshwater in the west. Two regiments of coastal artillery, with 6-inch and 9.2-inch guns, defended both locales.[3] However, the coastal forts had been designed prior to the World War I and had negligible protection against air attack. In June 1940, Beak established his brigade headquarters in Billingham, in the south-centre of the island, and decided to deploy most of his troops to defend the southern coasts. His brigade had served in France and been evacuated from Dunkirk, which made it critically short of transport. Even in September 1940, Beak's brigade relied upon civilian buses and bicycles for movement. Furthermore, Beak's brigade was not provided with field artillery support and there were no tanks or armoured vehicles on the Isle of Wight.

The 527th Coastal Artillery Regiment protected the west end of the Solent with four batteries and the River Yar helped to make this area defensible even from land attack. Beak left the 50th (Holding)

Battalion Hampshire Regiment, which included 200 militiamen from the Channel Islands, to assist the coastal gunners in defending this region. The eastern end of the island was defended by the 530th Coastal Artillery Regiment, whose main position was the Culver Down Battery, armed with two 9.2-inch guns in open concrete pits. Many of the coastal gunners were Territorial Army or reservists and these troops had yet to dig trenches or deploy barbed wire around their batteries. Nor did the batteries have more than token air defences, such as a Lewis Gun or two. Fort Bembridge, located near Bembridge airport (which was blocked with old cars), was garrisoned by just 14 support troops in 1940.[4] The RAF maintained the Chain Home station at Ventnor on the south coast but otherwise there was no other significant RAF presence on the island.

Although the British defences on the Isle of Wight were spread very thinly in 1940, the British could take some comfort from the fact that there were few decent beaches where an enemy could conduct an amphibious landing. The beaches on the south-west coast of the island were awful – narrow and overshadowed by steep cliffs. Indeed, the only practical invasion area was a 2½-mile-long stretch of beach between Shanklin and Sandown on the east coast. The beach was far from ideal but was close to two of the island's four civilian airfields. The Culver Downs Battery overlooked Sandown Bay with its two 9.2-inch guns, but otherwise British defences in this critical area were not strong. Dean's troops had installed Admiralty Scaffolding on some sections of beach but had only limited amounts of barbed wire and no mines. Access to the beach, or the Culver Downs Battery, was not yet blocked. The Yaverland battery overlooking the bay had a pair of old 6-pounder guns, a searchlight and a machine-gun bunker. Company C, from the 6th Battalion, Black Watch was assigned to defend the 4,500 yards of beach front.[5]

Hitler's main concern about *Seelöwe* was the potential for embarrassing heavy losses in a failed cross-Channel attack. Yet when he decided to postpone *Seelöwe*, Hitler still had the option to mount a raid on the Isle of Wight to divert attention away from the Luftwaffe's failure to subdue the RAF. A *coup de main* against the Isle of Wight could be conducted with much smaller forces, entailing far less risk. If the operation failed, it could be described as only a raid, not an invasion. If the *coup de main* succeeded, it would have both propaganda and tactical value for continuing the struggle against Britain in 1941.

A *coup de main* against the Isle of Wight would not have looked like the slow-going *Seelöwe*, but more like the landing at Narvik in April 1940. Bey's destroyers could cross the 75-mile stretch of Channel from Cherbourg to Sandown Bay in just three hours, arriving just before dawn with the vanguard of a *Gebirgsjägerregiment* from the 6. Gebirgs-Division. At dawn a battalion from Oberst Eugen Meindl's Luftlande-Sturm-Regiment 1 could land near Bembridge, with an assault company landing next to the Culver Down Battery in gliders and the rest by parachute near the airport. Unlike *Seelöwe*, this style of raid would very likely achieve tactical surprise; it would likely proceed as follows. The Luftwaffe would provide smoke for the landing and Stuka support to suppress any strongpoints. After the British coastal batteries were neutralized by glider troops, the Gebirgsjäger would land by Sturmboote and overwhelm the single British infantry company in the area. Bey's destroyers would beat a hasty retreat, with Luftwaffe fighter cover. Once the beach was secure – and the Gebirgsjäger would make no effort to clear it – they would link up with the Fallschirmjäger near Bembridge airport and push on to secure the town of Bembridge and the minor port of St Helens, which was only held by Home Guard. Several hours after the initial landing, Meindl would land a second Fallschirmjäger battalion to capture the Nodes Point battery north of St Helens. The coastal gunners, lacking much in the way of small arms, would be quickly defeated. By late afternoon, the Germans would have captured St Helens and Bembridge. During the day, the Luftwaffe would bomb the towns of Cowes and Fishbourne on the northern shore to disrupt ferry traffic across the Solent in order to isolate the island. The RAF would do well in several air actions over the Isle of Wight, but fail to strike Bey's destroyers or prevent the airborne operation. Uncertain about the enemy situation, Auchinleck would wait for more information on the enemy landing. Beak would be uncertain whether there would be more enemy landings and, lacking artillery or vehicles, could do little more than try to assemble a small reserve near Newport in the centre of the island. By nightfall, only a single company of the Black Watch and one company of Home Guard would be in contact with the enemy.

With the approach of dusk, two German convoys would depart Cherbourg. Bey's destroyers would cross with another battalion of Gebirgsjäger and land them during the night. At the same time, three torpedo boats would escort the transports *Moltkefels* and *Niedenfels*, modern freighters capable of 16 knots.[6] Each ship would carry a Panzer-Kompanie, an artillery battery, a Flak battery, engineers, wheeled vehicles and supplies. Although the Royal Navy would no doubt put out destroyer sweeps from Plymouth and Portsmouth, the odds of successfully intercepting fast transports would be low. Pulling into St Helens, both transports would begin unloading during the night. It is possible that RAF Coastal Command might sink these transports after dawn, but with a bit of luck and daring, the Germans would get some heavy equipment across the Channel. On day two, German engineers would begin restoring the captured batteries and airfield. Once they had even limited numbers of tanks and artillery ashore, the Germans could begin expanding their bridgehead. By the end of the second day, the Germans would have a firm lodgement with perhaps 3,000–4,000 troops ashore.

After the initial surprise wore off, Auchinleck would probably attempt to move another brigade across the Solent to reinforce Beak. Unfortunately, while there were plenty of ferries available to carry troops, few could carry vehicles or artillery. Any British reinforcements in the first few days would essentially be 'leg' infantry, with little artillery and no tanks. Bomber Command would doubtless bomb St Helens port, but poor accuracy would make this little more than a nuisance. Meanwhile, the Germans could continue to use their destroyers and small numbers of fast transports to bring small amounts

A Spitfire from the PRU photographed the port of Boulogne in early September 1940, revealing a large number of barges assembled for the invasion. The PRU gave the British an excellent indication of growing enemy amphibious capabilities, but could not reveal the timing of the invasion or the intended invasion beaches. Bomber Command attacked the invasion ports with some success, inflicting about 10 per cent losses on the assembled shipping. (IWM HU 93074)

A Tauchpanzer III being loaded aboard a ship in July 1940. The tanks were supposed to be launched about 200 yards offshore from special barges and rely upon an air hose while submerged. The Tauchpanzers were later successfully used in crossing the Bug River during the invasion of the Soviet Union in June 1941, but it is uncertain how they would have performed in the English Channel. However, it is likely at least some of the Tauchpanzers would have survived, giving the German first wave a powerful support force. (Bundesarchiv, Fotograf: Engelmeir)

The heavy cruiser *Admiral Hipper* was the only large surface warship the Kriegsmarine had available for *Seelöwe*, but Raeder was unwilling to risk it in the English Channel to escort barges. Instead, he assigned it to Operation *Herbstreise*, the diversionary operation, and then for an Atlantic raiding sortie. However, the Heer leadership was incensed that the *Hipper* was excluded from the invasion and attempted to get the Kriegsmarine to change its priorities. (Author)

General Sir Alan Brooke at his desk in the War Office in London. As commander of GHQ forces, Brooke would have been responsible for reacting to the German invasion and committing his limited armoured reserves. Despite his reputation from Dunkirk, Brooke was more of a desk soldier than a combat leader and Churchill quickly pulled him into the political realm. Brooke would likely have conducted a by-the-book fight for the beachheads, which the British Army was unprepared to win. (IWM TR 149)

Two sentries, possibly from the Somerset Light Infantry, on watch atop the chalk cliffs of the Seven Sisters at Birling Gap, near Beachy Head, on 28 October 1940. The sentries have a Bren Gun with two magazines. The British were forced to defend long stretches of beach with essentially a picket force. On S-Tag, the German 6. Gebirgsjäger-Division would have landed 1½ miles down the beach, at Cuckmere Haven. (IWM H 5108)

A Type 23 bunker on the English coast. The bunkers built between June and September 1940 were crude in design with walls offering protection only against small-arms fire and mortars. The wide apertures and brick construction would have made the occupants highly vulnerable to fire from either 2cm Flak guns or 3.7cm Pak guns. A bunker such as this was only intended to house a single light-machine-gun team, which meant limited range and firepower. Many of the bunkers were poorly positioned, with inadequate fields of fire. (Author)

A British fighting position overlooking a beach, August 1940. In many places the British 'crust defence' was rather thin. This position is equipped with an obsolete Lewis Gun (two drums of ammunition) and small arms. The lackadaisical attitude of the troops is evident. Note the absence of barbed wire in front of the position or any kind of bomb-proof defences. Lightly manned beach positions like this would have offered little resistance to the invaders. (IWM H 2724)

German Do 17Z bombers over England. The RAF succeeded in inflicting unacceptable losses upon German daylight bombing raids, but when the raids switched to night most of Fighter Command's defences were useless. The defeat of the Luftwaffe's daylight raiding tactics did not actually bring much of a respite from the German onslaught and only meant that Britain's cities were being bombed at night, instead of by day. The result was over 41,000 British civilian deaths by the end of May 1941. (Author)

A British 3.7-inch heavy anti-aircraft gun, which was the backbone of Britain's area defence system in 1940. Although this weapon, introduced in 1937, had the ability to engage German aircraft at medium altitudes, the fire control system that directed it was not particularly accurate. Before the introduction of radar fire control in mid-1941, it typically required 1,000 rounds fired to achieve a single hit. The relative ineffectiveness of British anti-aircraft defences is one of the facets normally omitted from standard Battle of Britain historiography. (Author)

German troops practising with Pioniersturmboote (assault boats) off the French coast, late June 1940. The Germans massed up to 800 of these small craft for Seelöwe and each could carry six troops. Although not particularly fast, the Sturmboote were very manoeuvrable and capable of being driven straight up on a beach. The Sturmboote would be carried across the Channel in larger vessels then unloaded offshore. The German advance units would then land at dawn on the British coast in dozens of these vessels. (Bundesarchiv, Fotograf: Bernhard Borghorst)

German troops training for *Seelöwe*. Had the invasion occurred, this would likely have been the appearance of the first wave as they approached the beaches in Kent and Sussex. (Bundesarchiv, Fotograf: Bernhard Borghorst)

German infantry leap ashore from Sturmboote on the island of Muhu on 14 September 1941. The first moments of a landing in England would likely have looked like this. Within a year of postponing *Sea Lion*, the Wehrmacht was able to successfully demonstrate its amphibious capabilities against the Soviets. (Author)

A Martello tower in Eastbourne, overlooking the German Landing Area D. In 1940, the British pressed these relics of the Napoleonic Wars back into service as observation posts. Each was provided a squad-sized garrison with a Lewis or Bren light machine gun and had wire communications to the nearest artillery units. While these solidly built structures would likely have become centres of British resistance nests near the beaches, they were highly vulnerable to air attack or even mortar fire. (Author)

The shingle beach at Pevensey Bay, just north of Eastbourne. According to the *Seelöwe* plan, the German 26. Infanterie-Division would have landed in this area on S-Tag. The beach was mined and obstacles consisted of barbed wire and Admiralty Scaffolding. The 4th Battalion, Duke of Cornwall's Light Infantry was responsible for defending this wide sector, with only about two companies watching the ocean front. Even with a small sea wall in place in 1940, the Germans would likely have secured this beach quickly and begun to push inland. (Author)

A 2cm Flak 30 gun on a German light warship. Unlike the Royal Navy, which only had 100 20mm dual-purpose guns in 1940, the Kriegsmarine had ample numbers of the Rheinmetall-built 2cm gun. Any British destroyer that approached the invasion convoys would be fired upon by many of these rapid-fire weapons, which could fire armour-piercing ammunition and high-explosive incendiary rounds. British gun crews in exposed mounts and crew on the unarmoured bridges would be highly vulnerable to 2cm fire. (Bundesarchiv, Fotograf: Vorländer)

R-Boats in the English Channel off Boulogne. This view gives a good impression of visibility conditions in the Channel even in daylight, with engagement ranges being only a few miles. The R-Boats lacked the torpedoes and speed of the Schnellboote, but they were capable of laying smoke and were highly manoeuvrable. (Bundesarchiv, Fotograf: Hasert)

A flotilla of R-Boats in the English Channel practising for *Seelöwe*. Each invasion convoy would have been led by a flotilla of five or six R-Boats, which would also sweep for mines. (Bundesarchiv, Fotograf: Dr. Feitel)

A group of Ju-52 transports coming in low over the Aegean in 1943. Unlike intercepting enemy bombers – which usually crossed the coast above 10,000 feet – the airborne echelon would have come in low across the Channel, reducing warning time and making intercept far more difficult. RAF Hurricanes that descended to intercept transports would risk being 'bounced' from above by the escorting Bf-109 fighters. (Bundesarchiv, Fotograf: Werner Bockelmann)

German Fallschirmjäger jumping from Ju-52 transports. The first wave of the airborne invasion would occur very quickly and land atop the 2nd London Infantry Brigade headquarters. Several British anti-aircraft units in the area would likely have caused losses to the transports, but the German airborne drop was likely to achieve its initial objectives without excessive casualties. Although the drop zones were not ideal, they were relatively close to the beaches of Landing Area B and would have helped to absorb any initial British counterattacks. (Bundesarchiv, Fotograf: Kleiner)

The fantasy. British Home Guard troops from the 5th Battalion (Doncaster) capture a simulated German paratrooper in a Yorkshire training exercise held in mid-October 1940. The War Office regarded the Home Guard as well suited to deal with enemy airborne landings. Unfortunately, the Germans intended to drop the 7. Flieger-Division into a fairly small area north of Hythe and opportunities to overwhelm isolated enemy paratroopers would have been rare. The simplistic infantry tactics demonstrated in this photo – all men converging upon a paratrooper armed with a submachine gun – are laughable. (IWM H 4755)

The reality. German Fallschirmjäger rounding up British prisoners on Crete, May 1941. The sudden descent of the 7. Flieger-Division into southern England would likely have caught a number of British troops from the 1st London Division by surprise. Well trained and tactically aggressive, the Fallschirmjäger were more than a match for poorly trained and equipped Territorials. (Bundesarchiv, Fotograf: Franz Peter Weixler)

Cuckmere Haven, southeast of Seaford, was one of the objectives for the German VIII Armeekorps in landing Area E. The 6. Gebirgsjäger-Division intended to land a reinforced regiment in this sector just after dawn on S-Tag, from a flotilla of motorized fishing boats. This area is known as 'the Seven Sisters' due to the series of steep chalk cliffs, but there is a small beach near the mouth of the river Cuckmere. In September 1940, this area was defended by a company-size force of recently raised British troops, with a motley collection of weaponry. (Author)

The beach at Cuckmere Haven seen from high ground on the eastern corner, on which British field works were located. The British defenders would have enjoyed enfilade fire against the landing Gebirgsjäger, but lacked the firepower to defeat a regiment-sized force. (Author)

The RAF's main weapon for use against the invasion convoys would be the Blenheim light bomber; Coastal Command had about 90 Blenheims and Bomber Command had 130. The Blenheim could only carry four 250lb bombs and had a single wing-mounted .303-cal machine gun, meaning that it had limited ability to strafe targets. Furthermore, the survivability of the Blenheim in the face of enemy fighters was poor, since the German Bf 109 fighter had a speed advantage of more than 100 miles per hour. Blenheims would likely have been committed in squadron-size attacks, at low level, making them vulnerable to Flak as well. (IWM HU 72753)

The Germans were able to fabricate 25 Siebel ferries in time for *Sea Lion*'s expected S-Tag in late September 1940. However, instead of using them to transport cargo, the Luftwaffe assigned them to carry the weapons of Flakkorps I and Flakkorps II. Equipped with four 8.8cm Flak and two 2cm Flak, the Siebel ferries would have provided a stable anti-aircraft platform to protect offshore shipping in the landing zones. No doubt, the 8.8cm guns might have provided fire support to ground forces, if needed. (Author)

Infantry of the 10th Battalion, Royal Berkshire Regiment and carriers in a simulated attack during a training exercise in Suffolk, June 1942. The British Army drew the incorrect lesson from the French campaign that carriers could be used in the attack rather than just as support vehicles, even though they were highly vulnerable to mortar and artillery fire. British counterattacks against the invasion bridgeheads would likely have seen such amateurish tactics as this. (IWM H 20536)

The British Army's main trump card against invasion was the 1st and 21st Army Tank Brigades, which together had a total of slightly more than 200 Matilda II tanks. Although this medium tank was impervious to the standard German 3.7cm Pak anti-tank gun, the newer 5cm Pak 38 could penetrate its armour. The Matilda II was a tough opponent, but it was slow and did not fire high-explosive ammunition, which limited what it could accomplish against infantry-heavy units. (IWM H 9527)

The 25-pounder gun was introduced at the start of the Second World War to replace the 18-pounder gun and the 4.5-inch howitzer. Each British infantry division was intended to have three field regiments with 24 25-pounders each, but in September 1940 most divisions only had a battery or two of the new guns. Here, 25-pounder guns of the 142nd Field Regiment, 45th Infantry Division, conduct a training shoot on a range near Eastbourne, 12 August 1940. This battery would have been involved in the beachhead battle from the opening hours of *Sea Lion*. (IWM H 2976)

The British submarine HMS *Tigris* at Holy Loch after returning from her second war patrol on 16 September 1940. The Royal Navy had more than a dozen modern submarines which could be committed against German shipping in the English Channel and this force may well have been best suited to interfering with the enemy's supply lines to its invasion force in England. (IWM A6586)

A Marinefährprahm (MFP) in harbour in 1943. The MFP incorporated lessons learned from the barge/ferry programmes of 1940 and resulted in one of the best all-around landing craft of the Second World War. The shallow draft of the MFPs made them difficult to hit with torpedoes and they were heavily armed with anti-aircraft weapons. (Bundesarchiv, Fotograf: Hirsche)

German troops crossing the Strait of Messina on a Siebel ferry in August 1943. The ability of heavy vehicles to drive straight onto the deck of a Siebel ferry, akin to a modern 'Ro-Ro' vessel, proved very handy for the Wehrmacht during the rest of the Second World War. (Bundesarchiv, Bild 101I-303-0580-04, Fotograf: Funke)

of troops and equipment across the Channel with relative impunity. Any naval actions in the Channel between opposing destroyers were not likely to be decisive. Within a week, the Germans could have most of a division on the Isle of Wight and would begin clearing the eastern half of the island, forcing the RAF to abandon the radar site at Ventnor. In London, Brooke would likely regard the Isle of Weight landing as a diversion and be opposed to committing too many forces onto the island. Over the course of several weeks, the British would retreat into the western end of the island while the Germans would content themselves with capturing the port of Cowes in the north and establishing a line along the River Medina. In time, the Germans might take the rest of the Isle of Wight by the end of 1940 or simply hold the eastern end of the island as a bargaining chip. In any event, the prevailing military factors suggest that the Germans had the capability to seize at least the eastern half of the Isle of Wight in 1940 and there was very little that the British could do to stop this.

Another potential possibility for a German raid, diversionary operation or a *coup de main* in September 1940 was the Isle of Sheppey, off the Kentish coast. The island, separated from the mainland by a wide channel known as the Swale, would be relatively easy to defend if it could be seized. A single bridge connected the island to the mainland and the garrison consisted solely of the 2/6th Queen's Royal Regiment from the 35th Infantry Brigade, 1st London Division. RAF Coastal Command had an airbase on the island, RAF Eastchurch, defended by a detachment of training personnel armed with eight Vickers machine guns.[7] The 518th Coastal Artillery Regiment had a few batteries on the island, protecting the Royal Navy dockyard at Sheerness and access into the River Medway. In late September 1940, the 2nd Cruiser Squadron was based out of Sheerness, with the light cruisers HMS *Aurora* and *Cardiff*. The Isle of Sheppey had excellent sandy beaches in the south-east, which were only defended by scattered sections and platoons. If the Germans could capture or destroy the sole bridge by glider assault, a British counter-attack across the Swale would have been very difficult. It is possible that the Isle of Sheppey could have been captured by a regiment of Fallschirmjäger and reinforced by destroyer-transports, in order to build up a lodgement on Britain's east coast. Nor could British armour be used to counter-attack across the Swale, which would effectively serve as a moat. A lightning raid on the Isle of Sheppey could have acquired a defensible airbase in Britain, but without the risks of a full-scale *Seelöwe* invasion.

CHAPTER 9

Siege Operations against Great Britain, October 1940–May 1941

German pressure upon Great Britain did not let up merely because the Luftwaffe failed to achieve daylight air superiority over southern England – far from it. The Luftwaffe kept up the pressure with regular night raids which inflicted considerable damage, while the Kriegsmarine's efforts to conduct anti-commerce operations against British trade increased during the winter of 1940/41. While still continuing to devote considerable resources for anti-invasion defences, the Royal Navy – with only modest help from the RAF – was forced to rapidly develop counter-measures to prevent these German campaigns from disrupting Britain's trade. Simultaneously, Churchill tried to respond to Germany's siege tactics by using RAF Bomber Command to pulverize critical targets, but Britain's resources were stretched too thinly to mount an effective strategic bombing campaign.

Despite British interference with X-Gerät signals, Luftwaffe night raids continued to intensify throughout the winter of 1940/41. A total of 23 major raids were flown in November–December 1940, but poor weather and low operational readiness rates of bombers reduced operations in January–February 1941. Luftwaffe losses on night raids averaged 1.5 per cent, which was far more sustainable than daylight raids. In total, the Luftwaffe lost about 500 bombers and 1,500 aircrew between November 1940 and May 1941 in order to inflict over 26,000 fatalities upon Britain. In contrast, RAF Bomber Command's offensive sputtered along through the winter months, achieving very little. Unlike the Luftwaffe, Bomber Command's raids were much smaller in size and frequency. In an effort to retaliate for the Coventry raid, the War Cabinet directed Bomber Command to conduct Operation *Abigail Rachel* on the night of 16/17 December 1940; 134 bombers were sent against the city of Mannheim in the largest British raid of the war to date. Lacking navigational aids, most of the bombs were dropped on the outskirts of the city, resulting in the deaths of only 34 Germans. Seven of the British bombers were lost – a 5.2 per cent loss rate.[1] Overall, Bomber Command lost 341 bombers and over 1,000 aircrew in the same period to inflict slightly over 1,000 fatalities upon Germany.

Table 12: Luftwaffe large-scale bomber raids on Great Britain, 1940–41

Month	Number of Bombers Involved					Total Large Raids	Bombers Lost*	British Deaths
	500+	400+	300+	200+	100+			
November 1940		1	4	1	6	12	84	4,588
December 1940		1	1	4	5	11	c. 36	3,793
January 1941					8	8	c. 42	c. 1,800
February 1941						0	c. 50	c. 900
March 1941		1	2	3	7	13	c. 80	c. 4,500
April 1941	2			4	9	15	c. 100	6,065
May 1941	1		1	3	5	10	c. 110	c. 5,000
TOTAL	3	3	8	15	40	69	500+	26,600+

Excludes non-combat losses and losses in the Mediterranean

Table 13: RAF Bomber Command large-scale bomber raids on Germany, 1940–41

Month	Number of Bombers Involved		Total Large Raids	Bombers Lost	German Deaths
	200+	100+			
November 1940			0	46	42
December 1940		1	1	40	34
January 1941		2	2	19	74
February 1941	1	2	3	48	N/A
March 1941		4	4	54	145
April 1941	1	3	4	87	286
May 1941		7	7	57	453
TOTAL	**2**	**19**	**21**	**351**	**1,035+**

Once Dönitz was able to get the French port of Lorient fully operational, the U-Boat campaign began to change dramatically and Wolfpack tactics became a reality. On 21–22 September 1940, Dönitz was able to concentrate several U-Boats against the unescorted convoy HX 72 west of Ireland. More U-Boats were quickly vectored in and the 43-ship convoy was assailed by seven U-Boats, although virtually all of the damage was inflicted by Kretschmer's U-99 and Schepke's U-100. In the ensuing action, 11 vessels (including three tankers) of 72,727 tons were sunk, for no loss to the Germans. Three weeks later, Dönitz was able to employ *Rudeltaktik* again against convoys SC 7 and HX 79; in a three-day battle, nine U-Boats sank 32 merchantmen of 154,591 tons for no loss. The British convoy escorts, who relied on ASDIC to prosecute underwater targets, were completely ineffective against the new German tactic of U-Boats attacking on the surface and from multiple directions. By October 1940, Dönitz knew that *Rudeltaktik* could maximize the effectiveness of his limited U-Boat force and inflict serious damage on British convoys. The U-Boats enjoyed one more major success in 1940, against convoy HX 90 in early December, before winter weather reduced the operational tempo. In the period September–December 1940, Dönitz was able to sink 191 ships of 1,033,850 tons for the loss of only four U-Boats – an impressive accomplishment and one which worried Churchill.

Another disturbing trend for the British was Dönitz's decision to start sending several U-Boat patrols at a time off West Africa, where the convoys were often unescorted. Although U-Boats had mounted occasional patrols off West Africa since the beginning of the war, the ability to operate from Lorient made these long-range patrols more practical. A single U-Boat, the U-65, made an 88-day patrol from Lorient and operated off Freetown in November–December 1940, where it sank seven ships of 56,326 tons. Given this success, Dönitz began regular patrols off West Africa in early 1941 and found a rich harvest. Two more U-Boats from Lorient, U-105 and U-106, made 112-day patrols off Freetown, where they sank a total of 20 ships of 117,938 tons. In addition, U-106 found the battleship HMS *Malaya* escorting convoy SL 68 on 20 March 1941 and torpedoed her; the British capital ship was out of action for five months. Increased German U-Boat activity off West Africa meant that the Royal Navy had to spread its escort forces even more thinly to cover convoys from Freetown to the Western Approaches. Although poor weather conditions in the Atlantic prevented Dönitz from successfully employing *Rudeltaktik* during the opening months of 1941, his U-Boats still managed to sink 99 ships of 545,782 tons in January–March.

Closer to home, the British had difficulty reining in German mines, destroyers and S-Boats in coastal waters. The new German acoustic mine was particularly difficult to sweep, since it could lie dormant for a time before activating; areas that appeared swept suddenly became active again. Nor did the previous degaussing efforts help to mitigate the acoustic mine threat. Consequently, German mines sank 48 Allied vessels in British waters in November 1940. On 12–19 December, the Luftwaffe mounted a major effort and dropped

300 mines in the Thames Estuary, which resulted in the loss of 12 ships of 20,675 tons. The Kriegsmarine's torpedo boats and minesweepers continued to aggressively mine British coastal waters as well. Another 18 ships were lost to mines in January 1941 and 13 in February. Altogether, German mines sank over 100 ships in British waters in the period November 1940–February 1941, including two destroyers and two submarines. The Royal Navy was forced to devote large resources to minesweeping efforts and yet the waters off the Thames Estuary, Liverpool and the Humber remained unsafe. However, the Royal Navy was able to retaliate with its own mine-laying campaign, which claimed two German torpedo boats and a number of merchant ships sunk in the same period.

Bey's destroyers enjoyed a run of success in the English Channel that highlighted the superior speed of the German warships. On the late afternoon of 17 October, Bey conducted a daring sortie from Brest with four destroyers into the South-west Approaches, hoping to catch one of several poorly escorted convoys in the area. RAF Coastal Command spotted Bey's destroyers and Force F (light cruisers HMS *Newcastle* and *Emerald*, plus five destroyers under Captain Louis Mountbatten) was dispatched from Plymouth to intercept. At 1707 hours HMS *Newcastle* opened fire on Bey's destroyers at a range of over 30,000 yards. Bey's destroyers fired a volley of torpedoes and turned away, using a smokescreen and their superior speed to escape. An attack by a Coastal Command Blenheim failed to score any hits on the fast-moving German destroyers. Bey successfully returned to Brest, without loss. On the night of 24 November, Bey conducted a sortie off the Lizard with three destroyers and sank a small Dutch tanker and sped off before Mountbatten's destroyers could intercept. Four nights later, Bey brazenly approached Plymouth with three destroyers, sinking a few small vessels, before turning south to return to Brest. Although the German destroyers had radar, at 0640 hours Mountbatten's five destroyers suddenly appeared on the port quarter at a range of just 1,650 yards. Mountbatten was coming on at 28 knots, in line-ahead formation, but when he spotted the German destroyers he mistakenly decided to steer a parallel course in order to bring all armament to bear. Bey responded as he had before – with a volley of 12 torpedoes then turning away, laying smoke and running off at 35 knots. HMS *Javelin* was hit by two torpedoes and crippled. Mountbatten pursued Bey for two hours, firing madly, but scored no hits. Bey made it safely back to Brest.[2] When it was over, Admiral Sir Dudley Pound, the First Sea Lord, conceded that the German destroyers 'were faster than ours'.[3] However, Bey's destroyers returned to Germany for engine overhauls during the winter of 1940/41 and there were no German destroyers in the English Channel again until April 1941.

The Kriegsmarine S-Boats remained very active in the English Channel and off the coast of East Anglia during the winter of 1940/1941, mounting raids against British coastal convoys. The Royal Navy formed a dedicated unit of four destroyers from Harwich to counter the S-Boat raids, which continued to pick off coastal merchantmen on the Southend to Methil route. A few destroyers were equipped with Type 286 search radar, but this could only detect an S-Boat at a range of 2 miles or less. On 19 November 1940, one German raid miscarried and S-38 was rammed and sunk by the destroyer HMS *Campbell* – this was the first S-Boat sunk in action. Nineteen of S-38's crew were captured, which yielded intelligence value as well.[4] Nevertheless, on 23 December the Kriegsmarine mounted an unprecedented massed raid with 11 S-Boats against convoy FN366, a lightly escorted group of seven merchantmen. An S-Boat managed to sink a 6,552-ton Dutch tanker and a trawler, before the British patrols in the area could respond. The German S-Boats continued to be a threatening presence in Britain's coastal waters throughout 1941, which was only gradually curbed as the Royal Navy introduced faster, better-armed Motor Gun Boats. However, the S-Boats were never truly defeated.

Despite a variety of tactical successes, the German siege strategy was not producing decisive results and British defences were slowly improving. After pursuing an uncoordinated overall strategy against

Britain for eight months, Hitler was finally persuaded to impose explicit strategic priorities upon Luftwaffe and Kriegsmarine operations. On 6 February 1941, he issued Führer Directive No. 23, providing guidance on how best to disrupt Britain's economy.[5] For the first time, the Luftwaffe was directed to assist the U-Boat campaign by focusing its raids against major ports, such as Liverpool, to disrupt the unloading of convoys. Hitler stated that once ports were successfully attacked, the attacks would be 'repeated again and again'. A special command, Fliegerführer Atlantik, was established to coordinate air operations with the Kriegsmarine. Initially, this command only had KG 40's limited number of Fw-200 Condors and a few He-111 bombers, but it would increase to about 150 aircraft by June 1941. Raeder and Dönitz were more optimistic once Hitler agreed to increase the priority of counter-trade operations, although the optimism was short-lived.

Meanwhile, the Royal Navy's response to the U-Boat threat was slow and measured, but finally began to produce results. In March 1941, the 5th Escort Group was formed under the command of Commander Donald Macintyre, consisting of five old destroyers and two corvettes. One of Macintyre's destroyers was equipped with a Type 286 surface search radar which gave it the ability to detect U-Boats on the surface out to several miles. Up to this point in the war, the Royal Navy had been rather slipshod in its convoy escort tactics and simply assigned whatever warships were available to the next convoy; there was no team cohesion and no standard tactics. The 5th Escort Group was the first attempt to build a dedicated escort group that remained together and was specifically trained to counter *Rudeltaktik*.

March 1941 began badly for the U-Boat force when Günther Prien's U-47 went missing on 7 March; the exact cause is unknown. Ten days later, the convoy HX 112 was detected south of Iceland and five U-Boats were vectored towards it. Macintyre's 5th Escort Group was protecting this convoy. Despite the presence of a strong escort, Otto Kretschmer's U-99 boldly penetrated the convoy on the surface on the night of 16 March and attacked. Amazingly, Kretschmer sank five ships (including three tankers) of 34,505 tons, then withdrew. At this point, HMS *Vanoc*, the one ship equipped with radar, detected Schepke's U-100 on the surface astern of the convoy and attacked. Kretschmer's U-99 bumped into HMS *Walker* on the way out and was also attacked. In short order, Schepke was killed and Kretschmer was captured. Churchill was exultant that three ace U-Boat commanders had been eliminated in March, but actually little had changed since most convoys remained poorly protected. The loss of five U-Boats in March 1941 was a heavy blow to Dönitz's U-Boat arm, but his U-Boats continued to sink well over 200,000 tons of shipping per month. In April and May, Dönitz was able to successfully employ *Rudeltaktik* against convoys SC 26 and HX 126.

While Royal Navy escort tactics slowly improved, it is important to note that RAF Coastal Command played very little role in countering the U-Boat threat prior to 1942. RAF Sunderland flying boats participated in the destruction of two U-Boats in 1940 and another in August 1941, but in each case the U-Boat had been detected by surface warships. Coastal Command equipped some of its aircraft with ASV radar in late 1940, but they achieved very little because the U-Boats simply moved their operations further away from shore. Aside from the fortuitous capture of U-570 in August 1941, RAF long-range patrol aircraft were too few in number to pose a serious threat to U-Boats on the surface until mid-1942.

The Royal Navy's ability to defend convoys from the low-level attacks of Fw-200 Condors also remained seriously deficient. In January 1941, KG 40 attacked British convoys off the coast of Portugal and sank 17 ships of 65,000 tons for the loss of only one Fw-200. Most of these attacks were conducted by a single Fw-200 at a time. RAF Coastal Command was unable to provide air cover over distant convoys and the air defences in most convoys were feeble – usually just old Lewis Guns and slow-firing 12-pounders. Without radar, air cover or decent anti-aircraft defences, Britain's convoys were wide open to air attack. In February 1941, Fliegerführer Atlantik coordinated multi-aircraft attacks against convoys, which inflicted serious damage on OB 290; seven ships of 35,107 tons were sunk. Condor attacks tended to scatter a convoy, which then made them easier targets for nearby U-Boats. Altogether, KG 40's Condors sank 21 ships of 84,301 tons in February. Furthermore, the Condors began shadowing convoys and passing spot reports to Dönitz, enabling him to vector U-Boats onto these convoys. At this point, the synergy of Condor and U-Boat posed a serious threat to the British convoy system.

Fortunately for Britain, inter-service rivalry between the Luftwaffe and the Kriegsmarine undermined the level of effort put into enacting Führer Directive No. 23. The Condor programme remained limited to a production rate of only four Fw-200s per month, which was barely enough to keep up with losses. Göring connived to starve Fliegerführer Atlantik of resources, in order to prevent the Kriegsmarine from establishing a de facto independent naval air arm. Meanwhile, Churchill pushed the Royal Navy to develop counter-measures to the Condor, and the first Catapult Aircraft Merchant (CAM) ships, using catapults to launch Hurricane fighters, were ready by May 1941. Each CAM ship could provide a grand total of one fighter sortie over a convoy. Nevertheless, a CAM-launched Hurricane succeeded in shooting down a Condor in August 1941. At the same time, the Royal Navy was building its first escort carrier, HMS *Audacity*, which was commissioned in June 1941. In September 1941, a Martlet fighter from HMS *Audacity* shot down an Fw-200. Although Fw-200 Condors sank 58 ships of 234,443 tons in 1941, 35 Condors were lost to all causes – a rate which was unsustainable. By 1942, the Luftwaffe pulled the remaining Fw-200 Condors off the anti-shipping mission and they were relegated to reconnaissance roles. Thus, the British were able to mitigate the Condor threat by late 1941.

Raeder decided to make his main play to sever Britain's Atlantic lifelines with Operation *Rheinübung* (Rhine Exercise) in mid-May 1941, by using the new battleship *Bismarck* and heavy cruiser *Prinz Eugen* to make a sortie into the Atlantic to attack the HX convoy routes. Raeder deployed nine covert support vessels into the Atlantic as part of the *Etappendienst* to support the operation. The *Bismarck* succeeded in penetrating the Denmark Strait and sinking the battle cruiser HMS *Hood* on 24 May 1941 but the Home Fleet gathered its strength and relentlessly hunted her down. On 27 May, the *Bismarck* was sunk before it could reach safety at St Nazaire. Yet even if *Bismarck* and *Prinz Eugen* had reached the convoy lanes, they could only have succeeded in mauling one or two convoys before being forced to run the gauntlet back to a friendly port. Raeder failed to appreciate that trading expensive surface warships for a dozen merchantmen was a losing trade.

Unknown to Raeder, the Royal Navy achieved an even larger game-changing victory in May 1941 when they captured the weather ship *Muenchen*, then the U-110. Between these two vessels, British intelligence acquired an intact Enigma machine with current settings, code books and other cipher material which enabled Bletchley Park to finally break into the *Heimisch* (DOLPHIN) code. The Royal Navy used intercepts from DOLPHIN to demolish Raeder's *Etappendienst* covert network of supply ships and tankers in the Atlantic.[6] After the loss of *Bismarck* and her supply network in May 1941, Raeder was even more reluctant to risk his remaining capital ships in raiding sorties into the Atlantic. Nevertheless, he made one last attempt in June 1941 to prepare the large cruisers *Admiral Scheer* and *Lutzow* for an Atlantic raid. Raeder was unaware that the British were now tipped off by their code-breaking and knew about the movement of the *Lutzow* off the coast of Norway. On the night of 12/13 June, 18 Beaufort torpedo bombers were sent to attack the *Lutzow*; only one Beaufort found the target, but managed to score a torpedo hit amidships. Consequently, *Lutzow* was out of action for six months – this was an amazing use of signals intelligence for operational purposes. British bombers relentlessly attacked the German capital ships in port, damaging both *Scharnhorst* and *Prinz Eugen*. Like the Home Fleet, Raeder became gun-shy about exposing his heavy ships to air attack and decided henceforth that they would only operate against convoys off Norway, where the risk of air attack was small. Thanks to

BONIFACE/Ultra and aggressive bombing of ports, Germany's capital ships were essentially neutralized as a serious threat to Atlantic convoys after mid-1941.

In contrast to the regular surface raiders, the disguised *Hilfskreuzer* remained a threat to British shipping in all oceans until late 1941. Due to their use of the more secure *Ausserheimisch* (Pike) Enigma code, the *Hilfskreuzer* were not directly put at risk by British code-breaking, although their support ships were gradually eliminated. The Royal Navy spent huge resources searching for the elusive *Hilfskreuzer* and did not succeed in eliminating one until *Pinguin* was sunk in May 1941. The *Kormoran* and *Atlantis* were sunk in November 1941, but the other four succeeded in returning to friendly ports. Altogether, the seven *Hilfskreuzer* succeeded in sinking or capturing 97 ships of 658,976 tons in 1940–41, which was double what the regular surface raiders accomplished. However, the second round of *Hilfskreuzer* patrols in 1942–43 only sank 214,000 tons of shipping and most of the raiders were lost. Thus, it was not until the fourth year of the war that the *Hilfskreuzer* threat was brought under control.

While the Kriegsmarine struggled to interdict Britain's maritime lines of communication, the Luftwaffe resumed its bombing offensive in full force in March 1941 and concentrated its raids against the ports of Liverpool, Portsmouth, Glasgow, Hull and Plymouth. Liverpool's anti-aircraft defences were still ineffectual, but on the night of 12 March 1941 improved night fighters succeeded in shooting down four of 316 German bombers that attacked the city. British night-fighter successes steadily increased, but the Luftwaffe still managed to kill over 15,000 British civilians in three months while keeping their losses to an acceptable level. The Luftwaffe offensive culminated with three massive raids against London on the nights of 16 and 19 April and 10 May, each involving over 500 bombers. More than 1,800 tons of high explosive were dropped in these three massive raids, inflicting major damage on the British capital, then the offensive faded away as the Luftwaffe was transferred eastward. However, unlike daylight bombing, the RAF had not defeated the Blitz nor prevented the

Luftwaffe from smashing British cities, one by one. Hitler's military reputation was built on quick, cheap victories but the siege operations against Great Britain did not fit in that model and were costly and time-consuming.

By the end of May 1941, Britain was still hard pressed by Germany's air and sea attacks, with no let-up in sight. Aside from making German daylight raids over Britain prohibitively expensive, the only real military success Britain had achieved was against Italian colonial armies, which could hardly lead to a favourable conclusion of the war with Germany. Reprieve, when it came in June, was due to Hitler's caprice, not any substantive change in the overall military balance between the Third Reich and Great Britain. Yet Hitler's turn to the east, to deal with Stalin, handed Churchill a strategic victory by default by reducing the effort put into siege operations.

CHAPTER 10

Sea Lion Redux, May 1941

Churchill and his War Cabinet were unaware that Hitler had postponed *Sea Lion* and fears of invasion persisted well into 1941. On 17 October, Brooke was still fretting about signs of 'impending invasion' and his fear of a surprise attack of some sort continued until nearly Christmas 1940.[1] In November, Admiral John Tovey, the new commander of the Home Fleet, stated that 'the danger of invasion will not disappear with the coming of winter and may confront us with novel possibilities in the coming year'.

Once the winter arrived, it was clear that Britain had gained a respite until the next spring to build up its defences. However, Churchill was not content with defensive measures and the success of General Sir Archibald Wavell's counteroffensive against the Italians in Egypt in December 1940 emboldened him. The victory of Lieutenant General Sir Richard O'Connor's Western Desert Force in Egypt led to Churchill's insistence that the counteroffensive continue into Libya, which meant more tanks and equipment were needed from Britain. O'Connor's success in Libya in January–February 1941 encouraged Churchill to push for an expeditionary force to Greece in March.

Instead of focusing on building up his army at home and making any future German invasion impossible, Churchill poured Britain's resources into colonial-style campaigns in the Mediterranean and East Africa. On 28 May 1941, Brooke continued to visit coastal defences in Britain and was alarmed at 'how desperately thin our defences are'.[2]

On 31 March 1941, the Germans responded to these British adventures with their own surprises: Generalleutnant Erwin Rommel's Afrika Korps launched a counteroffensive in Libya that demolished O'Connor's Western Desert Force, including the 2nd Armoured Division. In less than two weeks, Rommel routed British forces in Libya and surrounded the garrison in Tobruk. Adding to the defeat, O'Connor and four other British generals were captured. Shortly thereafter, the Germans invaded Greece and routed the 62,000-man Commonwealth expeditionary force by the end of April. In May, the Germans used 7. Flieger-Division to spearhead an invasion of Crete, which eliminated the Commonwealth garrison there as well. In the space of two months, the Germans had inflicted over 30,000 casualties on Commonwealth forces in the Mediterranean in these three defeats. Commonwealth forces lost over 200 tanks, 500 guns and nearly 10,000 vehicles as well. These equipment losses would have to be made good quickly and at the expense of Brooke's forces in the United Kingdom.

Meanwhile, the German preparations for *Seelöwe* continued throughout the winter of 1940/1941 – albeit at a slow pace. More importantly, the Kriegsmarine's surface fleet began to recover its strength as new units were commissioned and existing units were repaired. Churchill knew that the Germans were commissioning new warships and wrote in a letter to President Roosevelt on 8 December 1940 that 'the next six or seven months bring relative battleship strength in home waters to a smaller margin than is satisfactory. *Bismarck* and *Tirpitz* will certainly be in service in January. These two first-class modern 35,000 ton 15-inch gun German battleships force us to maintain a concentration never previously necessary in this war.'[3] In fact, *Bismarck* was ready by January 1941, but *Tirpitz* would not be fully operational for another year. In addition, the battlecruisers *Scharnhorst* and *Gneisenau* were repaired, and the heavy cruisers *Admiral Hipper* and *Prinz Eugen* were available. Five new Type 36A destroyers were also commissioned during the winter of 1940/41. By spring 1941, the Kriegsmarine would actually reach its peak operational strength in the World War II, with three battleships, two heavy cruisers and two dozen destroyers and torpedo boats potentially available. With surface escorts of this strength, the British plans of intercepting the invasion convoys with destroyers and light cruisers suddenly became impractical. The Home Fleet would have to commit its heavy units if it wanted to stop convoys escorted by these Kriegsmarine surface warships.

Over the course of the winter of 1940/1941, Siebel perfected his landing craft and the Heer began building Pionierlandungsboote. In mid-April 1941, the Kriegsmarine built its first MFP. By May, the Wehrmacht actually had real purpose-built landing craft and adequate surface escorts to cross the Channel. The Luftwaffe had also considerably built up its air transport forces and had the Me-323 heavy glider ready, although the heavy losses in the invasion of Crete would have reduced the number of veteran Fallschirmjäger available. In terms of air superiority, both sides were in the process of upgrading their primary fighters: the Luftwaffe had the improved Bf-109F-2 in service and the RAF was just introducing the Spitfire Mk V. The German introduction of drop tanks for the Bf-109F also slightly increased the aircraft's combat endurance. Nevertheless, the RAF still held the edge in daylight combat over the United Kingdom and the British were improving their radar and anti-aircraft defences in early 1941.

While the Kriegsmarine grew stronger over the winter, the Home Fleet's position was actually much weaker in June 1941 than it was in September 1940. Assuming that Operation *Rheinübung* (the sortie of the *Bismarck* into the Atlantic) had not occurred during May, Tovey's Home Fleet would consist of only four capital ships (HMS *King George V*, *Prince of Wales*, *Nelson* and *Hood*), a single heavy cruiser

(HMS *Devonshire*) and four light cruisers (HMS *Edinburgh*, *Manchester*, *Arethusa* and *Galatea*). The relentless attacks of *Hilfskreuzer*, U-Boats and surface raiders had forced the Royal Navy to disperse its strength across the globe to protect its trade, at the cost of weakening the Home Fleet. On the positive side, the Royal Navy's coastal forces were strengthened with the introduction of motor gunboats (MGBs) and improved MTBs in spring 1941, and a number of cruisers and destroyers had been re-fitted with search radar and 20mm and 40mm dual-purpose guns. Consequently, the Royal Navy had fewer, but better-armed warships to defend the home islands in June 1941. RAF Coastal Command was also improving, with better aircraft and more skilled aircrew.

Although Churchill apparently did not fear invasion in 1941, many other British leaders fully expected the Germans to attempt a landing in the spring or summer of 1941 and continued to press for improvement in home defences. In April 1941, Major General Henry H. 'Hap' Arnold, commander of the US Army Air Corps, visited England and reported that 'Dill, Beaverbrook, [Air Chief Marshal Sir Wilfrid] Freeman (Vice Chief of Air Staff) and [Archibald] Sinclair (Secretary of State for Air) all believe that it [a German landing] can be done and will be tried'. He also noted that the British did not expect to prevent an invasion outright but hoped to contain the beachhead so that the Germans could not break out.[4]

If Hitler had decided to delay *Barbarossa* and mount *Seelöwe* in June 1941, the Germans would have been in a much stronger position to mount an invasion than in September 1940. With the *Bismarck* and several other heavy warships, the Germans could potentially try to land on the better East Anglia beaches or mount an attack similar to the original plan. In either case, the ability of the Royal Navy to intercept and prevent an invasion would have been much less than in 1940. With lower losses in the crossing, the chances of the Germans landing a second wave with Panzer-Divisionen would have been much higher. On the other hand, British beach defences would have been stronger in June 1941 and the German first wave would have suffered heavier casualties. Key positions such as Folkestone and Dover would have been protected by more than Home Guard and training units in 1941, making the German expansion from their initial beachheads a much more arduous process.

Even with significant amounts of equipment going to the Middle East, Brooke had significantly better forces in June 1941 than he had had nine months prior. Unlike the bad days of 1940, British deficiencies in anti-tank guns, anti-aircraft, infantry weapons and artillery had been made good and units near the beaches would have the equipment to mount a robust defence in depth. Brooke also had more and better tanks than he did in 1940. Both the 1st and 6th Armoured Divisions were in England and less of their strength was based on obsolescent light tanks. The Valentine infantry tank was in series production with 120 being built per month and the Churchill tank was just starting low-rate production.[5] There were still shortages of tactical transport, but no longer severe. Rather than equipment, the one real factor that impaired the British Army's ability to successfully defend the United Kingdom was the lack of effective combined-arms training, which persisted until 1943–44. British armoured units were still likely to attack without proper support and impale themselves on German anti-tank guns, while British infantry units were being trained to conduct World War I-style set-piece assaults.

Without proceeding into further conjecture, we can deduce three important conclusions about the possibility of *Sea Lion* occurring in the early summer of 1941. First, while the Royal Navy had less chance of stopping a full-scale invasion, German losses in the landing phase and efforts to break out of the initial lodgements were likely to be much higher. Second, the British Army still did not have an assured ability to crush a German landing once established. Third, due to stronger Kriegsmarine support, the Germans would have a better chance of getting a substantial Panzer force ashore, which could greatly assist them in breaking out of the beachhead areas. As for the outcome, either an extended battle of attrition on the GHQ Line or a German breakthrough leading to a major British defeat were the two most likely scenarios. Consequently, it is clear that the standard interpretation that the German threat of invasion ended with the Battle of Britain is patently false and that the threat of invasion actually increased in spite of the Luftwaffe's failure in September 1940. Britain still had a knife at its throat throughout much of 1941 and the danger did not pass until Germany became bogged down in the Soviet Union.

CHAPTER 11

Hidden Benefits of *Sea Lion*: Germany Gains an Amphibious Capability for Other Theatres

---

Typically, it is suggested in Battle of Britain historiography that Germany gained nothing from the preparations for *Seelöwe*. In fact, the amphibious capabilities created for *Seelöwe* in 1940–41 were quickly put to use in other theatres and contributed to several notable Allied defeats. In particular, the creation of the Marinefährprahm (MFP), of which over 700 were built in 1941–45, was a major step forward for amphibious warfare technology. Unlike the motorized barges of 1940, the MFPs did not need to be towed by tugs and could land heavy vehicles and artillery directly onto a beach. The prototype MFP, designated F100, was commissioned on 16 April 1941 and series production of the MFP-A type began in July 1941. A total of 72 MFPs were built in 1941, followed by 303 in 1942, 177 in 1943, 173 in 1944 and 13 in 1945. Improved variants, known as the MFP-B and MFP-C types, were introduced in June 1942, followed by the larger

Type D in 1943. In addition to the basic landing craft model, the Kriegsmarine built MFPs to serve as coastal minelayers, anti-aircraft vessels and fire support vessels.

Germany's new amphibious capabilities were first demonstrated in the Baltic in 1941. Two experimental landing units, formed in Antwerp and Rotterdam in August 1940, remained on the Channel coast throughout 1941 as part of the deception effort to maintain the appearance of *Seelöwe* still being under consideration. However, the real potential was incorporated into an experimental unit known as the *Erprobungsverband* (EVO), which was formed to test the variety of landing craft available, including motorized barges, Siebel ferries and Pionierlandungsboote. In spring 1941, the EVO was transferred to the Baltic Sea to prepare for participation in Operation *Barbarossa*. Once the main forces of the Soviet North-west Front were defeated in the Baltic, the OKH decided to use the EVO to mount an amphibious landing known as Operation *Beowulf II* to clear several large islands off the Estonian coast. By late summer 1941, the EVO had grown to a large command with 12 MFPs, 21 Siebel ferries, 13 Pionierlandungsboote, 253 Sturmboote and 96 other vessels. The main German assault force was built around the 61. Infanterie-Division.

At 0500 hours on 14 September 1941, Operation *Beowulf II* began with a sudden descent upon Saaremaa (Ösel) and Muhu (Moon) islands, which were defended by approximately 24,000 Soviet troops. Prior to the operation, the Kriegsmarine conducted three diversionary operations which confused the Soviet defenders about the likely landing area. In an opening gambit, 50 *Brandenburger* troops from Sonderkommando Benesch landed on the southern tip of Saaremaa in five DFS 230 gliders; their mission was intended to disable a Soviet coastal battery equipped with four 130mm naval guns. Another 100 *Brandenburgers* were supposed to arrive by Sturmboote to reinforce the glider troops, but deteriorating weather conditions delayed their arrival and the glider troops were too few to capture the naval battery. Consequently, the main assault force of 1,000 troops from

I./Infanterie-Regiment 151 had to cross the 6-mile-wide Sur Väin Strait in 180 Sturmboote from the EVO under shell fire. German artillery from the mainland provided a 15-minute artillery preparation, followed by air strikes. Due to fog and light rain, one company landed in the wrong place, but the first wave was still able to establish a beachhead on the south side of Muhu Island. The 61. Infanterie-Division also sent its reconnaissance battalion across by Sturmboote to land on the northern side of Muhu. Two more waves followed, under heavy fire, bringing an artillery battery and the rest of Infanterie-Regiment 151 across. Almost half the Sturmboote were damaged or sunk and a battalion commander wounded, but the landing was a success. Later in the day, the EVO began using its landing craft to bring vehicles and more heavy weapons across. During the course of the operation, the Luftwaffe used four Me-321 Gigant gliders for the first time to deliver supplies and equipment to the island. It took three weeks of fighting, but the 61. Infanterie-Division cleared both Saaremaa and Muhu islands.

A follow-up landing, known as Operation *Siegfried*, was conducted at dawn on 12 October, using the EVO's landing craft to cross the 3-mile-wide Soela Väin Strait to Hiumaa (Dagö) Island. This time there was no resistance on the beaches and the island was secured within ten days. Operation *Beowulf II* was a landmark event that validated both German amphibious craft and tactics, as well as heavy gliders. Despite strong enemy coastal defences, the Germans had been able to conduct an opposed landing and quickly establish viable beachheads. The Kriegsmarine also demonstrated an ability to employ naval gunfire support from the light cruisers *Köln*, *Leipzig* and *Emden* to support the landing. As a result of both landing operations, thousands of Soviet troops were killed or captured.

As German forces surged across the Ukraine in 1941, the Kriegsmarine realized that they needed an amphibious capability in the Black Sea as well. In November 1941, the 1. Landungs-Flottille was formed at the port of Varna in Bulgaria. A facility was established in Vienna to fabricate MFP components and they were sent down the

River Danube to be assembled at Varna. By the time that the German 11. Armee began its final offensive to reduce the Soviet fortress of Sevastopol in the Crimea in June 1942, the Kriegsmarine had enough MFPs available in the Black Sea to provide logistical support to the army. After the fall of Sevastopol, the Kriegsmarine began planning an amphibious operation known as Operation *Blucher II* to cross the Kerch Straits and thereby support the invasion of the Caucasus. On the night of 1/2 September 1942, the 1. Landungs-Flottille, equipped with 24 MFPs, carried a Kampfgruppe from the 46. Infanterie-Division across the straits to the Taman Peninsula. Operation *Blucher II* was a low-key success, which helped to accelerate the German drive into the Kuban.

Later, after overrunning part of the Caucasus, the German 17. Armee was forced to conduct a fighting withdrawal to the Kuban, where it mounted a desperate defence from January to September 1943. By this point, the Kriegsmarine had amassed an amphibious force of more than 70 MFPs and several Siebel ferries in the Black Sea and they played a major role in sustaining the Kuban bridgehead for nine months. Hitler finally agreed to evacuate 17. Armee from the Kuban as the war situation deteriorated, and the four amphibious flotillas in the Black Sea were tasked with conducting an army-size evacuation. Dubbed Operation *Brunhild*, the evacuation of the Kuban began on 12 September 1943, and over the course of 38 days the landing flotillas were able to transport 15 Axis divisions with 239,000 German and Romanian troops to the relative safety of the Crimea. Soviet efforts to interfere with the evacuation were easily rebuffed by the Luftwaffe and a handful of aggressively led S-Boats. Germany's amphibious capabilities had saved an entire army that would otherwise have been isolated and destroyed.

Less than a month after the Kuban was abandoned, the Axis forces in the Crimea found themselves isolated by the advance of the Soviet 4th Ukrainian Front. An army of over 200,000 troops was dependent upon naval convoys from Romania; the MFPs played a key role in sustaining the Crimea and brought in replacement troops and equipment, including assault guns and heavy artillery. Amphibious supply runs managed to sustain the garrison through the winter of 1943/44, but when the Soviet spring offensive began on 8 April 1944 the German defences in the Crimea cracked. After three days of fighting, the troops of 17. Armee were compelled to retreat to Sevastopol, but Hitler baulked at authorizing another evacuation. The MFPs were used to move troops along the coast, but once the Luftwaffe pulled out of the Crimea Soviet fighter-bombers strafed them without mercy. On 23 April, a single over-loaded MFP attempting to carry 1,000 troops to safety was bombed and sunk, with over 300 troops drowned. Hitler ordered the 17. Armee to stand and fight in Sevastopol, which led to a hopeless battle. It was not until nightfall on 8 May that Hitler consented to the evacuation of the 17. Armee from the Crimea, just as Soviet tanks were poised to enter Sevastopol. The Kriegsmarine and Royal Romanian Navy mounted a last-minute evacuation, which managed to save 28,992 German and 15,078 Romanian troops from the Crimea between 10 and 13 May. Had the evacuation begun sooner, the majority of the 17. Armee could have been saved, along with much of its equipment.

German amphibious craft also played a major role in the Mediterranean theatre. In the summer of 1941, the Kriegsmarine established 2. Landungs-Flottille at Palermo in Sicily and began constructing MFPs in the port. By December 1941, this flotilla had eight MFPs and 20 more were built at Palermo in 1942. In the spirit of Axis collaboration, the Germans gave the Italians a licence to manufacture a copy of the MFP-A design, which entered service with the Italian Regia Marina as the Motozattera (or MZ) in February 1942. The Italians quickly put the MZ into serial production at several yards and were able to commission 98 landing craft in 1942–43. Both the German MFPs and the Italian MZs proved very handy in the Mediterranean, Adriatic and Aegean, particularly in maintaining sea lines of communication to Axis forces in Libya and German-occupied Crete. Unlike regular transports, which could only unload vehicles or cargo in ports, the ability of these landing craft to land vehicles and supplies on beaches near the front line was a major advantage.

By mid-1942, the Germans had about 30 MFPs in the Mediterranean and the Italians had 65 MZ, along with about two dozen Siebel ferries and Pionierlandungsboote, which gave the Axis a substantial amphibious capability. Generalfeldmarschall Albert Kesselring, *Oberbefehlshaber Süd* (commander-in-chief South), advocated an invasion of British-held Malta in order to reduce attacks on the Axis sea lines of communication to North Africa; this concept evolved into Operation *Herkules*, a joint German–Italian effort to seize Malta. Operation *Herkules* borrowed heavily from lessons learned during the preparations for *Seelöwe* as well as the airborne operation against Crete in 1941. If executed in July 1942 as Kesselring intended, Operation *Herkules* would have involved an airborne landing with two airborne divisions and an amphibious landing by five reinforced Italian divisions. Although Malta was well defended, Operation *Herkules* had excellent prospects for success and could have eased Rommel's supply situation in North Africa. However, the Luftwaffe assets required to make *Herkules* possible were instead diverted to support Rommel's drive into Egypt and the operation was postponed, then cancelled.

Nevertheless, the large amount of Axis amphibious shipping available in the Mediterranean was put to good use. When Hitler wanted to rush German units to Tunisia in response to Operation *Torch* in November 1942, the MFPs and Siebel ferries proved their worth. By January 1943, the Germans had a fleet of 45 MFPs and 45 Siebel ferries making continuous round trips from Sicily to Tunis.[1] The Royal Navy's Force Q succeeded in destroying one Italian convoy north of Tunis on 2 December 1942, but the shallow-draft ferries proved difficult targets. Had Hitler authorized a timely evacuation of Tunisia, there is little doubt that the amphibious forces could have saved part of Panzerarmee Afrika.

After the Axis surrender in Tunisia, the Allied invasion of Sicily began on 10 July 1943 and led to the rapid collapse of Italy's will to fight. The German XIV Panzerkorps was able to delay two Allied armies in a lop-sided battle for a month, but the outcome was never in doubt. This time, Hitler listened to reason and authorized an evacuation effort to save the XIV Panzerkorps. Operation *Lehrgänge* commenced on 11 August and employed three landing flotillas with a total of 33 MFPs, 12 Siebel ferries, 11 Pionierlandungsboote and 76 other landing craft to evacuate Axis troops across the 2- to 6-mile-wide Straits of Messina. Despite the strong Allied air and naval forces operating around Sicily, the Allies were not immediately aware of the German evacuation and were reluctant to send units into the narrow strait due to fear of mines. At least eight MFPs were sunk during the operation, but few troops were lost. The last Tiger tank belonging to Schwere Panzer-Abteilung 504 was shipped across the Strait on a Siebel ferry on 17 August, the final day of the evacuation. The week-long Operation *Lehrgänge* was a major success, resulting in 52,000 German troops, 14,105 vehicles (including seven tanks) and 94 guns being saved to fight again another day in Italy.[2]

Nevertheless, the successful evacuation of the XIV Panzerkorps did not prevent Italy from signing an armistice with the Allies on 3 September, leaving the German position in the Mediterranean quite vulnerable. While the main Anglo-American armies moved into mainland Italy, the British independently moved quickly to occupy several Italian-held islands in the Aegean, including Kos, Samos and Leros. The Royal Navy's Mediterranean fleet enjoyed naval superiority in this region, although the Luftwaffe retained a measure of local air superiority. In Athens, the German Heeresgruppe E responded to the British intervention in the Aegean by assembling an amphibious force of 30 vessels, including nine MFPs and five small transports in Greek ports. Operation *Eisbär* (Polar Bear) was planned to deal with the British battalion-size garrison inserted onto Kos and three small convoys – escorted by just three R-Boats and five armed fishing trawlers – sailed from Crete, Piraeus and the island of Naxos on 1 October. The German convoys had to cross distances of 100 to 230 miles to reach Kos, which exposed them to interception for over 24 hours. Although the Royal Navy had several destroyers in the area for just such an eventuality, they were all out of position when the

German invasion commenced. At 0300 hours on 3 October 1943, the MFPs landed the first wave of the assault force, a 1,200-man Kampfgruppe from the 22. Infanterie-Division, on Crete. A battalion of Fallschirmjäger also landed by parachute and glider. By the end of the first day, the Germans had 4,000 troops, light artillery and armoured cars ashore. The MFPs landed a number of Sd.Kfz. 10/4 half-tracks equipped with 2cm Flak guns, which provided the landing force with superior mobile firepower. Efforts by RAF aircraft to attack the German landing craft proved ineffective – the Germans had affixed 20mm-thick plates of armour on the MFPs' key areas, which made them proof against .303-calibre machine-gun fire. British resistance collapsed after 25 hours of fighting and 1,388 British troops surrendered. The German invasion force suffered only 14 killed – an incredibly small rate of loss for an opposed landing.[3]

Buoyed by this success, the Germans attempted to take Leros 'on the bounce' before it could be reinforced, but the Royal Navy returned to the Aegean in strength after the loss of Kos. A German convoy, consisting of the ex-Greek transport *Olympos*, six MFPs and a single armed trawler was detected by a British submarine, then intercepted at 0400 hours on 7 October 1943 by three Royal Navy light cruisers and two destroyers. Unlike 1940, most Royal Navy light cruisers and destroyers by 1943 were equipped with search radar and dual-purpose 20mm guns, which considerably increased their ability to intercept enemy convoys. In short order, the British squadron tore the convoy to pieces, with only one damaged MFP escaping. The *Olympos* convoy had been carrying the IX. Festungs-Infanterie-Bataillon 999, which lost 309 of its troops drowned. While the British interception was near-perfect in execution, the RAF still had difficulty providing air cover for Royal Navy surface action groups at sea. The Luftwaffe was able to bomb the light cruiser HMS *Penelope* later the same day, and then the next day sank a destroyer and damaged another light cruiser.[4]

Due to the Royal Navy's successful destruction of the *Olympos* convoy, the Germans were forced to delay the invasion of Leros for a month. Nevertheless, Heeresgruppe E was able to gather more landing craft and mount Operation *Taifun* on 12 November 1943. The British were alerted to the operation by Ultra intercepts and positioned six destroyers in the area, but failed to stop the enemy convoys. At 0430 hours, the Germans conducted three small battalion-size landings on Leros using five MFPs, five Pionierlandungsboote and some auxiliary craft. The British garrison on Leros was larger, consisting of the 234th Infantry Brigade, but its three infantry battalions were spread out trying to cover every possible beach. The 4th Battalion, Royal East Kent Regiment (the Buffs) was able to contain the landing at Parteni Bay and the 2nd Battalion, Royal Irish Fusiliers conducted a company-size counter-attack against the landing in Gurna Bay in an effort to prevent the Germans from establishing a beachhead. German losses among the landing troops were heavy, but intense German 8cm mortar fire kept the British at bay. At 1430 hours, the Germans dropped a 500-man airborne battalion (Kampfgruppe Kuhne) in the centre of the island, which disrupted communications between the three British battalions. Although the British had some anti-aircraft guns, the German Fallschirmjäger jumped at low altitude to minimize their risk from enemy ground fire. German casualties were heavy, but key terrain was seized. Gradually, the German numbers on Leros increased as more troops and equipment landed. The Royal Navy and RAF attempted to interdict the German resupply convoys, but without much success until the battle was nearly over. On the night of 14/15 November, the destroyer HMS *Eclipse* and three MTBs intercepted a convoy of 12 MFPs in Alinda Bay and sank three of them in a point-blank action. However, the typical confusion of a night action allowed most of the German landing craft to escape. The powerful Luftwaffe presence in the Aegean inflicted painful losses on the Royal Navy surface units in the area and ensured the success of the invasion. After four days of fighting, the British garrison surrendered and 3,200 British troops became prisoners. German losses during *Taifun* were much heavier, including 512 killed and 900 wounded – more than one-third of the invasion force.[5] Yet the successes of both *Eisbär* and *Taifun* indicate the ability of the Germans to plan and execute combined amphibious–airborne operations and then to overcome enemy coastal defences. The British defeat in the Aegean was humiliating, even though the loss of 4,800 troops was hardly catastrophic, since the Germans were able to pull off two long-distance amphibious operations in spite of stiff resistance by the RAF and the Royal Navy. Churchill's later claim that 'after Alamein we never had a defeat' conveniently omitted the Aegean in 1943.

However, after the capture of Kos and Leros, German amphibious capabilities were used exclusively to rescue isolated forces from destruction. Several of the amphibious units in the Mediterranean were disbanded by early 1944, while 2. Landungs-Flottille holed up in Genoa and remained operational until April 1945. In the Black Sea, the Kriegsmarine was forced to scuttle virtually all of its amphibious craft in August 1944 when Romania changed sides. Losses of German amphibious shipping rose sharply, with 101 MFPs lost in 1943 and 244 in 1944. Nevertheless, the Third Reich retained significant amphibious capabilities nearly up to the end of war.

In north-west Europe, the Allied invasion of France in June 1944 led to the rapid defeat of Germany's Atlantic Wall defences and a precipitate retreat to the German border. During the retreat, the bulk of the German 15. Armee was nearly isolated in the coastal regions of Holland, which left a huge gap in the German front line in Holland. As is well known, the British decided to exploit this gap by pushing northward in mid-September towards Arnhem and the Rhine bridges. However, Montgomery's 21st Army Group was overly focused on jumping the Rhine and paid little attention to the 15. Armee. In a desperate race against time, the Germans decided to evacuate the entire 15. Armee across the Scheldt Estuary using amphibious craft, despite complete Allied air superiority. Kapitän zur See Hermann Knuth was put in charge of the evacuation, which began on 7 September. Knuth had about 60 small vessels, including six MFPs and one Siebel ferry to transport an army. Two of the landing units involved, the 11. and 12. Landungs-Flottille, were the original units formed for *Seelöwe* in 1940. Amazingly, the Allies did little to interfere with the evacuation – aside from sporadic air attacks – and in 15 days Knuth succeeded in evacuating nine divisions with 100,000 troops, 6,000 vehicles and 750 guns across the Scheldt. He even managed to transport a 21cm railroad gun across the Scheldt. Once across the Scheldt, the 15. Armee was fed into positions just as Montgomery's Operation *Market-Garden* kicked off on 17 September. The unexpected reinforcements from the 15. Armee helped to tip the battle against Montgomery and contributed to the failure of *Market-Garden*.[6]

In the final months of the war, German amphibious craft from three different landing flotillas served on resupply runs to sustain the isolated Heeresgruppe Kurland, then to evacuate over 300,000 troops and 800,000 civilians from East Prussia. These final efforts were conducted under constant enemy air attack, through mine-infested waters. None of these final efforts altered the course of the war, but they were far from futile since they saved tens of thousands of German citizens who would otherwise have fallen into Soviet hands.

As a direct result of preparing for *Seelöwe*, Germany developed landing craft such as the Marinefährprahme and the Siebel ferries, as well as the amphibious tactics to use them, which greatly increased the Wehrmacht's operational and logistic capabilities for the rest of the war. The construction of over 1,000 landing craft was a major effort, which consumed 60,000 tons a year of iron and steel. Had Germany not made this investment beginning in 1940, the Germans would have suffered substantially larger losses in the Mediterranean theatre and on the Eastern Front.

CHAPTER 12

The Reckoning

'The man who sacrifices the possible in search of the impossible is a fool.'
Karl von Clausewitz, *Vom Krieg* (1832)

Was Hitler's postponement of *Seelöwe* on 17 September 1940 a decisive moment in the World War II? I have argued that it was not because nothing was really decided. Hitler still had a viable option to conduct the invasion in 1941 once the Kriegsmarine was stronger and improved landing craft were available. Nothing that the British achieved in 1940 prevented the enemy from selecting this course of action in 1941. Furthermore, Hitler had options short of full-scale invasion, such as a smaller landing on the Isle of Wight, which would have represented a partial victory for Germany. It is a fact that Britain remained in a position of great peril even after the air battles of September 1940, with Germany able to inflict substantially greater damage upon Great Britain's people and economy than vice versa.

Nor does the contention that Hitler committed Germany to a two-front war by shying away from *Seelöwe* appear viable. In *Mein Kampf*, Hitler made his intent to destroy Bolshevism evident, but there is nothing in his book about making political and economic deals with the Soviet Union. Yet Hitler did precisely that with the Ribbentrop–Molotov pact in 1939, indicating that he was not completely bound by a priori ideology. Hitler found the idea of destroying the Soviet Union increasingly attractive after the fall of France, but there is little to support the contention that he was inflexibly committed to a specific timetable. Maintaining the trade relationship with the Soviet Union was extremely valuable for the German economy and mitigated any effects of the Royal Navy's blockade. Hitler did not want the Heer to sit on its hands while the Kriegsmarine and Luftwaffe continued to chip away at Britain, but there was plenty of work for soldiers to do in the Balkans and North Africa. Even as Hitler began transferring much of the Heer to Eastern Europe, he committed a corps-size force to North Africa in February 1941 and two armies (including seven Panzer-Divisionen) to the invasion of Yugoslavia and Greece in April 1941. Soon after, he also authorized an expeditionary force for Iraq. These peripheral operations indicate that Hitler was an opportunist willing to exploit fleeting enemy vulnerabilities. He was also a leader who wavered between making bold decisions and deferring tough decisions for later. Had Rommel taken Tobruk in 1941, Hitler might well have decided to reinforce success – pushing into Egypt then overrunning the Middle East, deferring *Barbarossa* until the next year. Hitler's intent to ultimately destroy the Soviet Union was not pre-destined to supplant his immediate need to force Britain to the peace table by any means possible; an aggressive push into the Middle East, although logistically challenging, might have made *Seelöwe* unnecessary. However, as Clausewitz's comment suggests, Hitler sacrificed two real possibilities in 1940–41 (*Seelöwe* or Middle East) in search of something else which proved impossible.

Even after the Battle of Britain, the war was going against Britain, not Germany. In November 1940, the Germans held 39,956 British prisoners while the total number of Germans in British captivity was a mere 3,594 prisoners. Eight months later, the Germans held 50,717 British prisoners whereas the British held only 5,010 Germans prisoners.[1] The same was true in other categories – aircraft losses, shipping sunk and civilian deaths from bombing. Rather than the deferral of *Seelöwe* locking Hitler into an invasion of the Soviet Union, the real strategic fulcrum was that Churchill was locked into an extended and one-sided battle of attrition with Germany. Churchill's decision to stand up to *Sea Lion* in 1940 doomed the British Empire, rather than saved it – beginning with the loss of Hong Kong, Singapore and Burma to the Japanese in 1942. For centuries, it had been British strategic policy not to fight a protracted European war without allies – and Churchill threw this common sense policy out the window. By choosing to fight an open-ended war without major allies, Churchill committed the Commonwealth to a war that it could not win on its own and which reduced the world's largest empire to a state of penury. British industry could crank out tanks and planes to match Germany ad infinitum, but every weapon built or purchased only further depleted the British Empire's economic strength. By 1941, Britain was reduced to a hand-to-mouth financial existence and dependent upon American Lend-Lease. Churchill needed American or Soviet intervention to provide a means for Britain to join a war-winning coalition, but it came at the cost of further reducing Great Britain to the role of a junior partner. Hitler over-extended himself in the Soviet Union and doomed the Third Reich to a war of attrition that ultimately cost Germany the war, but Churchill also over-extended Britain in the name of uncompromising bravado. When it came to war-making, both Hitler and Churchill shared some of the same inflexible tendencies.

A more practical British strategy after Dunkirk would have been to adopt Halifax's suggestion of opening negotiations with Germany to seek a temporary armistice, thereby causing Hitler to cease preparations for *Sea Lion*, as well as U-Boat warfare and bombing of British cities. A renewed Phoney War period lasting into 1941 would have enabled the British military to gather its strength and prepare for a long-term war once it had powerful coalition partners. Instead, like Hitler,

Churchill sought an impossible victory rather than call for a time-out. Overall, Churchill proved himself a great wartime leader and advocate for liberal democracy, but that does not absolve him of the critical mistakes in strategic judgement he made in 1940.

As for *Sea Lion*, sober military analysis suggests that Germany might have used its nascent amphibious capabilities to achieve some kind of partial victory in either 1940 or 1941, but it was unlikely to overrun the British homeland. Rather, the result was likely to be a tactical stalemate and potentially gruesome city fighting in the outskirts of London. Neither Churchill nor any other British leaders were likely to negotiate an armistice as long as German troops were on British soil. Yet *Sea Lion* might have proved the tipping point, just as Britain was trying to fend off U-Boats, the Blitz and distant commerce raiders. Extended ground combat in England would have significantly altered the conduct of the war by forcing Britain to reduce the resources devoted towards Bomber Command and the Mediterranean theatre in favour of equipping the British home army with improved weapons. Germany would only be fighting to reach the off-ramp to peace negotiations and Hitler would be looking for tactical victories, not the destruction of the British army or state. If Britain eventually grew war-weary, Hitler would almost certainly have agreed to withdraw in return for a peace settlement. Once peace with Britain was achieved, Germany could have either turned its full attention to crush the Soviet Union or direct events on mainland Europe from a position of strength.

If executed, Operation *Sea Lion* would have changed the course of the World War II, but probably not decisively. Even with Britain out of the war, the Third Reich was unprepared to defeat either the Soviet Union or the United States. Nor did *Sea Lion*'s postponement in September 1940 determine the war's outcome any more than the Allied decision not to invade France in 1943 affected the outcome. Hitler missed an opportunity to impose greater military pressure on Britain, but Churchill missed an opportunity to reduce that pressure by eschewing negotiation. After *Sea Lion*, both sides opted for greater violence to fight their way out of their strategic conundrum, rather than to consider simply shifting to a defensive posture and letting the war fizzle out.

Glossary

AOK	Armeeoberkommando
BPC	British Purchasing Commission
CIGS	Chief of the Imperial General Staff
CSC	Chiefs of Staff Committee
EATS	Empire Air Training Scheme
GRT	Gross Registered Tons
OKH	Oberkommando des Heeres
OKL	Oberkommando der Luftwaffe
OKM	Oberkommando der Marine
OKW	Oberkommando der Wehrmacht
OKW/Chi	Oberkommando der Wehrmacht Chiffrierabteilung
RLM	Reichsluftfahrtministerium (Air Ministry)
Skl	Seekriegsleitung

Appendices

Appendix A: Order of Battle, 25 September 1940

Commonwealth Forces

ROYAL AIR FORCE

RAF Fighter Command (Air Chief Marshal Sir Hugh Dowding)
No. 10 Group (Air Vice-Marshal Sir Quintin Brand)
  4x Fighter Squadrons [Spitfire] (92, 152, 234, 609)
  4x Fighter Squadrons [Hurricane] (56, 87, 213, 238)
  1x Night Fighter Squadron [Blenheim 1F] (604)
No. 11 Group (Air Vice-Marshal Keith R. Park)
  7x Fighter Squadrons [Spitfire] (41, 66, 72, 79, 222, 602, 603)
  14x Fighter Squadrons [Hurricane] (1, 17, 43, 46, 73, 111, 249,
    253, 257, 501, 504, 601; 1 RCAF, 303 POL)
  2x Night Fighter Squadrons [Blenheim 1F] (25, 600)
No. 12 Group (Air Vice-Marshal Trafford Leigh-Mallory)
  6x Fighter Squadrons [Spitfire] (19, 64, 74, 266, 611, 616)
  6x Fighter Squadrons [Hurricane] (85, 151, 229, 242, 302 POL,
    310 CZ)

2x Night Fighter Squadrons [Blenheim 1F] (23, 29)
1x Night Fighter Squadron [Defiant] (264)
No. 13 Group (Air Vice-Marshal Richard E. Saul)
  3x Fighter Squadrons [Spitfire] (54, 65, 610)
  7x Fighter Squadrons [Hurricane] (3, 32, 145, 245, 605, 607, 615)
  1x Night Fighter Squadron [Blenheim 1F] (219)
  1x Night Fighter Squadron [Defiant] (141)

RAF Coastal Command (Air Chief Marshal Sir Frederick W. Bowhill)
No. 15 Group (Air Vice-Marshal Rey G. Parry)
  3x Patrol Squadrons [Anson] (217, 320 DUTCH, 321 DUTCH)
  1x Flying Boat Squadron [Sunderland] (210)
  1x Reconnaissance Squadron [Spitfire] (PRU)
No. 16 Group (Air Vice-Marshal John H. S. Tyssen)
  3x Bomber Squadrons [Blenheims] (53, 59, 235)
  1x Patrol Squadron [Hudson] (206)
  1x Patrol Squadron [Anson] (500)
  1x Torpedo Squadron [Beaufort] (22)
  1x Torpedo Squadron [Swordfish] (812)
  1x Torpedo Squadron [Albacore] (826)
No. 18 Group (Air Vice-Marshal Charles D. Breese)
  4x Bomber Squadrons [Blenheims] (21, 57, 248, 254)
  4x Patrol Squadrons [Hudson] (220, 224, 233, 269)
  1x Torpedo Squadron [Beaufort] (42)
  2x Flying Boat Squadrons [Sunderland] (201, 204)
  1x Flying Boat Squadron [Walrus] (700)

RAF Bomber Command (Air Marshal Sir Charles Portal)
No. 1 Group (Air Commodore John Breene)
  6x Light Bomber Squadrons [Fairey Battle] (12, 103, 142, 150,
    300 POL, 301 POL)
No. 2 Group (Air Vice-Marshal Sir James Robb)
  11x Light Bomber Squadrons [Blenheim] (15, 18, 40, 82, 101,
    105, 107, 110, 114, 139, 218)

No. 3 Group (Air Vice-Marshal Sir John E. A. Baldwin)
  9x Medium Bomber Squadrons [Wellington] (9, 37, 38, 75, 99, 115, 149, 214, 311 CZECH)
No. 4 Group (Air Vice-Marshal Arthur Coningham)
  6x Medium Bomber Squadrons [Whitley] (10, 51, 58, 77, 78, 102)
No. 5 Group (Air Vice-Marshal Arthur T. Harris)
  7x Medium Bombers [Hampden] (44, 49, 50, 61, 83, 106, 144)

GHQ HOME FORCES (GENERAL SIR ALAN BROOKE)

Scottish Command (Lieutenant General Harold Carrington)
  Royal Artillery: 61st, 71st and 79th Medium Regiments
5th Infantry Division (Major General Horatio Berney-Ficklin)
  13th, 15th and 17th Infantry Brigades
  9th, 91st and 92nd Field Regiments
46th (West Riding) Infantry Division (Major General Desmond F. Andersen)
  137th, 138th and 139th Infantry Brigades
  70th, 71st and 151st Field Regiments
51st (Highland) Infantry Division (Major General Sir Alan Cunningham)
  152nd, 153rd and 154th Infantry Brigades
  126th, 127th and 128th Field Regiments
Polish Corps (Major General Marian Kukiel)[1]
  1st and 2nd Rifle Brigades

Northern Command (Lieutenant General Ronald Forbes Adam)
  Royal Artillery: 65th and 80th Medium Regiments; 58th Heavy Regiment
24th Army Tank Brigade (Brigadier Arthur G. Kenchington)
  41st, 45th and 47th Royal Tank Regiment (very few tanks)
I Corps (Lieutenant General Harold Alexander)
  1st Infantry Division (Major General Kenneth Anderson)

1st Guards Brigade, 2nd and 3rd Infantry Brigades
2nd, 19th and 67th Field Regiments
2nd Infantry Division (Major General Daril Watson)
4th, 5th and 6th Infantry Brigades
2nd Battalion Manchester (MG)
10th, 16th and 99th Field Regiments
44th (Home counties) Infantry Division (Major General Arthur Percival)
131st, 132nd and 133rd Infantry Brigades
57th, 58th and 65th Field Regiments
2nd Motor Machine Gun Brigade (Brigadier Terence D. Murray)
Royal Artillery: 3rd and 53rd Medium Regiments
X Corps (Lieutenant General William Holmes)
54th (East Anglian) Infantry Division (Major General John H. T. Priestman)
161st, 162nd, 163rd Infantry Brigades
85th, 86th and 134th Field Regiments
59th (Staffordshire) Infantry Division (Lieutenant General Frederick V. B. Witts)
176th, 177th and 197th Infantry Brigades
61st, 110th and 116th Field Regiments
Royal Artillery: 1st Medium Regiment

Western Command (General Robert Gordon-Finlayson)
Royal Artillery: 51st, 76th and 78th Medium Regiments; 51st Heavy Regiment
III Corps (Lieutenant General James Marshall-Cornwall)
38th (Welsh) Infantry Division (Major General Aubry E. Williams)[2] [2TA]
113th, 114th and 115th Infantry Brigades
102nd, 132nd and 146th Field Regiments
2nd (London) Infantry Division (Major General Harry Willans)
4th London Infantry Brigade
11th and 12th Royal Fusiliers, 2nd London Irish Rifles

5th London Infantry Brigade
25th Infantry Brigade
117th and 138th Field Regiments
36th Independent Infantry Brigade (Brigadier Arthur L. Kent-
Lemon)
6th and 7th Battalions Queen's Own Royal West Kent
Regiment, 5th Battalion Buffs (Royal East Kent
Regiment)
Royal Artillery: 73rd and 75th Medium Regiments
23rd Army Tank Brigade (Brigadier Walter F. Murrogh)
40 RTR, 46 RTR, 50 RTR (very few tanks)
3rd Motor Machine Gun Brigade (Colonel Herbert Lumsden)
15/19th King's Royal Hussars
1st Czechoslovak Mixed Brigade (Brigadier General Bedrich
Neumann-Miroslav)[3]

Eastern Command (Lieutenant General Sir Guy Williams)
115th Field Regiment (mixed); 5th, 56th (4x 6in), 59th and 69th
Medium Regiments; 1st, 2nd and 3rd Super-Heavy Regiments
(9.2in howitzers)
II Corps (Lieutenant General Edmund Osborne)
18th (East Anglian) Infantry Division (Major General Merton
Beckwith-Smith)
53rd, 54th and 55th Infantry Brigades
52nd (Lowland) Infantry Division (Major General James Drew)
155th, 156th and 157th Infantry Brigades
37th Independent Infantry Brigade [2TA] (Brigadier Richard
J. P. Wyatt)
Royal Artillery: 2nd and 70th Medium Regiments
XI Corps (Lieutenant General Hugh Massy)
15th (Scottish) Infantry Division (Major General Robert C.
Money)
44th, 45th and 46th Infantry Brigades
55th (West Lancashire) Infantry Division (Major General Vivian

H. B. Majendie)
 164th, 165th and 199th Infantry Brigades
 87th, 109th and 136th Field Regiments
Royal Artillery: 72nd Medium Regiment
XII Corps (Lieutenant General Andrew 'Bulgy' Thorne)
 1st London Division[4] (Major General Claude F. Liardet)
  1st London Infantry Brigade (Brigadier Charles R. Britten)
   8th and 9th Royal Fusiliers, 1st Battalion London Irish Rifles
   90th Field Regiment (8x 75mm, 4x 18/25-pdr, 8x 4.5in)
  2nd London Infantry Brigade (Brigadier Guy M. Portman, TA)
   1st Queen's Westminsters, 1st London Scottish, 1st London Rifle Brigade
   64th Field Regiment (4x 75mm, 4x 25-pdr, 8x 4.5in)
   Attached: 6th Battalion (Home Defence) Royal East Kent (the Buffs)
  35th Infantry Brigade (Colonel E. K. Bolton)
   2/5, 2/6th and 2/7th Queen's Royal Regiment
  Princess Louise's Kensington Regiment (Machine Gun Battalion)
  113th Field Regiments (13x 75mm, 4x 4.5in)
 45th (Wessex) Infantry Division (Major General Sir Edmund C. Schreiber)
  134th Infantry Brigade (Brigadier Sir William G. Michelmore)
   6th and 8th Battalions Devonshire, 1st Battalion Royal Irish Fusiliers
  135th Infantry Brigade (Brigadier Arthur L. W. Newth)
   5th, 6th and 7th Somerset Light Infantry
   53rd Field Regiment
  136th Infantry Brigade (Colonel G. H. P. Whitfield)
   9th Battalion Devonshire, 4th and 5th Battalions Duke of Cornwall's Light Infantry; 8th and 10th Battalions Royal

Sussex (HD) attached

55th, 96th and 142nd Field Regiments

2nd New Zealand Expeditionary Force[5] (Major General Bernard Freyberg)

    5th New Zealand Infantry Brigade (Brigadier James Hargest)

    21st, 22nd, 23rd Infantry Battalions

    7th New Zealand Infantry Brigade (Brigadier Alexander S. Falconer)

    28th, 29th Infantry Battalions

    5th Field Regiment (16x 75mm, 8x 25-pounder)

    Milforce (Lieutenant-Colonel E. C. N. Custance): rapid reaction force composed of C/8 RTR (7 Mk VI light tanks), one machine-gun company (ten Vickers MG and 14 Bren Gun carriers), two companies of infantry and one cavalry/scout troop

    8 RTR (-) attached [27 Mk I Infantry tanks, 23 Matilda II]

1st Motor Machine Gun Brigade or 'Broc Force'[6] (Brigadier Montagu B. Burrows)

    16/5 Lancers, 17/21 Lancers, 2nd Lothians and Border Horse Yeomanry

29th Independent Infantry Brigade (Brigadier Oliver Leese)

    1st Battalion Royal Scots Fusiliers, 2nd Battalion East Lancashire, 2nd Battalion Royal Welch Fusiliers, 2nd Battalion South Lancashire, 17th Field Regiment (25-pounder), 88th Field Regiment (12x 75mm, 4x 4.5in)

11th Royal Marine Battalion

18th Pionier Battalion Royal Fusiliers

No. 3 Independent Company (Major Augustus C. Newman)

Royal Artillery: 60th Field Regiment, 88th Field Regiment, 74th Medium Regiment (4x 6in howitzers)

Coastal Artillery:

    St Mary's Battery (Dymchurch Battery): 358th Coastal Artillery Battery with 2x 6-inch Mk XII guns

    Hythe: 340th Coastal Artillery Battery with 2x 6-inch guns

Eastbourne: 342nd Coastal Artillery Battery with 2x 6-inch guns

Greatstone: 415th Coastal Artillery Battery with 2x 6-inch guns

Folkestone West Battery: 339th Coastal Artillery Battery with 2x 6-inch Mk XII guns

Folkestone East Battery: 338th Coastal Artillery Battery with 2x 6-inch Mk XI guns

St Margaret's: 411th Coastal Artillery Battery with 4x 5.5-inch naval guns

Folkestone Mill Point Battery: 412th Coastal Artillery Battery with 4x 5.5-inch naval guns

Grand Redoubt Battery: 2x 6-inch guns

Norman's Battery: 375th Coastal Artillery Battery, RA with 2x 4.7-inch guns

Hastings: 341st Coastal Artillery Battery with 2x 6-inch guns

Seaford: 343rd Coastal Artillery Battery with 2x 6-inch guns

Shoreham: 344th Coastal Artillery Battery with 2x 6-inch guns

Worthing: 345th Coastal Artillery Battery with 2x 6-inch guns

Brighton: 359th Coastal Artillery Battery with 2x 6-inch guns

Dungeness West: 374th Coastal Artillery Battery with 2x 6-inch guns

Bexhill: 385th Coastal Artillery Battery with 2x 6-inch guns

Kent Battery (Dungeness): Royal Marines with 3x 6-inch guns

Dover Garrison (Brigadier Christopher H. Gotto)

9th Battalion Green Howards

50th Battalion (Holding) Queen's Own Royal West Kent

3rd Battalion (Training) Irish Guards

15th Battalion Royal Fusiliers

No. 5 Commando

5th Field Regiment (Training)

519th and 520th Coastal Artillery Regiments (mixed)

Det./Royal Marine Siege Regiment (1x14-inch Mk VII gun, *Winnie*)

Kent Home Guard

1st Battalion (Ashford)

7th Battalion (Lyminge)
8th Battalion (Deal-Dover-Folkestone-Hythe)
Sussex Home Guard
    15th Battalion (Brighton)
    16th Battalion (Lewes)
    20th Battalion (Hailsham)
    21st Battalion (Eastbourne)
    22nd Battalion (Rye)
    23rd Battalion (Hastings/Bexhill)

Southern Command (Lieutenant General Claude Auchinleck)
    Royal Artillery: 4th, 58th and 63rd Medium Regiments; 54th
        Heavy Regiment
V Corps (Lieutenant General Bernard Montgomery)
    4th Infantry Division (Major General Ralph Eastwood)
        10th and 11th Infantry Brigades
        12th Infantry Brigade (Brigadier Daniel M. W. Beak, VC) –
            on Isle of Wight
            2nd Battalion, Royal Northumberland Fusiliers, 6th
            Battalion, Black Watch and 1st Battalion, Queen's Own
            Royal West Kent Regiment, 50th (Holding) Battalion
            Hampshire Regiment
        22nd, 30th and 77th Field Regiments
    50th (Northumbrian) Infantry Division (Major General Giffard
        'Q' Martel)
        69th, 150th and 151st Infantry Brigades
        74th, 90th and 124th Field Regiments
    Royal Artillery: 66th Medium Regiment
    Coastal Artillery on Isle of Wight:
        527th Coastal Artillery Regiment, RA: New Needles Battery
            (2x 9.2-inch Mk X), Warden Point Battery (2x 6-inch),
            Cliff End Battery (2x 6-inch)
        530th Coastal Artillery Regiment, RA: Culver Battery (2x
            9.2-inch Mk X). Nodes Port Battery (2x 9.2-inch, 2x

6-inch), Yaverland Battery (2x 6-pounder)

VIII Corps (Lieutenant General Harold Franklyn)

    3rd Infantry Division (Major General Sir James A. H. Gammell)

        7th Guards Brigade (Brigadier Arnold de Lerisson Cazenove) 1st and 2nd Battalions Grenadier Guards, 1st Battalion Coldstream Guards

        8th Infantry Brigade (Brigadier Christopher G. Woolner) 1st Battalion Suffolk, 2nd Battalion East Yorkshire, 4th Battalion Royal Berkshire (TA)

        9th Infantry Brigade (Brigadier Bryan G. Horrocks) 2nd Battalion Lincolnshire, 1st Battalion King's Own Scottish Borderers, 2nd Battalion Royal Ulster Rifles

        2nd Battalion Middlesex (MG)

        7th, 33rd and 76th Field Regiments

    48th (South Midland) Infantry Division (Major General Roderic L. Petre)

        143rd, 144th and 145th Infantry Brigades

        18th Field Regiment

GHQ Reserve

IV Corps (Lieutenant General Francis Nosworthy)

    2nd Armoured Division (Major General Justice C. Tilly)[7,8]

        1st Armoured Brigade (Brigadier Harold 'Rollie' Charrington): 3 RTR, 4th Queen's Own Hussars, 1st Kings Dragoon Guards (Mk VI)

        22nd Armoured Brigade: 2nd Royal Gloucestershire Hussars (Mk VI), 3rd and 4th County of London Yeomanry (Mk VI)

        2nd Support Group: 2 RHA, 1st Battalion Tower Hamlets Rifles, 1st Battalion Rangers

        Armour available: 54 cruiser tanks, 156 Mk VI light tanks

    42nd (East Lancashire) Infantry Division (Major General Henry B. D. Willcox)

        125th, 126th and 127th Infantry Brigades

52nd, 53rd and 111th Field Regiments

43rd (Wessex) Infantry Division (Major General Robert Pollok)
128th, 129th and 130th Infantry Brigades
94th, 112th and 141st Field Regiments

31st Independent Infantry Brigade (Brigadier Herbert E. F. Smyth)
2nd Battalion South Staffordshire, 2nd Battalion Oxfordshire
& Buckinghamshire Light Infantry, 1st Battalion Royal
Ulster Rifles, 75th Field Regiment (25-pounder)

Royal Artillery: 67th Medium Regiment

VII Corps (Lieutenant General Andrew McNaughton)

1st Armoured Division (Major General Charles W. M. Norrie)
2nd Armoured Brigade[9] (Brigadier Richard McCreery); the
Queen's Bays, 10th Royal Hussars, 9th Queen's Royal
Lancers

3rd Armoured Brigade: 5th RTR (A Squadron with A-9, B &
C Squadrons with A-13)

20th Armoured Brigade: 1st Royal Gloucestershire Hussars,
1st Northamptonshire Yeomanry, 2nd Northamptonshire
Yeomanry (64 Guy armoured cars)

Note: a few tanks, rest equipped with Bren carriers and
trucks

1st Support Group: 11 RHA, 1st Battalion, The Saskatoon
Light Infantry (MG), Royal Montreal Regiment (MG)

Armour Available: 125 Cruisers (A9/A10/A13), 23 Mk VI
light tanks

1st Canadian Infantry Division (Major General George R. Pearkes,
VC)
1st Canadian Infantry Brigade
The Royal Canadian Regiment, the Hastings and Prince
Edward Regiment, the 48th Highlanders of Canada

2nd Canadian Infantry Brigade
Princess Patricia's Canadian Light Infantry, the Seaforth
Highlanders of Canada, the Loyal Edmonton
Regiment

3rd Canadian Infantry Brigade
> Royal 22e Régiment, the Carleton and York Regiment, the West Nova Scotia Regiment

1st, 2nd and 3rd Field Regiments

1st Army Tank Brigade (Brigadier Harry R. B. Watkins)
> 4 RTR, 8 RTR (-)
>
> Armour: 125 Mk II Matilda

21st Army Tank Brigade (Colonel Reginald Naesmyth) [1TA]
> 42, 48 RTR [some Valentine I tanks]
>
> Armour: 80 Mk II Matilda/Mk III Valentine

Australian Imperial Force (Major General Henry Wynter)
> 18th Infantry Brigade (Brigadier Leslie Morshead)
>> 2/9, 2/10, 2/12 Infantry Battalions
>
> 25th Infantry Brigade (Brigadier William Bridgeford)[10]
>> 2/70, 2/71, 2/72 Infantry Battalions
>>
>> 2/3 Field Artillery (12x 25-pdr, 3x 18-pdr, 3x 4.5-inch), 2/1 Machine Gun Battalion, 2/1 Anti-tank Regiment

2nd Canadian Division (Major General Victor W. Odlum)[11]
> 4th Canadian Infantry Brigade
>
> 5th Canadian Infantry Brigade
>
> 4th, 5th and 6th Field Regiments

198th Infantry Brigade (Independent) (Brigadier James M. Rawcliffe)
> 8th (Irish) Battalion King's Regiment, 6th and 7th Battalions Border Regiment

London District:
> 20th Infantry Brigade (Guards) (Brigadier William Augustus Fox-Pitt)
>> 2nd Battalion Grenadier Guards, 2nd Battalion Welsh Guards, 1st Battalion Royal Norfolk
>
> 24th Infantry Brigade (Guards) (Brigadier William Fraser)12
>> 1st Battalion Scots Guards, 1st Battalion Irish Guards, 1st Battalion Welsh Guards
>
> 3rd London Infantry Brigade (Brigadier Hugh V. Combe)

2nd Battalion Tower Hamlets Rifles, 2nd Battalion Rangers
Headquarters, Anti-Aircraft Command (Lieutenant General Frederick
A. Pile)
1st, 2nd, 3rd, 4th 5th, 6th and 7th Anti-Aircraft Divisions

ROYAL NAVY/HOME FLEET[13]

Scapa Flow

Aircraft carrier HMS *Furious* (18 Swordfish, 6 Sea Gladiator, 9
Skua II)
Battlecruiser Squadron (Vice-Admiral William J. Whitworth)
Battlecruiser HMS *Repulse*
2nd Battle Squadron (Vice-Admiral Lancelot E. Holland)
Battleship HMS *Rodney*
1st Cruiser Squadron (Vice-Admiral John H. D. Cunningham)
Heavy cruisers HMS *Berwick, Norfolk,*
Destroyers: *Douglas, Duncan, Eskimo, Isis, Maori, Mashona,*
Matabele, Punjabi, Somali, Tartar, Versatile, Vimy
Destroyer-Escort HMS *Eglinton*
1st Minesweeper Flotilla: *Bramble, Britomart, Speedy, Hazard*

Methil, Scotland

Destroyers HMS *Scimitar, Valorous, Vega, Verdun, Vivien,*
Watchman, Westminster (convoy escorts)

Rosyth Command (Vice-Admiral Sir Charles Gordon Ramsey)

Rosyth

Battleship HMS *Nelson*
Battlecruiser HMS *Hood*
Light cruisers HMS *Cairo, Naiad*
Destroyers HMS *Ashanti, Bedouin, Cossack, Electra, Fame, Jackal,*
Kashmir, Kipling, *Sikh, Winchester, Zulu*

Dundee
   9th Submarine Flotilla (Dutch): HNLMS O-10, O-13, O-21,
      O-22, O-23, O-24
   Submarine HMS *Clyde*

Nore Command (Admiral Sir Reginald Drax)
Immingham/Humber (near Hull, on North Sea Coast)
   Light cruiser HMS *Curacao*
   Minelayers HMS *Plover*, HNLMS *Willem van der Zaan* [Dutch]

Tyne (Newcastle)
   Light cruiser HMS *Edinburgh*
   Destroyers HMS *Vanity, Witch, Wolfhound*

Harwich
   Destroyers HMS *Achates, Jaguar, Jupiter, Mackay, Malcolm,
      Windsor*
Sheerness
   2nd Cruiser Squadron (Rear-Admiral Alban T. B. Curteis)
      Light cruisers HMS *Aurora, Cardiff* and *Galatea*
   18th Cruiser Squadron (Vice-Admiral George F. B. Edward-
      Collins)
      Light cruisers HMS *Manchester, Southampton*
   Destroyers HMS *Campbell, Venetia, Venomous, Vesper, Veteran,
      Wild Swan, Wivern*
   Destroyer-Escorts HMS *Cattistock, Garth, Holderness*
   Minesweepers HMS *Salamander, Selkirk, Sutton*

Felixstowe
   1st Motor Torpedo Boat Flotilla (Commander Charles M.
      Donner): MTB 14, 16, 17, 18 [60-foot, BPB-type]
   10th Motor Torpedo Boat Flotilla (Lieutenant Charles F.
      Anderson): MTB 67, 68, 104, 106, 107 [Thornycraft-type]

Southend (Thames Estuary)
Destroyers HMS *Vimiera, Vivacious, Wallace, Wolsey, Woolston*

Dover
Destroyers HMS *Icarus, Impulsive, Intrepid*

Portsmouth Command (Admiral Sir William M. 'Bubbles' James)

Portsmouth
Destroyers HMS *Beagle, Bulldog, Harvester, Wolverine, Volunteer*
Destroyer-Escorts HMS *Atherstone, Berkeley, Fernie*
Minesweepers HMS *Elgin, Niger*
4th Motor Torpedo Boat Flotilla (Lieutenant Commander Antony
    B. Cole): MTB 22, 24, 25, 28, 29, 30, 32, 34 [all Vosper-type]
Submarines HMS *Swordfish, Ursula*

Plymouth
Battleship HMS *Revenge*
Light cruisers HMS *Emerald, Newcastle*
Destroyers HMS *Isis, Javelin, Kashmir, Kipling, Mackay, Westcott*

Falmouth
Submarine HMS *Cachalot*

Western Approaches (Admiral Sir Martin Dunbar-Nasmith VC)

Assigned as Convoy Escorts
Destroyers HMS *Active, Amazon, Ambuscade, Antelope, Broke,
    Vansittart, Whitehall, Witherington, Wolverine, Worcester,
    Viscount*; ORP *Blyskawica, Burza, Garland*

Liverpool
Light Cruiser HMS *Despatch*
Destroyers HMS *Havelock, Sabre, Vanoc, Verity, Wanderer, Warwick, Winchelsea* (convoy escort)

Glasgow
Destroyer HMS *Fearless*

Greenock/Northwest Approaches
Light Cruiser HMS *Dunedin*
Destroyers HMS *Anthony, Arrow*

Submarines Operating in or near Home Waters:
HMS *Porpoise, Sealion, Seawolf, Severen, Snapper, Sturgeon, Sunfish, Taku, Talisman, Tetrarch, Tigris, Tribune, Trident, Tuna, Upright, Ursula*

German Forces

LUFTWAFFE (REICHSMARSCHALL HERMANN GÖRING)

Luftflotte 2 (Generalfeldmarschall Albert Kesselring)
I. Fliegerkorps (Generaloberst Ulrich Grauert)
 I., II., III./KG 1 [He-111]
 I., III./KG 76 [Do-17], II./KG 76 [Ju-88]
II. Fliegerkorps (General der Flieger Bruno Lörzer)
 I., II., III./KG 2 [Do-17]
 I., II., III./KG 3 [Do-17]
 I., II., III./KG 53 [He-111]
 II., IV./St.G.1 [Ju-87]
 Erprobungsgruppe 210 [Bf-110/Bf-109]
 I.(Jagd)/LG2 [Bf-109], II.(Schl)/LG2 [Bf-109E-4B]
IX. Fliegerkorps (Generalmajor Joachim Coeler)

I., II./KG 4 [He-111], III./KG 4 [Ju-88]

I./KG 40 [Fw-200]

KGr 100 [He-111]

Küstengruppe 126 [He-111]

Jagdfliegerführer 2 (Generalmajor Theodor Osterkamp)

I., II., III./JG3 [Bf-109]

I., II., III./JG26 [Bf-109]

I., II., III./JG51 [Bf-109]

I., II./JG52 [Bf-109]

I., II., III./JG54 [Bf-109]

I., II., III./ZG26 [Bf-110]

II., III./ZG76 [Bf-110]

Luftflotte 3 (Generalfeldmarschall Hugo Sperrle)

IV. Fliegerkorps (Generalleutnant Kurt Pflugbeil)

I., II., III./KG 27 [He-111]

I., II., III./LG1 [Ju-88]

V. Fliegerkorps (General der Flieger Robert Ritter von Greim)

I., II., III./KG 51 [Ju-88]

I., II./KG 54 [Ju-88]

I., II., III./KG 55 [He-111]

VIII. Fliegerkorps (General der Flieger Wolfram Freiherr von Richthofen)

I., II./St.G.1 [Ju-87]

I., II./St.G.2 [Ju-87]

I., II., III./St.G.77 [Ju-87]

V./LG1 [Bf-110]

Jagdfliegerführer 3 (Oberst Werner Junck)

I., II., III./JG2 [Bf-109]

I., II., III./JG27 [Bf-109]

I., II., III./JG53 [Bf-109]

I., II./ZG2 [Bf-110]

Luftflotte 5 (Generalobest Hans-Jürgen Stumpff) [in Norway]

X. Fliegerkorps (Generalleutnant Hans Geisler)
  I., III./KG 26 [He-111]
  I., II., III./KG 30 [Ju-88]
  I./ZG76 [Bf-110]
  II./JG77 [Bf-109]

Transport Units

KG zb V1	185 Ju-52 (115 operational)
KG zb V9	30 Ju-52 (20 operational)
KG zb V106	53 Ju-52 (39 operational)
KG zbV172	45 Ju-52 (18 operational)

Fallschirmjäger

7. Flieger-Division (Generalleutnant Richard Putzier)
  Fallschirmjäger-Regiment 1 (Oberst Bruno Bräuer)
  Kampfgruppe Stentzler (Major Edgar Stentzler) – two battalions
  Kampfgruppe Bräuer – one FJ battalion, one pionier battalion,
    anti-tank company
  Fallschirmjäger-Regiment 2 (Oberst Alfred Sturm)
  Fallschirmjäger-Regiment 3 (Oberst Richard Heidrich)
  Luftlande-Sturm-Regiment 1 (Oberst Eugen Meindl)

KRIEGSMARINE (GROß ADMIRAL ERICH RAEDER)

Kiel

Heavy Cruiser *Admiral Hipper*
Light Cruisers *Koln*, ″″
U-Boat [Type IIC] U-56

Brest

Destroyers (2) 6th Destroyer Flotilla: *Erich Steinbrinck, Paul Jacobi*
2. R-bootsflottille (8)
7. Vorpostenflottille
40. Minensuchflottille

Cherbourg

Destroyers (5) 5th Destroyer Flotilla (Kapitän zur See Erich Bey)
Friedrich Ihn, Friedrich Eckoldt, Hans Lody, Karl Galster, Thiedor Riedel

2. Torpedobootsflottille (Riede) T5, T6, T7, T8

S-Boats (8) 1. S-Bootsflottille (Kapitänleutnant Heinz Birnbacher):
S18, S20, S21, S22, S25, S26, S27, S28

Minelayers (3) *Cobra*, Schiff 23/*Cairo*, *Tannenberg*

Minesweeper M4001

Motor Minesweeper R26

Le Havre

1. Torpedobootsflottille (Korvettenkapitän Edler von Rennenkampf) T2

5. Torpedobootsflottille (Korvettenkapitän Wolf Henne) *Greif, Seeadler, Kondor, Falke, Wolf, Jaguar, Iltis*

Minelayers (2) *Straslund, Skagerrack*

1. R-Bootsflottille

3. R-Bootsflottille: (8) R-33, R-34, R-35, R-36, R-37, R-38, R-39, R-40

4. Vorpostenflottille

13. Vorpostenflottille

20. Vorpostenflottille

Lorient

U-Boats [Type IIC] U-58, U-59, U-60, U-61; [Type VII] U-28,
U-47, U-48, U-99, U-100; [Type IX] U-38

St Nazaire

U-Boat [Type VII] U-46

Antwerp

Minelayer (3) *Brummer, Kaiser, Hansestadt Danzig*

15. Minensuchflottille

7. R-Bootsflottille: (11) R-151, R-152, R-153, R-154, R-155, R-156, R-157, R-158, R-159, R-160, R-161

Rotterdam
4. Minensuchflottille

Amsterdam
32. Minensuchflottille
34. Minensuchflottille

Ostend
S-Boats (7) 2. S-Bootsflottille (Korvettenkapitän Rudolf Petersen): S30, S33, S34, S36, S37, S55, S56
Minelayers (3) *Grille, Konigin Luise, Preussen*
16. Minensuchflottille
2. Vorpostenflottille (10): V202, V203, V204, V205, V206, V208, V209, V210, V211, V212

Calais
4. R-Bootsflottille
1. Minensuchflottille
32. Minensuchflottille

Dunkirk
11. R-Bootsflottille
3. Minensuchflottille
3. Vorpostenflottille (7): V302, V303, V305, V306, V307, V308, V309

Boulogne
2. R-Bootsflottille
2. Minensuchflottille
18. Minensuchflottille
16. Vorpostenflottille (6)

19. Vorpostenflottille

Fécamp

15. Vorpostenflottille (5): V1505, V1507, V1508, V1510, V1512[14]

Rotterdam

S-Boats (6) 3. S-Bootsflottille (Kapitänleutnant Friedrich Kemnade): S1, S10, S11, S12, S13, S54

Off West Coast Ireland

U-Boats [Type IID] U-137, U-138 (both en route to Lorient)

Off Norway

U-Boats [Type IX] U-103, U-123 (en route to Atlantic)

Operating along the North Sea/English Channel coast:

38. Minensuchflottille

42. Minensuchflottille

44. Minensuchflottille

18. Vorpostenflottille (6)

HEER (GENERALFELDMARSCHALL WALTHER BRAUCHITSCH)

Heeresgruppe A (Generalfeldmarschall Gerd von Rundstedt)

22. Luftlande-Division (Generalleutnant Hans Graf von Sponeck)

Arko 104 (Artillery Command 104) (Generalmajor Karl Böttcher)

Batterie Siegfried (2x 38cm gun), Cap-Gris-Nez

Batterie Grosser Kurfürst (4x 28cm guns), Cap-Gris-Nez

Batterie Friedrich August (3x 30.5cm
guns), Boulogne-Sur-Mer

Batterie Prinz Heinrich (2x 28cm), Calais

Batterie Oldenburg (2x 24cm), Calais

Eisenbahn-Artillerie-Batterie 710, 712, 713: 6x 28cm K 5
railroad guns

Eisenbahn-Artillerie-Batterie 701: 1x 21cm K 12 (E) railroad gun

16. Armee (Generaloberst Ernst Busch)
Flakkorps II (Generalmajor Otto Deßloch)
   Flak-Regiment 6, 136, 201, 202
First Wave
XIII Armeekorps (General Heinrich-Gottfried von Vietinghoff genannt Scheel)
   17. Infanterie-Division (Generalleutnant Herbert Loch)
   21., 55. and 95. Infanterie-Regimenter
   35. Infanterie-Division (Generalleutnant Hans Wolfgang Reinhard)
    34., 109. and 111. Infanterie-Regimenter
   Tauchpanzer-Abteilungen B, D
   Sturmgeschütz-Batterie 666
   Luftwaffe II./Flak-Regiment 14
   Corps Artillery: II./Artillerie-Regiment 66 (15cm), II./Artillery Regiment 67 (15cm)
VII Armeekorps (Generaloberst Eugen Ritter von Schobert)
   1. Gebirgs-Division (Generalleutnant Ludwig Kübler)
      Gebirgsjäger-Regiments 98, 99,100
   7. Infanterie-Division (Generalleutnant Eccard Freiherr von Gablenz)
      19., 61. and 62. Infanterie-Regimenter
   Tauchpanzer-Abteilung A
   Panzer-Abteilung (Fl.) 100
   Sturmgeschütz-Batterie 659 and one battery from Sturmgeschütz-Abteilung 184
   Luftwaffe I./Flak-Regiment 26

9. Armee (Generaloberst Adolf Strauss)
Flakkorps I (Generaloberst Hubert Weise)
   Flak-Regiment 101, 102, 103, 104

XXXVIII Armeekorps (General der Infanterie Erich von Manstein)
26. Infanterie-Division (Generalleutnant Sigismund von Förster)
39., 77. and 78. Infanterie-Regimenter
34. Infanterie-Division (Generalleutnant Werner Sanne)
80., 105. and 107. Infanterie-Regimenter
Tauchpanzer-Abteilung C
Sturmgeschütz-Batterie 667 and one battery from Sturmgeschütz-Abteilung 184
VIII Armeekorps (General der Artillerie Walter Heitz)
6. Gebirgs-Division (Generalmajor Ferdinand Schörner)
Gebirgsjäger-Regiments 141, 143
8. Infanterie-Division (Generalleutnant Rudolf Koch-Erpach)
28., 38. and 84. Infanterie-Regimenter
28. Infanterie-Division (Generalleutnant Johann Sinnhuber)
7., 49. and 83. Infanterie-Regimenter
Sturmgeschütz-Batterie 665 and one battery from Sturmgeschütz-Abteilung 184
Second Wave
V Armeekorps (General der Infanterie Richard Ruoff)
12. Infanterie-Division (Generalleutnant Walter von Seydlitz-Kurzbach)
27., 48. and 89. Infanterie-Regimenter
30. Infanterie-Division (General der Infanterie Kurt von Briesen)
6., 26. and 46. Infanterie-Regimenter
Sturmgeschütz-Batterie 660
XXXI Armeekorps (General der Panzertruppen Georg-Hans Reinhardt)
8. Panzer-Division (Generalleutnant Adolf Kuntzen)
Panzer-Regiment 10., Schützen-Regiment 8
10. Panzer-Division (Generalleutnant Ferdinand Schaal)
Panzer-Regimenter 7, 8; Schutzen-Regimenter 69, 86
29. Infanterie-Division (mot.) (Generalmajor Walter von Boltenstern)
15. and 72. Infanterie-Regimenter (mot.)

Infanterie-Regiment (mot.) *Großdeutschland*
Infanterie-Regiment Leibstandarte SS *Adolf Hitler* (mot.)
Sturmgeschütz-Batterie 640

Appendix B: German 1st Wave Composition on S-Tag, Landing Area B

TRANSPORTFLOTTE B [TRANSPORT FLEET B] (VIZEADMIRAL HERMANN VON FISCHEL)

Embarkation: Rotterdam, Ostend, Dunkirk
   Total: 64 transports, 425 barges, 100 tugs, 200 motorboats
Escort:
   2. Vorpostenflottille [Patrol Flotilla]
   3. Vorpostenflottille
   3. R-Bootsflottille
   11. R-Bootsflottille
   3. Minensuchflottille [Minesweeper]
   15. Minensuchflottille
Tow Formation 1 (from Dunkirk): 75 tows (150 barges, 75 trawlers/tugs, 150 pusher boats)
   4. Minensuchflottille
Tow Formation 2 (from Ostend): 25 tows (50 barges, 25 fishing trawlers, 50 pusher boats)
   Convoy 1 (from Ostend): 8 transports with 16 barges
   16. Minensuchflottille
Convoy 2 (from Rotterdam): 49 transports with 98 barges
(The transport fleet was expected to be 1,000 yards wide and 10 miles long)

Embarked:
XIII Armeekorps (General Heinrich-Gottfried von Vietinghoff genannt Scheel)

17. Infanterie-Division (Generalleutnant Herbert Loch)
21., 55. and 95. Infanterie-Regimenter
35. Infanterie-Division (Generalleutnant Hans Wolfgang Reinhard)
34., 109. and 111. Infanterie-Regimenter
Tauchpanzer-Abteilungen B, D
Sturmgeschütz-Batterie 666
Luftwaffe II./Flak-Regiment 14

XIII Armeekorps (General Heinrich-Gottfried von Vietinghoff genannt Scheel)
35. Infanterie-Division (Generalleutnant Hans Wolfgang Reinhard)
1st Echelon
  I. Gruppe (from Dunkirk): Vorausabteilung Bode: 4 reinforced infantry companies from IR 109, 4x Heavy Machine-gun platoons, 4x Panzerjäger platoons (3x 3.7cm each), 4x Flammpanzer II; 2 companies from Tauchpanzer-Abteilung D, 1 company from Lehrregiment *Brandenburg*
    Embarked on 4 minesweepers or Vorpostenboote, 8 fishing trawlers, 6 motorized barges (incl. 3 AS type), 56 Sturmboote
    3x light auxiliary gunboats (1x 7.5cm, 2x 3.7cm)
  II. Gruppe (from Dunkirk): 2 reinforced infantry battalions each from IR 109 and IR 111; Radfahr-Abteilung 35 (reconnaissance battalion); Pionier-Bataillon 35; 1 battery of Nebelwerfers (8x 15cm), 2 mountain batteries (8x 7.5cm); Division Staff
    Embarked on 28 motorized barges
  III. Gruppe (from Dunkirk/Ostend): 2 reinforced infantry battalions; II./AR 66 (15cm); 1 Panzerjäger Company (9x 4.7cm SP); 1 Reconnaissance Company, 1 Pionier Company
    Embarked on 68 barges, 2 transports
  Corps Troops: XIII Corps Headquarters, 1x Artillery Battalion (10cm); 2x Panzerjäger companies (4.7cm SP); 2x Flak

companies (2cm).

    Embarked on 2 transports and 1 or more R-Boats

2nd Echelon (from Rotterdam/Ostend)

    Infanterie-Regiment 34; Artillerie-Regiment 35; remainder of pionier and Panzerjäger troops, signal battalion

        Embarked on 2 transports

    Corps Troops: 1 Pionier-Bataillon embarked on 3 transports from Ostend; 1 artillery battalion (15cm), 2 Panzerjäger companies, Corps-level support troops from Dunkirk on 8 transports

3rd Echelon (from Dunkirk)

    Remainder of division support troops, embarked on 50 barges.

17. Infanterie-Division (Generalleutnant Herbert Loch)

1st Echelon

    I. Gruppe: Vorausabteilung Schuler (from Ostend): III./Infanterie-Regiment 21, Tauchpanzer-Abteilung B

    Vorausabteilung Pannwitz (from Dunkirk): II./Infanterie-Regiment 55

        Embarked on 24 motorized barges, 4 minesweepers, 4 VP, 4 R-Boats

        6x light auxiliary gunboats (1x 7.5cm, 2x 3.7cm)

    II Gruppe: Division Staff; 2 companies from IR 55, 2 companies from IR 21; 2 companies from Lehrregiment *Brandenburg*; Radfahr-Bataillon 17; Sturmgeschütz-Batterie 666; 2 pionier companies, 2 Flak companies, 1 mountain artillery battery (4x 7.5cm guns)

        Embarked on 62 barges

    III Gruppe: II./Artillery Regiment 67 (15cm), 3 pionier companies

        Embarked on 2 transports and 4 barges

2nd Echelon (from Rotterdam)

    Infanterie-Regiment 95; three infantry companies from IR 21/55; Artillerie-Regiment 17

        Embarked on transports

3rd Echelon (from Ostend)

    Remainder of division support troops, embarked on 50 barges

Notes

INTRODUCTION

1 John Keegan, *The Second World War* (New York: Viking Penguin, 1990), p. 102.
2. Leo McKinstry, *Operation Sea Lion: The Failed Nazi Invasion That Turned the Tide of War* (New York: the Overlook Press, 2014), p. 343.
3. Peter Fleming, *Operation Sea Lion* (London: Pan Books Ltd., 1957), p. 298.
4. Max Hastings, *Inferno: The World at War 1939–1945* (New York: Vintage Books, 2012), p. 100.

CHAPTER 1

1. David Edgerton, *Britain's War Machine: Weapons, Resources, and Experts in the Second World War* (Oxford: Oxford University Press, 2011), p. 56.
2. Michael M. Postan, *British War Production* (History of the Second World War, United Kingdom Civil Series, London, 1957), pp. 72–75.
3. Edward Smalley, *The British Expeditionary Force, 1939–40* (London: Palgrave Macmillan, 2015), p. 19.
4. C. P. Stacey, *The Canadian Army 1939–1945: An Official Historical Summary* (Ottawa: Department of National Defense, 1948), pp. 5–15.
5. Jon Cooksey, *Boulogne: 20 Guards Brigade's Fighting Defence–May 1940* (Barnsley, UK: Leo Cooper, 2002), p. 139.
6. Jon Cooksey, *Calais: A Fight to the Finish, May 1940* (Barnsley, UK: Leo Cooper, 2000), p. 140.
7. Hugh Sebag-Montefiore, *Dunkirk: Fight to the Last Man* (London: Penguin, 2007), p. 246.
8. Karl-Heinz Frieser, *The Blitzkrieg Legend: The 1940 Campaign in the West* (Annapolis, MD: Naval Institute Press, 2005), pp. 292–299.
9. Basil Liddell Hart, *History of the Second World War* (Boston: Da Capo Press, 1999), p. 83.

10. Sebag-Montefiore, p. 541.
11. Sebag-Montefiore, pp. 272–273.
12. Field Marshall Lord Alanbrooke, *War Diaries 1939–1945* (London: Phoenix Press, 2002), pp. 79–81.
13. Stacey, p. 15.
14. Sean Longden, *Dunkirk: The Men They Left Behind* (London: Constable, 2009).
15. L. F. Ellis, *War in France and Flanders 1939–1940: History Of The Second World War: United Kingdom Military Series: Official Campaign History* (Uckfield, UK: The Naval & Military Press Ltd., 2009), p. 327.
16. Mark Urban, *The Tank War* (London: Little, Brown Book Group, 2013).
17. According to *Survey of Allied Tank Casualties in World War II* by Alvin D. Coox, this included 29 Matilda II, 97 Matilda I, 134 A-13, 31 A-10, 24 A-9 and 407 Mk VI.
18. Postan, p. 186.
19. Urban.
20. Postan, pp. 176, 183.
21. Peter Knight, *The 59th Division: Its War Story* (London: Frederick Muller Ltd., 1954).
22. David French, *Raising Churchill's Army: The British Army and the War against Germany 1919–1945* (Oxford: Oxford University Press, 2000).
23. The selection of Bartholomew, a 63-year-old artillery officer, to review the lessons of the French campaign indicates the superficial approach to this effort. Bartholomew had not served in France and had little time to interview the commanders who had; after completing the report, Bartholomew retired.
24. David Kahn, *Hitler's Spies: German Military Intelligence in World War II* (Boston: Da Capo Press, 1978), p. 423.
25. On 17 May 1940, the 2nd Battalion Royal Marines was replaced by the 147th Infantry Brigade of the 49th Infantry Division (TA).
26. House of Commons Official Report of Sessions 1940.
27. James Owen, *Danger UXB: The Heroic Story of the WWII Bomb Disposal Teams* (London: Abacus, 2010), p. 22.
28. John Lukacs, *Five Days in London, May 1940* (New Haven: Yale University Press, 1999), pp. 89–94.
29. War Cabinet Meeting, W. M. (40) 140th Conclusions, Confidential Annex, 26 May 1940, p. 2.
30. War Cabinet Meeting, W. M. (40) 170th Conclusions, Suggested Approach to Signor Mussolini, Memorandum by the Secretary of State for Foreign Affairs, 26 May 1940.
31. David Reynolds, 'Churchill and the British "Decision" to Fight on in 1940: Right Policy, Wrong Reasons', in Richard Langhorne (ed.), *Diplomacy and Intelligence During the Second World War* (Cambridge: Cambridge University Press, 1985), pp. 147–167.
32. John Charmley, *Churchill: The End of Glory* (London: Hodder and Stoughton, 1993).

33. Reynolds, p. 154.
34. War Cabinet Meeting, W. M. (40) 181st Conclusions, 25 June 1940, p. 604.
35. Ibid.
36. Jerrard Tickell, 'Britain Gathers Strength', in *History of the Second World War* (New York: Marshall Cavendish, 1973), p. 250.
37. Peter Mangold, *Britain and the Defeated French: From Occupation to Liberation, 1940–1944* (London: I.B. Tauris & Co. Ltd., 2012), p. 122.
38. War Cabinet Meeting, W. M. (40) 181st Conclusions, 25 June 1940, p. 605.
39. War Cabinet Meeting, W. M. (40) 176th Conclusions, Minute 5, Confidential Annex, 22 June 1940.
40. War Cabinet Meeting, W. M. (40) 177th Conclusions, 23 June 1940, p. 569.
41. War Cabinet Meeting, W. M. (40) 177th Conclusions, 23 June 1940, pp. 571–572.
42. War Cabinet Meeting, W. M. (40) 184th Conclusions, Minute 5, Confidential Annex, 27 June 1940.
43. Mangold, p. 41.
44. War Cabinet Meeting, W. M. (40) 140th Conclusions, Confidential Annex, 26 May 1940, p. 5.
45. The Chiefs of Staff Committee was a sub-committee of the War Cabinet and included Admiral Sir Dudley Pound (First Sea Lord), Air Chief Marshal Sir Cyril L. N. Newall (Chief of the Air Staff), General Edmund Ironside (Chief of the Imperial General Staff) and their deputies, Admiral Sir Thomas Philipps, Air Chief Marshal Sir Richard Peirse and General John Dill. On 27 May 1940, Dill replaced Ironside.
46. War Cabinet Meeting, W. M. (40) 168th Conclusions, 25 May 1940, pp. 319–320.
47. War Cabinet Meeting, W. M. (40) 123rd Conclusions, Minute 2, Confidential Annex, 15 May 1940, pp. 72–73.
48. War Cabinet Meeting, W. M. (40) 173rd Conclusions, 20 June 1940, p. 525.
49. Reynolds, p. 156.
50. War Cabinet Meeting, W. M. (40) 191st Conclusions, Minute 2, Confidential Annex, 2 July 1940.
51. War Cabinet Meeting, W. M. (40) 175th Conclusions, 28 May 1940, Seizure of Crete in the Event of Italian Hostilities.
52. War Cabinet Meeting, W. M. (40) 168th Conclusions, 25 May 1940, pp. 319–320.
53. War Cabinet Meeting, W. M. (40) 168th Conclusions, 25 May 1940, pp. 319–320.
54. War Cabinet Meeting, W. M. (40) 128th Conclusions, 18 May 1940, p. 177.
55. Once the invasion scare was past, many of these internees were released and some assisted RAF Bomber Command in 'spoofing' Luftwaffe ground controllers.
56. Hugh Trevor-Roper, *Hitler's War Directives 1939–1945* (Edinburgh: Birlinn Ltd., 1964), p. 50.
57. Trevor-Roper, pp. 56–57.

58. Nevertheless, Hitler became aware of the memorandum and told Göring to get rid of Felmy. On 12 January 1940, Felmy was relieved of command ostensibly because of the Mechelen incident, which proved unfortunate for the Luftwaffe. Consequently, he missed the Battle of Britain and the Blitz. Felmy was one of the few senior Luftwaffe officers to understand the necessity of cooperation between air and sea forces in an offensive against England. However, he was returned to service in May 1941 and sent to command the German mission in Iraq.

59. Geisler transferred from the navy to the Luftwaffe in 1933 and he was a specialist in maritime aviation matters.

60. Horst Boog, 'German Air Intelligence in the Second World War', in Michael I. Handel (ed.), *Intelligence and Military Operations* (London: Frank Cass, 1990), p. 358.

61. Boog, p. 355.

62. Walter Ansel, *Hitler Confronts England* (Durham, NC: Duke University Press, 1960), pp. 43–46.

63. Ansel, p. 47.

64. Trevor-Roper, pp. 56–57.

65. Ansel, pp. 116–117.

66. Stephen Bungay, *The Most Dangerous Enemy: A History of the Battle of Britain* (London: Aurum Press, 2001), pp. 110–113.

67. Klaus A. Maier et al., *Germany and the Second World War*, Volume 2 (Oxford: Oxford University Press, 2015), p. 368.

68. War Cabinet Meeting, W. M. (40) 178th Conclusions, Civil Defence Report No. 19, 13 July 1940, p. 336.

69. Maier, p. 375.

70. Ansel, p. 103.

71. Trevor-Roper, p. 74.

72. About 15 Landwehr and static divisions were disbanded after the French campaign, but few of the troops were actually de-mobilized and returned to the labour pool. Instead, many of the troops were either shifted to occupation duty or sent to join new divisions. By December 1940 the Heer had actually increased to 192 divisions.

73. Albert Speer, *Inside the Third Reich* (New York: Simon & Schuster, 1970), p. 177.

74. Rolf-Dieter Müller, *Enemy in the East: Hitler's Secret Plans to Invade the Soviet Union* (London: I.B. Tauris & Co., 2015), pp. 193–194.

75. Charles Burdick and Hans-Adolf Jacobsen (ed.), *The Halder War Diary 1939–1942* (Novato, CA: Presidio Press, 1988), pp. 209–210.

76. Karl Ries, *Deutsche Luftwaffe über der Schweiz, 1939–1945* [*German Luftwaffe over Switzerland, 1939–1945*] (Mainz: Dieter Hoffmann, 1978).

77. Christian Leitz, *Nazi Germany and Neutral Europe during the Second World War* (Manchester: Manchester University Press, 2000), p. 14.

78. Adolf Hitler, *Mein Kampf: Volume I and Volume II*, p. 519.

79. Patrick Osborn, *Operation Pike: Britain Versus the Soviet Union, 1939–1941* (Westport, CT: Greenwood Press, 2000), pp. 198–199.

80. Müller, p. 202.
81. Ansel, p. 132.
82. Karl Klee, *Das Unternehmen Seelöwe, Vol. 2, Die geplante deutsche Landung in England 1940. Dokumente zum Unternehmen „Seelöwe"* (Göttingen: Musterschmidt, 1958).
83. Ansel, p. 141.
84. Geirr H. Haarr, *The German Invasion of Norway, April 1940* (Annapolis, MD: Naval Institute Press, 2009), pp. 6–10.
85. Ansel, p. 136.
86. Egbert Kieser, *Operation Sea Lion: The German Plan to Invade Britain, 1940* (London: Cassel & Co., 1997), p. 128.
87. Ansel, p. 169.
88. *The Halder War Diary 1939–1942*, pp. 235, 240–241.
89. Halder made great efforts after the war to conceal his own involvement in planning Operation *Barbarossa* and appeared as a witness for the Allied prosecutors at the Nuremburg Tribunals.
90. Müller, pp. 208, 231.
91. *The Halder War Diary 1939–1942*, p. 242.
92. *The Halder War Diary 1939–1942*, pp. 244–245.
93. Walter Warlimont, *Inside Hitler's Headquarters 1939–1945* (Novato, CA: Presidio Press, 1991), pp. 111–112.
94. Peter Schenk, *Invasion of England 1940: The Planning of Operation Sealion* (London: Conway Maritime Press Ltd., 1990), pp. 12–14.
95. Klee, pp. 345–350.
96. Schenk, p. 319.
97. Klee, pp. 360–367.
98. Klee, pp. 370–372.
99. Klee, pp. 360–367.

CHAPTER 2

1. Michael B. Barrett, *Operation Albion: the German Conquest of the Baltic Islands* (Bloomington, IN: Indiana University Press, 2009).
2. Schenk, p. 25.
3. Schenk, p. 133.
4. Schenk, pp. 19, 148.
5. Roger Jordan, *The World's Merchant Fleets 1939* (Annapolis, MD: Naval Institute Press, 1999), p. 66.
6. Schenk, pp. 93–94.
7. Schenk, p. 67.
8. Schenk, p. 151.
9. Schenk, p. 157.
10. Schenk, pp. 129–130.
11. Ansel, p. 137.
12. Schenk, pp. 119–124.

13. Schenk, p. 128.
14. Schenk, pp. 94–98.
15. Ansel, p. 136.
16. Schenk, pp. 76–88.
17. Thomas L. Jentz, *Panzertruppen: The Complete Guide to the Creation & Combat Employment of Germany's Tank Force, 1933–1942*, Vol. 1 (Atglen, PA: Schiffer Military History), pp. 142–143.
18. Ansel, p. 159.
19. Kieser, pp. 119–120.
20. Lars Hellwinkel, *Hitler's Gateway to the Atlantic: German Naval Bases in France 1940–1945* (Barnsley, UK: Seaforth Publishing, 2014), pp. 17–18.
21. Schenk, pp. 166–169.
22. Schenk, pp. 171–172.
23. Ansel, pp. 229–230.
24. The British could at least be thankful that the Dutch shipped 1,295 captured German Fallschirmjäger and troops from 22. Luftlande-Division (incl. Oberst George Friemel, commander of IR 65 and the battalion commander of I./FJR 2) to England on 13 May, just before Holland capitulated. On 21 June, they were shipped to Canada.

CHAPTER 3

1. Purvis was a very successful negotiator who was killed in a plane crash on 14 August 1941.
2. Martin Gilbert, *The Second World War: A Complete History* (New York: Henry Holt & Co., 1989), p. 25.
3. In March 1940, the British Government set the official exchange rate as £1 = $4.03, which remained in effect until 1944.
4. Finlo Rohrer, 'What's a Little Debt Between Friends', *BBC News Magazine*, 10 May 2006.
5. Jerrard Tickell, 'Britain Gathers Strength', in *History of the Second World War* (New York: Marshall Cavendish, 1973), p. 247.
6. A P-40B fighter cost about $24,600 (£6,100) in 1940, against $40,000 (£9,900) for a Spitfire Mk I. However, the P-40B's performance at altitudes about 15,000 feet was significantly inferior to that of the Spitfire or the Bf-109F fighters.
7. Reynolds, p. 164.
8. Norman Moss, *Nineteen Weeks: American, Britain and the Fateful Summer of 1940* (New York: Houghton Mifflin Co., 2003), pp. 119–121.
9. Moss, p. 120.
10. Tickell, p. 246.
11. Reynolds, p. 162.
12. According to German historian Oliver Lubrich in *John F. Kennedy, Unter Deutschen: Reisetagebücher und Briefe 1937–1945* (2013), the ambassador's son and future US president visited the Third Reich twice before the war and made several favourable comments about Hitler and Fascism.

13. Stephen Conn and Byron Fairchild, *The Framework of Hemisphere Defense*, *The Western Hemisphere*, The United States Army in World War II (Washington, DC: Center of Military History, United States Army, 1989), pp. 35–37.

14. Clay Blair, *Hitler's U-Boat War: The Hunters, 1939–1942* (New York: Random House, 1996), pp. 742–743.

15. War Cabinet Meeting, W. M. (40) 324th Conclusions, 21 August 1940.

16. Website:http://www.americanrhetoric.com/speeches/fdrarsenalofdemocracy. html.

17. Mark E. Dixon, 'The Great Marcus Hook Swindle', in *Main Line Today* (November 2009).

18. Derek Wood, *The Narrow Margin: The Battle of Britain and the Rise of Air Power 1930–1940* (Barnsley, UK: Pen & Sword Aviation, 2010), p. 305.

19. 'British Order Sixty 10,000 DWT Cargo Steamers', *Pacific Marine Review*, Volume 38, No. 1 (January 1941).

20. Brian J. Ford, *Allied Secret Weapons: The War of Science* (New York: Ballantine Books, Inc., 1971), p. 102.

21. Stereoscopic photography requires two images to be taken of the target at the same time, but from slightly offset lenses. When viewed through a stereoscope, the resulting stereo images appear three-dimensional and enable a skilled photo interpreter to better determine the height and shape of a target.

22. On 14 November 1940, it was re-designated as No. 1 PRU.

23. Taylor Downing, *Spies In the Sky: The Secret Battle for Aerial Intelligence During World War II* (London: Little, Brown Book Group, 2013).

24. The PIU was renamed the Central Interpretation Unit in April 1941.

25. Geirr H. Haarr, *The Gathering Storm: The Naval War in Northern Europe September 1939–April 1940* (Barnsley, UK: Pen & Sword, 2013), p. 265.

26. Cox, p. 427.

27. Douglas C. Dildy, *Fall Gelb 1940: Airborne Assault on the Low Countries* (Oxford: Osprey Publishing, 2015), p. 45.

28. Bungay, p. 192.

29. Hugh Sebag-Montefiore, *Enigma: The Battle for the Code* (Hoboken, NJ: John Wiley & Sons, Inc., 2000), p. 19.

30. Michael Smith, *The Bletchley Park Codebreakers* (London: Biteback Publishing, 2011).

31. The code name for Enigma decryption was changed from BONIFACE to ULTRA in 1942.

32. Ronald Lewin, *Ultra Goes to War* (New York: McGraw-Hill Book Company, 1978), pp. 76–81.

33. Lewin, pp. 84–85.

34. War Cabinet Meeting, W. M. (40) 244th Conclusions, Imminence of German Invasion of Great Britain, Report by the Joint Intelligence Sub-Committee, 4 July 1940.

35. Data fusion is a modern concept but it has been occurring since the Second World War. It entails merging information from multiple and diverse collection means in

order to answer priority intelligence requirements. Britain pionieered data fusion for intelligence, whereas Germany's collection means lacked a central coordinating and analysis mechanism.

36. War Cabinet Meeting, W. M. (40) 244th Conclusions, Imminence of German Invasion of Great Britain, Report by the Joint Intelligence Sub-Committee, 4 July 1940.

37. Kahn, pp. 302–303.

38. Kahn, p. 347.

39. Kahn, pp. 303–305.

40. James Hayward, *Hitler's Spy: The True Story of Arthur Owens, Double Agent Snow* (London: Simon & Schuster, 2012).

41. Kahn, p. 367.

42. Monika Siedentopf, *Unternehmen Seelöwe: Widerstand im deutschen Geheimdienst* [*Operation Sea Lion: Resistance Inside the German Secret Service*] (Munich: Deutscher Taschenbuch Verlag, 2014).

43. Bryan Clough, *State Secrets: The Kent-Wolkoff Affair* (Hove, UK: Hideaway Publications Ltd., 2005).

44. US Army Security Agency, *European Axis Signals Intelligence in World War II as Revealed by TICOM Investigations and by Other Prisoner of War Interrogations and Captured Material, Principally German*, Volume 3, DOCID 3560827 (Washington, DC, 1 May 1946), pp. 50, 54 (hereafter TICOM).

45. TICOM, p. 61.

46. TICOM, p. 97.

47. The intelligence cycle consists of four primary phases: direct, collect, analyse and disseminate. In essence, the OKW was lacking the organizational component to conduct one of the key phases.

48. Blair, p. 125.

49. David Kahn, *Hitler's Spies: German Military Intelligence in World War II* (Boston: Da Capo Press, 1978), pp. 216–218.

50. Kahn, pp. 388–389.

51. Sebastian Cox, 'A Comparative Analysis of RAF and Luftwaffe Intelligence in the Battle of Britain, 1940', in Michael I. Handel (ed.), *Intelligence and Military Operations* (London: Frank Cass, 1990), p. 439.

52. Boog, p. 361.

53. Maier, pp. 381–382.

54. Kahn, pp. 382–384.

55. Cox, p. 437.

56. Boog, pp. 394–396.

57. Kahn, pp. 420–423.

58. Schenk, p. 235.

59. Denis Smyth, *Diplomacy and Strategy of Survival: British Policy and Franco's Spain, 1940–41* (Cambridge: Cambridge University Press, 1986), p. 130.

60. Richard Wigg, *Churchill and Spain: The Survival of the Franco Regime, 1940–1945* (Abingdon: Routledge, 2005), pp. 5–14.

61. Richard Norton-Taylor, 'MI6 Spent $200 million Bribing Spaniards in Second World War', *The Guardian*, 22 May 2013.
63. Smyth, pp. 74–75.
63. Stanley G. Payne, *Franco and Hitler: Spain, Germany, and World War II* (New Haven, CT: Yale University Press, 2008), p. 72.
64. Michael Mueller, *Canaris: The Life and Death of Hitler's Spymaster* (Annapolis: Naval Institute Press, 2007), p. 194.
65. Payne, p. 78.
66. Payne, p. 51.
67. The best equipped Spanish Air Force units were one fighter squadron with Bf-109B and four bomber squadrons with He-111, all equipment left behind in Spain by Legion Condor.
68. Payne, p. 90.
69. Payne, p. 83.
70. Payne, p. 93.
71. Payne, p. 93.
72. Payne, p. 103.
73. Payne, p. 51.

CHAPTER 4

1. Edward Warner, 'Douhet, Mitchell, Seversky: Theories of Air Warfare', in Edward M. Earle (ed.), *Makers of Modern Strategy: Military Thought from Machiavelli to Hitler* (Princeton: Princeton University Press, 1971), pp. 485–503.
2. Williamson Murray, *Strategy for Defeat: The Luftwaffe 1933–1945* (Maxwell AFB: Air University Press, 1983), p. 40.
3. Ferenc A. Vajda and Peter Dancey, *German Aircraft Industry and Production, 1933–1945* (Warrendale, PA: SAE International, 1998), p. 145.
4. Robin Higham, *Unflinching Zeal: The Air Battles Over France and Britain, May–October 1940* (Annapolis: Naval Institute Press, 2012), p. 107.
5. Manfred Griehl, *German Bombers over England 1940–1944* (London: Greenhill Books, 1999).
6. James S. Corum, *The Luftwaffe: Creating the Operational Air War, 1918–1940* (Lawrence, KS: University Press of Kansas, 1997), p. 172.
7. It was not until the Lofte 7C bombsight – based on stolen technology from the American Norden bombsight – became available in February 1941 that Luftwaffe bombers gained increased accuracy.
8. Mike Spick, *Luftwaffe Bomber Aces: Men, Machines, Methods* (London: Greenhill Books, 2001), p. 32.
9. Chris Goss, *Luftwaffe Fighters & Bombers: The Battle of Britain* (Mechanicsville, PA: Stackpole Books, 2011), p. 250.
10. Bungay, p. 204.
11. James Owen, *Danger UXB: The Heroic Story of the WWII Bomb Disposal Teams* (London: Abacus, 2010), pp. 163–164.
12. Spick, p. 60.

13. Jerzy B. Cynk, *The Polish Air Force at War: The Official History, 1939–1943* (Atglen, PA: Schiffer Publishing, 1998).

14. Spick, p. 62.

15. Higham, p. 122.

16. The PAC used a rocket to carry a 300–400 foot steel cable into the air, which descended slowly by parachute. The concept was to fire the PAC as enemy aircraft approached and, with luck, to snag a cable on one of the wings.

17. Richard Hough and Dennis Richards, *The Battle of Britain: The Greatest Air Battle of World War II* (New York: W. W. Norton & Co., Inc., 1989), p. 144.

18. Owen, pp. 19–21.

19. Owen, p. 81.

20. Owen, p. 95.

21. Owen, p. 143.

22. Owen, p. 213.

23. Owen, p. 157.

24. BBC, 'Bethnal Green WW2 bomb: Attempts continue to defuse device', 11 August 2015.

25. Knickebein enabled German bombers to get within about a mile of two intersecting navigation beams, although this was clearly inadequate to attack anything smaller than cities. The Germans intended to drop their bombs within a 330-yard area around where the X- and Y-axis beams intersected.

26. Allan W. Kurki, *Operation Moonlight Sonata: The German Raid on Coventry* (Westport, CT: Praeger Publishers, 1995), pp. 113, 116–117, 123.

27. Alfred Price, *Instruments of Darkness: The History of Electronic Warfare* (New York: Charles Scribner's Sons, 1978).

28. Francis K. Mason, *Battle over Britain: A History of the German Air Assaults on Great Britain 1917–18 and July–November 1940, and of the Development of Britain's Air Defences between the World Wars* (London: McWhirter Twins Ltd., 1969), p. 615.

29. Basil Collier, *The Defence of the United Kingdom*, History of the Second World War, United Kingdom Military series (Uckfield, UK: The Naval and Military Press Ltd., 2004), pp. 494–505.

30. Ken Ford, *Run the Gauntlet: The Channel Dash 1942* (Oxford: Osprey Publishing, 2012), pp. 29–42.

31. Kurki, pp. 109–112.

32. The Centre of Gravity (COG) is usually defined in modern military parlance as a moral or physical factor upon which the enemy's ability to successfully conduct its primary missions rests. A COG can exercise Critical Capabilities (CC) against an opponent and is dependent upon Critical Requirements to exercise that CC. Critical Vulnerabilities (CV) are factors which put the COG at risk of failure.

33. Directive issued by Göring on 15 August 1940 to all Luftwaffe commanders.

34. Spitfire production dropped from 268 to 151 in October due to the Southampton raids.

35. Boog, p. 369.

36. The most important yards were Vickers-Armstrong and Swan Hunter in Newcastle

and John Brown & Co. in Glasgow.

37. Corum, pp. 256–258.

38. M. J. Whitney, *Destroyer! German Destroyers in World War II* (Annapolis: Naval Institute Press, 1983), p. 106.

39. OP 1673A, *German Underwater Ordnance Mines* (US Department of the Navy, June 14, 1946).

40. David Isby (ed.), *The Luftwaffe and the War at Sea 1939–1945* (Mechanicsburg, PA: Stackpole Books, 2005), pp. 180–181.

41. Lawrence Peterson, *The First U-Boat Flotilla* (Annapolis: Naval Institute Press, 2002), pp. 12–15.

42. Dönitz was promoted to Konteradmiral on 1 October 1939 and Vizeadmiral on 1 September 1940.

43. Blair, p. 126.

44. Whitney, p. 104.

45. Chris Goss, *Sea Eagles: Luftwaffe Anti-Shipping Units, 1939–1941* (Hersham: Ian Allan Publishing Ltd., 2005), p. 5.

46. Corum, p. 281.

47. Goss, p. 5.

48. Haarr, p. 267.

49. Haarr, p. 268.

50. Jak P. Mallmann Showell, *Fuehrer Conferences on Naval Affairs, 1939–45* (London: Greenhill Books, 2006), p. 81.

51. Blair, p. 127.

52. Isby, p. 184.

53. Jürgen Rohwer, *Chronology of the War at Sea, 1939–1945* (Annapolis, MD: Naval Institute Press, 2005), p. 52.

54. Showell, p. 142.

55. Robert Jackson, *The Royal Navy in World War II* (Annapolis: Naval Institute Press, 1997), p. 40.

56. Jean-Philippe Dallies-Labourdette, *S-Boote: German E-Boats in Action, 1939–1945* (Paris: Histoire & Collections, 2003), pp. 42–44.

57. Haarr, p. 287.

58. By July 1941, Baumbach had claimed to have sunk 240,000 tons of Allied shipping.

59. Isby, pp. 193–194.

60. H. Herbert Hughes (ed.), *The Minerals Yearbook 1940* (Washington, DC: United States Government Printing Office, 1940).

61. Edgerton, pp. 51–54.

62. Blair, pp. 98–99.

63. Karl Dönitz, *Memoirs: Ten Years and Twenty Days* (Annapolis, MD: Naval Institute Press, 2012), pp. 29–31.

64. Blair, pp. 39–40.

65. A total of 27 ocean-going submarines – two Type I, 18 Type VII and seven Type IX – and 30 coastal submarines: all Type II.

66. Blair, p. 48.

67. Data from Convoyweb database. Of the five ships sunk, two by U-Boats, two by mines and one by aircraft.

68. After the war, Churchill would comment, 'The only thing that ever really frightened me during the war was the U-Boat peril. I was even more anxious about this battle than I had been about the glorious air fight called the Battle of Britain.'

69. Kieser, p. 117.

70. Blair, pp. 167–168.

71. Blair, pp. 176–177.

72. Roughly $100 million in 1934 prices. In contrast, most heavy cruisers cost about $8–12 million at the time and U-Boats ranged from RM 1.5 million for a Type II U-Boat to RM 4.1 million for a Type VII. All 57 submarines in the U-Boat service at the start of the war only cost about RM 170 million.

73. Richard Woodman, *The Battle of the River Platte: A Grand Delusion* (Annapolis: Naval Institute Press, 2008).

74. WW2 People's War (BBC), 'The Cyclamen Incident', 26 November 2004.

75. M. J. Whitley, *German Cruisers of World War Two* (Annapolis: Naval Institute Press, 1987), pp. 109–117.

76. Heinz J. Nowarra, *Focke-Wulf 200 'Condor'* (Koblenz: Bernard & Graefe, 1988).

77. The Royal Dutch Shell Santa Anna refinery on Curacao was the largest in the world (capacity: 6 million barrels/month). On Aruba, the Lago Refinery (Esso), producing 9 million barrels per month, was located at San Nicolas harbour and the smaller Eagle Refinery (Shell), producing 240,000 barrels per month was located at Oranjestad harbour. The Lago refinery was a key source of 100-octane aviation fuel. On Trinidad, the Pointe-à-Pierre refinery produced 2.4 million barrels per month and was the largest in the British Empire; this refinery was expanded in 1940 to begin producing high-octane fuel for the RAF.

78. John Knape, 'British Foreign Policy in the Caribbean Basin 1938–1945: Oil, Nationalism and Relations with the United States', *Journal of Latin American Studies* 19 (November 1987): 279–280.

79. Edgerton, pp. 183–194.

80. Entry for 21 May 1940. I SKL, Teil CVII, Überlegungen des Chefs der SKL und Niederschriften über Vorträge und Besprechungen beim Führer, September 1939–Dezember 1940, PG 32184 Case 230, BA-MA, 146–147.

81. Showell, p. 114.

82. David J. Bercuson and Holger H. Herwig, *Long Night of the Tankers: Hitler's War against Caribbean Oil* (Calgary: University of Calgary Press, 2014).

83. D. J. Payton-Smith, *Oil: A Study of War-time Policy and Administration* (London: H.M. Stationery Office, 1971), p. 201.

84. Bercuson and Herwig, p. 11.

CHAPTER 5

1. Edgerton, pp. 89–92.

2. Sandys was a member of parliament and a Territorial officer assigned to the 51st (London) Anti-Aircraft Brigade. In July 1941, he was appointed to a position in the War Office.
3. Edgerton, pp. 109–111.
4. Alan Brooke, *War Diaries 1939–1945* (London: Phoenix Press, 2002), p. 98.
5. War Cabinet Meeting, W. M. (40) 225th Conclusions, 13 August 1940.
6. In War Cabinet meetings in early August, Churchill claimed that a German Dornier flying boat had flown to Dakar for liaison purposes in order to suggest that Germany was contemplating some type of operation in West Africa.
7. Colin Smith, *England's Last War against France: Fighting Vichy 1940–42* (London: Phoenix, 2009), p. 112.
8. War Cabinet Meeting, W. M. (40) 219th Conclusions, 5 August 1940.
9. Brooke, p. 105.

CHAPTER 6

1. Collier, p. 223.
2. Four Hudsons were lost to enemy action in August–September 1940 and nine more were lost in accidents.
3. Collier, p. 225.
4. Schenk, p. 349.
5. Ford, p. 65.
6. Wood, pp. 309, 312.
7. T. C. G. James, *The Battle of Britain* (London: Frank Cass Publishers, 2000), pp. 365–366.
8. Tony Holmes, *Spitfire vs. Bf 109: Battle of Britain* (Oxford: Osprey Publishing, 2007), p. 72.
9. Holmes, p. 46.
10. In the Sandhurst exercise, the German forces tried to execute the 'Broad Front Landing', including landings at Deal and Lyme Bay – even though these were cut from the final *Seelöwe* plan. The simulation included numerous inaccuracies in the Royal Navy order of battle and judged that the Luftwaffe had 600 Ju-52 transports, which was double the actual amount.
11. Sir Arthur Hezlet, *Aircraft and Sea Power* (New York: Stein and Day Publishers, 1970), p. 154.
12. Derek Robinson, *Invasion 1940* (London: Robinson Publishing Ltd., 2006), p. 252.
13. McKinstry, p. 270.
14. Schenk, pp. 330–333.
15. The British 4.7-inch HE round had a 5lb bursting charge while the SAP round had about a 2lb charge. Furthermore, the SAP round was less likely to explode against unarmoured targets.
16. Britain imported 100 20mm Oerlikon guns from Switzerland before June 1940, but did not begin licensed production in England until November 1941. Similarly, the Swedish-designed Bofors 40mm gun was adopted by the British Army, but the

Royal Navy did not see any need for it until late 1941.

17. In a Cabinet meeting on 15 July 1940 (CAB 65/57), the First Sea Lord stated that the Royal Navy's destroyers were not likely to be effective against S-Boats or other light craft.

18. Donald A. Bertke and Gordon Smith, *World War II Sea War, Volume 3: The Royal Navy is Bloodied in the Mediterranean* (Dayton, OH: Bertke Publications, 2012), p. 43.

19. Vincent O'Hara, *Struggle for the Middle Sea* (Annapolis: Naval Institute Press, 2015), pp. 119–121.

20. Timothy Harrison Place, *Military Training in the British Army, 1940–1944, From Dunkirk to D-Day* (London: Frank Cass, 2000), pp. 9–10.

21. Robert Gardner, *Kensington to St. Valery en Caux: Princess Louise's Kensington Regiment, France and England Summer 1940* (Stroud, UK: Spellmount, 2012).

22. Karl G. Larew, *The Royal Navy in the Battle of Britain*, The Historian, Vol. 54, Issue 2 (December 1992), pp. 243–254.

23. Foynes, p. 56.

24. Brooke, p. 122.

25. Instructions for Milforce, No. 4 (20 September 1940), War Diary 8 RTR, WO 166/1408.

26. Brooke, pp. 164, 388.

27. Place, p. 114.

28. Place, pp. 236–241.

29. Peter Beale, *Death by Design: British Tank Development in the Second World War* (Stroud, UK: The History Press, 1998).

30. The 8th Army mounted three multi-brigade attacks against the Afrika Korps in July 1942. In Operation *Bacon*, the 4th New Zealand Brigade was destroyed due to failure of the supporting armoured brigade. In Operation *Splendour*, another armour-infantry debacle, two Commonwealth infantry brigades were mauled and the supporting 23rd Armoured Brigades lost 99 of its 106 tanks. The performance of the 1st Armoured Division in these battles was very poor. Finally, Operation *Manhood* cost the 8th Army three complete infantry battalions due to inadequate support. The basis of these fiascos was a reliance on brigade-size attacks rather than division-level operations.

31. Niall Barr, *Pendulum of War: The Three Battles of El Alamein* (New York: The Overlook Press, 2004), pp. 133–137, 173–182.

32. Robert Harris and Jeremy Paxman, *A Higher Form of Killing: The Secret History of Chemical and Biological Warfare* (New York: Random House, 2002), p. 109.

33. Tim Jones, *The X Site: Britain's Most Mysterious Government Facility* (Rhyl: Gwasg Helygain Ltd., 2000), pp. 7–10.

34. OS(40) 790, 2 October 1940, E. L. Davies Collection, Official History.

35. Harris and Paxman, pp. 111–112.

36. Harris and Paxman, pp. 39, 48–49.

CHAPTER 7

1. Ansel, p. 273.
2. Schenk, pp. 330–333.
3. Schenk, p. 305.
4. Ansel, p. 240.
5. Four Type IX U-Boats (U-37, U-38, U-103, U-123), one Type VII (U-46) and five Type IIC (U-56, U-58, U-59, U-60, U-61).
6. Schenk, p. 218.
7. Robert A. Doughty, *The Breaking Point: Sedan and the Fall of France, 1940* (Mechanicsburg, PA: Stackpole Books, 1990), p. 157.
8. Schenk, p. 269.
9. Based upon casualty estimates from HERO; typically 5 per cent daily casualty rates in high-temp. attacks down to about 1 per cent for positional warfare.
10. Trevor N. Dupuy, et al., *Handbook on Ground Forces Attrition in Modern Warfare* (Fairfax, VA: Historical Evaluation & Research Organization, 1986), pp. 69, 75.
11. Ansel, p. 299.
12. Brian Johnson, *The Secret War* (Barnsley, UK: Pen & Sword, 1978), pp. 254–255.
13. Schenk, p. 355.

CHAPTER 8

1. Ansel, p. 140.
2. Adrian Searle, *The Isle of Wight at War 1939–1945* (Stanbridge, UK: The Dovecote Press, 1989), pp. 92–94.
3. Searle, pp. 98–100.
4. Searle, p. 103.
5. David Sutherland, *He who Dares: Recollections of Service in the SAS, SBS and M15* (Annapolis, MD: Naval Institute Press, 1999).
6. Schenk, p. 32.
7. Gardner.

CHAPTER 9

1. Martin Middlebrook, *The Bomber Command War Diaries* (Hinckley, UK: Midland Publishing, 1985), p. 111.
2. Whitley, pp. 142–143.
3. War Cabinet Meeting, W. M. (40) 299th Conclusions, 2 December 1940, p. 149.
4. Foynes, p. 94.
5. Trevor-Roper, pp. 102–104.
6. John Winton, *Ultra at Sea* (New York: William Morrow & Co. Inc., 1988), pp. 33–39.

CHAPTER 10

1.   Brooke, p. 116.
2.   Brooke, p. 161.
3.   War Cabinet Meeting, W. M. (40) 466th Conclusions, 8 December 1940, pp. 3–4.
4.   Reynolds, p. 266.
5.   Benjamin Coombs, *British Tank Production and the War Economy, 1934–1945* (London: Bloomsbury, 2013), p. 111.

CHAPTER 11

1.   Alan J. Levine, *The War against Rommel's Supply Lines, 1942–1943* (Westport, CT: Praeger, 1999), p. 84.
2.   Samuel W. Mitcham Jr., *The Battle of Sicily: How the Allies Lost their Chance for Total Victory* (Mechanicsburg, PA: Stackpole Books, 1991), pp. 291, 307.
3.   O'Hara, p. 220.
4.   O'Hara, p. 222.
5.   Peter C. Smith, *War in the Aegean: The Campaign for the Eastern Mediterranean in World War II* (Mechanicsburg, PA: Stackpole Books, 2008), pp. 209–226.
6.   S. J. DeGroot, *Escape of the German Army across the Westerscheldt, September 1944,* Canadian Military History, Vol. 6, Issue 1 (23 January 2012), pp. 109–117.

CHAPTER 12

1.   Vasilis Vourkoutiotis, *Prisoners of War and the German High Command: The British and American Experience* (New York: Palgrave Macmillan, 2003).

APPENDICES

1.   The Polish Corps consisted of 14,382 personnel and was assigned to defend the Firth of Forth coastline.
2.   Retired later in 1940.
3.   The Czech brigade had a total of 3,274 personnel and consisted of two infantry battalions and several support companies. It was stationed near Chester, re-training and re-equipping for the rest of 1940.
4.   Re-named 56th (London) Infantry Division on 18 November 1940.
5.   Remained in UK until January 1941, but General Freyburg was flown to Egypt on 25 September 1940. Total strength of the 2NZEF was about 7,000 personnel.
6.   Three Motor Machine Gun Brigades were created between 30 May and 23 June from existing light armoured units that had no tanks. Each brigade had three regiments, equipped with a motley mix of Bren Gun carriers and civilian vehicles. On 12 October 1940 the MMG Brigades were converted back to armoured brigades.
7.   Killed in action, North Africa, 5 January 1941. The 2nd Armoured Division was

demolished in North Africa and disbanded on 10 May 1941.

8. The 2nd Armoured Division was sent to North Africa in October 1940 and arrived 1 January 1941.

9. Equipment abandoned at Brest in June 1940

10. The Australian 25th Infantry Brigade was formed in England in July 1940, primarily from service support personnel, and it was significantly understrength.

11. The Canadian 2nd Infantry Division's main body arrived in England on 4 September 1940 and three battalions remained in Iceland until the end of October. The division was not fully formed until December.

12. The 24th Guards Brigade served in Norway until June 1940 and its commander, Brigadier Fraser, was wounded there.

13. Only operational ships are included.

14. These Vorpostenboote were all former *Walfangboote* (whaling boats) of 340-350 tons. They were armed with a single 3.7cm PaK in the bow, a 2cm Flak and a pair of machine guns.

Bibliography

Primary Sources

Copies of the minutes of British War Cabinet meetings for 1940–41 are available at the website http://www.ukwarcabinet.org.uk/time/1940.

Secondary Sources

Walter Ansel, *Hitler Confronts England* (Durham, NC: Duke University Press, 1960).

Kurt Aßman, 'Sea Lion', *Naval Institute Proceedings* (January 1950).

Clay Blair, *Hitler's U-Boat War: The Hunters, 1939–1942* (New York: Random House, 1996).

Stephen Bungay, *The Most Dangerous Enemy: A History of the Battle of Britain* (London: Aurum Press, 2001).

Basil Collier, *The Defence of the United Kingdom*, History of the Second World War, United Kingdom Military series (Uckfield, UK: The Naval and Military Press Ltd., 2004).

Anthony J. Cumming, *The Royal Navy and the Battle of Britain* (Annapolis, MD: Naval Institute Press, 2010).

David Edgerton, *Britain's War Machine: Weapons, Resources, and Experts in the Second World War* (Oxford: Oxford University Press, 2011).

Martin Matrix Evans, *Invasion: Operation Sea Lion 1940* (Harlow, UK:

Pearson Education Ltd., 2004).

Peter Fleming, *Operation Sea Lion* (London: Pan Books Ltd., 1975).

Julian P. Foynes, *Battle of the East Coast* (J. P. Foynes, 1994).

Geoff Hewitt, *Hitler's Armada: The Royal Navy & the Defence of Great Britain, April–October 1940* (Barnsley, UK: Pen & Sword Books Ltd., 2008).

Robin Higham, *Unflinching Zeal: The Air Battles Over France and Britain, May–October 1940* (Annapolis: Naval Institute Press, 2012).

E. R. Hooten, *Phoenix Triumphant: The Rise and Rise of the Luftwaffe* (Arms & Armour, 1996).

Richard Hough and Dennis Richards, *The Battle of Britain: The Greatest Air Battle of World War II* (New York: W. W. Norton & Co., Inc., 1989).

Stuart Hylton, *Kent and Sussex 1940: Britain's Front Line* (Barnsley: Pen & Sword, 2004).

Egbert Kieser, *Operation Sea Lion: The German Plan to Invade Britain, 1940* (London: Cassel & Co., 1997).

Karl Klee, *Das Unternehmen Seelöwe*, Vol. 2, *Die geplante deutsche Landung in England 1940. Dokumente zum Unternehmen 'Seelöwe'* (Göttingen: Musterschmidt, 1958).

Kenneth Macksey, *Invasion: The Alternative History of the German Invasion of England, July 1940* (London: Greenhill Books, 1999).

Jak P. Mallmann Showell, *Fuehrer Conferences on Naval Affairs, 1939–45* (London: Greenhill Books, 2006).

Leo McKinstry, *Operation Sea Lion: The Failed Nazi Invasion That Turned the Tide of War* (New York: The Overlook Press, 2014).

David J. Newbold, *British Planning and Preparations to Resist Invasion on Land, September 1939–September 1940* (Unpublished thesis, King's College, London, 1988).

Stanley G. Payne, *Franco and Hitler: Spain, Germany, and World War II* (New Haven, CT: Yale University Press, 2008).

Alan Philson, *Order of Battle of the Land, Sea and Air Forces of the United Kingdom 30th September 1940* (Westoning, UK: Military Press, 2010).

Michael M. Postan, *British War Production* (History of the Second World War, United Kingdom Civil Series, London, 1957).

Derek Robinson, *Invasion 1940* (London: Robinson Publishing Ltd., 2006)

Peter Schenk, *Invasion of England 1940: The Planning of Operation Sealion* (London: Conway Maritime Press Ltd., 1990).

Adrian Searle, *The Isle of Wight at War 1939–1945* (Stanbridge, UK: The Dovecote Press, 1989).

Monika Siedentopf, *Unternehmen Seelöwe: Widerstand im deutschen Geheimdienst* [*Operation Sea Lion: Resistance Inside the German Secret Service*] (Munich: Deutscher Taschenbuch Verlag, 2014).

Index